How Bad Is It?

"So ridiculous, you wouldn't believe me if I told you."
—*Washington Post* on *Indecent Proposal*

"Disney nature porn."
—*The New Yorker* on *The Blue Lagoon*

"The funniest film of the decade . . . I laughed my head off."
—*New York Times* on *The Concorde: Airport '79*

"The most enjoyably awful of Madonna's many awful movies."
—*Movieline* on *Body of Evidence*

"Promises us the moon and delivers Bruce Willis's butt."
—*Washington Post* on *Color of Night*

"The cinematic equivalent of Cheez Whiz!"
—*New York Times* on *From Justin to Kelly*

THE OFFICIAL RAZZIE MOVIE GUIDE

The Official RAZZIE MOVIE GUIDE

Enjoying the Best of Hollywood's Worst

by
John Wilson,
CREATOR OF THE RAZZIE® AWARDS

WARNER BOOKS

NEW YORK   BOSTON

If you purchase this book without a cover you should be aware that this book may have been stolen property and reported as "unsold and destroyed" to the publisher. In such case neither the author nor the publisher has received any payment for this "stripped book."

Copyright © 2005 by John Wilson
Foreword copyright © 2005 by Peter Travers
All rights reserved.

Warner Books

Time Warner Book Group
1271 Avenue of the Americas, New York, NY 10020
Visit our Web site at www.twbookmark.com.

Printed in the United States of America

First Printing: January 2005
10 9 8 7 6 5 4 3 2 1

Library of Congress Cataloging-in-Publication Data
Wilson, John, 1954 –
    The official Razzie movie guide : enjoying the best of Hollywood's worst / John Wilson.
    p. cm.
    Includes index.
    ISBN: 0-446-69334-0
1. Motion pictures—Catalogs. 2. Motion pictures—Plots, themes, etc. I. Title.
    PN1998.W548 2005
    791.43′75—dc22
        2004017405

Book design and chapter illustrations by Mada Design, Inc.
Cover design by Brigid Pearson
Cover photo courtesy of Worldwide Entertainment Corp.

This book is dedicated to my father,
Donald Drew Wilson,
who gave me my lifelong love of movies,
and to my son,
Parker Drew Wilson,
to whom I have passed it along . . .

Contents

Foreword by Peter Travers of *Rolling Stone* — xi

Acknowledgments — xiii

A Brief History of the Razzies and Introduction — xv

Key to Symbols — xix

ALL GOD'S CREATURES, LARGE AND LAME
Anaconda — 3
A*P*E — 7
The Beach Girls and the Monster — 10
The Giant Spider Invasion — 13
Goliath and the Dragon — 16
Jaws: The Revenge — 18
King Kong Lives — 21
Trog — 23

CAN'T STOP THE MUSICALS
Body Rock — 29
Can't Stop the Music — 32
From Justin to Kelly — 35
Glitter — 38
Lost Horizon (1973) — 40
The Pirate Movie — 44
Rhinestone — 46

Roller Boogie	49
Spice World	52
Staying Alive	55

DISASTERS... IN EVERY SENSE

Airport 1975	61
Avalanche	64
The Concorde: Airport '79	67
On Deadly Ground	70
The Poseidon Adventure	73
The Swarm	76
The Ten Commandments (1956)	79

DOOFY TWOSOMES

The Bodyguard (1992)	85
Indecent Proposal	88
The Jayne Mansfield Story	91
Shining Through	93
Sincerely Yours	96
The Specialist (1994)	99
Sweet November (2001)	102
White Comanche	105

NOW *THAT'S* A DUMB IDEA!

The Car	111
Cocktail	114
Color of Night	117
Eegah	120
Fever Pitch	123
High School Confidential	125
Impulse	127
Perfect	130
Road House (1989)	132
Sinbad of the Seven Seas	135
Yor, the Hunter from the Future	153
Zardoz	155

THE ROLES THAT MADE THEM SHAMELESS

The Betsy	159

Beyond the Forest	162
The Conqueror	165
The Godfather: Part III	168
Harum Scarum	171
The Jazz Singer (1980)	173
Julie	175
Rambo: First Blood Part II	177
She (1935)	180
Strait-Jacket	183

SHOWBIZ LAID BARE ...

Beyond the Valley of the Dolls	189
The Carpetbaggers	191
The Greatest Show on Earth	194
The Legend of Lylah Clare	197
The Love Machine	201
Valentino	204
Valley of the Dolls	208
The Wild Wild World of Jayne Mansfield	211

THEY CAME FROM PLANET RAZZIE

The Astounding She-Monster	217
Barbarella	219
The Creeping Terror	221
Devil Girl from Mars	223
The Green Slime	226
Mac and Me	229
Robot Monster	232
Santa Claus Conquers the Martians	235
Supergirl	238

WELL, *SOMEONE* THOUGHT IT WAS SEXY!

Barb Wire	243
The Blue Lagoon (1980)	245
Duel in the Sun	248
Ghosts Can't Do It	251
Kitten with a Whip	254
Love Crimes	256
The Naked Kiss	259

A Night in Heaven	262
Orgy of the Dead	264
The Scarlet Letter (1995)	266
Sextette	269
Sheena	271
Where Love Has Gone	273

WHEN MAD SCIENTISTS GO BAD

The Brain That Wouldn't Die	279
Frankenstein's Daughter	282
The Island of Dr. Moreau (1996)	284
Maniac (1934)	286
The Tingler	289

THE VERY BEST OF THE BERRY WORST

The Adventurers	295
Battlefield Earth	299
Body of Evidence	302
Exorcist II: The Heretic	305
Glen or Glenda	309
The Lonely Lady	311
Mommie Dearest	314
The Oscar	317
Showgirls	321
Xanadu	323

Appendix I How to Get Your Hands on the Films	327
Appendix II The Complete Razzie Award History	331
Index	363
About the Author	380

Foreword

The dirty little secret about film critics such as myself is that the movies we watch for fun most often suck. Sure, we admire the landmarks from *Citizen Kane* to blah blah blah, but for kicking back at home, there's nothing like getting hold of a classic stinker on DVD, ripping off the wrapping with your teeth—it sharpens reflexes for the attack—and settling in to feast on choice cinematic junk food.

That's where the Razzies come in. Since 1980, the Golden Raspberry Award Foundation, headed by John Wilson, has been sticking it to Hollywood by awarding Razzies to the stars and filmmakers who shamelessly bite the big one. That the ceremony always takes place the day before the Academy Awards is particularly appropriate. Oscar night always finds the major studios taking bows for quality when we know that 90 percent of what they grind out is indisputable hoo-hah. The Razzies, in which Wilson and his cohorts dis-honor gutless winners who rarely show up—unlike Tom Green, who admirably appeared with five feet of his own red carpet—are the antidote to the Oscars and thereby indispensable. Nothing is better than a Razzie to burst the balloon of Tinseltown pretension.

What you have in your hand, fellow film freaks, is a book that celebrates all that is gloriously godawful about movies. Wilson couldn't be bothered with the glut of dull formula flicks that clog our multiplexes. A movie is only Razzie-worthy when its intrinsic awfulness sinks to levels so low that the pain of watching it turns to pleasure. You can't appreciate great movies without also learning how to savor the fabled fiascos. I don't trust any film buff who says different, just as I wouldn't trade my debates with fellow critics over whether a particular film is bad enough to deserve Razzie consideration.

In addition to listing all the Razzie nominees and winners since the award's inception—a go-to list for unintentionally hilarious home entertainment unrivaled anywhere—this book lets John Wilson fly on the essence of putrescence in cinema. To read Wilson on 1992's *Body of Evidence*, starring Madonna—who scored the third of her five Razzies as Worst Actress for this debacle—is to experience critical writing at a level of mad inspiration. Who else is going to tell you that the infamous sex scene in which Madonna pours hot wax and cold champagne on Willem Dafoe's nether region is chapter 7 on the DVD?

With Wilson as guide, it's a kick to take a trip through Razzie history—my favorite stops being at *Mommie Dearest, Showgirls, Battlefield Earth,* and *Swept Away.* As a proud voting member in the Razzie Awards, I look forward to weighing in with my choices for years to come. There's something cathartic about giving the razzle to a memorably dreadful movie. You know how to razzle, don't you? To redirect Bacall's line to Bogie in *To Have and Have Not,* you just put your lips together and blow. Then let Wilson do the rest. He can take down a movie with a single phrase that gives you the munchies for more, more, more. That's what makes his affection for cinema's bottom rung contagious. Wilson only kills the things he loves.

Peter Travers
Rolling Stone

Acknowledgments

So many people have been a part of the Razzies over the years that an entire book could be filled just acknowledging their contributions and support. In terms of this book itself, I must first thank Sean Desmond for lighting the fire that got the project going, and my wife, Barbara Jean, for granting me the indulgence of pursuing the project to the exclusion of husbandly and fatherly duties. For their direct involvement in this book, its midwifing and birth, I must acknowledge my editor Jason Pinter of Warner Books and my agent Rob Robertson of Princeton Literary Management. For his gracious and enthusiastic agreement to write an intro and add his classy credential to this tome, I am Berry Grateful to Peter Travers of *Rolling Stone*. For their help in getting graphics, screener DVDs, and other materials helpful to creating the manuscript I must also thank Sue Procko (PR maven for Anchor Bay Entertainment), Spencer Savage of Image Entertainment, Sam Toles of Rhino Video, "The Gang" at Something Weird Video, too many Internet film critics to mention (who, to a one, when asked, were quick to respond with permission to quote their amusing reviews of various films in this book), and the many auctioneers and sellers at Amazon.com and eBay who rushed "screeners" to me from the four corners of the United States. On a personal level, I also need to thank Angie and Billy Hall, Allison Jo at Bernard B. Norman Pictures, Razzie stalwart Nancy Lilienthal (a.k.a. "NLBP"), Chuck Moran for *Robot Monster*, Kathryn R. at The Margaret Dumont Library, and Tom Higgins for giving me *The Naked Kiss* many years ago (and if you read something salacious into that last one, you're *way* too into Harold Robbins novels!). Lastly, I'd like to once again mention my son, Parker, whose company in sitting through endless hours of Tinseltown trash made this project enjoyable in ways I'll remember for years to come.

A Brief History of the Razzies and Introduction

It all started in my tiny living room alcove, in what *People* magazine would later call "a run-down apartment in a seedy section of Hollywood." Twenty-five years later, the Razzies have grown into an annual media event that is covered by television, radio, newspapers, and magazines, amusing millions of people all over the world.

The Razzie Awards began at an Oscar-night potluck I hosted on Tuesday, March 31, 1981. You may recall that was the year the Oscars were postponed for twenty-four hours because John Hinckley shot newly inaugurated president (and retired B-movie star) Ronald Reagan. Immediately following that year's 53rd Annual Academy Awards, my potluck party guests were hauled up to a hand-painted cardboard podium and asked to present or accept "awards" in eight categories. Both of the films that had inspired me to create the Razzies won "dis-honors" that evening. Olivia Newton-John's roller-disco disaster *Xanadu* "won" Worst Director, while the Village People's *Can't Stop the Music* took Worst Screenplay and Worst Picture. The evening ended with an audience sing-along of lyrics I had written for "Dead Entertainers," a tribute to all the stars who died in 1980, rhyming their names to the tune of "That's Entertainment." Every one of those guests later told me how much fun they'd had—and what a great idea I'd come up with.

The next day, more out of curiosity than expectation, I sent a press release to a handful of newspapers and radio and TV stations, announcing the "winners" of what I was already calling the 1st Annual Golden Raspberry Awards. A few days later, the *L.A. Daily News* ran a story with the headline "And the Winners Aren't." The Razzies were officially launched.

The following year, we moved the ceremony to a mansion in Bel Air and I sent out an advance press release announcing nominations in nine categories. While the Academy of Motion Picture Arts and Sciences chose *Chariots of Fire* as Best Picture that year, *Mommie Dearest* swept the 2nd Annual Razzies with five dis-honors, including Worst Picture. Two Los Angeles newspapers, a TV station, and a radio station ran stories. And for the first time, a "winner" was informed of her award: A London newspaper claimed that when they told Mommie herself Faye Dunaway that she was named 1981's Worst Actress, she "flew into a litigious rage"!

Speaking of mothers, I realized by our fourth year that if the Razzies were ever going to get major media attention, they couldn't go head-to-head with the Mother of All Awards Shows. So we moved from Oscar night to Oscar eve—and the coverage suddenly exploded: UPI, CNN, and *USA Today* all did stories on us. Pia Zadora swept the 4th Annual Razzies with her hilarious Harold Robbins vehicle *The Lonely Lady,* and my creation went overnight from being a private Oscar party joke to being the logical antidote to Hollywood's annual orgy of self-congratulatory, over-the-top awards show hype.

Over the years, only a handful of "winners" have graciously accepted Razzie Awards. They include Bill Cosby (who had us flown up to Lake Tahoe, where his three Razzies for *Leonard Part 6,* made of 24-karat gold and Italian marble at a cost to Fox Television of more than $27,000, were presented to him), *Showgirls* director Paul Verhoeven (who became the first "winner" to actually attend our ceremonies and accept his dis-honors in person), Robert Conrad (who cleverly used our 20th Annual ceremonies to express just how much he despised Barry Sonnenfeld's movie remake of Conrad's TV series *Wild Wild West*), and Tom Green (whose *Freddy Got Fingered* swept the 22nd Annual Razzies, where he ended up accepting Worst Picture while holding a rubber dead rat).

As big a media event as the Razzies now are, it's surprising that the publicity-hungry movie business has yet to embrace or accept them as part of the annual avalanche of awards overkill. But the fact that the public and the press seem to appreciate us makes it worthwhile. And the fact that the so-called Industry loathes us . . . actually makes the Razzies all the funnier.

The Joy of Bad Movies
One of the secrets to the ongoing success of the Razzies is Hollywood's knack for making horrible movies. Unlike all those 357 *other* awards purportedly honoring "The Best," we've never lacked for contenders for Worst Achievements.

But in a quarter century of presenting the Razzie Awards, I've also learned that every once in a while a movie somehow gets made that is so bad it's actually wildly entertaining. The acting in these movies isn't merely wretched, it's laughable. The writing is deliriously dunderheaded. And the direction sails beyond the mediocre into the stratosphere of meteoric misfires. There aren't many of these Berry Funny Movies out there, but for this book I've compiled 100 of my personal favorites.

By the time you finish *The Official Razzie Movie Guide: Enjoying the Best of Hollywood's Worst,* you too will be an expert on the Worst Movies Ever Made—and how the right attitude can make watching truly terrible movies one of life's best and most entertaining pleasures.

Hey, these days, you've gotta take your entertainment however you can get it!

Key to Symbols

- 🍋 = Razzie nominee
- 🍋 = Razzie "winner"
- O = Oscar nominee
- 𝑂 = Oscar winner

Anaconda

(1997/Columbia Pictures)   **DVD / VHS**

Who's to Blame   CAST: **Jon Voight** ☺ (*Paul Sarone*); **Jennifer Lopez** (*Terri Flores*); **Ice Cube** (*Danny Rich*); **Eric Stoltz** (*Dr. Steven Cale*); **Owen Wilson** (*Gary Dixon*); **Jonathan Hyde** (*Warren Westridge*); **The Audioanimatronic Anaconda** ☺ (*Himself*)
CREW: **Directed by Luis Llosa** ☺ **Screenplay** ☺ **by Hans Bauer, Jim Cash, and Jack Epps Jr.**

Rave Reviews

"No single movie in the annals of cheesy aquatic flicks fashioned after *Jaws* . . . has ever provided more unintentional laughs than *Anaconda*."
— **Edward Margulies,** *Movieline* **magazine**

"*Anaconda* is so desperate and silly that . . . it's a lot of fun. The ultimate crowd-pleaser!"
— **Mick LaSalle,** *San Francisco Chronicle*

"A trashily entertaining reptilian version of *Jaws* . . . crosses the line from drama into farce."
— **Stephen Holden,** *New York Times*

Plot, What Plot? Few genres offer the giggle potential of horror movies gone wrong. Perhaps it's because we go to them all keyed up and expecting to be terrified—and when they *do* make us scream, but with laughter, the release just explodes from us in uncontrollable gales. Gale conditions prevail for most of the 89-minute running time of *Anaconda,* the Razzie choice as Best Bad Horror Movie of the 1990s.

This one has it all: an Oscar-winning star (Jon Voight) giving a performance that begs for a Worst Actor nomination; a cast of characters you actually look forward to seeing get gobbled up by the gargantuan snake; over-the-top camera work that in itself is giggle-worthy; and a "creature" that is one of the biggest hoots ever to slither across the screen. The title character in *Anaconda,* played by a combination of audioanimatronics, primitive digital effects, and elements with all the sophistication of a Halloween hand puppet, is almost as funny as the performance of its equally ridiculous screen mate Voight. Anacondas are, we are told by a title card at the very beginning of the film, "unique among snakes. They are not satisfied after eating a victim. They will regurgitate their prey in order to kill and eat again."

Our story opens as an Amazon River captain confronts the terrifying choice of facing down an anaconda the size of a Boeing airliner or taking his own life. The persistent predator crashes through the floorboards of his cabin, and pursues the captain up the mast while the boat slowly sinks around him. The captain winds up atop the mizzenmast, arranged like Christ on the cross, and chooses to blow his brains out with a pistol. Given what's to come in *Anaconda,* he made a wise choice.

Next, we join a young, hip documentary film crew boarding a barge to head into the South American jungle in pursuit of a tribe called "The People of the Mist." The head of the expedition, in the film's most thankless role, is Eric Stoltz as the documentary's director. His assistant and main squeeze, played by Jennifer Lopez, is one of those braver-than-she-has-to-be females who overpopulate post–Women's Lib horror films. Rounding out the crew are an English narrator, played with shameless abandon by Jonathan Hyde, an angry black soundman in the person of rapper Ice Cube, and the requisite happy-young-couple-who-are-both-destined-to-die, Owen Wilson and Kari Wuhrer.

Before you can say "snakes and snails and anaconda tails," the barge runs across a stranded stranger whom they will come to regret picking up: Jon Voight as snake hunter extraordinaire Paul Sarone. Voight clearly relishes the excesses he brings to this role, including an accent critics compared to that of everyone from Ricky Ricardo to ancient *Wolfman* crone Maria Ouspenskaya, and facial expressions that constantly leave you expecting him to bark "Aargh!" like a cartoon pirate. Something is clearly afoot as Sarone deliberately misleads our film crew into parts of the Amazon that look like they were shot on location at Disneyland's Jungle Cruise ride, then expedition head Stoltz is stung in the mouth by a big whopping wasp that leaves him laid up and mute for the rest of the film. We eventually learn that Voight planned all of this because his current prey is a legendary anaconda whose shed skin, when unrolled on deck by Voight, exceeds forty feet in length.

We are now halfway into the film and, according to Bad Horror Movie Rules, it's time to start dispatching characters one by one. First to go is the boatman, secretly in cahoots with Voight. He gets slithered and squished while investigating the very boat where we saw the captain blow his brains out at the beginning of the film. Undulating, hissing, and occasionally squealing like a stuck pig, the anaconda next manages to slither *up* a waterfall in pursuit of the Englishman, then comes up on deck to swallow Wilson, a bas-relief of whose face is later seen in the belly of the beast as it swims by underwater. Throughout all of this, Voight's accent keeps getting thicker and thicker, Lopez's temper gets shorter and shorter, Mr. Cube's facial expressions get snarlier and snarlier . . . and Stoltz sleeps fitfully in his cabin.

At a conveniently abandoned foundry located in the middle of the jungle, Voight comes face-to-face with the creature of his dreams (and his nightmares) and must, in the tradition of Captain Ahab, be destroyed by his obsession. But Voight's consumption by constrictor tops all the others that came before it: When Sarone is swallowed by the slithering menace, we actually see him enter the mouth of the snake . . . from a POV inside its throat!

Just when you think *nothing* could possibly top the pink-tunnel image from inside our Monster, Lopez is cornered by the snake, which rears back . . . and vomits up Voight, whose stomach-juice-covered, partially decomposed visage stares at Lopez . . . and winks!

But wait, don't stop laughing yet, because in the film's final moments Lopez and Cube plot to lure it into the foundry's chimney and blow it to bits with lighted barrels of fuel. As the chimney explodes, Fangs à la Flambé comes coiling down right next to Lopez, and it's up to Cube to finally dispatch it with a meat axe. As its flaming face slowly sinks into the water, and it squeals its last plaintive wild-boar squeal, we can almost hear the snake screeching, "What a world! What a world! Who would think Jennifer Lopez could destroy my beautiful wickedness!"

For laughs per minute, gasping-for-air giggle fits, *great* bad acting, and the sheer joy of its unintended humor, *Anaconda* can't be topped. They say snake meat tastes like chicken, but in *Anaconda,* it has a distinct aftertaste . . . of Razz-berries.

Dippy Dialogue
Terri Flores (*Jennifer Lopez*): "This film was supposed to be my big break . . . but it's turned out to be a big disaster!"

Choice Chapter Stops
Chapter 26 ("On the Rocks"): The anaconda climbs the waterfall . . . which is later seen flowing *up*!
Chapter 30 ("A Wink and a Smile"): The anaconda regurgitates Voight.

(1976/Worldwide Entertainment—Korean) **DVD / VHS**

Who's to Blame CAST: **Rod Arrants** (*Tom Rose*); **Joanna Kerns** (*Marilyn Baker*); **Alex Nicol** (*Colonel Davis*); **Lee Nak Hoon** (*Captain Kim*); **Bob Kurcz** (*The Actor*); **Paul Leder** (*Dino, the Director*)
CREW: **Directed by Paul Leder; Written by Paul Leder and Reuben A. Leder**

Rave Reviews
"Shockingly bad—Laughable in every respect!" — **Richard Scheib, Science Fiction, Horror and Fantasy Film Review (Web site)**

"A cheap, ludicrous picture marked by laughable special effects."
— **Ken Begg, Jabootu.com**

"Painfully funny . . . a very memorable and wildly entertaining movie experience!" — **Adam Tyner, DVDTalk.com**

Plot, What Plot? Men in monkey suits have been a staple of bad moviemaking since the days of silent movies. Totally fake-looking toy cities were perfected by the makers of pagoda-stomping Japanese monster movies in the late 1950s and early 1960s. But these two elements of cinematic silliness have rarely come together in so laughably lame a combination as in the 1976 Korean production *A*P*E*. To give you some idea of how utterly incompetent the producers of *A*P*E* are in the ways of moviemaking, they made this film to cash in on what they expected to be an international box-office bonanza: Dino De Laurentiis's ultimate man-in-a-monkey-suit movie, the awful 1976 remake of *King Kong*, starring Jeff Bridges and a then unknown Jessica Lange.

Print ads for *A*P*E* even went so far as to warn viewers that their film was "not to be confused with *King Kong*." Surely, it could never have been—as silly as Rick Baker in an ape suit was in Dino's dog of a movie, this stinker is worlds worse. First of all, the landscapes across which this "36 foot tall monster" stomps are so obviously miniatures that a five-year-old could spot them as phony. Secondly, the fur part of the suit looks more like your grandmother's lamb's wool collar than an actual simian. Thirdly, the seam at the neckline keeps threatening to literally come apart during the action. And lastly, the guy inside the monkey suit has a belly and tush that look amazingly like Homer Simpson in the episode where he dreamed *he* was Kong.

Things start off badly when we realize the first shot *isn't* supposed to be a toy boat floating in some kid's bathtub—it's supposed to be a full-sized oil tanker, inexplicably transporting a giant ape across the ocean. Two crew members, whose lips don't match a single word they speak, discuss what's in the cargo hold—and suddenly A*P*E makes a break for it, tossing the toy boat aside. He then thrashes in the "ocean" (which has no visible horizon) fighting a great white shark. Okay, it actually looks more like a great white shark carcass. And the monkey does all the thrashing. But the filmmakers, we're sure, thought they'd brilliantly blended elements of both *Kong* and *Jaws*—how could it miss?

When A*P*E reaches land, he wreaks havoc on the first of dozens of Matchbox-scale villages and buildings, tossing oil barrels (which resemble emptied Campbell's soup cans) at a power plant and starting a raging fire. Crowds and Korean extras (a dozen or more in some instances) flee in panic—many of them sporting smirky smiles and "Gee-it's-fun-to-be-an-extra" expressions on their faces.

Now it's time to introduce A*P*E's future love interest: *Growing Pains* sitcom mom Joanna Kerns (making her screen debut, billed here as Diana de Verona). Just so you *don't* confuse this film with Dino's big money/big monkey movie, Kerns plays an actress shooting a movie (wait—didn't Jessica Lange play the same thing in the Dino *Kong*?). And to further clarify that this is *not* a blatant rip-off of that *other* 1976 ape opus, Kern's human love interest/fiancé is a wisecracking, gruff know-it-all. (Say, I think *Kong*'s Jeff Bridges was one of those too!) And whenever Monkey Man reaches into a frame with full-sized humans, it's the exact same badly mechanized fake hand every time (Carlo Rambaldi's Oscar-winning effects for *Kong* also featured a single, full-sized monkey's paw). And finally, when confronted with her super-sized simian love interest, Kerns declares, "Be gentle, big fella!" (Almost word for word what Lange said to the Gorilla of Her Dreams). No *wonder* they were worried audiences might be "confused"!

By this point in the film, you'll also have noticed A*P*E's got one of the worst soundtracks of all time—for the first hour, an incessant five-note "love theme" ("Don't Monkey with My Love"?) loops endlessly. For the "action-packed" climax, a redundant seven-note "action theme" takes over. And the actual "production sound" features big patches where the entire audio track is literally blank, scene changes where outgoing music suddenly stops at picture cuts, and dialogue lines that get chopped off by the editing. You begin to wonder, "How did a director this incompetent find someone even *more* incompetent than himself to cut the film?" A quick check of the credits tells you the director actually cut this film *himself*—otherwise his "auteur's vision" might have been mangled in postproduction!

One of the most amusing things about *A*P*E* is that every time you think you've seen what *has* to be the lamest bit of model work or monkey business, it tops itself just moments later. Perhaps the high point of the film is when our Primate Pal carefully steps over the most obvious plastic toy cow you've *ever* seen onscreen.

It all leads up to the point where Kong—I mean A*P*E—takes Kerns hostage and tries to have his way with her. As he carries her across a blatantly man-made desert landscape, toy jets and helicopters swirl around his head, and Kerns looks suspiciously like a Barbie doll in his hands. Putting Barbie/Joanna down, he swats at the planes attacking him, doing what looks for all the world like a Watusi dance. When their bullets first start to pierce his fake-fur hide, he turns to the camera and . . . *flips them the bird*!

Now thoroughly enraged, Fur Boy heads into the city, where entire blocks full of four-foot-tall cardboard buildings await his unstoppable wrath. Finally done in on a sand dune (rather than atop the World Trade Center), A*P*E gets an epitaph from Kerns's fiancé that is, if possible, even hokier than that spoken by Bridges in the Dino *Kong*: "He was too big for a small world like ours!" But the last word belongs to the fanatical Colonel Davis, whose army of toy tanks have cut down the Great Beast. As the dust settles, Davis declares, "Let's see him dance for his organ grinder now!" Actually, had they cast an organ grinder's monkey in the title role instead of the man in the A*P*E suit, it would have been more convincing.

Dippy Dialogue
Tom Rose (*Rod Arrants*): "I'm a reporter—not Charlton Heston!"

Choice Chapter Stop
Chapter 11 ("Flipping a Chopper"): A*P*E flips the birdie.

The Beach Girls and the Monster
(1965/American International Pictures) **DVD / VHS**

Who's to Blame **CAST:** **Jon Hall** (*Otto Lindsay*); **Sue Casey** (*Vicky Lindsay*); **Walker Edmiston** (*Dick Lindsay*); **Elaine Dupont** (*Janie*); **Arnold Lessing** (*Mark*); **Tony Roberts** (*Brad*); **and introducing "Kingsley the Lion"**

CREW: **Directed by Jon Hall; Screenplay by Joan Gardner; Additional dialogue by Robert Silliphant and Don Marquis**

Rave Reviews
"A cheap laugh riot, with lots of bongos, murders and girls in bikinis!"
—Michael Weldon, *The Psychotronic Encyclopedia of Film*

"Maintains the philosophical depth and production values of 60s beach bimbo fare . . . a hybrid horror with acres of flesh!"
— *VideoHound's Golden Movie Retriever*

"A movie for morons . . . about as scary as one of those rubber baby toys that squeak when you squeeze them."
— Kevin Thomas, *Los Angeles Times*

Plot, What Plot? Jon Hall was once one of Hollywood's most handsome leading men, costarring with his female equivalent, Dorothy Lamour, in a series of exotic sandals-and-sarongs hits, including *Hurricane* and *Aloma of the South Seas*. But by the time Hall directed and starred in *Beach Girls and the Monster*, both his career and his looks had seen better days. An attempt to combine elements of drive-in horror movies, those horrible Frankie-and-Annette *Beach Party* films, and the plotless rock 'n' roll romps that were popular at the time, *Beach Girls* is a great big mess, obviously made on a teeny-tiny budget.

As the film begins, you may think your DVD player is malfunctioning: Surely the feature can't start with a random shot of four bikini-clad babes bop-dancing on the beach with no setup, no master shot, no nothin'. But since nothin' is what they spent on this little know-nothin' gem, nothin' is what they figured we'd expect. About the only name you might recognize superimposed over the wriggling, jiggling bimbos is Frank Sinatra Jr., who did the music . . .

The plot, such as it is, begins with a group of teenagers having a hot dog hootenanny on the beach when one couple runs off to be alone. The blonde girlfriend, who practically has the words "First Victim" stamped on her forehead, tosses sand at the guy and runs laughing into a cave. Little does she know, the cave is home to . . . The Monster! Okay, the "monster" actually looks like a ten-cent baby bathtub toy of the Creature from the Black Lagoon, with googling eyes made from goofballs. But before you can say "Bye-bye, Bimbo," the monster has offed the girl and taken off on a wild killing spree. A killing spree which, due to budgetary constraints, consists of three further attempts to imbibe bimbo burger—only two of them successful.

Despite all this horror, and further contributing to it, is the teens' insistence on continuing to hold hot dog parties and dance sessions on the beach—at night. At one of these, the bikini babes bop to a truly bizarre tune called "There's a Monster in the Surf," performed by a hand puppet of a severed head called Kingsley the Lion. Its lyrics, written by the "actors" who perform it, include such brilliant rhymes as, "Everybody's sleepin', monster comes a creepin' Yeah! Yeah! Yeah!" Clearly intended to be odd, this one song is so far off the charts in its lunacy that it achieves a surreality that has likely left zombied-out late-night TV viewers dazed for decades.

After much wasted screen time diverting suspicion to a crippled sculptor as "the man in the monster suit," all is resolved when the monster turns out to be Hall himself, nursing a grudge against "those surfers that hang around the beach all the time." When the teens are defended by a cop as being "a nice bunch of kids just trying to find themselves," Hall snorts: "They'll find themselves in your jail one day! The boys are nothing but a bunch of loafers and the girls are little tramps! They contribute absolutely nothing to a decent society!"

Hall's reward for speaking the truth, and possibly saving the world from a sequel to this film? Two cop cars chase him through an obviously rear-projection Malibu, still wearing the body suit of the monster. Finally, his fancy little MG sports car crashes through a guardrail overlooking the ocean—and on its way over the cliff (thanks to the magic of stock footage) the 1956 MG turns into a 1937 roadster before bursting into flames. And when the cops arrive to survey the wreck, yet a third blatantly different vehicle is seen overturned in flames.

Although Robert Silliphant, cowriter of *The Creeping Terror*, was brought in to do "additional dialogue," the final proof of just how low-budget this film is is the fact that the producers couldn't even afford to pay for a pithy last line, something everyone expects from a movie like this. Instead we fade out on the stock footage of the burning car, and a cheapo THE END title appears. But we bet what you'll still remember for days (or weeks!) is the "Monster in the Surf" song. Weird, man, weird!

Dippy Dialogue
Dick (*Walker Edmiston*): "Bunny's dead—doesn't that mean anything to you?"
Vicky (*Sue Casey*): "What *should* it mean to me??"

The Giant Spider Invasion

(1975/Group 1 Releasing)   **DVD / VHS**

Who's to Blame   CAST: **Steve Brodie** (*Dr. J. R. Vance*); **Barbara Hale** (*Dr. Jenny Langer*); **Alan Hale Jr.** (*Sheriff Jeff Jones*); **Robert Easton** (*Dan Kester*); **Kevin Brodie** (*Dave Perkins*); **Diane Lee Hart** (*Terry*); **Bill Williams** (*Dutch*); SPECIAL GUEST STAR: **Leslie Parrish** (*Ev Kester*)
CREW: **Directed by Bill Rebane; Written by Richard L. Huff and Robert Easton; From a story by Huff**

Rave Reviews
"Lots of laughs ... there hasn't been a movie with special effects so bad since *The Giant Claw*!"
—**Michael Weldon,** *The Psychotronic Encyclopedia of Film*

"RATED: BOMB ... [a] tacky horror opus filmed in Wisconsin."
—*Leonard Maltin's Movie & Video Guide*

"Perversely entertaining."
—**The Amazing World of Cult Movies (Web site)**

Plot, What Plot? If you've ever wondered why Wisconsin is the capital of American cheesemaking rather than moviemaking, *The Giant Spider Invasion* should answer your query. Produced in the small town of Gleason, on an obvious shoestring budget, *Giant Spider* features a collection of has-beens and never-really-weres, presents some of the least special "outer space special effects" since Rocket Man hung up his helmet, and stars the silliest "giant creature" *ever* created in movie history. It takes this film almost an hour for the "giant spider" to show up, and when it does, it's so blatantly a VW beetle with fake legs attached that you won't believe your eyes.

The first familiar face in *Invasion*'s parade of "Didn't he used to be so-and-so" actors is Alan Hale Jr., playing the town sheriff. Just in case you don't recognize him as The Skipper from *Gilligan's Island,* the screenplay has him call an eager young newspaper reporter "little buddy."

The whole town is abuzz about a revival meeting that night, during which no one seems to notice "comets from space" streaking into farm fields just outside of town. As seen in the first of this film's 237 cheesy special effects, the trajectories of these comets are suspiciously straight—almost like someone took an eraser and a ruler to the film's negative. Within a day or two, geodes found around town start cracking open, and normal-sized tarantulas walk out of them. In one of the film's few intentionally funny moments, town boozer Leslie Parrish fails to notice a spider in her blender, and whips up a truly Bloody Mary.

Parrish's husband is a hillbilly who makes Jed Clampett seem like a Rhodes scholar. Considering how lame his southern accent is, it's amazing that he's played by Robert Easton, who made a career of teaching countless actors how to do "believable" accents. But then, he's not only this film's worst actor, he's also the film's coauthor. It seems that Dippy Dan is so dumb he thinks the sparkly insides of those geodes are "diamonds from space," and goes off to gather them up like so many Easter eggs. He thus winds up being the first character "eaten" by a giant spider, which "devours" him in much the same way Bela Lugosi wrestled with the rubber octopus in *Bride of the Monster.*

Two "NASA scientists," played by *Perry Mason*'s Barbara Hale and Steve Brodie from TV's *Wyatt Earp,* figure out that if they "shower the monster with neutrons," it may die from energy overload. The scene where they try to explain this theory to Alan Hale by telephone is a classic: Brodie is clearly standing just off camera feeding his "over-the-phone" dialogue to Hale, who revives several of his I'm-a-likable-doofus expressions from *Gilligan* to convey that he has no idea what he's being told. Impatient with scientific solutions, the townsfolk then meet up at a bar to fight the annoying arachnids via vigilantism, and a wide shot of a mob of armed Wisconsinites rushing from the bar looks like a cattle casting call for *The Ed Grimley Story.*

Soon a single "giant spider" is seen crossing farmlands at 37 miles an hour, headed for the local Gleason Days Festival, where innocent children and toothless old men have gathered to gum undercooked chicken, knock over Coke bottles with baseballs, ride on rinky-dink carnival rides—and eventually become so many spider snacks. When the giant spider finally attacks the crowd at a local baseball field, you'll swear you can see VW tire tracks on the infield as the local yokels flee in panic.

Finally convinced that he *does* have a problem, Sheriff Hale calls in the National Guard, but not before that old horror-movie standby an "angry mob" gathers in the town square. As Hale tries to disperse the mob, our single "giant spider" shows up again, this time with red lenses on its VW headlights. The mob tries to fight back, but hand-tossed rocks prove useless against the beast . . . which nevertheless turns tail and heads out of town.

In a too-little-too-late attempt to hide how hideously humorous their title character is, the action suddenly shifts to day-for-night, with some of the spider shots so underexposed you literally can't see what's going on. Before the two scientists can dispatch the spider, it has one final snack: the deputy sheriff, whose brave final words are, "Eat lead, you!" as he fires his gun and pulls himself up into the monster's maw. A single highway flare is then lit and tossed into the "spider's nest," causing a mini mushroom cloud which the filmmakers were so impressed with they then show it again in slo-mo reverse. As it expires, the "giant spider" spews gick that looks like projectile-fired, melted chocolate ice cream.

Relieved that it's over, Dr. Hale hugs Dr. Brodie and asks, "Can it happen again?" But just as Brodie replies, "I don't know," everything freeze-frames and the titles pop on, leaving us to wonder: Given how ultra-hokey the entire film was, what was wretched enough that they'd resort to a freeze-frame instead of showing it? Perhaps someday, when the "restored director's cut" of *Giant Spider Invasion* is released on DVD, we'll finally know . . .

Dippy Dialogue
Sheriff Jones (*Alan Hale Jr.*): "Did you ever see that movie *Jaws*—this makes that shark look like a goldfish!"

Choice Chapter Stops
Chapter 4 (*About 35 minutes*): The Spider-in-the-Blender scene.
Chapter 6 (*About 1 hour, 6 minutes*): The "Giant Spider" (actually a VW) attacks a local baseball game.

Goliath and the Dragon

(1960/American International Pictures) **DVD / VHS**

Who's to Blame CAST: **Mark Forest** (*Emilius/Goliath*); **Broderick Crawford** (*King Eurytheus*); **Eleanora Ruffo** (*Dejanira*); **Wandisa Guida** (*Alcinoe*); **Sandro Moretti** (*Illus*); **Claudio Undari** (*Satyr*)

CREW: **Directed by Vittorio Cottafavi; Screenplay based on a story by Mario Piccolo and Archibald Zounds Jr.**

Rave Reviews

"A must for fans of ridiculous movies with ridiculous monsters!"
—*VideoHound's Golden Movie Retriever*

"Very enjoyable and full of cheesy goodness."
— Duane L. Martin, B-MovieCentral.com

"A real potboiler. . . . Get ready for a great late-night schlockfest!"
— "The Vid," IMDb.com

Plot, What Plot? Any movie that opens with a camera angle peering up a bodybuilder's backside as he climbs into a volcano immediately qualifies for entrance into the "anals" of Bad Movie Nirvana. *Goliath and the Dragon,* filled with badly dubbed English dialogue, cheesy-looking creatures, and costumes that could've been borrowed from a Hollywood High School production of *Medea,* is perhaps the funniest of the dozens of Italian-made "sword and sandal" epics that tumbled across American drive-in movie screens in the early 1960s.

Originally entitled *La Vendetta di Ercole,* this one was picked up for U.S. distribution by American International, the company best known for *Beach Party* movies and Edgar Allan Poe rip-offs. Since Warner Bros. owned the rights to the name Hercules, AIP simply renamed this film's hero "Goliath," spent what appears to be about $57 on a new English dialogue track, and threw in another $112 to "upgrade" the scene where "Goliath" takes on the "dragon" of the title.

The first of the film's many laughable beasties shows up just over three minutes in. Supposedly a three-headed dog, this "terrifying" creature snaps, snarls, swivels its multiple heads, and breathes fire (courtesy of three flame throwers visible in its snout)—and is then dispatched in less than one minute, but not before we have ample chance to notice it looks more like a three-headed bearskin rug than any identifiable breed of dog.

The first of the film's many abrupt scene and audio changes comes before the steam stops rising from "Fluffy's" three dead heads: Suddenly we find ourselves staring at Broderick Crawford, in a two-sizes-too-big toga and sporting a facial scar that looks like he recently went through a windshield. Then he speaks—and it ain't the "10-4, good buddy" voice of Oscar winner Crawford we hear, it's some low-budget imitator, who sounds remarkably like Mel Blanc voicing a Looney Tunes cartoon gangster.

Meanwhile, back on another Italian soundstage, "Goliath" has found "the bloodstone." But he is blocked from simply grabbing it by yet another lame beastie. Looking like *Star Wars*'s Chewbacca trick-or-treating as a bat, this half-man/half-bat thing doesn't even last 35 seconds up against Ol' Bare Butt-Cheeks. Having defeated two terrifying creatures in only ten minutes, "Goliath" returns triumphantly to his homeland.

The so-called plot finally gets going as Big Broddie plans to kidnap Goliath's best pal and deliver the muscleman's missus into the mouth of his pet dragon. Much muscle flexing ensues, culminating in the Cave of Horrors, where Goliath goes head-to-head with the fearsome (read: incredibly fake-looking) dragon of the title. Given how unconvincing the Final Beastie is, even with AIP's upgrading, one wonders how much more amusing the original Italian monster must have been.

Dippy Dialogue
Goliath (*Mark Forest*), addressing his barbecue guests: "I ask your pardon for my absence, friends, but the unpleasantness is over now! Let us enjoy our dinner..."

Choice Chapter Stops
Chapter 1 ("Main Titles and Cave of Horrors"): Close-ups of Goliath's backside, followed by the Three-Headed-Dog-Rug.
Chapter 12 ("Goliath vs. the Dragon"): Gourmet fromage.

Jaws: The Revenge

(1987/Universal Pictures) **DVD / VHS**

Who's to Blame CAST: **Lorraine Gary** ☺ (*Ellen Brody*); **Michael Caine** ☺ (*Hoagie Newcomb*); **Lance Guest** (*Michael Brody*); **Mario Van Peebles** (*Jake*); **Karen Young** (*Carla*); **Judith Barsi** (*Thea Brody*); **Bruce the Rubber Shark** ☺ (*Himself*)
CREW: **Directed by Joseph Sargent** ☺, **Screenplay by Michael De Guzman; Based on characters created by Peter Benchley**

Rave Reviews:
"Not simply a bad movie, but also a stupid and incompetent one—a rip-off." — **Roger Ebert**, *Chicago Sun-Times*

"There's more suspense in *On Golden Pond*. Some sequences among the humans . . . are so pathetic that you begin rooting for the shark."
— **Desson Howe**, *Washington Post*

"The attack sequences, full of jagged cuts and a great deal of noise, more closely resemble the view from inside a washing machine." — *Variety*

Plot, What Plot? With most of the titles in this book, we recommend that you watch the *entire* film to achieve maximum enjoyment. But with *Jaws: The Revenge,* its last half hour is so funny, and its first hour is so excruciatingly awful, we suggest that you take advantage of the DVD chapter stops and skip immediately to chapter 17, where Ellen Brody (Lorraine Gary) sails off alone to face Bruce the Shark fin-to-fin.

The fourth film in the *Jaws* series, *The Revenge* came four years after 1983 Worst Picture nominee *Jaws 3-D*. And as bad as *3-D* was, it was still superior to this chum-bucket chuckle fest. The first hour establishes the Brody family as still living in Amity, still grieving over the deaths and near-deaths from the previous films, and still swimming in the estuary where almost every family member has had a run-in with Bruce, thus continuing to offer themselves as shark bait. Sure enough, one of the sons *does* get chomped during that first hour, but this film's makers were too cheap to hire John Williams to adapt his classic *Jaws* theme once more, and too incompetent to stage the feeding frenzy in an even remotely frenzied way. So the results are lame in the extreme.

But losing another son to that snarky shark sends Mrs. Brody off the deep end. In fact, she's so upset by it that she forgets to ever put on any makeup, and thus looks like the result of a failed gene-splicing experiment using material from both Joan Rivers and Elsa Lanchester as the Bride of Frankenstein. In a line that strains credibility, to say the least, she tells surviving son Michael: "It came for him . . . it waited all this time and it came for him!" Where else can Michael send his bonkers mom but the Bahamas to "get over" her loss? And who should decide to join them in paradise but . . . Ol' Rubber Teeth himself.

Mrs. B then heads off to meet her fate, boarding a boat the size of a glorified dinghy (with the macho-sounding name *Neptune's Folly* emblazoned on its side) and daring Brucie with the immortal line, "Come and get me, you son of a bitch!" Just to show she means business, Gary removes her jacket to reveal a pair of shoulder pads that make her look like an anorexic Green Bay Packer. Of course, since it's been "after" her since 1975, the shark can't resist, and soon shows itself by jumping out of the water onto the back of the boat. The fact that it's no more convincing a fake fish than the one attacking trams regularly on the Universal Studios Tour may explain why this film "won" a Razzie for Worst Special Visual Effects.

Flying over the backlot water tank at Universal searching for Mrs. B are Mario Van Peebles, Oscar winner Michael Caine, and Lance Guest (the fourth actor to play Michael Brody in four films). Belly-flopping into the water beside Mrs. B's dinghy, Caine and crew stupidly swim across from their airplane to help her. At least Caine thought to wear drip-dry clothes, as he emerges from the ocean crisply, dryly dressed. As the shark swings by for one more bite, Van Peebles heads out to the prow to throw a sonic device into its mouth—and winds up being Brucie Chow, along with the beeper. Now Mrs. B is *so* mad, she starts remembering incidents from previous *Jaws* films that happened when she wasn't even there. She spins the ship's wheel wildly toward the shark, impales it on the broken prow—and it *explodes,* for no clear reason.

Then comes the most blatant test-market ending of all time as (on the Universal/MCA DVD) Van Peebles is suddenly found alive, and everybody gets to go home happy. Everybody but the paying patrons, that is. On opening night in Hollywood, *Jaws: The Revenge* was regularly greeted with audience guffaws. And when it ended, an extensive, angry "BOO!" was left lingering in the air.

In large part because of his Worst Actor–nominated "performance" here, Bruce the Shark received our 1987 Worst Career Achievement Razzie Award. And no one found our choice fishy in the least . . .

Dippy Dialogue
Hoagie (*Michael Caine*), getting out of his plane as Bruce the Shark pops up: "Aww . . . shit!"

Choice Chapter Stop
Chapter 17 ("*Where's Mother?*"): In which Mrs. Brody decides to go off and get that pesky shark herself . . .

Fun Footnote
At one time Universal was considering doing a *deliberate* comedy sequel in conjunction with National Lampoon. It was to be entitled *Jaws 5, People Zero.*

King Kong Lives

(1986/De Laurentiis Entertainment Group) **DVD / VHS**

Who's to Blame **CAST:** **Brian Kerwin** (*Hank Mitchell*); **Linda Hamilton** (*Dr. Amy Franklin*); **John Ashton** (*Col. Nevitt*); **Peter Michael Goetz** (*Dr. Ingersoll*); **Peter Elliott** (*King Kong*); **George Yiasomi** (*Lady Kong*)
CREW: **Directed by John Guillermin; Story and screenplay by Ronald Shusett and Steven Pressfield**

Rave Reviews
"Hilarious . . . some of the funniest scenes imaginable!"
— **John Stanley, *Creature Features Movie Guide Strikes Again***

"The proximity of two Kongs prompts these primates to discover what comes naturally. . . . Mindless!" — ***Variety***

"There are sequences that are guaranteed to have audiences rolling on the floor . . . one of the funniest sights in modern cinema history!"
— **Richard Scheib, Science Fiction, Horror and Fantasy Film Review (Web site)**

Plot, What Plot? Only producer Dino De Laurentiis, the one person on earth who thought his wretched 1976 remake of *King Kong* was any good, would be dumb enough to produce a sequel ten years later. But what can Kong do in this one that he hasn't done before? How about fall in love! The result, an ersatz *Kong* equivalent of *Bride of Frankenstein,* is one of the most incredibly asinine, unnecessary sequels ever made. It's also one of the most idiotically entertaining.

We begin with the ending from the '76 *Kong,* in which everyone remembers the big ape died . . . or did he? We suddenly switch to a facility in Georgia (subtitled "Ten Years Later") where Kong has been kept on life support, and is still awaiting a blood donor so an artificial Kong-sized heart can be implanted. Luckily (!) a female Kong is found in Borneo and their "blood types" match, so the operation can proceed. Despite complications during surgery, Ol' King recovers so quickly that for the rest of the film, no scar is seen on his chest.

But once Kong gets a whiff of Kongarella, there's no keeping them apart. Together, they break free and run off into the wilderness for a humongous honeymoon, with U.S. Army battalions in hot pursuit. The rest of the film is basically a chase, with Kongarella captured and kept in a silo while Kong fights his way back to her. Along the way, King eats a few crocodiles, chomps on a Cajun hunter or two, and falls from a cliff into a raging river where he bonks his head on a rock. "Not even your Kong can survive that!" declares the colonel, who wants this monkey to cry uncle!

Of course, the colonel is wrong, and our Ape Couple *are* reunited. We then discover that Kongarella is "in a family way." As the Army fills the Daddy-to-Be full of bullets, Mommy goes into labor, and what is supposed to be a touching ending finds Baby Kong arriving just as Daddy dies. We guarantee there won't be a dry eye in the house—you'll have tears streaming down your face from laughing so hard.

Mere description cannot do this film justice. Neither the brain-dead dialogue nor its delivery help us to resist deriding it at every turn. And in scene after scene, little touches like the Buick-sized artificial heart, the squishy/sucky sound effects during Kong's surgery, or the dopey lovesick smiles on the apes' faces prompt fits of disbelieving snickers. This is one film whose existence cannot be explained in a sane universe. And as it ends, you realize . . . the birth of Baby Kong was intended as a setup for a *third* Dino/*Kong* movie. Maybe it didn't get made because Mama Kong's agent asked too much for reprising her role?

Dippy Dialogue
Dr. Amy Franklin (*Linda Hamilton*): "We're not lancing a hemorrhoid here, we're replacing a heart!"

Choice Chapter Stop
Chapter 4 ("*Surgery*"): In which Kong gets an artificial heart—the size of a Volkswagen!

Razzie Credential *King Kong Lives* was nominated for one award, Worst Special Visual Effects, which it lost to 1986's Worst Picture "winner" *Howard the Duck*.

(1970/Warner Bros.) **VHS**

Who's to Blame Cast: **Joan Crawford** (*Dr. Brockton*); **Michael Gough** (*Sam Murdock*); **Bernard Key** (*Inspector Greenham*); **Kim Braden** (*Anne Brockton*); **Thorley Walters** (*Magistrate*); **Joe Cornelius** (*Trog*)
Crew: **Directed by Freddie Francis; Screenplay by Aben Kandel; Story by Peter Bryan and John Gilling**

Rave Reviews
"Super-ridiculous. . . . *Trog* is a dog!"
— **John Stanley,** *Creature Features Movie Guide Strikes Again*

"A fascinating Golden Turkey—[has] a wonderfully hysterical camp value." — **Richard Scheib, Science Fiction Horror and Fantasy Film Review (Web site)**

"Crawford has done more than her share of crappy movies . . . however, the ridiculous *Trog* has to be the absolute worst!"
— **Ned Daigle, BadMovieNight.com**

Plot, What Plot? The bottom of the barrel for former screen queen Joan Crawford proved to be a steeper drop than even she could have imagined. Having already played a psychopathic axe murderess in *Strait-Jacket* and an aging carnival barker in *Berserk,* Crawford would end her career with a film so embarrassing she reportedly once joked that if it weren't for her end-of-life conversion to Christian Science, she might have committed suicide just thinking about it.

In *Trog,* Crawford basically plays straight man to a guy who's supposed to be the proverbial Missing Link, but instead looks like someone in a badly glued-on dime-store monkey mask. "Trog" is short for troglodyte, but the creature is so utterly unconvincing as to elicit guffaws every time he's shown. Joan plays a famous woman scientist who befriends Trog, teaches him to play ball, cuddle dolls, and say "Wah-wah!" She also discovers that Trog enjoys classical music, but whenever he hears rock 'n' roll, he literally goes ape. You think we're making this stuff up?

It's either a tribute to her devotion as an actress, or a side effect of the heavy doses of vodka that she reputedly laced her Pepsi with by this point in life, but Crawford plays this entire film with a sincerity that's both laudable and laughable. If any dignity could be brought to this slumming role, Crawford *almost* pulls it off. But her appearance finally does her in. Dressed in custom-made outfits that run the rainbow of pastel colors, with her hair dyed that odd, old-lady red American women past sixty seem to favor, and sporting enough mascara to play *Bride of the Beast with 10,000 Eyes,* the ever vain Crawford looks every day of her age in this film.

Almost as scary-looking as Joan, Trog is first discovered in an underground cave in the countryside of England, and, being the "foremost authority" on such things, "brilliant woman scientist" Crawford is called in to both determine what the creature is, and how best to handle it. Since she is now best remembered as the subject of both the book and movie versions of *Mommie Dearest,* the maternal instincts Crawford displays toward Trog have an even more laughable quality today than when the film was made.

Using her considerable expertise, Dr. Joan concludes that, properly trained and handled, Trog could prove her theory that primitive man had many of the same abilities and instincts as his modern counterpart. To make her point, she holds a press conference at which an irrelevant, odd (and blatantly time-filling) short film is shown, explaining Trog's world and origins. Apparently, Trog comes from Irwin Allen's *Animal World,* since most of the short "explanatory" film's footage is borrowed from it. Dr. Joan then takes a tip from Gene Wilder in *Young Frankenstein,* staging a demonstration of her protégé's progress. But things go awry when a photographer's flash sets off Trog's temper, and again later when an angry neighbor (barkingly overacted by Michael Gough) sets Trog free to go on a killing spree, after which Trog returns to his cave.

Naturally, Dr. Joan rushes to convince authorities not to destroy her new friend, even though Trog now appears to have taken a little girl hostage. The scene where the perfectly coiffed Crawford, clad in a designer "spelunking ensemble," lures the kidnapped child from Trog's clutches in the dark, dank cave evokes both uncontrollable laughter and great pity—a bizarre experience, to say the least. If you've seen *King Kong* (or *A*P*E*) we probably don't need to tell you how *Trog* ends. That it was both the end and the nadir of her mother's movie career must have made daughter Christina Crawford one of *Trog*'s biggest fans.

Dippy Dialogue
Dr. Brockton (*Joan Crawford*): "Get the ball! Good boy, Trog!"

(1984/New World Pictures) **VHS**

Who's to Blame CAST: **Lorenzo Lamas** ☉ (*"Chilly"*); **Vicki Frederick** (*Claire*); **Cameron Dye** (*"E-Z"*); **Michelle Nicastro** (*Darlene*); **Ray Sharkey** (*Terrence*); **La Ron A. Smith** (*"Magick"*); **Grace Zabriskie** (*Chilly's Mom*); **Oz Rock** (*Ricky Ricardo*)
CREW: **Directed by Marcelo Epstein; Screenplay by Desmond Nakano; Story by Nakano and Kimberly Lynn White**

Rave Reviews
"Watching Lamas as the emcee/break-dancing fool is a hoot."
— *VideoHound's Golden Movie Retriever*

"The dancing in the movie is so hilariously bad that . . . it's the stuff camp classic fans dream of."
— **Keith Bailey, The Unknown Movies Page (Web site)**

"Watching Lamas chomp to the beat is like watching Victor Mature boogaloo." — *Leonard Maltin's Movie & Video Guide*

Plot, What Plot? Among the flash flood of knockoffs, rip-offs, and jerk-offs that inundated movie theatres in the wake of the phenomenal 1983 success of *Flashdance,* most people think the absolute nadir of mid-'80s dance flicks has gotta be Cannon Films's *Breakin'* (or its even more oafish sequel, *Breakin' 2: Electric Boogaloo*). But that's because most people have never even heard of, let alone seen, the true champ/chump among super-lame street-dancing musicals: Lorenzo Lamas in *Body Rock*.

Best known for playing "Lance Cumson" on TV's *Falcon Crest,* today Lamas is nearly forgotten. But twenty years ago, everyone thought this lug with a nice mug was really hot stuff—and nobody thought Lorenzo was hotter than Lorenzo himself, which makes watching Lamas make an utter ass of himself on and off the dance floor in *Body Rock* such a singular pleasure.

Our story begins as Chilly D (Lamas) is trying to decide what to do with his life. We meet him attending an interview at the unemployment office, dressed in colorful ragtag clothing with his hairy chest exposed to his navel. Asked, "Do you usually dress like this for interviews?" Chilly replies, "Oh, yeah—I always like to look fresh!" His secret dream, which neither the unemployment people (nor the best dance coach on earth) can help him achieve, is to be a break-dancing "star" on the New York club scene. Since Lamas has all the natural rhythm and panther-like grace usually associated with Wayne Newton, we realize immediately that this film is going to be a fantasy.

Grabbing opportunity by the short hairs, Chilly gets promoter Ray Sharkey to attend a performance by his dance group Body Rock at their local hangout Rhythm Nation. Only problem is, now Lorenzo must actually learn to dance—yes, the film is at least sentient enough to admit that its star needs a little help in the terpsichorean department. His main coach is little ten-year-old "Magick," a truly talented little pop-n-locker who moves like a precision wind-up toy and openly declares Lamas's case to be hopeless.

But before long, Lorenzo/Chilly is rilly bustin' moves and blowing away audiences with routines that look alarmingly like what happens when test dummies crash into walls in auto safety tests. Only problem is, when Starkey calls Chilly back, it's *only* Chilly he wants to promote—*not* any of his street-dancin' pals.

Chilly decides to go for it, explaining his need to move out and up with, "I need to be in a creative environment, Ma. I need to be around other artists." Pursuing his dream turns out to encompass giving "break-dancing lessons" to Darlene, a skanky gal pal of Sharkey's, whom he moves in with. His new "upper crust" lifestyle also includes leather designer outfits with his name spray-painted on them and, in the film's guffaw-full musical highlight, his own theme song performed with sequins glued to his face and green smoke being blown up his backside.

The film's funniest "dramatic" moment comes when Chilly is kissed by Sharkey's friend Donald in a gay bar, punches him out . . . and then discovers that it was Donald's money that was to pay for Chilly's recording session. Told that he's been sacked for refusing to share the sack with Donald, Chilly yells, "Screw him, he kissed me!"

So, will Chilly do right by his former bros from the 'hood? Will he achieve his dreams, even if he's not willing to suck face or kiss ass to get ahead? If you're feeling resistant to the idea of seeking out this amazingly awful film, perhaps Chilly/Lorenzo's philosophy of breakdancing will help sway you: "Don't move. Just open your mind . . . and let your body follow."

Loopy Lyrics
Chilly (*Lorenzo Lamas*) sings his signature tune, "Smooth Talker," at the dance club: "I'm a hard situation, I'm a sensual relation and I'm harder than a rock—I've got a hole in my pocket where I keep my rocket, and it shows in the way I walk!"
Chorus: "Smooth talker!"

Can't Stop the Music

(1980/AFD)

Who's to Blame   CAST: **The Village People** (*Themselves*); **Valerie Perrine**☺ (*Samantha Simpson*); **Bruce Jenner**☺ (*Ron White*); **Steve Guttenberg** (*Jack Morell*); **Paul Sand** (*Steve Waits*); **Barbara Rush** (*Norma White*); **Altovise Davis** (*Alicia Edwards*); **Marilyn Sokol**☺ (*Lulu Brecht*)

CREW: **Directed by Nancy Walker**☺; **Screenplay**● by Bronte Woodard and Allan Carr

Rave Reviews

"Undeniably the absolute worst musical in film history!"
— Ned Daigle, BadMovieNight.com

"With regard to character, plot, and dialogue, *Can't Stop the Music* . . . is too campy to describe . . . it's priceless kitsch."
— Troy Patterson, *Entertainment Weakly*

"Both awful and immensely enjoyable—the ideal party movie!"
— Wade Major, *Box Office* magazine

Plot, What Plot? The enormous and largely unexpected success of *Grease* in 1978 may be responsible for more bad 1980s movies than any other film. As the producer of *Grease,* elfin entrepreneur Allan Carr was able to mount several Worst Picture contenders over the next five years. But few of them achieved the status of legendary awfulness now accorded *Can't Stop the Music,* the film that not only "won" our first ever Worst Picture ack-olade, but helped inspire the entire idea of the Razzies in the first place.

    In 1978, when the deal for this film was being negotiated, the Village People were America's disco darlings, a sextet of gay stereotypes whose string of hits included "Macho Man," "In the Navy," and their signature tune, "Y.M.C.A." But disco was to die a swift and merciless death before *Can't Stop* and its equally awful evil twin, *Xanadu,* ever hit theatres. Sold as "the movie musical event of the '80s," and produced at an estimated cost of $20 million, *Can't Stop* proved instead to be one of the most miserable financial events of the '80s, grossing a humiliating $2 million before becoming one of the first quick-to-video titles in Hollywood history.

Based on the "true" story of how the Village People came about, *Can't Stop* is basically a reworking of those old Mickey-and-Judy MGM musicals, in this case a boys-meet-boys version. Standing in for Jacques Morali (the Village People's founder who's credited as coproducer of the film) is a very young, very dorky (but not very endearing) Steve Guttenberg as "Jack Morel." By day he works in a giant New York record emporium, but by night he and roomie Samantha (sexy but slutty Valerie Perrine) conspire on ways to get Jack's songs heard by a public that yearns to dance to tunes like "Magic Night." Batting around ideas while throwing a lasagna singalong party one night (yes, the Razzie-"winning" screenplay is *that* hokey!), Jack and Sam hit on the idea of holding open auditions in Greenwich Village. Among the contestants who answer the call of booty are a leather biker man, a blond construction worker, a black cop, a soldier, a sequined cowboy, and a scantily clad Indian in full-feathered regalia.

Now that they've got their "group," it's time to record their first song, "Liberation," a paean to Gay Lib in the days before AIDS existed. Like the film itself, their first recording session is a total disaster. So the meat of the film deals with Perrine's efforts to get "Marakesh Records" executive Paul Sand to sign the boys to a contract, and aging publicist Tammy Grimes's efforts to get Perrine and the Village People to agree to do a commercial for milk. Along the way, the VP sing such "original" tunes as "I Love You to Death," "Samantha," and, in the film's high-camp highlight, "Y.M.C.A." This number, staged in the steam rooms, locker rooms, swimming pools, and hot tubs of a men's gym, combines elements of old Esther Williams pictures, *Rocky, Lonely Lady,* and countless other tacky movies to create an eye-popping, mind-boggling sequence that is the epitome of 1980s tastelessness.

By film's end, the Village People are set to debut in concert in San Francisco with the Ritchie Family as their opening act. Backstage, Guttenberg rallies his traipsing troops with the announcement, "Hey, guys—we're a *group!*" They then take to the stage in glitter-glommed versions of their each-one-a-gay-cliché costumes for what feels like a 19-minute dance remix/reprise of the film's Razzie-nominated title tune, "(You) Can't Stop the Music."

Now that it's on DVD and you can skip and jump through the boring stretches (namely, anything with 1980 Worst Actor nominee Bruce Jenner as a "square" lawyer courting Perrine), *Can't Stop the Music* is almost as enjoyable as its double-feature-mate that co-inspired the Razzies, *Xanadu*.

Dippy Dialogue
Jack (*Steven Guttenberg*), to Samantha (*Valerie Perrine*): "Anyone who can swallow two Sno Balls and a Ding Dong shouldn't have any problem with pride."

Choice Chapter Stop
Chapter 16 ("Y.M.C.A."): The Village People's signature song. (Try freeze-framing at 1:16:00 to spot both of Perrine's nipples clearly in view.)

From Justin to Kelly ☻

(2003/20th Century-Fox)   **DVD / VHS**

Who's to Blame   CAST: **Kelly Clarkson** ☻ (*Kelly*); **Justin Guarini** ☻ (*Justin*); **Katherine Bailess** (*Alexa*); **Anika Noni Rose** (*Kaya*); **Greg Siff** (*Brandon*); **Brian Dietzen** (*Eddie*); **Theresa San Nicholas** (*Officer Cutler*)
CREW: **Directed by Robert Iscove** ☻; **Screenplay** ☻ **by Kim Fuller**

Rave Reviews
"The cinematic equivalent of Cheez Whiz!"
— **Stephen Holden,** *New York Times*

"*Xanadu* revisited!" — **Greg Braxton,** *Los Angeles Times*

"So outrageously poor, so cluelessly conceived, [that it's] a campy delight for audiences looking for a *Plan 9 from Outer Space*–style film to mock." — **Phil Villareal,** *Arizona Daily Star*

Plot, What Plot? Movies as wonderfully dunderheaded as *From Justin to Kelly* are rare indeed. Watching the winner and runner-up from the first year of TV's *American Idol* make total asses of themselves in this vehicle tailor-made for their "talents" personifies what Bad Film Appreciation is all about.

Concocted as a fast-buck chance to cash in on the 15 minutes of fame Kelly Clarkson and Justin Guarini experienced as a result of *American Idol, From Justin to Kelly* was shot in three weeks, rushed into theatres in less than three months . . . and was dead in the water within three days. Essentially a combination of those Frankie-and-Annette *Beach Party* movies and a wholesale rip-off of the old Connie Francis vehicle *Where the Boys Are, From Justin to Kelly* "borrows" elements from every bad beach musical ever made. Its plot is both simple and simpleminded: Two groups of young singles on vacation in Florida keep miscommunicating and misconnecting until "romance" finally blossoms at film's end. That absolutely nothing in *J2K* (as its releasing studio referred to it in press materials) would seem out of place in a 1960 beach musical is only one of its problems.

The biggest problem is that the onscreen "chemistry" between its stars is practically nil. It's obvious they actually like each other, but any thought of their sharing a sexual relationship, as the *L.A. Weekly* put it, "makes one think not of romantic destiny but of unseemly sibling affection." Add to this problem the fact that either one would be in over their head handling the second lead in a high school senior play, and you begin to see the Razz-able possibilities.

We first see Kelly in a Texas beer joint, singing "I Won't Stand in Line" (and yes, many critics did pick up on how prophetic that song title was). Seems her gal pals Alexa and Kaya are planning a spring break trip to Florida, and want to include her. When her lummox of a "steady boyfriend" comes on too strong, Kelly is ready to quit her job and head south. Justin, on the other hand, hangs out with his "posse" using promotional gimmicks like a "Whipped Cream Bikini Contest" to get access to girls. If you're wondering why on earth anyone with an IQ over 27 should care, you've already got one up on this film's makers.

Interspersed with the entirely predictable plot of their destined love being short-wired by Kelly's blonde vixen of a best friend Alexa are some of the clumsiest, most clod-footed musical numbers imaginable. Behind-the-scenes footage on the official Web site for *J2K* had both stars mentioning that they "weren't natural dancers," and expressing gratitude that the film's choreographer, Travis Payne, came up with moves they could handle. Since both stars seem to have trouble putting one foot in front of the other without stumbling, you can imagine how "inspired" Payne's work is. Featuring isometric moves with oversized beachballs, moves that look like flocks of spastic ducks painfully molting, and guys-grabbing-gals moves that wind up with the gals' crotches in the guys' faces, the dance routines in *J2K* inspired a Special Governor's Award at the 24th Annual Razzies, specifically to dis-honor Mr. Payne's "Distinguished Under-Achievement in Choreography."

Creating still more problems is the fact that the camera seems to actively dislike both leads: Guarini bears an unfortunate resemblance to Krusty the Clown's sidekick on *The Simpsons,* Sideshow Bob, and Clarkson swiveling her hips in a skirt made entirely of men's ties reminds us of the rumors about J. Edgar Hoover, the late FBI director, liking to play dress-up.

Then there's the dialogue. Written by the same screenwriter as the Spice Girls' execrable *Hard Day's Night* rip-off, *Spice World*, *J2K* is chock-full of things that no one in real life would be geeky or goofy enough to say out loud. When Justin finally meets Kelly, fleeing into a ladies' room chased by girls wanting free passes to the bikini contest, Kelly comes up with this second-grade put-down: "Do you spend a lot of time in the girls' room?" And when the two have a first outing on a small boat, and Justin mentions that he "comes out here a lot to think," the audience can't help noticing that the boat looks like it's almost never been used.

Stupid when it means to be clever, garishly clubfooted when it wants to be graceful, and bearing no resemblance to anything a modern teenager would be caught dead watching, *From Justin to Kelly* is a modern classic now credited with taking the rebirth of the movie musical impelled by the success of both *Moulin Rouge* and *Chicago* . . . and killing it. But it makes for one truly fun funeral!

Dippy Dialogue
Brandon (*Greg Siff*) does his "How to Get Chicks" rap: "To impress these chicks, ya gotta be smoother than ever. No need to sweat, I'm your mentor, I'm clever. But it's cool, 'cause I rule, multiple chicks you'll be landin', just listen to Brandon and soon they'll be standin' with you . . ."

Choice Chapter Stop
Chapter 27 ("That's the Way I Like It"): The "big" finale, featuring the Painfully Molting Ducks moves.

Glitter

(2001/Columbia Pictures & 20th Century-Fox)　**DVD / VHS**

Who's to Blame　CAST:　**Mariah Carey** (*Billie Frank*); **Max Beesley** (*Julian Dice*); **Tia Texada** (*Roxanne*); **Da Brat** (*Louise*); **Eric Benet** (*Rafael*); **Dorian Harewood** (*Guy Richardson*); **Ann Magnuson** (*Kelly*)
　　　　　　　　　CREW:　**Directed by Vondie Curtis Hall**; **Screenplay by Kate Lanier; Story by Cheryl L. West**

Rave Reviews

"Unintentionally hilarious ... the audience erupted repeatedly into laughter at scenes intended to carry emotional weight."
　　　　　　　　— **Lawrence Van Gelder,** *New York Times*

"That old chestnut *A Star Is Born* gets another workout in this hilariously inept showcase for soul diva Mariah Carey."
　　　　　　　　— **Neil Smith, BBC Films (Web site)**

"Helplessly clichéd, predictable and unaware of its own lameness, it could easily become a camp classic." — **Jonathan Foreman,** *New York Post*

Plot, What Plot? Poor Mariah Carey. Only New York City had a worse year in 2001 than she did. First, she had to cancel a concert tour due to "exhaustion." Then her album sales plummeted so low that her label bought her out of her recording contract. Then things really got bad for her—on September 21, 2001, *Glitter* was released.

To say that Mariah's dramatic debut didn't do well would be like saying the *Titanic* sprung a minor leak. Backed by both Columbia Pictures and 20th Century-Fox, *Glitter* grossed less than $2.5 million its first weekend in release. It then dropped off 61 percent in its second weekend, 87 percent in its third, and another 71 percent the fourth. By the fifth weekend, it was gone. On an investment estimated at $30 million, *Glitter* grossed barely $5 million ... worldwide. By the time all was said and done, the only people even remotely interested in Carey's movie debut were Razzie voters, who awarded her our 2001 Worst Actress statuette by a landslide.

Looking like the child of one of those Bratz fashion-model dolls and Italian mouse puppet Topo Gigio, Carey brings to the screen a degree of self-involvement and acting incompetence unseen since Pia Zadora divorced her billionaire first husband. Add to that a singing voice that, in its upper registers, could set dogs to barking for miles around, and you have an eminently resistible star package. And make no mistake, *Glitter* was packaged to showcase what someone thought were Mariah's assets. Other than the two that are constantly threatening to tumble from the bodice of her gowns (and her cleavage was, after all, nominated as Worst Screen Couple), Carey doesn't have an asset to fall back on here.

The central character in *Glitter,* "loosely based" on Carey herself, is Billie Frank, the child of a lady lounge singer who clearly paid no attention to the lyrics if she ever sang "Don't Smoke in Bed." After Mom burns down their home, Billie is taken to an orphanage and, in a quick montage, grows up to be buxom, chipmunk-faced Mariah, who dreams of being the success her mother never was. If you're even remotely questioning whether she'll make it, you obviously haven't seen any of the three versions of *A Star Is Born* that this film's makers must have endlessly screened before "creating" this clump of clichés for Carey. Of course she becomes a star. Of course, there are complications along the way. And of course, she ends the film with a teary-eyed tribute concert to the guy she should've stayed with all along.

As predictable as a jigsaw puzzle with the completed picture on its box cover, *Glitter* has an interesting parallel with what most critics consider the greatest movie ever made: *Citizen Kane. Glitter* is every bit as embarrassing, unprofessional, and laughable as the sequence where Kane builds an opera house to "showcase" his mistress's "talents." Except that in *Glitter,* unlike *Kane,* it's not just two technicians in the rafters holding their noses as she performs . . . *Glitter* had almost everyone in America holding their noses.

Dippy Dialogue
Music video director (*James Allodi*): "Is she black, is she white—we don't know. She's exotic! I want to see more of her breasts . . ."

Choice Chapter Stop
Chapter 10 ("The Video Shoot"): In which we learn that, even though the rest of this movie proves otherwise, "The glitter shouldn't overpower the artist."

Lost Horizon

(1973/Columbia Pictures)

Who's to Blame   CAST: **Peter Finch** (*Richard Conway*); **Liv Ullmann** (*Catherine*); **Sally Kellerman** (*Sally Hughes*); **George Kennedy** (*Sam Cornelius*); **Olivia Hussey** (*Maria*); **Michael York** (*George Conway*); **Bobby Van** (*Harry Lovett*); **Charles Boyer** (*The High Lama*); CREW: **Directed by Charles Jarrott; Screenplay by Larry Kramer; Based on the novel by James Hilton**

Rave Reviews
"You can't help laughing at it—its Shangri-La . . . is about as alluring as Forest Lawn!" — **Pauline Kael,** *The New Yorker*

"A misbegotten mishmash of mystical musings and '70s stylings . . . [an] ungainly kitschfest."
— **David Marc Fischer,** *Entertainment Weakly*

"Hungry for [a] memorably, side-splittingly bad [movie]? Here's 143 minutes' worth!"
— **Edward Margulies and Stephen Rebello,** *Bad Movies We Love*

Plot, What Plot? Perhaps Rodgers and Hammerstein could have made a palatable musical out of James Hilton's *Lost Horizon,* given its vague thematic similarities to both *South Pacific* and *The King and I.* Instead, schlocky '70s songmeisters Burt Bacharach and Hal David, together with schmaltz-and-kitsch king Ross Hunter, created a legendary box-office bomb so awful that it has never been released on video in the United States and is rarely even shown on cable. If you're a bad-movie buff, this is one film you've always heard ranks among the worst ever made—and rank it is. And reek it does.

For its first half hour, this wholly unnecessary retelling of Frank Capra's 1937 classic follows its progenitor almost shot-for-shot in establishing five characters whose plane escapes a war-torn Asian nation, only to crash in the Himalayas. In the midst of a snow-covered wilderness, they are rescued by a team of monks who bring them through the mountains to the legendary Valley of the Blue Moon, and to the paradise known as Shangri-La. Up to this point, you are left to ponder: Why did they bother to make this pale imitation of a classic film?

But once inside Shangri-La, such nonsinging stars as Peter Finch, Liv Ullmann, Olivia Hussey, Sally Kellerman (!), and George Kennedy (!!) start bursting into song as if there's LSD in the water. And they begin expressing their innermost (and mostly inane) thoughts in ludicrous lyrics courtesy of Mr. David. And they start hopping about like injured birds, hopelessly trying to pull off what they believe are dance numbers, under the direction of dinosaur Hermes Pan (whose past credits *do* include one Oscar thirty-six years earlier, but also include the similarly wretched 1959 remake of *The Blue Angel*).

Woven in and around this incredible collection of terpsichorean calamities is the basic plot of both Hilton's novel and Capra's film: Finch, as a world-renowned peace negotiator, has actually been kidnapped and brought to the Valley of the Blue Moon to take over for the 260-year-old high lama, played by Charles Boyer. You know Boyer's important because he's never forced to sing . . . and because whenever he appears onscreen, he has his own syrupy string section, screeching away to tug at our heartstrings. When Boyer dies, he slumps over in his chair, a flatulent breeze flaps at the curtains—and we know he *must* be dead, because those damned violins finally go silent.

To call this *Horizon* a lost cause would be an understatement. What saves it from the tedium of mere mediocrity are the unbelievably awful musical sequences, eleven in all. Each song sneaks up on the audience like a mugger on the subway, until you get leery every time you see a filtered shot of sunshine or two characters holding hands. "Oh my God," you start thinking, "here comes another one!" But once you realize that not only is every one of them going to be lame, but that they progressively top one another in laughability, you'll find yourself awaiting the next number in a perverse, goggle-eyed, giggle-induced stupor.

Olivia Hussey kicks things off with "Share the Joy," which looks and sounds like it was concocted to launch a new line of perfume at

Macy's. Then it's Liv Ullmann's turn: She leads a gaggle of gag-inducing moppets in the irksomely repetitive "The World Is a Circle." By the time you get to the fifth fiasco, a duet in the Shangri-La library between Hussey and Kellerman, you're inoculated and ready for any ditzy dance move or risible rhyme Bacharach, David, or any club-footed, tone-deaf cast member can throw at you. Up to this song, you may have noticed that Finch is the only poorly dubbed nonsinger who never lip-syncs. All his numbers are heard echoing inside his head, as he adopts poses he thinks resemble those Richard Burton struck in *Camelot*. And when, in the restored version (!) of the film available on foreign DVD, his big number "If I Could Go Back" is seen for the first time in over thirty years, you'll realize why he rarely lip-syncs: He quite simply cannot. The combination of the banal blather posing as lyrics and the utter insincerity with which Finch flaps his lips will astound you. But wait—Kellerman and Kennedy have a duet still coming up. When you see the two of them conversing at a river-side rock, make sure you're *not* drinking milk—otherwise it'll be spraying out your nose when you see the gawky/awkward hip-hopping "dance" Kellerman performs while advising goy George, "Your reflection reflects in everything you do, and everything you do . . . reflects on you!"

Lost Horizon reflected poorly on everyone associated with it. In fact, it is so widely reviled that it's next to impossible to actually see for yourself. And once you *have* seen it, you still won't believe what you've seen. This is one notoriously numbskulled Hollywood remake that gloriously lives *down* to its reputation.

Loopy Lyrics
Richard Conway (*Peter Finch*) doing an astonishingly awful job of lip-syncing, accompanied by a "Woo-Woo" chorus, blatting horns, and thump-and-pish drums:
"How do I know this is part of my real life?
If there's no pain can I be sure I feel life? . . .
And what I thought was living is just confusion,
the chance to live forever is no illusion . . .
Can I accept what I see all around me—
have I found Shangri-La . . . or has it found me?"

Availability

To see this famously failed film, you'll have to go to extreme efforts: We suggest trying to find it on eBay, or watching it on some all-night/all-movie cable channel with very low standards and two and a half hours to fill at 3 a.m.

Fun Footnote

The version of *Lost Horizon* shown to the crowd that fled its Hollywood premiere included an extended "fertility dance" sequence which, as the reputed comedic highlight, was almost immediately cut out of the film—and has never been seen since.

The Pirate Movie

(1982/20th Century-Fox) **VHS**

Who's to Blame **CAST:** **Kristy McNichol** (*Mabel*); **Christopher Atkins** (*Frederic*); **Ted Hamilton** (*The Pirate King*); **Linda Nagle** (*Aphrodite*); **Bill Kerr** (*The Modern Major General*); **Maggie Kirkpatrick** (*Ruth*); **Marc Colombani** (*Dwarf Pirate*)

CREW: **Directed by Ken Annakin**; **Screenplay by Trevor Farrant;** **"Inspired" by the Gilbert and Sullivan opera** *The Pirates of Penzance*

Rave Reviews

"Rated: BOMB. Not only trashes the original, but fails on its own paltry terms. It should have been called *The Rip-off Movie*."
— **Leonard Maltin's Movie & Video Guide**

"So bad it's delightful to watch. If you're a musical fan or just a glutton for punishment, definitely go rent this horribly wonderful movie."
— **"Andie," MutantReviewers.com**

"*Pirate Movie* may be bad, but it's definitely a good kind of bad . . . definitely entertaining!" — **Tom Panarese, BadMovieNight.com**

Plot, What Plot? Sometimes, just doing a lame remake isn't enough for Hollywood. Instead, they'll take the kernel of something that's been done before—and done better—and combine it with "contemporary" elements, then rework it into the filmic equivalent of a mongrel dog. An excruciating example of this "breed" of bad film is 1982's *The Pirate Movie,* essentially a rock 'n' roll updating of Gilbert and Sullivan's *The Pirates of Penzance.*

About half a dozen of the opera's original songs remain, but surrounding them—and arguably stomping all over them—are seven "original" songs, two of which were deemed wretched enough by our voting members to be Worst Song nominees. And the film's so-called script is every bit as inept and indefensible as those songs: Two modern teens get bonked on the head, and dream they're back in the days of galleons, doubloons, and skullduggery. Or, as Worst Actress nominee Kristy McNichol puts it, "Pirates! You mean like walking the plank? Buried treasure? Hack, slash, off with his head, and the Jolly Richard, and everything?" Kristy's leading man here, hot from his "success" in the Razzie "winning" *Blue Lagoon,* is vacuous pretty boy Christopher Atkins, who looks like he couldn't buckle his own swash if he had written directions. This performance would net Atkins the first of many Razzie nominations as Worst Actor.

Torn between being an outright rip-off of *Penzance* or a backhanded homage (the French term for rip-off), *Pirate Movie* basically treads water during most of its running time. Whether staging incredibly inept "modern" dance numbers in Kmart-quality period costumes, slathering every situation with slapstick and pratfalls that all fall flat, or touting a trumped-up "romance" between McNichol and Atkins that never rings true, *Pirate Movie* is an astounding example of just how low Hollywood will stoop in its attempts at "youth appeal." But just when you think it can't possibly sink any lower, the action moves underwater for the film's most inimitable, unforgettable moment: the Razzie-"winning" Worst Song "Pumpin' and Blowin'," with lyrics that bald-facedly point out that it isn't a nautical term we're talking about here. Accompanied by animated fish and clad in only a diaper and diving helmet, Atkins "dances" under the sea as McNichol lyricizes topside about how sometimes in romance "you have to swallow more than water—it's your pride."

By film's end, Atkins and McNichol are back to being their modern selves (someone's idea of a happy ending) and you may well try to forget everything that's come before. But we defy you ever to forget "Pumpin' and Blowin'," which to this day remains the lamest of *all* the "winners" of our Dippiest Ditty Dis-Honor.

Dippy Dialogue
Mabel (*Kristy McNichol*): "You'll be hung!"
Pirate King (*Ted Hamilton*): "Oh, I am, I am! And very well, thank you!"

Rhinestone

(1984/20th Century-Fox)

Who's to Blame **CAST:** **Sylvester Stallone** 🍋 (*Nick Martinelli*); **Dolly Parton** (*Jake*); **Ron Leibman** 🍋 (*Freddie Ugo*); **Robert Farnsworth** (*Noah*); **Tim Thompson** (*Barnett*); **Stephen Apostle Pec** (*Father Martinelli*)
CREW: **Directed by Bob Clark** 🍋; **Screenplay** 🍋 **by Phil Alden Robinson and Sylvester Stallone; Screen story by Robinson; Based on the song "Rhinestone Cowboy" by Larry Weiss**

Rave Reviews
"Stallone sings like he's punch-drunk. He can't carry a tune, he can't even hold a note. And rhythm? Forget it. . . . Instant hysterics!"
— *Dennis Hunt*, **Los Angeles Times**

"Less a movie than a frame for Stallone's super ego."
— *Arthur Knight*, **Hollywood Reporter**

"Stallone belts like a basset hound in heat—I've never had a better time watching someone make an utter fool of himself!"
— *Michael Dare*, **L.A. Weekly**

Plot, What Plot? If you were ever bored enough to make a list of all the movie stars you'd *never* want to see in a musical, it's a pretty good bet that Sylvester Stallone would place near the top of the list. And if you were asked to name the one type of music you wouldn't want to hear the Yo-Man tackle, it'd likely be yodeling a country-and-western song. Yet, inexplicably, someone at Fox *did* green-light the first and (hopefully) last musical starring Duh Sly Guy. The result: *Rhinestone*.

Costarring Dolly Parton, *Rhinestone* basically "lifts" its plot from, of all things, *My Fair Lady* . . . er, George Bernard Shaw's *Pygmalion*. By giving it a "country twist," they turn Shaw's literate battle of the sexes into a cornpone clump of crud worthy of the title *Pig-Male-ion*.

CAN'T STOP THE MUSICALS

Big-busted Dolly, dressed in gowns that further emphasize her assets, plays a New York nightclub country singer who bets "everything" that she can take any stranger off the street and train him to win the club's talent contest in a matter of weeks. If she wins, she gets out of her contract, but if she loses, she has to have sex with Worst Supporting Actor nominee Ron Leibman—truly a fate worse than death. The catch is that Leibman gets to pick the trainee. And whom does he pick for Dolly to tutor? A loudmouthed New York City cabbie with an even bigger bust than Dolly's, Sylvester Stallone.

The humor is supposed to arise from Dolly teaching this Brooklynite the ways of Bubba Land and, of course, some of Sly's city-slicker ways rubbing off on backwoods belle Parton. But the two stars couldn't be less attracted to one another if they wore signs admitting their mutual loathing. And while Dolly gets away relatively scot-free (she was the only main character *not* Razzie-nominated for her "acting" here), Stallone is so clearly uncomfortable doing humor at his own expense that he gives one of the least funny "comic" performances ever committed. It's as though, having taken this idiotic project—and cowritten it—he still thought he had some dignity to defend, and defends it with a gigantic chip on his shoulder. It was for this film that Stallone "won" the first of his numerous Worst Actor Razzie Awards.

The film hits its so-bad-it's-good high point when Stallone is first heard singing. A Razzie-"winning" ditty written by Parton for the film, the song is entitled "Drinkenstein," and is a paean to Budweiser beer. Sly delivers it in a guttural, caterwauling voice while dressed in a neon yellow-and-blue leisure suit, with a coonskin cap on his head. Every time this clip is shown at a Razzie event, it elicits giggles, groans, and gasps of utter disbelief.

Several dumb plot complications and awful Dolly-and-Sly duets later (including the other Worst Song nominee from this film, "Stay Out of My Bedroom"), it's time for Rambo's singing debut in New York. In yet another failed stab at being funny, the filmmakers stack the deck in Sly's favor by having acts they think are even worse precede Stallone's song. The problem is, even though these performers are being putrid on purpose, every one of them has more musical talent than Sylvester could ever muster. If you have to ask how the film ends, then you don't know your Hollywood musical clichés.

For their efforts here, Stallone was paid $5 million against 10 percent of the eventual gross, Dolly reportedly got $3 million against another 10 percent and *Porky's* director Bob Clark, who took over the project after filming began, was paid $1 million. But when the film was released, it played to vacant theatres nationwide—the *New York Times* reported counting 21 patrons in a 1,300-seat theatre in Manhattan—and Fox lost a fortune. Which may have dissuaded Fox from doing their *other* planned remake of *My Fair Lady,* starring Madonna as Eliza Doolittle and Ah-Nuld Schwarzenegger as Professor Higgins. Just kidding! But if *Rhinestone* had made money, the Material Girl and the Terminator in *Mein Fair Lady* might have been next!

Dippy Dialogue
Jake (*Dolly Parton*), to lecherous Freddie Ugo (*Ron Leibman*): "There are two kinds of people in this world . . . and you ain't one of 'em!"

Fun Footnote
Stallone, as quoted in *Halliwell's Film & Video Guide* regarding *Rhinestone*: "You'd have thought we all got together and decided how we could fastest ruin our careers."

Roller Boogie

(1979/United Artists) **DVD / VHS**

Who's to Blame CAST: **Linda Blair** (*Terry Barkley*); **Jim Bray** (*Bobby James*); **Beverly Garland** (*Lillian Barkley*); **Roger Perry** (*Roger Barkley*); **Jimmy (James) Van Patten** (*Hoppy*); **Chris Nelson** (*Franklin*); **M. G. (Machine Gun) Kelly** (*The Disco D.J.*)
CREW: **Directed by Mark L. Lester; Screenplay by Barry Schneider; Story by Irwin Yablans**

Rave Reviews
"WOOF! Truly awful. . . . Everything about this one reeks amateur."
— *VideoHound's Golden Movie Retriever*

"If Fisher Price made a toy called My First Film Editor, this is what the output would resemble." — **Reed Hubbard, BadMovieNight.com**

"Like a combination of *Charlie's Angels* and *CHiPs* on skates."
— **John Allen, New Orleans Worst Film Festival**

Plot, What Plot? Rarely are the words "narcissistic" and "nerdy" applicable to the same subject. But in the doofy disco classic *Roller Boogie*, almost every single character is both a narcissist . . . and a nerd. From their so-tight-even-the-guys-suffer-from-VPL disco short-shorts to their "lookit-me-I'm-flyin'" skate-cum-dance moves, every "actor" in this film achieved the nanoseconds-long apex of their lives in this geeky, freaky, squeaky-clean paean to the flash-in-the-pan fad that was roller disco.

Focused on a roller boogie skate-dancing competition at a club called Jammers, *Roller Boogie* takes its basic conflict from *Romeo and Juliet*: A rich girl defies her parents to fall in love with a street guy who happens to be the man of the moment because of his prowess on roller skates. The rich girl is perennial Razzie contender Linda Blair, fresh off her phenomenal "success" tap-dancing in *Exorcist II* and now ready to boogie on wheels. The street guy is one of the most amazingly amateurish actors ever to be offered a lead role in Hollywood, a disco roller-skating champion named Jim Bray, whose gawkiness here no doubt contributed to his never making another film.

She's buxom, chipmunk-faced, and no better an actress here than she was when she got an Oscar nomination for *The Exorcist* in a role whose every dramatic moment was dubbed by Mercedes McCambridge. He's pencil-neck thin, with a toothy grin and a bushy headful of disco hair that makes him look like a human Q-Tip on wheels. And together they're . . . astoundingly ordinary. In the tradition of the old MGM teenager musicals, they not only plan to win the roller boogie contest, but must also convince her parents and his friends that they belong together, as well as thwarting a thug's plot to shut down the roller rink and put up a shopping mall. From frame one, you know how everything's gonna turn out, so just sit back and wallow in the film's world-class oafishness.

Start with the songs. The one played under the opening titles, for example, featuring lyrics like, "I used to hate to skate . . . now, I can't wait!" We all know disco was hardly the zenith of American songwriting, but this stuff makes *Pirate Movie*'s melodies look professional. Then there are those costumes, authentic to the '70s styles of the period, but now so retro they seem almost ancient, with not a natural fiber anywhere in sight. Then there's the dialogue, including such putdowns as, "I swear, you've got more hands than a poker game!" and "Our little genius is throwing a tantrum!"

But crowning it all are the roller disco "dance" numbers. Occasionally going for balletic moves, but for the most part showing the strain and stress necessary to pull them off, each of the "boogie interludes" in *Roller Boogie* is a hoot for a different reason. The one introducing the street characters, staged on the Venice Beach boardwalk, personifies the self-impressed, self-involved nature of roller disco itself, and features more gratuitous T&A than any episode of *Charlie's Angels*. The one in which Blair and Bray finally connect at the rink includes the kind of pop-n-lock moves popular back then that now seem pathetically passé. The one in which everyone in the club forms a line and performs "The Coonga" shows just how utterly idiotic roller disco truly was. The one in which Bray "emotively" pays roller-skating tribute to the rink's broken-down drunk of an owner is a marvel of sincere ineptitude. But the one in which Blair and Bray finally win the Roller Boogie Trophy is the most amusing of all, in part because you can't help noticing that every time Bray has to hold Blair in midair, his face is frozen into an I-don't-dare-breathe-or-I'll-drop-her smile, and every time we should see him heft her over his head, they conveniently cut away . . . so they could bring in a crane?

Beloved by bad movie mavens for decades, *Roller Boogie* is the kind of film for which Linda Blair will never be forgiven, and for which Jim Bray is long since deservedly forgotten. So put on yer skates and boogie on over to eBay to bid on a copy now!

Dippy Dialogue
Terry (*Linda Blair*): "So what, I'm a musical genius! Whatta drag! Whatta bummer!!"

Choice Chapter Stop
Chapter 15 (*"Boogie Night"*): In which the big roller disco skate-off is held . . .

Razzie Credential
Roller Boogie missed being a Razzie nominee solely by being released the year *before* we began the awards. It did, however, contribute to Linda Blair's 1987 Worst Career Achievement Razzie.

Spice World

(1998/Columbia Pictures) **DVD / VHS**

Who's to Blame **CAST:** **The Spice Girls** 🌀: **Melanie Brown, Emma Bunton, Melanie Chisholm, Geri Halliwell, and Victoria Adams** (*Themselves*); **Meat Loaf** (*Dennis*); **Richard E. Grant** (*Clifford*); **Alan Cumming** (*Piers Cuthberton-Smyth*); **George Wendt** (*Martin Barnfield*); **Roger Moore** 🌀 (*The Chief*)
CREW: **Directed by Bob Spiers; Screenplay** 🌀 **by Kim Fuller; Based on an idea by the Spice Girls and Fuller; Additional writing by Jamie Curtis**

Rave Reviews
"Let's face it, the Spice Girls could be duplicated by any five women under the age of 30 standing in line at Dunkin' Donuts."
— **Roger Ebert,** *Chicago Sun-Times*

"Striving for the comic sensibility of *A Hard Day's Night,* the Spice Girls instead achieve a below-average episode of *The Monkees*."
— **Christine James,** *Box Office* **magazine**

"The Spice Girls: They can't sing, they can't dance, they are not amazingly good-looking and—as they prove in their first movie—they can't act, either." — **Craig Marine,** *San Francisco Examiner*

Plot, What Plot? Given how successfully *A Hard Day's Night* helped launch the Fab Four in 1964, no wonder it's been endlessly imitated ever since. But the furthest from fab of all the *Hard Day's Night* imitators is the Spice Girls' vehicle *Spice World,* a movie so inane that even when referencing its own inanity it doesn't deserve to be cut any slack.

The human equivalent of Barbie dolls, the five Spice Girls (can anyone still name all five?) were a quintet distinguishable from one another only by the costumes and accessories each wore, who proved so instantly forgettable that they were at 14 minutes, 58 seconds into their 15 minutes of fame by the time Columbia Pictures released *Spice World* in the United States in early 1998. Promoting itself as a girl glam romp, the film was instead widely greeted by American critics as a clear sign of the coming of the Apocalypse.

An example of how stupid people admitting they're stupid doesn't make them any less stupid, *Spice World* wants desperately to be hip, self-deprecating, and devastatingly funny. It actually *is* devastatingly funny, but almost none of the laughs come where the filmmakers were seeking them. Chockablock with jokes that fall flat, dramatic moments that aren't even vaguely dramatic, and songs of a quality you'd expect to get for putting 25 cents into a gumball machine, *Spice World* does at least realize its own lameness. But it never quite realizes just *how* incredibly lame it truly is.

Mel B, Emma, Mel C, Geri, and Victoria, also known as Scary Spice, Baby Spice, Sporty Spice, Sexy Spice, and Posh Spice, are five working-class girls as astounded by their success as the critics are confounded by it. So far, so good. But the filmmakers also wanted to do a tie-in album to cross-promote the film, meaning a minimum number of songs were needed. And however lame the girls are at slapstick and verbal humor, they're at their ultra-lamest when seen in concert. Lip-syncing every lyric with excessively overglossed lips, constantly looking lasciviously into camera, and sporting "theme costumes" that could've been dreamed up by Mattel, the Spice Girls in concert make TV's the Monkees seem like prodigies by comparison. Throw in their repeatedly stated "message" of "girl power" (which boils down to "Girls have the right to be bimbos—who treat all boys like boy toys") and you've got the makings of something no one over the age of ten should be able to watch with a straight face.

What few elements of "plot" there are to *Spice World* deal with their being the subject of a documentary being made by prissy Alan Cumming, and their being at the beck and call of pickled-looking former James Bond Roger Moore as a quintet of female 007s—though seven might also be the combined IQ of everyone involved in making this film. Wildly funny in spite of itself—and never when it means to be—*Spice World* is a crash course in British pop culture that is arguably the 1990s equivalent of *Can't Stop the Music*. But in the case of the Spice Girls, thank God somebody *did* stop the music.

Dippy Dialogue
The Director (*Alan Cumming*) after hearing the Spice Girls rehearse: "That was absolutely perfect—without being actually any good."

Choice Chapter Stop
Chapter 12 ("Come On"): In which the Spice Girls appear in concert singing the biker song "Come On!" with bared-bottom male dancers undulating in the background.

Fun Footnote
The executive producer of this film was caustic *American Idol* judge Simon Fuller, whose brother Kim wrote *Spice World*'s atrocious screenplay.

(1983/Paramount Pictures) **DVD / VHS**

Who's to Blame   CAST: **John Travolta** ☉ (*Tony Manero*); **Cynthia Rhodes** (*Jackie*); **Finola Hughes** ☉ (*Laura*); **Steve Inwood** (*Jesse, the Director*); **Julie Bovasso** (*Mrs. Manero*); **Frank Stallone** (*Carl*)
CREW: **Directed by Sylvester Stallone; Written by Stallone and Norman Wexler; Based upon characters created by Nik Cohn**

Rave Reviews
"A camp classic . . . a musical trip through Hell!"
— *Leonard Maltin's Movie & Video Guide*

"Constantly falls flat on its face . . . [take] *Saturday Night Fever,* add some bad hair, too tight pants and too much glitter and you have a disaster!" — **Ali Barclay, BBC Films (Web site)**

"An impossibly funny series of overproduced production numbers. It's high-tech camp heaven!"
— **Edward Margulies and Stephen Rebello,** *Bad Movies We Love*

Plot, What Plot? Hollywood has yet to find the cure for the disease called "sequelitis," the uncontrollable urge to make a sequel to a successful film, even if it's six years later, the sequel costs three times as much as the original film did, and historically sequels are lucky to gross even 60 percent of what the previous film did at the box office.

A perfect example of the deadly side effects of sequelitis is *Staying Alive,* the utterly unnecessary 1983 follow-up to John Travolta's first monster hit, 1977's *Saturday Night Fever.* Not only did *SNF* gross $142 million and become the best-selling sound track album of all time, but Travolta's performance was actually nominated for a Best Actor Academy Award. For his performance in this sequel, he was also nominated . . . for Worst Actor at the 4th Annual Razzies.

Staying Alive made numerous avoidable errors on its way to the screen, the first one being that it took too long to arrive. By the time of its release, disco was long since dead and buried. Second, it completely misunderstood the appeal of Travolta's Tony Manero character, thinking he was analogous to Rocky, which may be why they turned the screenwriting and directing of this second film over to . . . Sylvester Stallone. Thirdly, Sly either didn't watch (or just as likely, didn't "get") the first film and its appeal: True, Tony is a lug, but he's basically likable and honorable at film's end. He's also a cliché of macho bravado, someone who wouldn't be caught dead being dressed by Cher's favorite costumer, Bob Mackie . . . so guess who did the costumes for the big musical sequence at the end of *Staying Alive*?

On the disco floor in *Saturday Night Fever,* Manero discovered a place where his own talents made him special. But as *Staying Alive* opens, he's living in a seedy Manhattan hotel, working nights as a tight-pantsed cocktail waiter and running around to cattle-call auditions all day for Broadway musical dancers. The fact that the Tony Manero from the first film would never even consider wearing tights is lost on this film's creators. But throwing a Broadway musical into this film allowed Sly to hire his little brother Frank Stallone to create no fewer than *seven* songs, as well as play the bass guitar player in Manero's girlfriend's band.

As the film opens, Manero's main squeeze is Jackie. Played by Cynthia Rhodes, she's the only really likable character in the film. So naturally, when Tony is smitten with the star of a musical that features Jackie as a backup dancer, Manero tramples all over Jackie's feelings for him. The new object of Tony's affections is a smug, self-impressed rich bitch, played by soap opera veteran (and Worst Supporting Actress nominee) Finola Hughes. In the dance scenes, Hughes moves like Catherine O'Hara doing Lola Heatherington on *SCTV.* And in the "dramatic" scenes, she comes off like Pia Zadora attempting a British accent. Her character is summed up by her line "We met, I liked you, we made it. What do you think it was, true love?" She later inadvertently serves as the mouthpiece for what may be Stallone's philosophy of life: "Everybody uses everybody—don't they?"

The utterly predictable plot follows Travolta through his wham-bam-nice-dancin'-witcha-ma'am relationship with Hughes, his breakup with Rhodes, and his eventually being cast opposite Hughes as the lead male dancer in a big-budget musical entitled *Satan's Alley.* As the show's director, who looks like a community theatre version of

Kenny Loggins, accurately describes the show, "It's a journey through Hell . . ."

Literally overfull with smoke, mirrors, and chrome, *Satan's Alley* looks like a spectacularly tasteless Best Song production number from a 1970s Oscarcast. Mackie's costumes include blood-spattered leotards, metallic silver headbands, and what look like pairs of men's extra-large gym socks stuffed into the crotches of every male dancer. There's lots of thrusting, leaping, straining, and loud grunting throughout the "show" as we watch its opening-night performance. At intermission, the director comes backstage to berate Travolta with a comment every viewer has also been thinking: "What were you doing out there? You call that dancing?" Travolta's response? He literally flings Hughes offstage near the end of the show, and launches into an improvised dance solo. In the real world, this would get him fired and drummed out of the Broadway Dancers' Union. But in this film, it's greeted by a standing ovation and the realization that tomorrow morning Tony will be a star.

Thus Stallone and his coconspirators on *Staying Alive* have taken Tony Manero, a macho man looking for his own identity, and turned him into a male Ruby Keeler. *Staying Alive* plays like a comedy. But then, neither Travolta nor his "mentor" for this film, Stallone, has ever been funnier than when they *weren't* trying to be.

Dippy Dialogue
Tony Manero (*John Travolta*), upon meeting snooty Laura (*Finola Hughes*): "Did you hear the way she talks? It's so intelligent-like . . . I love it!"

Razzie Credential
Travolta was dually nominated as Worst Actor for both this film and his *other* 1983 bomb, *Two of a Kind.*

Choice Chapter Stop
Chapter 14 ("Satan's Alley"): The "big dance number" from Tony's Broadway debut vehicle, this is often cited as one of the funniest, lamest dance sequences ever committed to film.

(1974/Universal Pictures) **DVD / VHS**

Who's to Blame CAST: **Charlton Heston** (*Murdock*); **Karen Black** (*Nancy*); **George Kennedy** (*Joe Patroni*); **Efrem Zimbalist Jr.** (*Captain Stacy*); **Helen Reddy** (*Sister Ruth*); **Linda Blair** (*Janice Abbott*); **Dana Andrews** (*Scott Freeman*); **Myrna Loy** (*Mrs. Devaney*); **Erik Estrada** (*Julio*); **and Gloria Swanson** (*as Herself*)
CREW: **Directed by Jack Smight; Written by Don Ingalls; "Inspired" by the movie *Airport* and the novel by Arthur Hailey**

Rave Reviews
"Aimed squarely at the yahoo trade." — ***Variety***

"Processed schlock—one can have a good time laughing at it."
— **Pauline Kael,** ***The New Yorker***

"Proof that nothing's worse than . . . disaster films, of which this is the funniest example—a high point of unintentional hilarity!"
— **Kevin Hennessey,** ***Movieline***

Plot, What Plot? Most film historians cite 1972's *Poseidon Adventure* as the first big hit of the so-called disaster movie genre—but they're wrong. The first was 1970's *Airport,* which not only was one of the first films ever to top $100 million at the box office, but also snagged a Best Picture Oscar nomination. With such a stellar pedigree, it was only natural that *Airport* would sire a series of sequels and knockoffs, culminating in one of the funniest movie parodies ever, 1980's *Airplane!* But many of the jokes in *Airplane!* were lifted directly from the first actual *Airport* sequel, *Airport 1975*—and most of them are even funnier in this film, precisely because they weren't *meant* to be funny.

True to Hollywood's formula for sequels, *Airport 1975* assembles what *Leonard Maltin's Movie & Video Guide* calls "a *Hollywood Squares* type cast," then places them all in peril for the audience's pleasure.

Since the law of diminishing returns applies to sequels, this second *Airport* outing downsizes über-hero Burt Lancaster into Charlton Heston, pilot Dean Martin into Efrem Zimbalist Jr., and sexy stewardess Jacqueline Bisset into cross-eyed, badly wigged Karen Black. The role of the old biddy, which won Helen Hayes a Supporting Actress Oscar in the first *Airport,* in this film becomes a *pair* of crones: Myrna Loy as a boozy busybody and Gloria Swanson (in her final film role) as the Grandma Moses of movie stars—literally playing herself. Others along for this flight into filmic oblivion include: chubby-cheeked Munchkin-with-mumps Linda Blair (fresh off *The Exorcist*) as a teenaged dialysis patient; Helen Reddy as a singing nun whose guitar cannot be pried from her hands (starting to see the *Airplane!* parallels?); a weathered and withered Dana Andrews as a private pilot who suffers an in-flight heart attack; Norman Fell, Jerry Stiller, and Conrad Janis as a trio of drunk-and-disorderlies; the only actor desperate enough to appear in all four *Airport* movies, George Kennedy; and an eclectic passenger and crew list that must have emptied half the beds at the Motion Picture Country Home, including Sid Caesar, Erik Estrada, Beverly Garland, Sharon Gless, Ed Nelson, Nancy Olson, Martha Scott, Guy Stockwell, Larry Storch, and Roy Thinnes.

Columbia Airlines Flight 409 is headed with a full passenger load from Washington, D.C., to Los Angeles when they are diverted to Salt Lake City. Upon descent into the Mormon capital, they literally "run into" Dana Andrews' private plane in a head-on collision that blows a hole in the cockpit big enough for an inflatable dummy of Thinnes to be sucked through it. Estrada is also killed, and pilot Zimbalist is blinded and left looking like an entire bottle of ketchup exploded in his face. Stewardess Karen Black heads to the cockpit, appraises the situation, and then hysterically (in *both* senses) informs flight control via headphones, "Something hit us—there's no one left to fly the plane! Help us . . . *Oh my God—help us!*"

Karen's paramour happens to be Moses himself, Charlton Heston, who is enlisted to "talk the plane down" with Black at the controls, much like Doris Day did in *Julie* (except that Day wasn't cross-eyed). When Black gets all choked up over finding Thinnes's empty coffee cup, they realize that Karen's rampant overacting may endanger everyone aboard. So they come up with a backup plan that an Air Force spokesman calls "One hell of a stupid idea!" George Kennedy then barks, "Well, that's all we've got!"

What rescue remedy could be even more ridiculous than having an overwrought stewardess land a 747 via headphones? How about lowering someone on an umbilical cord into the cockpit while the plane is still aloft? And how about having top-billed Heston be the one who eventually has to do it? "This is just plain suicide, sir!" declares one of Chuck's cohorts. It's unclear whether he's referring to what Heston's character is about to do, or to the prospects for Charlton's future career after this fiasco.

Despite the dangers of badly staged rear-projection effects, Heston manages to climb into the cockpit. And when the passengers are informed he's aboard, they break out into applause—perhaps because they know the film is finally about to end. As Charlton negotiates the landing strip, making sharp turns to avoid obstacles, the passengers careen from side to side, and the 747 takes out a model building or two before it finally stops. Inflatable escape ramps burst from the exit doors, and as the plane is evacuated we get the chance to check out the undergarments of nearly every female passenger as they slide to safety. For most of them, their awful ordeal is over. But for George Kennedy, *The Concorde: Airport '79* was yet to come.

Dippy Dialogue
Sister Ruth (*Helen Reddy*), seeing Gloria Swanson surrounded by reporters: "Who is she, Sister Beatrice? Do you recognize her?"
Sister Beatrice (*Martha Scott*): "I believe it's one of those Hollywood persons."
Ruth: "*Oh!* You mean an actress?"
Beatrice: ". . . or worse!"

Choice Chapter Stop
Chapter 8 ("Impact"): Andrews' small plane collides with the 747's cockpit.

Razzie Credentials
Airport 1975, along with *Airport '77* and *The Concorde: Airport '79,* was inducted into the Razzie Hall of Shame at our 3rd Annual Awards.

(1978/New World Pictures) **DVD / VHS**

Who's to Blame CAST: **Rock Hudson** (*David Shelby*); **Mia Farrow** (*Caroline Brace*); **Robert Forster** (*Nick Thorne*); **Jeanette Nolan** (*Florence Shelby*); **Barry Primus** (*Mark Elliott*); **Steve Franken** (*Henry McDade*)
CREW: **Directed by Corey Allen; Screenplay by Allen and Claude Pola; Story by Frances Doel**

Rave Reviews
"Goofy pleasure [is] to be derived from Roger Corman's big star snowjob."
— **Edward Margulies and Stephen Rebello**, *Bad Movies We Love*

"Stupid entry in one of the worst genres ever created, the disaster film." — *TV Guide's Movie Guide*

"No better than TV movies of this same kind, especially as it resorts for its climaxes to scratched old stock film."
— *Halliwell's Film & Video Guide*

Plot, What Plot? The true all-star disaster movies of the 1970s each had their own guilty pleasures. I still recall with relish the nasty look I received from an elderly couple when I applauded wildly as Jennifer Jones fell to her death from a flaming elevator in *The Towering Inferno*. But any genre that proves as successful as Irwin Allen's round-up-a-bunch-of-big-names-and-put-'em-all-in-peril formula eventually engenders ever cheaper, cheesier, and more chowder-headed imitations. And perhaps the nadir of the disaster genre is king-of-the-cheapies Roger Corman's *Avalanche*.

Having produced his first film, *Monster from the Ocean Floor,* for the staggeringly low budget of just $18,000, Corman clearly knew how to squeeze blood from a nickel. And if anyone involved with this film received more than five cents for their efforts, they were overpaid.

Our central character is a starting-to-sag Rock Hudson, as a blowhard developer about to open a multimillion-dollar mountain ski resort. The first of many budget-conscious effects is the view of the looming mountain outside Hudson's office window: It looks about as convincing as the Paramount logo (except that logo actually has *stars* in it!). Beyond the pressures of being, as Rock's devoted mom, Jeanette Nolan, puts it, "up to his ass in celebrities" planning his gala event, Hudson is also all atwitter because his ex-wife will be attending the festivities. But if Hudson is starting to sag, Mia Farrow as Rock's ex-wife is already decomposing. With purplish, paper-thin skin hanging in bags below her eyes, Farrow looks like the mommy of *Rosemary's Baby* may be sleep-deprived and expecting again.

Enter Robert Forster as a nature photographer and environmentalist, who tries to warn everyone about a potential avalanche by declaring, "There's a heaviness and it's growing. I can feel it!" Among those contributing to that heaviness are stock/stick figures like a studly male champion skier, a nymphomaniacal figure skater who looks (intentionally, we're sure) like Peggy Fleming and talks like Marie Osmond, a TV reporter covering the "excitement" whose loony lush of an ex-wife is carrying on with the male skier, and assorted other has-beens, never-weres, and never-coulda-beens.

Hudson himself brings about the big snow job when he orders an associate to fly through a blizzard to the mountaintop, whereupon the tiny jet crashes into the mountain. The ensuing 10-minute sequence depicting the actual avalanche is a marvel of spend-next-to-nothing thriftiness. Stock shots of actual avalanches are intercut with double exposures showing people buried under "chunks of ice" (which actually look like giant Sugar-Frosted Shredded Wheats). There are several moments where it looks like powdered sugar pumped through a vacuum in reverse is inundating crowds of "terrified" victims. Once the snow has hit the fan, the digging-out process begins, getting off to a bang when a gas pipe in the resort's kitchen blows, resulting in the single funniest over-the-top explosion stunt in cinema history.

Dug out from an ice cave, Nolan is loaded into an ambulance, demanding a Bloody Mary instead of an oxygen mask. Farrow rides with her ex-mother-in-law, but the ambulance, apparently being driven by Evel Knievel, spins out of control and careens off a mountain bridge. Nolan and the driver wind up as toast in the crevasse below, and Farrow is left hanging by a thread, much like her career after this turkey. Will Rock or Robert—or both of them—save 78-pound Mia from falling to her death? Will Rock and Mia be reunited at the end? And most importantly, will anyone be able to sit through this *Avalanche* of overacting without laughing so hard they could make their own yellow snow?

Dippy Dialogue
Hudson's assistant (*Steve Franken*): "It's always uphill to get to the top!"
Hudson's mom (*Jeanette Nolan*): "If I had the strength, I'd write that down..."

Choice Chapter Stop
Chapter 10 ("Avalanche!"): The meat and potatoes of the film, including the hilarious kitchen-help-blown-all-to-hell stunt sequence.

The Concorde: Airport '79

(1979/Universal Pictures) **DVD / VHS**

Who's to Blame CAST: **Alain Delon** (*Captain Paul Metrand*); **Susan Blakely** (*Maggie Whelan*); **Robert Wagner** (*Kevin Harrison*); **Sylvia Kristel** (*Isabelle*); **George Kennedy** (*Joe Patroni*); GUEST STARRING: **Eddie Albert, Bibi Andersson, Charo, Sybil Danning, John Davidson, Andrea Marcovicci, Mercedes McCambridge, Martha Raye, Cicely Tyson, Jimmy J. J. Walker,** *and* A Human Heart in a Box CREW: **Directed by David Lowell Rich; Screenplay by Eric Roth; Story by Jennings Lang; "Inspired" by the novel** *Airport* **by Arthur Hailey**

Rave Reviews
"It could hardly be funnier if it were intended as a comedy!"
— *Halliwell's Film & Video Guide*

"For people who treasure expensive, supremely tacky Hollywood claptrap.... Sheer Joy, the funniest film of the decade.... I laughed my head off!" — **Vincent Canby,** *New York Times*

"123 minutes of aerodynamic howls from beginning to end.... All that's missing is Lassie bound for a cataract operation and The Vienna Boys' Choir." — **Sheila Benson,** *Los Angeles Times*

Plot, What Plot? The Razzies, and the frosty reception they've always received among "Industry types," stand in mute tribute to how rarely Hollywood admits to having made mistakes. Arguably only two instances exist in which studios admitted in their own paid advertising that something intended as a drama played to paying customers as a comedy. One was *Mommie Dearest,* with its "Biggest Mother of Them All" ad. The other is another all-time-so-bad-it's-good classic, *The Concorde: Airport '79.*

The fourth and final entry in the progressively less plausible *Airport* series, *Concorde* seems concocted by someone congenitally plot-impaired, then mounted by graduates of a film school for the blind, with casting sessions conducted exclusively during meetings of Overactors Unanimous. *Concorde*'s screenwriter is eventual Oscar winner Eric Roth, whose Academy Award for *Forrest Gump* was, after all, bestowed in part for his having written the line "Stupid is as stupid does." Its director is TV hack David Lowell Rich, whose next fiasco was the flatly unfunny *Chu Chu and the Philly Flash*. And its cast, as many a critic was happy to point out, could easily have been found at a *Fantasy Island* guest stars' reunion picnic.

Having already staged the comically priceless helicopter-to-cockpit rescue stunt in *Airport 1975*, then saved a sunken airliner with giant balloons in *Airport '77*, the makers of *Concorde* should have had a difficult time topping their predecessors' lunacy. But *Airport '79* comes through with flying colors, in part by staging not one, not two, but a whole series of ludicrous near misses involving a supersonic jet ferrying a decidedly motley list of passengers from Washington, D.C., to Moscow by way of Paris. The fact that the basic plot is predicated on Americans' attending the 1980 Moscow Olympics, which the United States chose to boycott after this film was finished—and that this is actually one of *Concorde*'s lesser flaws—should give you some idea of just what a juicy joyride you're in for.

First off, there isn't one credible character, situation, or line of dialogue in the entire film. Examples: Robert Wagner plays a billionaire industrialist so boneheaded he's willing to use his own deliberately misguided missile to blow up the Concorde in order to prevent his mistress, TV reporter Susan Blakely, from revealing his involvement in illegal arms deals. And Blakely isn't exactly playing with a full deck either. After finding out it was Wagner's "Buzzard" missile that came after the SST on its way to Paris, she agrees not to break the story until the plane lands in Moscow. The film's other "fun couples" include: Alain Delon as the copilot dallying with stewardess Sylvia Kristel (neither of whose dialogue can be understood without enabling closed captioning); helmet-haired TV reporter John Davidson and overaged Olympic gymnast Andrea Marcovicci, whose love is forbidden by her less-than-feminine female coach Mercedes (I'm-pixie-from-Hell) McCambridge; Eddie Albert as the head of the airline that's just bought the SST and sex bomb Sybil Danning as his nubile new bride; Avery Schreiber as a Soviet Olympic coach, traveling with his deaf daughter (who at least is spared the agony of hearing her father's blatantly phony Russian accent); Cicely Tyson and her dourly serious family doctor, traveling with a Styrofoam chest labeled "Human Heart, Handle with Care"; and for intentional comic relief, there's Charo smuggling a Chihuahua, and bladder-challenged Martha Raye, whose character has an unhealthy relationship with the SST's in-air toilet.

With so many morons all on one plane, it's hard to make a case against seeing it shot down. But in the course of its two-legged trip from the capital of the U.S. to that of the USSR, Delon and copilot George Kennedy (reprising his role of Joe Petroni from all three previous *Airport* films) repeatedly "rescue" the passengers—by putting them through midair barrel rolls, engine cutoffs that send the plane plummeting toward either the ocean or the Alps, and zigzag maneuvers even a Formula One race driver would never attempt. When a heat-seeking missile is fired at the SST, Kennedy easily deflects it . . . by opening the cockpit window (!) at 20,000 feet, and firing a flare for the missile to chase instead. The disastrous first leg of the trip culminates in the Concorde's being brought to a stop by using gigantic rubber bands—we kid you not! Then, in the film's single funniest Mount Everest–sized plot hole, almost every ticketholder reboards the same plane for the continued flight to Moscow.

Wall-to-wall with laugh-a-minute implausibilities, *Concorde* was released to such high-decibel howls of derision that Universal Pictures cried uncle. First promoted with the phrase "Fasten your seatbelts, the thrills are terrific," *Concorde*'s newspaper ads soon added the phrase ". . . and so are the laughs!" Indeed, they are.

Dippy Dialogue
Joe Petroni (*George Kennedy*): "They don't call it the cockpit for nothing, honey!"

Razzie Credentials
Concorde: Airport '79, along with *Airport 1975* and *Airport '77,* was inducted into the Razzie Hall of Shame at our 3rd Annual Awards.

Choice Chapter Stop
Chapter 10 ("Scramble Jet Fighters"): Kennedy barrel-rolls the plane, then deflects a heat-seeking missile by firing a flare out the open cockpit window.

Fun Footnote
The fifth *Airport* film was to have been *Airport '82: UFO.*

On Deadly Ground 🍅

(1994/Warner Bros.) **DVD / VHS**

Who's to Blame CAST: **Steven Seagal** 🍅 (*Forrest Taft*); **Michael Caine** (*Michael Jennings*); **Joan Chen** 🍅 (*Masu*); **John C. McGinley** (*MacGruder*); **Billy Bob Thornton** (*Homer Carlton*); **Chief Irvin Brink** (*Silook*)
CREW: **Directed by Steven Seagal** 🍅 ; **Screenplay** 🍅 **by Ed Horowitz and Robin U. Russin**

Rave Reviews
"Awesomely incoherent, a mixture of poorly staged violence and *Dances with Wolves*–style astral musings." — **Janet Maslin,** *New York Times*

"Seagal's directing ability is crude and occasionally downright silly [and] fails to mute the plethora of unintentional laughs."
 — **Chris Hicks,** *Deseret News* **(Salt Lake City)**

"One of those movies that is so bad it causes jaws to drop and stay agape until the closing credits." — **Scott Foy, BadMovies.net**

Plot, What Plot? There are few things funnier than watching a "message picture" made by an inept filmmaker: Ed Wood's cross-dressing camp classic *Glen or Glenda* is a perfect example, and, at the exact opposite end of the macho-meter of bad movies, Steven Seagal's *On Deadly Ground* is another.

While Mr. Wood's *Glenda* tried to make the case for wearing his fiancée's pink panties, Mr. Seagal's *Deadly* wants to convince us that oil companies drilling in the pristine Alaskan wilderness are not good guys. An easy task, you say? By the time Stone-Faced Steve makes an impassioned speech in the last reel, you may well find yourself rooting for the oil rig to blow our hero to smithereens, instead of rooting for Seagal to get revenge.

The film opens with a shot of a bald eagle, symbol of the wilderness (something Seagal learned in Moviemaking 101?), and under the main titles, listing all the people you'll want to get your own revenge on by film's end, the camera soars over mountaintops and frozen lakes, with Basil Poledouris's bogus Native American musical score prompting us to think, "Wow! That Steve, he sure is a nature-lovin' kinda guy!" As the credits end, we find ourselves landing at the site of a huge oil rig fire.

Our first glimpse of the Eco Avenger is his alligator-skin boot climbing from a helicopter (wait a minute, aren't ecologists against making boots out of alligators?). Next we pan up the back of Seagal's buckskin jacket (another beast bites the dust for Steve's vanity). The jacket is emblazoned with an embroidered "dream catcher," thus further establishing Steve as a Friend of the Friendless. To complete the tableau of Just How Much He Cares About the Environment, we finally see Seagal's face as he engages in that most ecologically sound of habits, lighting a cigar—which he soon tosses into one of those pristine snowbanks he's supposedly so hot on defending.

Changing into a bright yellow firefighting jumpsuit that makes him look like Big Bird's evil twin, Seagal has arrived just in time to save the day. He is greeted by a decrepit old prospector who barks the prophetic dialogue line "This is a disaster!" Then Steve's big entrance is almost topped by costar Michael Caine's. The ancient oil-rigger kvetches about the fire, blaming it all on Seagal's "Goddamned pal Jennings . . ." Right on cue, the copter door slams open to reveal Caine as Jennings, his hair dyed the color of a pit bull's fur and his face that odd shrimp pink one usually associates with open-casket funerals. Caine barks back at the old man, meaning he *must* be the villain of the piece. Such brilliant, economical filmmaking: We're barely four minutes in and all our basic conflicts have been established.

In the course of this incredible exercise in superstar self-ego stroking, Steven routs a bunch of ethnically insensitive louts in a barroom brawl, takes a mystic journey with the help of an Inuit female who is supposed to be his love interest (just how much did they pay Joan Chen for trying to pull off that one?), and eventually decides that in order to save the local environment, he has no choice . . . but to blow up Jennings's biggest oil rig.

Once the flotsam and shrapnel from the explosion have settled into the pristine wilderness, it's time for Seagal's big spiel at the Alaska state capitol expressing his concern for our ecosystem—a scene reputedly three or four times longer before it caused mass fleeing by audiences at sneak previews. As the music swells for the

1,357th time, we see Steve standing before an audience made up almost entirely of Native Americans in feathered headdresses and colorful native costumes. With a look on his face meant to be sincere concern (but possibly the result of irritable bowel syndrome) Steven launches into a four-minute diatribe against fossil fuels and those rilly bad gize who pollute our world to make profits. It obviously hasn't occurred to Seagal that the smoke being blown out of every orifice of a noxious gasbag such as himself also impacts our environment. When the speech ends, Steve is hugged by a mumbling Eskimo shaman, who blows literal smoke Steve's way, and declares, "The Earth is our grandma!"

Your eyes are likely to have glazed over by this point, but hang in there: About halfway through the end titles, we get to hear the Worst Song Razzie nominee "Under the Same Sun," a faux John Lennon ballad that lyricizes such utter banalities as "We all live under the same sun (yeah!), we all walk under the same moon, so why (why-y-y-y-h?) can't we live as one?"

One of my fondest Razzie recollections is seeing this film at a nearly empty matinee in the San Fernando Valley, and just as I thought to myself, "About the only category this one hasn't got covered is Worst Song," up came this tune, like some kind of Razzie epiphany.

Dippy Dialogue
Forrest Taft (*Steven Seagal*) warning his colleagues: "If you smell anything, get out of here!"

Choice Chapter Stop
Chapter 33 ("To Do What's Right"): Stevie's big Sierra Club spiel.

The Poseidon Adventure

(1972/20th Century-Fox) **DVD / VHS**

Who's to Blame CAST: **Gene Hackman** (*Rev. Frank Scott*); **Ernest Borgnine** (*Mike Rogo*); **Stella Stevens** (*Linda Rogo*); **Red Buttons** (*James Martin*); **Carol Lynley** (*Nonnie Parry*); **Roddy McDowall** ("*Acres*"); **Jack Albertson** (*Mannie Rosen*); **Shelley Winters** O (*Belle Rosen*); **Pamela Sue Martin** (*Susan Shelby*); **Leslie Nielsen** (*Captain Harrison*)
CREW: **Directed by Ronald Neame; Screenplay by Stirling Silliphant and Wendell Mayes; From the novel by Paul Gallico**

Rave Reviews
"The script is the only cataclysm in this water-logged *Grand Hotel*."
— ***The New Yorker***

"Works best as a Bad Movie to Laugh At!"
— **Andrew Hicks, Internet Movie Critic-at-Large**

"The disaster movie touchstone, a laughathon that . . . deliver[s] the 'so-bad-it's-good' goods."
— **Edward Margulies and Stephen Rebello,** ***Bad Movies We Love***

Plot, What Plot? Okay, okay! We know—*everybody* loves *The Poseidon Adventure*. But if you think about it, you love it for all the *wrong* reasons: hokey situations, hammy acting, and ham-fisted direction. A huge box-office behemoth, it is often mistakenly cited as the film that started the whole all-star disaster film cycle. But the title that *Poseidon does* deserve is Most Successful Trash Film of All Time.

For the three of you reading this book who don't already know *Poseidon*'s plot, it involves a mammoth tidal wave capsizing an ocean liner at straight-up midnight on New Year's Eve, and ten survivors' efforts to find their way to daylight in what ads proclaimed, "Hell, upside down."

Leading the plucky group of diehards slogging through hell and heading "up to the bottom" is Gene Hackman, giving what *Movieline* magazine called "a perfect impersonation of man-of-action blowhard Charlton Heston." Hackman, who won his Best Actor Oscar for *The French Connection* while *Poseidon* was filming, plays an irreverent reverend who spends most of the movie yelling—at the situation, at his cohorts, and in one way-over-the-top scene, at God himself. Among Hackman's motley group of walking, talking stickboard characters are fellow Oscar winners Red Buttons as the Lonely Old Man, Ernest Borgnine as the Gruff Cop Who Resents Being Ordered Around, Jack Albertson as the Loving Husband Who Loses His Wife, and, most memorably, Shelley Winters as the Unlikely Heroine Who Dies to Save the Others. Others along for this wild and wooly ride include Stella Stevens as the Prostitute with a Heart of Gold, Roddy McDowall as the Timid Survivor Who Finds Love, Carol Lynley as the Timid Survivor's Love Interest, and Leslie Nielsen as the Ship's Captain, giving a performance indistinguishable from his self-parodies in the *Airplane!* and *Naked Gun* movies.

The technical aspects of this film—its pacing, costumes, art direction, and special effects—are admittedly all top-notch. But they service a script that features about a cliché a minute. Just try keeping count of how many times characters say "We're all gonna die!" And we dare you to come up with even one line of "character exposition" that you haven't heard in at least a dozen other earlier movies.

Don't get us wrong, though: We love *Poseidon* too. It's just that we're aware the whole time that this is an Irwin Allen production and, as such, should *not* be taken too seriously. So throw in the DVD, sit back, capsize a bowl of popcorn in your lap, and enjoy this most entertaining—and tacky—of all the all-star disaster movies. Using the upside-down/inside-out logic that pervades *Poseidon*, it truly *is* a great film.

Dippy Dialogue
Lookout to captain: "Off the port bow—I don't know, I never saw anything like it. An enormous wall of water coming towards us!"
Captain Harrison (*Leslie Nielsen*): "Oh ... my ... God! Hard left!" (*Klaxons sound.*)

Choice Chapter Stop

Chapter 10 ("Oh, My God!"): In which the enormous wall of water hits, and the *Poseidon* is capsized during a New Year's Eve party.

NOTE: Best Stunt—29:39: A man in a tuxedo plummets into a huge skylight and gets electrocuted.

The Swarm

(1978/Warner Bros.) **DVD / VHS**

Who's to Blame   CAST: **Michael Caine** (*Brad Crane*); **Katharine Ross** (*Helena*); **Henry Fonda** (*Dr. Walter Krim*); **Olivia de Havilland** (*Maureen*); **Fred MacMurray** (*Clarence*); **Ben Johnson** (*Felix*); **José Ferrer** (*Dr. Andrews*); **Richard Chamberlain** (*Dr. Hubbard*); **Patty Duke Astin** (*Rita*); **Richard Widmark** (*Gen. Slater*)

CREW: **Directed by Irwin Allen; Screenplay by Stirling Silliphant; Based on a novel by Arthur Herzog**

Rave Reviews
"Well-known actors try to outdo each other while reading terrible dialogue and being stung [in] this multi-million-dollar flop."
— **Michael Weldon,** *The Psychotronic Encyclopedia of Film*

"The story is of a banality matched only by the woodenness of the acting!" — **Barry Took,** *Punch* **magazine (United Kingdom)**

"The movie must rank as one of the most ludicrously, if enjoyably silly, large budget Hollywood projects ever conceived."
— **Almar Haflidason, BBC Films (Web site)**

Plot, What Plot? Producer/director Irwin Allen "won" a 1984 Worst Career Achievement Razzie naming him "The Master of Disaster." And *The Swarm* is the single biggest disaster on his less-than-distinguished résumé. After producing *The Poseidon Adventure,* then codirecting *Towering Inferno,* Allen decided that he alone should direct his next big-budget picture featuring an all-has-been cast. But Allen's "directing" abilities, best displayed in his 1957 hysterical/historical opus *The Story of Mankind,* were from the Frying Pan School of Filmmaking: When in doubt, hit the audience in the head with a frying pan instead of bothering to be subtle. And under Allen's firm hand, and despite its enormous pro-

DISASTERS...IN EVERY SENSE

duction budget, *The Swarm* turned the tale of an invasion by killer bees into the ultimate B movie.

Allen's cast, none of whom willingly list *The Swarm* on their own résumés, included no fewer than nine former Oscar nominees or winners: Michael Caine, Olivia de Havilland, Patty Duke, José Ferrer, Lee Grant, Henry Fonda, Ben Johnson, Katharine Ross, and Richard Widmark. Every one of them, along with Slim Pickens, Richard Chamberlain, and Cameron Mitchell, knowingly signed on to appear in a movie in which they would spend most of their screen time either mouthing inane dialogue concocted by Oscar-winning screenwriter Stirling Silliphant, or dodging a swarm of imaginary "killer bees" that would later be optically added to their "dramatic" scenes. And every one of them spends almost every screen moment with a look on their face like they'd rather confront real killer bees than appear in the career-killing buzz bomb in which they find themselves trapped.

Throughout the film, various scientists and military bigwigs try in vain to find some way to either counteract the African killer bees' venom, or at least to waylay the fake-looking cloud of bees that shows up like clockwork every few minutes to liven up the action. In the course of the film, the bees attack a military base, a grade school, a town picnic, and a nuclear power plant. Hoping to prevent another poorly executed bee attack sequence, Henry Fonda then stupidly injects himself with the equivalent of six beestings in order to test the anti-bee serum he's just formulated. Fonda somehow keeps a straight face while declaring, "Smells just like bananas!" and then goes into cardiac arrest, seeing an imaginary giant bee before he dies. But it's kinky-haired Caine who comes up with the final solution: luring the swarm out of Houston by using the sound of the killer bees' "mating ritual" played on several buoys, and then setting fire to the ocean where the swarm lands. Like Steven Seagal in *On Deadly Ground,* Caine has come up with a way to preserve the environment by "blowing it up real good."

Just in case any American bees were offended while buzzing past drive-in theatres, Allen included the following title card at the end of *The Swarm*: "The African killer bees portrayed in this film bear absolutely no relationship to the industrious, hard-working American honey bee, to which we are indebted for pollinating vital crops that feed our nation." But it turned out to be moviegoers who were offended. When *The Swarm* proved to be his biggest bomb,

Allen decreed a policy that no journalist was ever to mention it in his presence again. Years later, a pair of wisecracking reporters from the *L.A. Times* brought it up upon entering Allen's backlot office—and were both immediately escorted out the studio gates by Warner Bros. security guards.

Dippy Dialogue
General Slater (*Richard Widmark*) watching Houston burn outside his window: "You wonder, don't you: Will history blame me . . . or the bees?"

Choice Chapter Stop
Chapter 34 ("Nuclear Nightmare"): In which José Ferrer and Richard Chamberlain flee in slo-mo from a cloud of what looks like Killer Puffed Wheat . . . and a miniature nuclear power plant blows up real good.

Fun Footnote
Caine claimed that he ate "the little yellow stuff" left on his jacket by the bees throughout filming, thinking it was honey. It was actually bee BMs.

The Ten Commandments O

(1956/Paramount Pictures)　**DVD / VHS**

Who's to Blame　CAST: **Charlton Heston** (*Moses*); **Yul Brynner** (*Ramses*); **Anne Baxter** (*Nefretiri*); **Edward G. Robinson** (*Dathan*); **Yvonne De Carlo** (*Sephora*); **John Derek** (*Joshua*); **Debra Paget** (*Lila*); **Sir Cedric Hardwicke** (*Pharaoh*); **Cecil B. DeMille** (*Narrator*)
CREW: **Directed by Cecil B. DeMille; Screenplay by Aeneas MacKenzie, Jesse Lasky Jr., Jack Garris, and Fredric M. Frank; Based on "Ancient Texts"**

Rave Reviews
"De Mille's riotously flatulent Exodus epic . . . hysterically campy."
— Eric Henderson, *Slant* **magazine**

"A great big wallow, sublime hootchy-kootchy hokum."
— *TV Guide's Movie Guide*

"What DeMille has really done is to throw sex and sand into the moviegoers' eyes for almost twice as long as anyone else has ever dared to." — *Time* **magazine**

Plot, What Plot? Before movies even learned to talk, legendary director Cecil B. DeMille learned the one unbeatable box-office combination: stories from the Bible featuring scads of sex and oodles of orgies. This theory of tantalizing tales from the Good Book reached its zenith in DeMille's multimillion-dollar 1956 remake of *The Ten Commandments*. Beloved by many, and taken way too seriously by most, *Ten Commandments* is basically a carnival sideshow of devilry and debauchery, swathed in the protective blanket of being based on the Bible.

We first know we're in for a Holy Hoot when the film opens with DeMille himself stepping out from behind a curtain to tell us how carefully and accurately his film tells the biblical tale of Moses. Once the master showman steps back behind the drape, his film belies everything he's said. The central story concerns the age-old eternal triangle, this one between Charlton Heston as the stone-faced Hebrew prince Moses, Princess Nefretiri, a slithering sex goddess steamily overplayed by Anne Baxter, and bald-headed Yul Brynner as Moses' "half brother" Ramses, who wants Baxter to bear his children. The only problem is, neither history books nor the Good Book make any mention of this trio of love turtles.

Never mind, the film also features state-of-the-art, Oscar-winning special effects, including John Carradine turning Moses' staff into a snake, a green-fingered plague misting its way through the streets of Egypt at night, and the legendary "parting of the Red Sea" sequence (an effect achieved by melting two blocks of blue Jell-O, then running the footage backwards). When it's trying to be spectacular, *Commandments* indeed is. But whenever two characters are onscreen speaking, purple prose keeps popping up, made all the purpler by the actors speaking it.

DeMille always insisted he cast Heston in the lead role because of his resemblance to Michelangelo's statue of Moses—little did he know that Charlton's every move and line reading could be mistaken for granite. "Your fragrance is like the wine of Babylon," Chuck tells the badly bewigged Baxter, restraining himself from mashing his lips to hers. "Oh, Moses!" she declaims, playfully grabbing his helmet, "I am Egypt!" She then performs the lip-lock Chuck was too restrained to do.

As the third side of this triangle, Yul Brynner's Ramses is the most consistently interesting character in the film—which isn't to say he doesn't overact, merely that he does so with greater gusto than most of the rest. In proposing marriage to Baxter (or rather, commanding that she marry him), Brynner declares, "You will be mine, like my dog, or my horse, or my falcon. Except that I shall love you more . . . and trust you less!" Apparently finding the prospect of being walked on a leash irresistible, Baxter acquiesces.

In typical 1950s epic fashion, DeMille also cast a gallery of character actors and ingénues (both male and female) in supporting roles. Among the more amusing faces in this overcrowded cast of thousands are: Lily Munster (Yvonne De Carlo) as Mrs. Moses; a vampish Vincent Price as bad boy Baka; the DeMille of the Razzies John Derek as hunky stonecutter Joshua; and, constantly swallowing scenery whole, then spitting it right back into the camera, Edward G. Robinson as the heavy of the piece (and the leader of the Golden Calf Gang) Dathan. An interesting factual note is that Nina Foch, cast as Moses' adoptive mother who rescues him from the bulrushes, is in real life all of *seven months* older than Charlton Heston.

Nearly four hours long, with every minute of that last hour making your backside throb, *Ten Commandments* is widely considered the finest of DeMille's many sand-and-sex epics. But for those of us who know kitsch when we see it, *Ten Commandments* is CB's supreme masterpiece of biblical bloviation.

Dippy Dialogue
Nefretiri (*Anne Baxter*): "Oh, Moses, Moses! You stubborn, splendid, adorable fool!"

Choice Chapter Stops
Chapter 17, Disc One ("The Royal Barge"): Baxter lords it over Heston, now reduced to making bricks out of straw and mud.
Chapter 13, Disc Two ("The Parting of the Red Sea"): In which The Jell-O of God smites those evil Egyptians.

Special Recommendation
If you get the DVD, try watching it with the French dialogue track and English subtitles enabled—you'll miss none of the nostril-flaring "subtleties" of the performances, and experience the rare treat of hearing a Bible tale told by Pepé Le Pew.

The Bodyguard

(1992/Warner Bros.) **DVD / VHS**

Who's to Blame   CAST: **Kevin Costner** ☺ (*Frank Farmer*); **Whitney Houston** ☺ (*Rachel Marron*); **Gary Kemp** (*Sy Spector*); **Bill Cobbs** (*Bill Devaney*); **Debbie Reynolds** (*Herself*); **Robert Wuhl** (*Oscar Host*)
CREW: **Directed by Mick Jackson; Screenplay** ☺ **by Lawrence Kasdan**

Rave Reviews

"Overblown dual-star vehicle, makes no sense, but has many... moments of high kitsch." — *Leonard Maltin's Movie & Video Guide*

"A jumbled mess... feels like a music video interrupted by a movie." — *Variety*

"A great silly mess of a luv story, a multimedia circus of music videos, entertainment journalism, action thriller and '60s movie melodrama." — **Rita Kempley,** *Washington Post*

Plot, What Plot? A testament to the ability of "star power"—and one monster hit song—to propel even the most risible of romances to box-office gold, *The Bodyguard* paired Kevin Costner (fresh off his Worst Actor "win" as *Robin Hood: Prince of Dweebs*) and Whitney Houston (making her screen debut) as a professional protector and a top-of-the-charts pop star, threatened by a deranged fan. Like *Titanic* five years later, *Bodyguard* was helped enormously at the ticket booth by its gazillion-copy-selling love theme, Houston's version of "I Will Always Love You." *Bodyguard* eventually grossed over $410 million worldwide, yet today is best remembered for the clownish, close-cropped haircut Costner wore in it.

Frank Farmer (whose name sounds like he should be making sausages) is "the very best" in the bodyguard business, but as he himself professes, he "doesn't do celebrities." Rachel Marron is America's biggest recording star, but she has a problem: Someone recently sent her a Barbie doll dressed like her that exploded in her dressing room. Will Frank take on the task of protecting Rachel if she begs hard enough? Will Costner and Houston fall in love? Will Rachel's appearance at the Oscars prove to be a comic highlight? Will anyone have the nerve to tell Kevin how utterly nerdy that haircut makes him look? These and other pressing questions all get answered as this by-the-numbers romance plods its way toward its inevitable big shootout finale.

Along the way, Houston gets to sing two Oscar-nominated Best Songs and one Razzie-nominated Worst Song ("Queen of the Night," with hilarious single-entendre lyrics). During one of them, Costner is watching a Rachel music video on a projection TV, and finds himself sitting up at attention . . . in more ways than one. Soon, they wind up at his place, where she "symbolically" grabs his Samurai sword and plays with it, and he then splits her scarf with his blade. But there's trouble in paradise, as Kevin tells Whitney the next morning: "I can't protect you like this. You can live with it, or you can fire me." And she, oh so romantically, replies, "I can fire you . . . but I can't fuck you?"

Everything culminates when, in a moment that could happen only in the fantasy world of chick flicks, Houston (who was a Worst Actress nominee for this performance) finds herself up for Best Actress at the Academy Awards. That year's Oscarcast must be on WB, though, because it's hosted by total nobody Robert Wuhl, and the only star we see backstage is Debbie Reynolds. When it comes time for her category, Rachel's name is read from the envelope, and she rises slowly from her seat, wearing a grin more appropriate for having won a PTA bake-off than an Academy Award. Suddenly, we go into hilarious slo-mo as the stalker aims a rifle—disguised as a TV camera—right at Whitney's head, Costner is temporarily blinded by the klieg lights, the would-be assassin aims and shoots . . . and Kevin tackles Whitney football-style in a fake Oscar moment worthy of Stephen Boyd in *The Oscar*. Does he die? Does she die? Do we *all* die laughing? To find out, you'll have to see *The Bodyguard*. Yes, it *was* one of 1992's biggest-grossing films. But we figure that's because in 1992, no other movie had more laughs.

Dippy Dialogue
Rachel (*Whitney Houston*): "While you were protecting her, she got killed, right?"
Frank (*Kevin Costner*): "Nobody's perfect . . ."

Razzie Credential
Bodyguard entered the 13th Annual Razzies at the top of the charts, with seven nominations, including Costner's awful new haircut competing as Worst New Star. It wound up as empty-handed as the movie was empty-headed, failing to "win" a single spray-painted statuette.

Choice Chapter Stop
Chapter 35 ("The Winner Takes the Stage"): In which Kevin goes down on Whitney, live on the Academy Awards . . . in slo-mo yet!

Fun Footnote
The screenplay for *Bodyguard* was first written in 1975. Its original stars were supposed to have been Steve McQueen and Diana Ross.

Indecent Proposal

(1993/Paramount Pictures) **DVD / VHS**

Who's to Blame   CAST: **Robert Redford** ☉ (*John Gage*); **Demi Moore** ☉ (*Diana Murphy*); **Woody Harrelson** ● (*David Murphy*); **Oliver Platt** (*Jeremy*); **Seymour Cassel** (*Mr. Shackleford*); **Billy Bob Thornton** (*Day Tripper*)

CREW: **Directed by Adrian Lyne** ☉; **Screenplay** ● **by Amy Holden Jones; Based on the novel by Jack Engelhard**

Rave Reviews
"So ridiculous, you wouldn't believe me if I told you."
— Desson Howe, *Washington Post*

"Sports an idiotic conclusion that looks like Test Market Ending #6."
— *Variety*

"Comes on like *Honeymoon in Vegas* with a bad case of the sniffles."
— Peter Travers, *Rolling Stone*

Plot, What Plot? Every once in a while, Hollywood produces a box-office smash of such staggering banality that it almost seems the filmmakers set out to prove H. L. Mencken's adage: "Nobody ever went broke underestimating the intelligence of the American public." *Indecent Proposal,* one of 1993's biggest hits, is such a film. As several critics were quick to point out, it's actually a feature-length version of an old joke: A man walks up to a woman in a bar and whispers, "Would you sleep with me for a million dollars?" When the woman answers, "Yes," the man adds, "Would you sleep with me for one dollar?" Repulsed, the woman responds, "What kind of woman do you take me for?" The man then one-ups her with, "We've already established that. Now we're negotiating the price." But in the case of *Indecent Proposal,* it's not meant as a stand-up comedian's joke, it's meant as A Serious Issue Drama. And amazing numbers of American moviegoers (mainly women) were willing to overlook the film's idiocies in exchange for a chance to fantasize that Robert Redford might also offer *them* a million dollars for a one-night stand. But we're getting ahead of ourselves . . .

"Losing Diana," whines Woody Harrelson in voice-over as the film opens, "was like losing a part of me." Just as you're thinking he sounds like maybe he's lost his cerebral cortex, the film shifts into that old standby of mediocre moviemaking, the flashback. Woody and Demi Moore once deeply loved one another, but things somehow went wrong, maybe because they're both greedy, materialistic assholes who'd literally sell their own asses to get ahead in life. Their touching dilemma begins when they're stupid enough to gamble away their last dollar in Las Vegas, hoping to win the money needed to hang on to their about-to-be-repossessed dream house. The fact that the house is on a cliff in Malibu, and would be hard for the real Harrelson or Moore to afford even on their movie-star salaries, is lost on this film's dim-bulb creators.

Enter Robert Redford (who looks like he should be playing Prune Face in Warren Beatty's *Dick Tracy*) as the billionaire who makes the "indecent proposal" for which the film is named: In exchange for one million dollars, would Harrelson agree to "lend" him Moore for one night of sex? That the couple is sleazy enough to even entertain the offer should give you some idea of how off-center this film's supposed moral compass is. That they'll accept the offer goes without saying, since if they didn't, the movie would be under 45 minutes long. That it will create complications for all concerned is to be anticipated. That the movie now goes from banal to unbearable, resorting to quoting T-shirt slogans as if they're the wisdom of the ages and showing us all just what boneheads Demi and Woody are (and just how desperate Redford must have been for a hit film), is what made this an eventual Razzie "winner."

Reunited on the very pier where Woody made *his* proposal to Demi in that first flashback, with Moore sporting hair swept behind her ear and looking like Dopey from The Seven Dwarfs, our happy doofy couple finally work things out, and at the end we freeze-frame on their hands clasped as tears stream down Demi's cheeks. All of this is underscored by the most syrupy, manipulative music score imaginable, and sentient audience members will realize this film isn't just yanking our emotional chain, it's torn the chain right out of the wall and is beating us over the head with it.

Perhaps the most shocking thing about *Indecent Proposal* is that it was taken to heart by millions of moviegoers, grossed over $106 million, and sparked a national debate about the "moral dilemma" its characters faced. But if you're a lover of bad movies (and, hey, you bought this book!) we defy you to sit through this treacly treatise on love and greed with a straight face. And during the slow parts, we encourage you to make your own list of which billionaires you would or wouldn't have sex with for a million dollars: Donald Trump? Ross Perot? Mister Magoo? Montgomery Burns?

Dippy Dialogue
Diana (*Demi Moore*), after David bids the entire million dollars at a zoo charity auction: "I really wanted you to have that money . . ."
David (*Woody Harrelson*): "I really wanted you to have that hippo . . ."

Choice Chapter Stop
Chapter 15 ("Paradise Cove"): In which Demi quotes T-shirt wisdom one last time, then gets to play Dopey again to Woody's Happy.

Fun Footnote
If Redford's monologue about seeing a beautiful girl on the subway thirty years ago sounds familiar, that's because it was taken almost verbatim from a similar monologue in *Citizen Kane*.

The Jayne Mansfield Story

(1980/TV movie) **VHS**

Who's to Blame **CAST: Loni Anderson** (*Jayne Mansfield*); **Arnold Schwarzenegger** (*Mickey Hargitay*); **G. D. Spradlin** (*Gerald Conway*); **Raymond Buktenica** (*Bob Garrett*); **Kathleen Lloyd** (*Carol Sue Peters*)
CREW: Directed by Dick Lowry; Teleplay by Charles Dennis and Nancy Gayle; Based upon the book *Jayne Mansfield and the American 50s* by Martha Saxton

Rave Reviews
"Living Barbie doll Loni Anderson...at times bears an uncanny resemblance to Lady Penelope in *Thunderbirds*." — SkyMovies.com

"Semi-fictional, romanticized account of the world's most famous decapitated dumb blonde, leading up to her fatal car crash."
— **Michael Weldon, *The Psychotronic Encyclopedia of Film***

"Arnold's voice for the off-screen narration...[is] about as lucid as a subway announcer speaking through a sandwich."
— **Nigel Andrews, *The Life and Times of Arnold Schwarzenegger***

Plot, What Plot? For Ah-Nuld, the chance to play former Mr. Universe Mickey Hargitay, one of his childhood role models, must have seemed the dream of a lifetime. But Arnie not only costars in the film, he also narrates it. And since his command of "Inklitch" was "ferry limbited" in 1980, for audiences, it's the scream of a lifetime. This 1980 TV movie also stars 1983 Worst Actress Razzie nominee Loni Anderson (*Stroker Ace*) as screen sex goddess and '60s joke Jayne Mansfield, covering both the tragedy that was her life and the travesty that passed for her career.

Starting the film as an ambitious brunette, Loni wiggles and woowoo's her way from Texas to Hollywood, where Jayne longs to be taken seriously, even though she's got front bumpers like a 1957

Cadillac, bleaches her hair platinum, and shamelessly trades on her sexuality to get ahead. Attending Mae West's Latin Quarter show, she meets her match in terms of brains and narcissism, Mickey Hargitay, played by Ah-Nuld. Greased up and smiling with a mouthful of crooked teeth, Ah-Nuld is equally smitten by this sex kitten.

Structured in that hoary old device of the flashback, the story of Jayne Mansfield is entirely told to us by Ah-Nuld, reminiscing with a reporter after Jayne's death. Since it was made for TV, this film can't actually tell us just *how* trashy Mansfield got, or how low she sunk before dying in a famous road accident that left her decapitated. For details on the depths to which Jayne actually *did* sink, check the listing for *The Wild Wild World of Jayne Mansfield.*

This version of her life is so badly written that it *begins* with the car crash, and so has nothing to build up to. But watching Loni and Ah-Nuld go through the paces of "dramatically" portraying a disintegrating marriage, complete with alcoholism and spousal abuse, is a wondrous sight to behold. Chock-full of lines like Loni declaring, "I have a 160 IQ!" or Ah-Nuld perpetually mispronouncing Mansfield's first name as "Chayne," *Jayne Mansfield* is the movie equivalent of reading a yellowing old fan magazine. No more than fifteen words of it are probably true, but it so sincerely buys into the B.S. that it's shocking that it *is* entertaining. Our only regret: that they didn't stretch the truth enough to put Ah-Nuld in the Oldsmobile with "Chayne" on that foggy road outside Biloxi.

Dippy Dialogue
Mickey Hargitay (*Arnold Schwarzenegger*), speaking of his late wife in voice-over: "Ass Chayne always sayed apout her caweer . . ."

(1992/20th Century-Fox) **VHS**

Who's to Blame CAST: **Melanie Griffith** ☻ (*Linda Voss*); **Michael Douglas** ☼ (*Ed Leland*); **Liam Neeson** (*Franz-Otto Dietrich*); **John Gielgud** (*Konrad Friedrichs*); **Joely Richardson** (*Margrete von Eberstein*)
CREW: **Directed by David Seltzer** ☻; **Screenplay** ☼ **by Seltzer; Based on the novel by Susan Isaacs**

Rave Reviews
"As silly as they come... and every time you think it can't get any dumber, along comes something that proves you wrong."
— **Chris Hicks**, *Deseret News* **(Salt Lake City)**

"Fun, in an extravagant, hopelessly retrograde fashion."
— **Janet Maslin**, *New York Times*

"An insult to the intelligence... the movie would be over in 10 minutes if everyone in it weren't an idiot." — **Roger Ebert**, *Chicago Sun-Times*

Plot, What Plot? A spy "thriller" that's also a chick flick of the worst kind, *Shining Through* tells the story of Linda Voss, a woman whose way with strudel nets her a job behind enemy lines in Nazi Germany, where she hopes to rescue family members threatened by Hitler's extermination of the Jews. But as the *Washington Post* pointed out in its review of the film, only cartoon vamp Betty Boop would have made a less credible spy than *Shining Through*'s Worst Actress–"winning" star Melanie Griffith.

With her voice still breathy and babylike at the age of eighty, Griffith is first seen in utterly unconvincing "old age" makeup, being interviewed by the BBC for a documentary on "Women in the War." In the course of the film, she is supposed to age from early adolescence through dotage, but her eyes, voice, and flat line deliveries never change one iota. In the novel, Voss was apparently a gutsy, go-get-'em kinda broad who experienced the real-life equivalent of a Harlequin romance novel. But in the film, as played by monotone Melanie, she comes off more like someone auditioning to play Lucy Ricardo's even klutzier cousin.

Taking a job as assistant to Michael Douglas, who she quickly figures out *must* be a spy, Griffith can't wait for her chance to convince him what a terrific spy *she'd* make. Seizing her chance when a German diplomat's nanny quits and a new double agent is needed to take her place, Melanie quickly whips up a batch of apple strudel ("Just like they make it in Berlin!") and rushes it over to Douglas's house in the middle of the night. Not only can she cook kuchen, she can also sprechen Deutsch, so with little or no training she finds herself on her way behind enemy lines, by way of an airport scene blatantly knocked off from *Casablanca* but far funnier than even *The Carol Burnett Show*'s parody of that film.

In Berlin, she meets fellow spy John Gielgud (who really has no excuse for appearing in this drivel) and befriends her Nazi boss's children à la Julie Andrews in *The Sound of Music*. But when she bungles the task of smuggling a coded message at a fish market in a scene right out of *I Love Lucy*, things get sticky. And because he was the one who sent her in, Douglas must now come to her rescue. Never mind that he's disguised as a Nazi soldier and neither speaks nor understands German; by now he's in love and willing to take idiotic risks for the sake of the film's puerile plot.

Griffith and Douglas end up on a train near the Swiss border when they finally get caught. In a stroke of pure genius (NOT!), Douglas grabs Melanie in his arms, points to the bloody bandage around his throat to explain his inability to speak—and runs like hell for the borderline. Riddled with bullets, he barely staggers across the painted line . . . and the Nazis stop firing (we all remember from history class how well they respected international borders, don't we?) . . .

Overheated, underlogical, and underscored by music that often makes the already hokey dialogue and performances seem even hokier, *Shining Through* was a popular choice for our 1992 Worst Picture Razzie. And since Melanie assayed both this asinine role and the lead in *A Stranger Among Us* that same year, she too was a landslide choice, beating out both Whitney Houston in *The Bodyguard* and Kim Basinger in *Final Analysis* as Worst Actress.

When life hands you Razz-berries, sometimes you've just gotta make strudel . . .

Dippy Dialogue
Linda Voss (*Melanie Griffith*): "After all, Ed, what is war for if not to hold on to the things we love?"

Fun Footnote
While doing a publicity tour for this film, Melanie Griffith responded to a reporter's question about the Holocaust, saying, "Wow! Six million... that's a lot of people!" Which led us to wonder: Is *Shining Through* what happens when you hold a flashlight up to one of Ms. Griffith's ears?

Sincerely Yours

(1955/Warner Bros.) **VHS**

Who's to Blame CAST: **Liberace** (*Anthony Warrin*); **Dorothy Malone** (*Linda Curtis*); **Joanne Dru** (*Marion Moore*); **William Demarest** (*Sam Dunne*); **Lori Nelson** (*Sarah*); **Lurene Tuttle** (*Mrs. McGinley*)
CREW: **Directed by Gordon Douglas; Screenplay by Irving Wallace; Based on the play *The Man Who Played God* by Jules Eckert Goodman**

Rave Reviews
"RATED: BOMB! A camp classic . . . a ludicrous vehicle for Liberace."
— *Leonard Maltin's Movie & Video Guide*

"Given sufficient intoxication, you could find this movie amusing."
— *Saturday Review*

"Insipidly sentimental, hopelessly hokey, stiflingly hothouse-flowery. . . . But, oh, how [Liberace] does twinkle!"
— **Michael Sauter,** *The Worst Movies of All Time*

Plot, What Plot? Half a century later, Hollywood still hasn't learned one of the biggest lessons taught by Liberace's film debut in the infamous fiasco *Sincerely Yours*: The moviegoing public, as a general rule, is not willing to pay the price of a ticket to see someone on the big screen that they're used to seeing at home for free.

The other big lesson this film *did* manage to teach was that Liberace was no actor, and every frame of this film provided further argument for his never starring onscreen again. Despite his enormous success as a TV entertainer, as a movie star Liberace was a total washout. Bouncing merrily at his piano keyboard (often moving like there *must* be an earthquake going on), smiling broadly with his piano-keyboard-like pearly whites, or, toward the end of the film, clumsily tap-dancing (!), Liberace screams campy, fey appeal. But to old ladies of the naïve 1950s, he was an icon and "dream lover" to whose blatant "flamboyance" they were laughably oblivious. Warner Bros. naturally assumed his TV appeal would transfer well to motion pictures, and he was signed to a two-picture contract. The fact that the second film never got made and that—other than a gut-bustingly funny musical cameo in 1965's *When the Boys Meet the Girls*—Liberace never appeared in movies again should give you some idea of how well *Sincerely Yours* went over.

Poor choices and even poorer execution plagued this project from its beginnings. Firstly, it was based on a rickety old stage play entitled *The Man Who Played God,* which had previously been filmed in 1932, with the similarly prissy George Arliss in the title role. The story of a famed concert pianist who goes deaf, it was thought to be the perfect vehicle to launch Liberace's movie career. To adapt and update the material, Warners selected Irving Wallace—later a highly successful novelist, but then just another struggling hack screenwriter. To direct it, they picked Gordon Douglas, fresh off the 180-degrees-different *Them!* (and later the director of *Call Me Bwana* and Jerry Lewis's *Way . . . Way Out*).

The basic material has Liberace being pursued by his female assistant Joanne Dru while also "romancing" future Oscar winner Dorothy Malone. The fact that in real life Liberace would have been likelier to go after costar William Demarest than either of these two dames seems lost on the filmmakers. With a glint in his eye, a quart of brilliantine in his hair, and his fingers flying across the keyboard like wildly mating rabbits, Liberace spends almost half the film playing piano in his inimitable style. This element, though undeniably silly, is at least watchable. But when he stands up from this piano stool, the real problems begin . . . because without the Steinway to hide behind, Liberace is a cipher as a screen persona. Flat line readings, odd vocal inflections, and silent-movie-style "eye acting" are only a few of his problems. The funniest sequence in the film—the one where he realizes he's going deaf during a concert performance—finds our star making facial expressions more appropriate to locating the source of a flatulent outburst than to experiencing the loss of his hearing.

Given the overall hokiness of the script, we assume he'll have to face one of those only-in-the-movies "risky operations" where he'll either get his hearing back or be left deaf for life. Of course, he does. And while ruminating on his choice, he learns to lip-read, using binoculars and spying on strangers in Central Park. Bored, he decides to "play God" by giving some of his "subjects" what he thinks they need most. Eventually his lip-reading skills tell him something he'd rather not know about Malone. Naturally, the film has a happy ending, with an extensive concert at Carnegie Hall by Ol' Sequin Toes himself.

In today's more gay-assimilated society, it's almost impossible to believe that Liberace's personal preferences could ever have been so ludicrously overlooked. But the fact that they once were did at least create *Sincerely Yours,* a classic "romantic triangle" in which at least one of the sides was decidedly *not* straight.

Dippy Dialogue
Howard (*Alex Nicol*), referring to Liberace's character: "He respects the classics, but from a sitting position, not from his knees!"

Fun Footnote
For the Ultimate Liberace Musical Experience, check TV listings for *When the Boys Meet the Girls* and catch him performing the pricelessly suggestive song "Arruba Liberace!"

The Specialist

(1994/Warner Bros.) **DVD / VHS**

Who's to Blame CAST: **Sylvester Stallone** ☺ *(Ray Quick)*; **Sharon Stone** ☺ *(May/Adrian)*; **James Woods** *(Ned Trent)*; **Rod Steiger** ☺ *(Joe Leon)*; **Eric Roberts** *(Tomas Leon)*
CREW: **Directed by Luis Llosa; Written by Alexandra Seros; Suggested by the *Specialist* novels by John Shirley**

Rave Reviews
"With all the preening, posing and stretching, it's hard to know if *The Specialist* is an action movie or an exercise video. Or a porn movie without the sex." — **Hal Hinson,** *Washington Post*

"Mr. Stallone and Ms. Stone . . . a meeting as disastrous as the Hindenburg crashing into the Titanic . . . the biggest bomb is the movie itself." — **Caryn James,** *New York Times*

"Cheesecake meets beefcake." — *The New Yorker*

Plot, What Plot? In the Bizarro World where movies like *The Specialist* take place, Sylvester Stallone is a "brilliant" but hangdog-eyed explosives expert and Sharon Stone is a "bitter but beautiful" woman determined to avenge the murder of her parents, which she witnessed as a child. After an opening sequence in which Sly is seen trying to defuse a bomb which threatens the life of a drug czar's innocent daughter, Sylvester finds himself in "Miami Beach, present day" being courted via pay phone by silken-voiced Stone, who wants to give him the honor of offing her parents' killers.

Constructed like a paint-by-numbers kit for creating the impression of a thriller, *The Specialist* is one of those "packaged" pairings of two stars that from its inception should have seemed foolish to its financial backers. Neither Stallone nor Stone had a hit film in quite a while when this movie came along—and its critical and box-office reception, as well as its five Razzie nominations, did nothing to further either star's career.

For one thing, the screenplay requires its two narcissistic stars to waste more than half the film before meeting face-to-face, leaving the audience to assume that when they do finally meet, it will prove to be memorable. It is, but not in the way director Llosa or screenwriter Seros intended. The "climax" of all that buildup is a suds-and-sex shower scene that is one of the wonders of modern bad cinema. Both Sly and Mizz Sharon spend several minutes in carefully framed, revealing-but-not-*too*-revealing nude slo-mo shots, sudsing up and sizing up each other and themselves. When they finally come together, it has all the sexual heat . . . of a corporate merger.

Crashing and burning around our two stars is a convoluted plot that almost no one can follow, involving double crosses, switches-on-switches, and the old "red wire or green wire" cliché. About the only thing one can say in the stars' favor is that they're not the hammiest actors onscreen. James Woods, as Sly's former Army partner and current nemesis, is clearly having a ball making fun of the film while also being its most interesting element. Eric Roberts plays the target of the hit, who has apparently found the Fountain of Youth, since he hasn't aged a single day in the twenty years since he killed Stone's parents. And, possessed by the tormented spirit of Ricky Ricardo, Rod Steiger plays an old Cuban don with an accent and gestures that make Al Pacino in *Scarface* seem subtle.

Greeted with hoots of laughter in its initial release, *The Specialist* is the kind of "action/adventure" movie only a studio focused on its bottom line could think audiences would take seriously, and only *SCTV*'s "Farm Film Report" could love. Yes, things do "blow up real good"—but the movie itself also blows up right along with them.

Dippy Dialogue
May (*Sharon Stone*), on pay phone to Stallone: "I heard that you control your explosions, that you . . . shape your charges . . ."

Razzie Credential
Specialist "won" Worst Actress for Stone, and the pairing of Stone and Stallone tied for Worst Screen Couple with Tom Cruise and Brad Pitt in *Interview with the Vampire*.

Choice Chapter Stop
Chapter 22 ("May/Ray Close-Up"): In which Sylvester and Sharon,

helping the environment by sharing a shower, prove their passionate love . . . for themselves.

Fun Footnote

Although he lost out on a Razzie to O. J. Simpson in *The Naked Gun 33⅓*, Steiger "won" the *other* bad movie award, a Golden Turkey as Worst Supporting Actor, for this performance.

Sweet November

(2001/Warner Bros.) **DVD / VHS**

Who's to Blame CAST: **Keanu Reeves** ☯ (*Nelson Moss*); **Charlize Theron** ☯ (*Sara Deever*); **Jason Isaacs** (*Chaz*); **Greg Germann** (*Vince*); **Frank Langella** (*Edgar Price*)
CREW: **Directed by Pat O'Connor; Screenplay by Kurt Voelker; Story by Voelker and Paul Yurick; Based on a 1968 screenplay by Herman Raucher**

Rave Reviews
"An extra-thick vanilla schmalted with just the right amount of raw sugar to summon the awwwws of high school girls."
— Michael Atkinson, *Village Voice*

"Couldn't be more artificial if every object on the screen were molded from plastic. That includes leading man Keanu Reeves, who's widely believed to be made of wood."
— Robert W. Butler, *Kansas City Star*

"Beware all male viewers who enter here, you are in chick-movie hell."
— Peter Travers, *Rolling Stone*

Plot, What Plot? Imagine *Love Story* retold by a theatre group for the dramatically challenged. Okay, Ryan O'Neal and Ali McGraw weren't exactly Lunt and Fontanne, but compared to Keanu Reeves and Charlize Theron in the blatant *Love Story* rip-off *Sweet November,* Ryan and Ali are master thespians. A remake of the deservedly obscure 1968 Anthony Newley/Sandy Dennis tearjerker of the same name, *Sweet November* follows two colossally uninteresting people through a preposterous affair that can only end in tragedy for everyone involved, including the audience.

Sara Deever (Theron) is a woman with a secret who just loves life and people *so* much that every month she chooses a new man to share her joy with, remold ... and then move on. Sounds like a long-term escort service to me, but screenwriter Kurt Voelker (who, interestingly, had done nothing before, and did nothing again for years after this film) considered this a viable premise for a romance. Enter "Mr. November," Nelson Moss (Reeves), a stuffy, stuck-up, success-oriented prig who desperately needs saving by Miss Twinkletoes. So they move in together, the only rules being that they must not fall in love, and that Nelson must agree to move out once November ends.

Darn it all if Nelson, played by the notoriously thickheaded Keanu, doesn't break both rules, not only falling in love and refusing to go away, but asking Sara to marry him. It is at this point that Sara's secret is finally revealed: Like Ali in *Love Story*, she suffers from "movie cancer," the always incurable disease that never shows any signs of its presence until the plot requires them. We're sure that it's just an unfortunate coincidence, but when Reeves proposes to Theron, he then finds her one minute later vomiting on the bedroom floor. While we're thinking, "That'd be my response, too!" Keanu finally busts open Charlize's locked medicine cabinet and discovers about 387 vials of medication hidden in there. See, Charlize knew she wasn't long for this world, and just wanted to share herself with perfect strangers, one man at a time, until the Big Man came to get her.

So what can Keanu do, once Charlize throws him out, but show up on her fire escape at Thanksgiving in a red Santa hat, lugging a sackful of early Christmas presents that include a perfume named for her, a bubble machine, the puppy she's always wanted, a rainbow-colored fright wig . . . and a portable dishwasher (!).

But all the dishwashers in the world—sorry, we were getting into the cliché-ridden tone of the film there for a moment . . . Anywaze, nothing can save Sara. But at least Nelson has learned to live life to the fullest. And besides, we bet he'll get some use out of that dishwasher.

Sappy in the extreme, laughable when it's meant to be dramatic, and so predictable you'll spot every plot "surprise" six reels before they spring it on you, *Sweet November* exemplifies just how dead and gone true romance is in modern, big-budget Hollywood. Its makers want tears streaming down your face by the time *Sweet November* ends. You *will* be teary-eyed, but it'll be because you're laughing so hard!

Dippy Dialogue
Sara Deaver (*Charlize Theron*): "You live in a box . . . I could lift the lid . . ."
Nelson Moss (*Keanu Reeves*): "Wow . . . that's deep . . ."

Choice Chapter Stop
Chapter 29 ("Early Christmas"): In which Nelson/Keanu delivers that dishwasher in a knapsack, then dons a white tuxedo to sing (!) "Time After Time."

White Comanche

(1968/RKO General Pictures) **DVD / VHS**

Who's to Blame   CAST: **William Shatner** (*as twins: Johnny Moon and Notah*); **Joseph Cotten** (*Sheriff Logan*); **Rosanna Yani** (*Kelly*); **Perla Cristal** (*White Fawn*)

CREW: **Directed by Gilbert Lee Kay (José Briz); Written by Robert I. Holt and Frank Gruber**

Rave Reviews

"A cheap, visually ugly Spanish western . . . with a morose sincerity. . . . A sagebrush version of Dr. Jekyll and Mr. Hyde."
— **Robert Monell, VideoForum.com**

"The most electrifying of bad westerns . . . delivering some of the worst dialogue in movie history." — **Nate Nichols, www.ooze.com**

"Ultra cheap spaghetti western filmed in Spain . . . For the William Shatner fan who has everything." — **Michael Weldon, *Psychotronic Video Guide***

Plot, What Plot? If you think William Shatner is one of the great bad actors of our time, then this one's for you. In *White Comanche*, which he made during hiatus from overacting on a regular basis as Captain Kirk on TV's *Star Trek*, Shatner gets to ham it up as not one but *two* characters: half-breed twin brothers who square off in the old West.

    Some reviews suggest that this film was shot in about one week, and it certainly seems a credible accusation, given the film's quality. Even on DVD, the print looks like it was tap-danced on by the entire U.S. Olympic golf team. Instead of Leo the Lion roaring (or any studio logo) we open with a stock shot of a snowy mountain, with a stock sound effect of a wolf howl under it. Then the music comes up—if Sheriff Dillon from *Gunsmoke* had ever played Vegas, this is what his pit band would've sounded like. Finally, a title appears: "Producers' International Corporation presents. . ." With this inauspicious a start, we know already what we're in for. Made in Spain on a budget apparently under 2,317 pesos, *White Comanche* is supposed to be that country's answer to the so-called spaghetti westerns that were all the rage at the time. Think of it as the world's first sangria western.

As the main titles end, Shatner is being chased by a band of desperadoes, determined to string him up from the nearest tree (and they haven't even seen him in his other role as the Indian half-breed brother, Notah!). Barely escaping with his life, Johnny Moon realizes it must be his half brother they want to hang, and so goes to Notah's village, entirely populated by Spaniards in dime-store Indian wigs. Notah's wife, who wears the traditional excessive mascara of her people, tells her half-brother-in-law: "There has never been good between you!" To which Moon retorts, "Has there ever been good between Notah and anyone?"

Suddenly we're following a stagecoach through a canyon, in which rides a blonde with a 1967 *Playboy* centerfold hairdo. From the hills above ride a raiding party of Indians, led by Notah—Shatner in the same haircut as Moon, a headband on his forehead, his pale white chest bare, wearing buckskin pants and little booties, with his face streaked with "war paint" that looks like someone at the office attacked him with a bottle of Wite-Out. He lets out an Indian war whoop (as only Shatner can do an Indian war whoop) and one of the coach passengers intones, "It's the White Comanche!"

When Notah gets home from "work," Johnny is waiting for him with the welcoming remark: "Notah is well named. His liver is white, like his Yankee father, his heart burns blacker than the skin of his Comanche mother, and he's white-bellied, like his name, the snake!" Popping a button of peyote, Notah replies, "Notah's brother talks like the white man he thinks he is. He is afraid to be Comanche." The comeback? "Eat the peyote, drug of the devil—dream your dreams of hate!"

Obviously, these brothers don't get along. And how they work out their differences, through 93 minutes of ugga-mugga and broken English dialogue, is the meat and potatoes of this film. To accompany Shatner's name above the title, the producers hired Joseph Cotten to play the local sheriff. After having started his career with *Citizen Kane*, and skidding down from there to *Duel in the Sun* and *The Oscar*, Cotten reached his nadir with this role: You can almost smell his disdain for the words the screenwriters put in his mouth.

Deservedly obscure, and remembered today only because of Shatner's pricelessly hammy dual performance, *White Comanche* should be Exhibit A if Captain Smirk ever finds himself on trial for overacting in the first degree.

Dippy Dialogue
Johnny Moon (*William Shatner*), after winning a gun-drawing contest: "Next time, don't eat the peyote. Maybe then you'll be quick enough!"

Choice Chapter Stop
Big Shootout at End of Film: In which Shatner/Johnny challenges Shatner/Notah to a gun duel—and no one can tell which brother is which, until one of them dies.

The Car

(1977/Universal Pictures) **DVD / VHS**

Who's to Blame   CAST: **James Brolin** (*Wade Parent*); **Kathleen Lloyd** (*Lauren*); **John Marley** (*Everett*); **R. G. Armstrong** (*Amos Clements*); **John Rubinstein** (*John Morris*); **Ronny Cox** (*Luke*)
CREW: **Directed by Elliot Silverstein; Screenplay by Dennis Shryack, Michael Butler, and Lane Slate; Story by Shryack and Butler**

Rave Reviews
"Unintentional laughs highlight this 'thriller' patterned after *Jaws*."
— **Michael Weldon, *The Psychotronic Encyclopedia of Film***

"The audience starts laughing even before the titles . . . and the laughter never subsides." — *New West* **magazine**

"Dumb story, poor acting, bad direction . . . *The Car* is a total wreck!"
— *Variety*

Plot, What Plot? You'd think after the box-office bomb *Gable and Lombard,* in which he impersonated Clark Gable by squinting one eye and sporting an eyebrow-pencil mustache, James Brolin's career had nowhere to go but up. You'd be wrong, though, because the next picture starring the future Mr. Barbra Streisand was an even bigger flop: *The Car.*

Whoever convinced Brolin to make *The Car* probably sold it to him as a cross between *Jaws* and Steven Spielberg's classic TV movie *Duel.* What it turned out to be was a bad rip-off of both *The Exorcist* and the talking-car TV series *My Mother the Car,* with touches of *Mister Ed* thrown in for bad measure. The central character isn't Brolin's laid-back small-town sheriff, but a chromium and deep black automobile that deliberately starts running down cyclists, hitchhikers, pedestrians, and members of a school band for the simple reason that . . . it's possessed by the devil. Call it a Cadillac d'Evil, Satan's Saturn, whatever—*The Car* was supposed to be one hell of a terrifying ride. Instead, it's one hell of a funny accidental comedy.

For such an uninspired idea to work at all, the film would have to be perfectly done. Unfortunately, like the idea itself, *The Car* turned out to be . . . perfectly dumb. The title automobile, styled like a cartoon limo Bruce Wayne might drive, is a big, long, and, thanks to its too-often-tooted horn, overloud vehicle that's no more terrifying than your average road hog. About the most threatening things it's capable of doing before going for the kill are revving its engine and throwing road dust in people's faces. That it manages to terrorize an entire town for several days speaks more about the townsfolk (and the filmmakers) than it does about Beelzebub's Buick. But watching people cower in fear from an automobile, or conjecture if it might be "Satan himself" who's possessed (or is it "repossessed"?) this vehicle is a big part of this film's amusement quotient. And when various characters begin conversing with the car in the second half, you'll begin to understand why it was laughed off the screen at a 1977 press screening.

"Let us all see what a lunatic son of a bitch you are!" schoolteacher Lauren yells at the car after it's chased her school's marching band into the local cemetery. "You know what you are? You're a chicken!" When the car finally withdraws (because, we're told later, it can't enter the "hallowed ground" of the cemetery), Lauren's fellow teacher yells one last, odd epithet at it for good measure: "Tadpole!"

But once they've accepted that it's "an evil spirit" behind the wheel of the car, how do they get rid of it once and for all? Do they call Max von Sydow? Cut up its gasoline credit cards? Ask General Motors to do a recall? What they come up with is even sillier: Sheriff Brolin and his surviving cohorts lure the car up a mountain road, where they entice it over a cliff and simply . . . blow it up with dynamite. If it was that easy, why didn't anyone think of it days ago?

Possibly because the citizens of Santa Ynez have less brains than your average Detroit-made lemon. And by putting their idiocy on display in *The Car,* they helped create one of the all-time funniest "The Devil Made Me Do It" movies. Seriously, if Satan were going to possess an automobile, don't you think he'd go for something a little more stylish than *The Car*? About the only upside is that *The Car does* get very high mileage . . . for something that runs on laughing gas.

Dippy Dialogue
Old Woman: "Do you think it's healthy for a thirteen-year-old boy to imagine his teacher naked?"
The Teacher (*Kathleen Lloyd*): "Absolutely!"

Choice Chapter Stop
Chapter 18 ("Wade's Confrontation"): In which Sheriff Brolin confronts The Car with his pistol on a desert road . . . and is outsmarted by it.

Fun Footnote
The title role in *The Car* was played by a Lincoln Mark III, customized for the film by George Barris, who also created TV's Batmobile, Monkeemobile, and Munster Koach.

Cocktail

(1988/Touchstone Pictures) **DVD / VHS**

Who's to Blame **CAST:** **Tom Cruise** (*Brian Flanagan*); **Bryan Brown** (*Doug Coughlin*); **Elisabeth Shue** (*Jordan Mooney*); **Laurence Luckinbill** (*Mr. Mooney*); **Kelly Lynch** (*Kerry Coughlin*); **Gina Gershon** (*Coral*)
  CREW: **Directed by Roger Donaldson**; **Screenplay by Heywood Gould; Based on the book by Gould**

Rave Reviews

"Written, directed and acted on automatic pilot ... there is not a moment in this movie that is not borrowed from other movies."
— **Roger Ebert,** *Chicago Sun-Times*

"Cruise is walking in the footsteps of Troy Donahue here. It's a performance with all the integrity of wax fruit."
— **Rita Kempley,** *Washington Post*

"An inane romantic drama that only a very young, very naive bartender could love ... upscale and utterly brainless ... the hoot of the year!"
— **Vincent Canby,** *New York Times*

Plot, What Plot? During the "I'm a Boy Bimbo" phase of his career, Tom Cruise made more than his share of embarrassingly empty-headed male centerfold movies. But none of them was more embarrassing, or more empty-headed, than his 1988 Worst Picture Razzie "winner" *Cocktail*.

A remake of *Flashdance* with Cruise in the Jennifer Beals role, *Cocktail* tells the tale of Brian Flanagan, a pretty boy with low aspirations, a dazzling smile, and a talent for shaking his tail while juggling bottles of booze. It is the latter debatable "talent" that brings Flanagan fame, minor fortune, and the chance to face some tough life choices. Discovered by hustling Manhattan bartender Bryan Brown, Cruise's character soon adopts Brown as his lifestyle guru, enjoying all the empty perks of demi-celebrity we all know can only lead to eventual ruin. But while he's riding high, nobody (but nobody) can put on a drink-mixing show like the team of Bryan and Brian. The idiocy of this concept—that rhythmically tossing back and forth bottles of brandy while boogying to a beat, like male-strippers-cum-jugglers, could make someone a "star"—is the central conceit (and single most deliciously doofyheaded element) of *Cocktail*.

Because Brian is a "deep" character who's actually attended college, and longs for some of the "more important" things out of life, it's only a matter of months (though it may seem like years) before he tires of having his every whim catered to by drunken customers. Brian and Bryan then have a big falling-out, and Cruise winds up cruising all the way down to Jamaica to find a new life—and maybe snag a millionaire wife. In a plot device borrowed from Shakespeare (and those old Doris Day/Rock Hudson movies), Elisabeth Shue plays an appealing young woman Cruise meets in Jamaica and repeatedly shines on because he doesn't think she's got money. If you've already guessed that (a) she's loaded, (b) they'll first connect and then part before he finds out she's rich, and (c) when they *do* reconcile, there's an issue of whether it's for love or money, then you've either already seen this movie—or at least one of the thirty-seven previous films from which it blatantly cadges plot elements, dialogue, and situations.

The fun part of *Cocktail* is watching just how schizophrenic it is—at the same time it wants you to believe it's disparaging the hedonistic lifestyle of the Manhattan bar scene, it wallows so totally in that milieu that its so-called message gets muddled. And of course, at the film's center there's Cruise's star turn, a performance so vacuous and vacant that he comes off like a Calvin Klein underwear model come to life. He too seems to really be enjoying the middle of the film, when he's having his way with every lady he shakes his martinis for, and he's utterly unconvincing in the later, "serious" section.

Cruise made *Cocktail* the same year he made *Rain Man*. One of them won Best Picture, the other "won" Worst Picture. So from this point on, Cruise used *Rain Man* as the blueprint for the rest of his career. But *Cocktail* was a fitting end to those years when Cruise was appearing almost exclusively in dreck like this, and relying largely on the appeal of *both* his pairs of cheeks: one pair of which he smiled with, and the other pair of which he simply shook into the camera.

Dippy Dialogue
Doug Coughlin (*Bryan Brown*): "A bartender is the aristocrat of the working class. He can make all kinds of moves if he's smart. There are investors out there, there are angels, and there are suckers. And there are rich women with nothing to do with their money."

Choice Chapter Stop
Chapter 3 ("Bartenders & Poets"): In which Brown lays down his philosophy, and both men first demo their cocktail-shaker moves to "Hippy-Hippy Shake."

Color of Night

(1994/Hollywood Pictures) **DVD / VHS**

Who's to Blame CAST: **Bruce Willis** ⊙ (*Dr. Capa*); **Jane March** ⊙ (*Rose, Bonnie, and Richie*); **Lesley Ann Warren** ⊙ (*Sondra Dorio*); **Rubén Blades** (*Lt. Martinez*); **Scott Bakula** (*Dr. Moore*); **Brad Dourif** (*Clark*)
CREW: **Directed by Richard Rush** ⊙; **Screenplay** ⊙ **by Matthew Chapman and Billy Ray; Story by Ray**

Rave Reviews
"So lurid in its melodrama and so goofy in its plotting that with just a bit more trouble, it could have been a comedy."
— **Roger Ebert,** *Chicago Sun-Times*

"Enthusiastically nutty . . . has the single-mindedness of a bad dream, and about as much reliance on everyday logic."
— **Janet Maslin,** *New York Times*

"A convoluted psychosexual thriller that promises us the moon . . . and delivers Bruce Willis' butt." — **Rita Kempley,** *Washington Post*

Plot, What Plot? During its brief reign as a subsidiary of Disney, Hollywood Pictures' distinctive Egyptian sphinx logo prompted the industry bon mot: "If it's the Sphinx, it stinks!" The one film that best exemplifies that remark is the lame-o lascivious "thriller" *Color of Night*.

We open on an overly distraught Kathleen Wilhoite, slathering lipstick all over her face, until she looks like Faye Dunaway as Mommie Dearest. Suddenly she pulls a pistol from her purse, puts it in her mouth . . . and begins fellating it. So we're hardly surprised when her appointment turns out to be with a psychiatrist. Deciding her analyst's analysis isn't helpful, Wilhoite takes a literal flying leap out of his 85th-story window, sailing to her death with a casaba-melon-like thud on the street below. Cue the knockoff Hitchcock music and cut to the psychiatrist, staring out the shattered window in disbelief . . . the same disbelief the audience feels when we recognize him. No wonder this woman offed herself—she was seeking psychiatric counseling from Bruce Willis!

Seeing his patient do a double gainer from his office so hysterically upsets Willis's character that he goes literally color-blind. But Brucie's temporary blindness won't be the only hysterical thing about this film. Populated almost exclusively with miscast actors, miscreants, and people missing more than a few bricks from their mental load, *Color of Night* is not so much a psychological thriller as a psychotic one. Its central plot twist, which any five-year-old could spot from the first "clue," involves one actress playing three different characters—and playing them badly enough that she was nominated for Razzies as both Worst Actress *and* Worst Supporting Actor. Oops! We just gave away that twist . . . Oh well, it's not like you'll care anyway.

The few people who showed up in theatres to see *Color of Night* (besides dues-paying Razzie members) were lured by its lurid ads, promising hot-'n'-heavy nudity between Bruce and costar Jane March. But when the MPAA got a load of director Richard Rush's rough cut, they threatened the film with an X rating, and an infamous shot of Willis's wagging willy had to be cut. Thank goodness the "unrated" home video version has the integrity to restore not only Brucie's nudity, but also an additional 15 minutes of never-seen-in-theatres material, all of which is equally execrable and effusively unerotic.

To recover from seeing his patient do a Lady Louganis, Willis comes to L.A. to visit fellow analyst Scott Bakula (in this film's Bizarro World reality, only former TV stars are suited to be psychiatrists). When Bakula is stabbed in the chest "thirty-eight times," Willis agrees to help detective Rubén Blades solve the murder by *Moonlighting* as substitute psychologist for Bakula's therapy group. And whatta group it is—a collection of nutzoids that make the inmates of *Cuckoo's Nest* look well adjusted. In fact, the angriest of the group actually *was* an inmate in *Cuckoo,* Brad Dourif, who chews scenery on an epic scale throughout this film. Joining him on the ceiling are Lesley Ann Warren as a sexpot who can't decide if she's a lesbian or not, Lance Henriksen as a control freak (emphasis on the word "freak"), Kevin J. O'Connor as a tightly wound mama's boy, and one "boy" who secretly could *be* a mama—Ritchie, played by (we just keep ruining the surprise again and again!) Jane March.

Solidly convinced of its own cleverness—and bald-facedly displaying its own ineptitude at almost every turn—*Color of Night* believes it's a modern Hitchcock. But Sir Alfred's basic rule of thumb was to leave things to the audience's imagination. And this film's in-your-face nudity, graphic violence, and absurd psychobabble dialogue all violate Hitch's proviso. In fact, this is a film in which literally everything—including the furniture in one scene involving a patient's freakout—is hopelessly, helplessly hilarious.

Dippy Dialogue
Martinez (*Rubén Blades*): "Tell me about the patients in this group—five cuckoos?"
Doctor Capa (*Bruce Willis*): "No . . . four neurotics of varying degrees—and one killer!"

Choice Chapter Stops
Chapter 3 ("A Look in the Mirror"): In which Wilhoite goes out the window.
Chapter 12 ("Rose Returns"): In which Willis's weenie plays a teeny bit part.

Razzie Credential
Color of Night was nominated for nine awards, and was the first film to be a Worst Picture "winner" and take no other dis-honors.

Eegah

(1962/Fairway International Films) **DVD / VHS**

Who's to Blame   CAST: **Richard Kiel** (*Eegah*); **Arch Hall Jr.** (*Tommy Nelson*); **Marilyn Manning** (*Roxy Miller*); **William Watters (a.k.a. Arch Hall Sr.)** (*Robert Miller*)

CREW: **Directed by Arch Hall Sr.; Screenplay by Bob Wehling; Original story by Nicholas Merriweather (a.k.a. Arch Hall Sr.)**

Rave Reviews
"A staple in All-Time Worst Film festivals."
— *Leonard Maltin's Movie & Video Guide*

"Will leave you on the floor in hysterics."
— **David Sindelar, Fantastic Movie Musings & Ramblings (Web site)**

"Amazing. Idiot cave man falls in love . . . [a] laugh riot."
— **Michael Weldon,** *The Psychotronic Encyclopedia of Film*

Plot, What Plot? Some movies achieve a level of incompetence and ineptitude that is actually endearing. *Eegah,* made by the notoriously untalented Arch Hall Sr., is such a film. A horror movie of sorts whose central character is chased away by a barking poodle in one scene, *Eegah* maintains its level of goofiness with a golly-gee-whiz sincerity that make it far more enjoyable (read: laughable) than mere run-of-the-mill bad moviemaking.

    Eegah, a hairy caveman, lives just outside Palm Springs in a cavern chock-full of his dead ancestors (who look like coconut-headed voodoo dolls). He is played with blank expressionlessness by Richard Kiel, who would later achieve fame as James Bond's silver-toothed nemesis Jaws. As frightening as Kiel was in the Bond role, he's utterly unterrifying here. His fur Neanderthal suit literally hangs from his undernourished body, and the beard he wears at the beginning of the film looks like it was created using a cut-up ponytail wig and kindergarten paste. It doesn't help matters that the entire film, including

Eegah's "dialogue," was obviously recorded long after the film was done—or that Eegah's muttering gibberish sounds embarrassingly similar to the rantings of the Tasmanian Devil.

Poor Eegah's life is changed forever when he meets Roxy, a nasal-voiced, beehived bimbo in stilettos whose yellow sports car nearly runs him over. From the moment he sees this temptress, and realizes she's an even worse actor than he is, it's love at first sight. But before Eegah can introduce Roxy to his dead ancestors, Roxy's modern boyfriend must be established to create a love triangle. And Tommy, played by Hall Sr.'s incredible slug of a son Arch Hall Jr., is one of the most astoundingly smug, dimwitted boyfriends in all of filmdom. Given to wrinkling his nose like a puppy and blurting our declarations like "Wowzie wow-wow," Tommy also considers himself a rock singer. But the moment you hear him sing the first lyric of "Vicki" (backed up by a hilarious heavenly choir) you'll beg to differ. Two more songs follow, each bringing the film to a grinding halt, but providing comic relief in a movie whose inadvertent humor almost never lets up.

Roxy's dad, played by Hall Sr. under the pseudonym "William Watters," is an "adventure story writer," fascinated at the prospect of meeting Eegah, whom he likens to the giants in the book of Genesis. When Dad heads off to find Eegah and doesn't return, Roxy and Tommy go after him in Tommy's dune buggy, squealing "Whee!" as they bounce over each and every sand dune. But it's Eegah's turn to squeal with delight when he kidnaps Roxy and brings her to his cave. As Dad looks on, Eegah sniffs every inch of Roxy, then lays out a fur for her to sleep on. Being a virtuous bimbo, she refuses. When Eegah goes out to fetch a fistful of flowers and a dead rabbit for his new fiancée, Roxy and Daddy escape.

The film's final scene, in which a clean-shaven Eegah climbs the fence to join the kids at a poolside sock hop, and winds up being gunned down by two (count 'em, two!) policemen, is meant to elicit the same emotions as the ending of the 1933 *King Kong*. Instead, it prompts the same kind of laughter as the Korean *Kong* rip-off *A*P*E*. After seeing this, you too may long for the never-made sequel, *Eegah and Roxy: The Honeymoon Years*.

Dippy Dialogue
Roxy (*Marilyn Manning*), upon seeing Eegah's mummified relatives: "They're dead!"

Choice Chapter Stop ☉
Chapter 6 ("A Moonlight Serenade"): Tommy sings and whistles "Valerie" (with full chorus and orchestral accompaniment) in the middle of the desert.

(1985/MGM/UA) **VHS**

Who's to Blame CAST: **Ryan O'Neal** (*Steve Taggart*); **Catherine Hicks** (*Flo*); **Chad Everett** (*The Dutchman*); **Giancarlo Giannini** (*Charley Peru*); **Bridgette Anderson** (*Amy*); **Patrick Cassidy** (*Desperate Marine*)
CREW: **Directed by Richard Brooks** ☹ ; **Screenplay** ☹ **by Brooks**

Rave Reviews
"Delivers its message at a level of hysteria that reaches the frantic heights of *Reefer Madness*." — **Julie Salamon, *Wall Street Journal***

"*Fever Pitch* may be the best bad film of the year!" — ***Variety***

"You could live a long time and never see anything as awful as *Fever Pitch,* [a] shrill, hysterical, enjoyably silly peek at the world of compulsive gambling." — **Janet Maslin, *New York Times***

Plot, What Plot? If you're going to make a movie about compulsive behavior, it helps if you yourself aren't compulsive. This important filmmaking lesson is lost on Richard Brooks, whose "hard-edged" look at the world of compulsive gambling is one of the most compulsively watchable bad movies ever made.

Starring melodramatic mannequin Ryan O'Neal as a sportswriter "covering the gambling scene" for the *Los Angeles Herald-Examiner*, *Fever Pitch* is a wild ride of skewed camera angles, screwball dialogue, and even screwier situations that's supposed to be a recruiting poster for Gamblers Anonymous. Instead, it winds up a royal flush—a recruiting poster for Razzie membership, and a Worst Picture nominee.

O'Neal narrates the entire film in a Jack-Webb-on-steroids style that will have you constantly rewinding the film to be sure he said what you think he just said. He did. And so did Catherine Hicks, as an often hysterically preachy cocktail waitress who becomes O'Neal's "good luck trinket." "Let's just have some laughs," Hicks declares as they head out on their first gambling spree, "and just . . . crack their walnuts!"

Chad Everett is a loan shark with his hooks into O'Neal to the tune of $31,000. "I could easier get a French kiss," bemoans Everett of his debtors in one scene, "out of the Statue of Liberty!" O'Neal's savior, who buys his marker from Everett, turns out to be Giancarlo Giannini as Charley Peru, a high-rolling gambler who takes a shine to O'Neal in spite of his hangdog looks and the fact that over-the-top, jazzy finger-snapping theme music follows Ryan wherever he goes.

To list every funny moment in *Fever Pitch* could fill this entire book. Some of the highlights: O'Neal's wife dies in a car wreck while rushing to bring him $5,000 to pay off his debtors. As she's being pried from her car by the Jaws of Life with the bloody five Gs grasped in her dying hand, hubby is being roughed up by thugs while an elevator music version of "Singin' in the Rain" plays in the background. In another scene, O'Neal's eight-year-old daughter accompanies him to the horse races and witnesses him being socked in the kisser by someone he owes $400 to. Covered with mustard from a trash can he fell into, Ryan limps away in shame. And in the film's single most screw-loose sequence, after joining Gamblers Anonymous and declaring himself "bet free" for over a hundred days, O'Neal is accompanied to a casino by the head of the GA meeting, and is then cheered on as he spends the entire evening betting wildly to win back his losses, which now total $89,000.

Concluding with O'Neal having "made good" on every bad bet he'd ever lost, *Fever Pitch* can't even resist ending on a hokey line. As O'Neal boards the airplane back to L.A. from Vegas, Giannini tells him, "You'll be back!" With a wink and a nod, O'Neal declares, "Wanna bet?"

A well-respected filmmaker with titles like *Looking for Mr. Goodbar, Cat on a Hot Tin Roof,* and *Elmer Gantry,* plus eight Academy Award nominations and one Oscar among his credits, Brooks went off the deep end with this one. One almost wonders if he bet someone he could pull off a serious drama about this most uncinematic of compulsions. If so, odds are he lost. But at least the audience gets to laugh all the way to the cashier's cage.

Dippy Dialogue
Hotel towel boy to O'Neal at poolside: "Any idea what a real gambler is? He's the dumbbell who'd rather have luck . . . than fuck!"

High School Confidential

(1958/MGM) **DVD / VHS**

Who's to Blame CAST: **Russ Tamblyn** (*Tony Baker/Mike Wilson*); **Jan Sterling** (*Arlene Williams*); **Mamie Van Doren** (*Aunt Gwen*); **Jackie Coogan** (*Mr. A*); **Michael Landon** (*Steve Bentley*); **Special appearance by Jerry Lee Lewis** (*as Himself*)
CREW: **Directed by Jack Arnold; Screenplay by Lewis Meltzer and Robert Blees; Story by Blees**

Rave Reviews

"It's hard to believe that there could be a *better* Bad Movie [than *Reefer Madness*] But . . . *High School Confidential* is even funnier."
— **Edward Margulies,** *Movieline* **magazine**

"A must for midnight movie fans, thanks to high camp values."
— *VideoHound's Golden Movie Retriever*

"Hilariously awful marijuana exposé [with] a most fascinating cast."
— *Leonard Maltin's Movie & Video Guide*

Plot, What Plot? The juvenile delinquent drama—or juvie movie—was a mainstay of 1950s drive-in fare aimed at the teenaged trade. And they rarely come as desperately hip yet hopelessly square as exploitation king Albert Zugsmith's 1958 antidrug classic, *High School Confidential.* Made as the first film under a grind-'em-out-and-ship-'em multipicture pact Zugsmith had with MGM in the late '50s, this tale of an undercover cop exposing a dope ring at "a typical American high school" features some of the most interesting casting (and some of the funniest "coolsville" hip dialogue) you'll ever see.

Jive-talking, kewpie-faced "tough guy" Tony Baker (Russ Tamblyn of *West Side Story*) shows up for his first day at a new high school in a luxury convertible, ready to rumble on a moment's notice. Within minutes, he's so insulted his homeroom teacher that she sends him to the principal's office, where we discover that this is his "seventh year of high school." Putting out mixed signals, Tony is constantly "looking to graze on some grass" while simultaneously telling horror stories about the risks of getting hooked on "weed." What gives with this cat? Is he schizophrenic, a double agent . . . or is it because he's just plain *dumb* that he's spent so long matriculating? In truth, Tamblyn is an undercover cop, seeking to uncover a "dope ring" operating in or near the school. His search necessitates his living with his horny "Aunt Gwen" (wonderfully overplayed by the hilariously hormonal Mamie Van Doren) and investigating local teen hangouts like the airport where kids drag race, and a nightclub where Beat poets expound bleakly, and in bop-ese, about the future of our planet. He soon discovers that "shy" Doris is actually a heroin addict (she "graduated from weed") and that pretty blonde Joan is well on her way to the same fate. It takes him a little longer to find out that the big pusher in the area is the nightclub's owner, played by Jackie Coogan (who later was Uncle Fester on TV's *Addams Family*).

Like Tony himself, the film is torn about whether to condemn the sexual freedoms and "cheap kicks" of "Mary Jane," or simply exploit them for their box-office value. The end result is a ridiculously muddied "message" that makes an already silly concept all the sillier. Of course, you should *never* condemn something without knowing all the facts (yeah, right!). But when you spend as much time showing the awful (yet awfully enticing) effects of something as *High School Confidential* does, you naturally run the risk of making the very thing you are "condemning" seem appealing. Shocking though the thought may be, we're sure at least a few people have giggled their way through this film toked to the gills on the very "weed" it was made to warn them about.

Dippy Dialogue
Beat Poetess (*Phillipa Fallon*): "Tomorrow is a drag, Pops, the future is a flake!"

Choice Chapter Stop
Chapter 10 ("Dragging the Beat"): In which the Beat Poetess and Uncle Fester put on their floor show.

(1974/Conqueror Films) **VHS**

Who's to Blame CAST: **William Shatner** (*Matt Stone*); **Ruth Roman** (*Julia Marstow*); **Jennifer Bishop** (*Ann Moy*); **Kim Nicholas** (*Tina Moy*); **James Dobson** (*Clarence*); SPECIAL GUEST STAR: **Harold Sakata** (*Karate Pete*)
CREW: **Directed by William Grefe; Written by Tony Crechales**

Rave Reviews
"What a find! It's a sleaze classic."
— **Michael Weldon**, *The Psychotronic Video Guide*

"Shatner at the nadir of his career . . . for trash buffs and masochistic Trekkies." — ***TV Guide's Movie Guide***

"A hilariously awful mix of kitsch and sleaze that no self-respecting bad movie fan should go without seeing." — **Albert Walker, AgonyBooth.com**

Plot, What Plot? If you've ever wondered just how far down the scale of Hollywood failure William Shatner stumbled in the years between the end of *Star Trek* the series and the first of the *Star Trek* movies, *Impulse* provides your answer: absolute rock bottom. Shot on what looks to be a $357 budget, featuring fabulously funky mid-'70s clothes and with Shatner cast as a mentally deranged ladykiller, *Impulse* is one of those rarely mentioned gems that only True Trash Film Buffs seem to know about.

The film opens in black-and-white/flashback mode, as eight-year-old Matt Stone witnesses a drunken soldier roughing up his mom in the middle of the night. When the soldier gets belligerent, the son picks up the soldier's Samurai sword . . . and runs him through. Traumatized by what he's just done, the boy stands for several moments chewing on his extended pinkie in shock—a master gesture that the adult Shatner will later repeat several times, to snicker-inducing effect.

Caught leaving a belly dancer's performance after the main titles, the now grown-up Shatner denies everything to his rich girlfriend, and when she calls the belly dancer a "tramp!" about seventy-three times, he strangles her.

Suddenly we're having breakfast with a snotty little girl and her semi-attractive single mother, a seemingly irrelevant pair of characters who will turn out to be Shatner's next victims. The former Captain Kirk and the girl who's such a jerk meet when Shatner picks her up in his Oldsmobile as she walks to school. Like most of the character development in this film, this scene is so jumbled and badly handled, for a few minutes we're left assuming the girl must be Shatner's estranged daughter. Shatner then runs over a German shepherd, and tells little Tina, "It'll be okay—dogs lick their wounds and get all better." Unlike every adult in the film, Tina immediately pegs Shatner as a psycho . . . and before you can say "Stepdad from Planet Hairpiece," Tina's mom is dating Shatner, and the plot finally gets going.

But just when we're getting used to director Grefe's awful sense of time, place, and motivation, yet another seemingly irrelevant character arrives—and this one's a doozy. Puffing on a pipe and speaking broken English, Karate Pete (played by Harold Sakata, Odd Job from *Goldfinger*) turns out to be Shatner's old cellmate from prison, wanting Willie to help him pull off a robbery. Instead, Pete is lured to a closed car wash where Shatner tries to hang him, then mercilessly (and pointlessly . . . and S-L-O-W-L-Y) chases him through the car wash before running him over . . . twice. Unbeknownst to Bill, Tina has been hiding in the backseat and has seen everything. Now the film becomes a battle of wits between the hideous child actress, who plants her feet and speaks every line like she's addressing a stadium full of people with no microphone, and Shatner, who keeps sucking on his pinkie at important plot points. Guess who wins in the end.

It's the little touches Shatner brings to this performance that make this one of the best of his many worsts. After strangling the first girlfriend, he collapses on the roof of her car and makes moaning sounds like someone seriously constipated. About to kill fellow has-been Ruth Roman for what he thinks is the jewelry in her safe, Shatner gets so excited he literally jumps up and down like a kid who has to go potty. And when he finally cracks the safe, the look on his face is more disappointed than anyone the Easter Bunny ever royally ripped off.

Barely released theatrically, and admittedly hard to find, *Impulse* is one of those films you simply *must* see to disbelieve... if only because it also features a series of ever-changing toupees atop Shatner's knuckleheaded noggin.

Dippy Dialogue
Tina (*Kim Nicholas*) to mad killer Matt: "I'm not crazy—*you* are!"
Matt Stone (*William Shatner*): "Oh yeah!?!?!"

Razzie Credential
It was precisely because of performances like this one that William Shatner was nominated for Worst Actor of the 20th Century at our 20th Annual Razzie Awards.

Fun Footnote
Director Grefe supposedly talked Shatner into doing this film when the two had a chance meeting at an airport.

(1985/Columbia Pictures)　**DVD / VHS**

Who's to Blame　**CAST:** **John Travolta** (*Adam Lawrence*); **Jamie Lee Curtis** (*Jessie Wilson*); **Jann Wenner** (*Mark Roth*); **Marilu Henner** (*Sally*); **Anne De Salvo** (*Frankie*); **Laraine Newman** (*Linda*)
　　CREW: **Directed by James Bridges; Screenplay by Aaron Latham and Bridges; Based on *Rolling Stone* articles by Latham**

Rave Reviews
"So obnoxiously over-hyped that its dismal failure made it the laughingstock of 1985!" — **Michael Sauter,** *The Worst Movies of All Time*

"Best horror film of 1985, [featuring a] great three-minute Dueling Pelvises scene."
　— **Joe Bob Briggs,** *Joe Bob's Ultimate B-Movie Guide* **(Web site)**

"A camp classic . . . an unintentionally hilarious mixture of muddled moralizing and all-too-contemporary self-promotion."
　　　　　　　　　　　　— **Vincent Canby,** *New York Times*

Plot, What Plot? Few things are funnier than a dumb movie with "serious film" intentions. *Perfect,* cloaking itself pretentiously in the garb of being a "serious film" about journalistic ethics, is actually a lame framework onto which are hung a series of ever more overtly sexual (and irresistibly silly) riffs on the 1980s fitness craze. Audiences, which laughed the film out of theatres in its initial release, clearly chose not to take this film seriously at all.

　The main character is John Travolta, playing an ambitious reporter who works his way up from the obit desk of the *Jersey Journal* to being a star reporter for *Rolling Stone,* stomping on people's feelings and rights of privacy every step of the way. When he's assigned to do an "in depth" article suggesting that fitness gyms are "the singles bars of the '80s," Travolta gets way too attached to his subject. Setting down roots in L.A. (the epicenter of all fads and crazes), Travolta decides to focus specifically on one subject, hot-bodied aerobics instructor Jamie Lee Curtis. But before you can say "clichéd movie plot #137," Johnny has fallen in love with Jamie, and finds himself torn between doing his job as a journalist . . . or just doing Jamie.

Chock-full of lines like "She's the most overused piece of equipment in the gym," *Perfect* was clearly written by men who appreciate women only as the subject of wet dreams, then are nonplussed when women resent being objectified by them. As the only character not immediately impressed with Travolta, Curtis should be someone we admire. But then, every time Travolta asks to attend one of her aerobics classes, there she is in a leotard with its crotch open practically to her navel, thrusting away to awful '80s pop music and grinding her pelvis into the camera with a big, satisfied smile on her face. And across the classroom, with about six pairs of socks stuffed into his shorts and matching Curtis pelvic thrust for pelvic thrust, is Travolta. These scenes are the . . . um, meat of the film, and were supposed to keep audiences in their seats while the actors waded through the "message" parts of the picture.

And the message seems to be: Standing by your journalistic principles is good for your sex life. While working on the fitness article, shtupping Jamie, and pumping her for info, Travolta is also writing a piece about a millionaire accused of drug trafficking. When the rich man's case comes to trial and Johnny refuses to turn over his interview tapes on principle, he winds up in jail, with Jamie literally waiting for him outside the gates. All ends happily (doesn't it always in movies this dumb?) as the millionaire is acquitted, Travolta is released, and everyone is reunited for one more aerobics class, shown under the end titles. It's the *Perfect* ending to one of the most smugly self-important movies of the 1980s, which in reality was as empty as a pair of smelly gym socks tossed into a hamper.

Dippy Dialogue
Jesse (*Jamie Lee Curtis*): "What is so *wrong* with wanting to be perfect?!?!"

Choice Chapter Stop
Chapter 13 ("Shock Me"): In which Johnny and Jamie follow up great sex with a different kind of pelvic-thrusting workout, this time at the gym.

Road House

(1989/United Artists) **DVD / VHS**

Who's to Blame CAST: **Patrick Swayze** ☻ (*Head Bouncer Dalton*); **Ben Gazzara** ☻ (*Brad Wesley*); **Kelly Lynch** (*Dr. Elizabeth Clay*); **Sam Elliott** (*Wade Garrett*); **Red West** (*Red Webster*); **Kevin Tighe** (*Frank*)
CREW: **Directed by Rowdy Herrington** ☻; **Screenplay** ☻ **by Hilary Henkin and David Lee Henry; Story by Henry**

Rave Reviews
"Plays creepily like something made by and for horny 14-year-old boys."
— **Peter Travers,** *Rolling Stone*

"Was it intended as a parody? I have no idea, but I laughed more during this movie than during any of the so-called comedies I saw the same week." — **Roger Ebert,** *Chicago Sun-Times*

"An ugly commingling of old Westerns, Zen chic and kung fu movies . . . lays out its story with the subtlety of a wrestling match."
— **Hal Hinson,** *Washington Post*

Plot, What Plot? As a bouncer, Dalton has no equal—he's *so* good, in fact, that in the course of *Road House,* he gets promoted from mere bouncer to "cooler," the guy *other* bouncers call on when things get out of hand. "It's my way," original thinker Dalton is fond of saying, "or the highway!" Since he is played by *Dirty Dancing* alumnus Patrick Swayze as a man equally at home spouting Zen or gouging eyeballs, Dalton's way proves good for many a laugh.

A perfect example of a "nine-year-old-boy movie," *Road House* looks, sounds, and acts like it could have been conceived by any nine-year-old given a stack of *Playboy* magazines and the right set of crayons. Its plot skeleton owes a lot to such classic one-man-against-the-crowd classics as *High Noon, Enter the Dragon,* and *Godzilla versus the Smog Monster.* When Dalton figures out that one evil man basically runs the entire town where his bar of employment, the Double Deuce, is located, he decides to take on the crime boss single-handed. Of course the boss, played by Worst Supporting Actor contender Ben Gazzara with all the subtlety of a freight train, doesn't intend to fight Swayze single-handed. He plans to call in his army of goons. And the dramatic tension created by anticipation of this ultimate, inevitable showdown... could be cut with a soup spoon.

In the leading role, Swayze is so stoic one wonders if he's suffering from rigor mortis. Badly cut in an early-on brawl at Double Deuce, he goes to the local lady doctor and requests she sew up his wound without anesthetic. "Pain don't hurt none," Swayze insists. When Kelly Lynch, as the medical equivalent of the town schoolmarm in a John Wayne movie, asks about Dalton's past, he tells her he has a PhD from NYU. "What in?" she asks in dead earnest. "Philosophy... shit like that," Swayze answers.

The philosophy background also comes in handy when it's time for Swayze to address his staff of bouncers. His "philosophy" boils down to: Don't kill anybody... unless you have to. A series of brawls, in which Swayze's rules of engagement are sometimes adhered to and sometimes not, makes up the bulk of the film's running time. Whenever drunk-and-disorderlies aren't having pool cues, beer bottles, or other blunt implements broken over their heads, the film pauses for a bit of romance, more philosophy, or both. And before you can answer the question "How come Dalton has his shirt off so much of the time?" it's time for that last big brawl. Involving motorcycles, lots of kung fu kinda leaping, and artfully placed blood smears on each combatant's face, this is the movie's main course. And of course it ends as you knew it would... No, we won't ruin it for you, but if you can't guess, you haven't seen the 713 other films this one swipes riffs from.

Intended as mindless entertainment of the sort that used to be a staple of the drive-in trade, *Road House* has the mindless part down pat. And thanks to the poker face it keeps no matter how rough, rowdy, or ridiculous the proceedings get, it manages the entertaining part fairly well too. We're just never sure if its makers meant us to laugh as many times, and in as many places, as we do.

Dippy Dialogue
Jimmy (*Marshall Teague*) to a drunken patron: "I used to fuck guys like you in prison!"

Choice Chapter Stop
Chapter 4 ("The Rules"): Swayze lays down his "philosophy" of The Art of Bouncing to his barroom staff.

Sinbad of the Seven Seas
(1989/Cannon Films) **VHS**

Who's to Blame CAST: **Lou Ferrigno** (*Sinbad*); **John Steiner** (*Jaffar*); **Roland Wybenga** (*Ali*); **Alessandra Martines** (*Alina*); **Yehudi Efroni** (*Ahmed*); **Stefania Girolami** (*Kyra*); **Leo Gullota** (*Nadir*)
CREW: **Directed by Enzo G. Castellari; Written by Casterllari and Tito Capri**

Rave Reviews
"May be the most inept fantasy ever put onto celluloid. Yes, it's bad, but it's a laugh riot." — **Keith Bailey, The Unknown Movies Page (Web site)**

"So far over the top, it's hilarious. I recommend it highly to those who like to laugh at bad movies."
— **Samuel Stoddard, At-A-Glance Film Reviews (Web site)**

"One of the best bad movies I have ever seen. If you only see one bad movie this year, make it this one. You'll thank me for it later!"
— **David J. Parker, It's a Bad, Bad, Bad, Bad Movie (Web site)**

Plot, What Plot? In the mid to late 1980s, Cannon Films was a major supplier of Razzie contenders. *Bolero, Sahara, Tough Guys Don't Dance,* and the Lou Ferrigno version of *Hercules,* Razzie "winners" all, were all made by Cannon Films. Given the low-level tripe Cannon was willing to release, one has to wonder just *how* bad something would have to be in order for them *not* to release it. You'll find your answer in Cannon's second Ferrigno vehicle, produced in 1989, and released direct-to-video in 1990, *Sinbad of the Seven Seas.*

Starring as Sinbad, with a different dubbed voice than he had in his Worst New Star–"winning" screen debut as *Hercules,* Ferrigno seems like a perfectly nice, overly muscled fellow. What he doesn't seem even remotely like is an actor ... or a "star" worthy of having even a cheap-jack vehicle like this built around him. Looking like they slathered his torso with olive oil before every take, and carrying himself with an awkwardness befitting a bodybuilder who's in way over his head, Ferrigno romps and stomps his way through this 99-Cents-Only version of the Sinbad legend, in which only one actor appears to be speaking with his own voice.

Unfortunately, that character is played by one of the hammiest thespians ever to portray a villain in too-tall turban and excess eyeliner. John Steiner as Jaffar is incapable of merely speaking his lines. Instead, he twiddles his obviously glued-on fingernails through his obviously glued-on goatee, then delivers each word as though he were addressing the severely hearing impaired. His eyes wildly widening with every syllable, his voice soaring into the stratosphere, and his actual readings sounding identical (whether he's expressing anguish, ennui, or devilry), Steiner is an astounding example of an "actor" totally out of control.

Further undermining *Sinbad*'s credibility is literally every one of its technical aspects. The cinematography is grainy, the costumes look like community theatre cast-offs, the "special effects" wouldn't pass muster in a 1947 Maria Montez movie, the postproduction audio seems unconcerned with *ever* matching dialogue to lip movement, and the sets . . . wow, the sets! Sinbad's ship is so cartoonish-looking, you expect one of his shipmates to yell, "Crunch-itize me, Cap'n Crunch!" The palace in which much of the action takes place looks suspiciously like the lobby of some overly ornate Moorish movie palace. And the "secret hideaway" from which Jaffar operates looks like a cross between a set salvaged from the Dumpster behind a 1980s Golden Globes ceremony and the ultra-lame laboratory from *The Brain That Wouldn't Die*.

When something fails as utterly and miserably as this, one cannot help but watch it with a combination of disrespect, disbelief, and dumbfounded bemusement. If Cannon Films has any other still unreleased titles in its vaults . . . On second thought, let's not go there.

Dippy Dialogue
The Sorceress Soukra (*Teagan Clive*) to Jaffar: "There you go again, basking in your bubbles of fiction."

Razzie founder John Wilson emcees the 1st Annual Razzie Awards. (Credit: Barbara Wilson, © 1981/G.R.A.F.)

"Norma Desmond" (Sarah Folger) accepts a kiss from John Wilson at the 5th Razzies.
(Credit: Michael Q. Martin, © 1985/G.R.A.F.)

Rambo's grandfather, "Grampo," (Drew Wilson, father of Razzie founder John Wilson) accepted Worst Actor for Sylvester Stallone at the 6th Razzies. (Credit: John Wilson, © 1986/G.R.A.F.)

John Wilson and Nancy Lilienthal presenting Bill Cosby with three Razzie Awards for *Leonard Part 6*. (Credit: Barbara Wilson,© 1988/G.R.A.F.)

Dan E. Campbell (as Divine) presenting Worst Actor of the Decade at the 10th Razzies. (Credit: Jon Charbonneau, © 1990/G.R.A.F.)

"Human Searchlight" Jon Mullich greets arrivals at the 11th Razzies. (Credit: Barbara Wilson, © 1991/G.R.A.F.)

Kelie McIver (Princess Jasmine) and Jon Haddorff (Aladdin) perform "A Whole New Worst," the opening number at the 14th Razzies. (Credit: Barbara Wilson, © 1994/G.R.A.F.)

Showgirls director Paul Verhoeven accepts the Worst Picture award at the 16th Razzies.
(Credit: Billy Hall, © 1996/G.R.A.F.)

John Wilson presents *The Postman* screenwriter Brian Helgeland with his Worst Screenplay Razzie.
(Credit: Barbara Wilson, © 1998/G.R.A.F.)

Robert Conrad accepts the Worst Picture award on behalf of the remake of *Wild Wild West* at the 20th Razzies. (Credit: Barbara Wilson, © 2000/G.R.A.F.)

A TV crew "interviews" the nine-inch Terl action figure (from *Battlefield Earth*) at the 21st Razzies. (Credit: Mike Medlock, © 2001/G.R.A.F.)

Tom Green, writer, director, and star of *Freddy Got Fingered* accepting Worst Picture with his "basket full of berries" at the 22nd Razzies.
(Credit: Barbara Wilson, © 2002/G.R.A.F.)

Tom Green launching into a five-minute harmonica solo while accepting his awards. (Credit: Barbara Wilson, © 2002/G.R.A.F.)

A cardboard cutout of Madonna accepting an award at the 23rd Razzies. (Credit: Barbara Wilson, © 2003/G.R.A.F.)

Chip Dornell, Kelie McIver, and Glenn Simon performing the opening number "All That Razz" at the 23rd Razzies.
(Credit: Barbara Wilson, © 2003/G.R.A.F.)

Kelie McIver, Glenn Simon, and Chip Dornell pay tribute to Dr. Seuss—and the most famous line of dialogue from Worst Picture winner *Gigli*—at the 24th Razzies. (Credit: Barbara Wilson, © 2004/G.R.A.F.)

Yor, the Hunter from the Future

(1983/Columbia Pictures) **VHS**

Who's to Blame CAST: **Reb Brown** ☉ (*Yor*); **Corrine Clery** (*Ka-Laa*); **John Steiner** (*The Overlord*); **Luciano Pigozzi** (*Pag*); **Ayshe Gul** (*Roa*)
CREW: **Directed by "Anthony M. Dawson" (Antonio Margheriti); Screenplay by Robert Bailey and "Dawson," based on the novel by Ray Collins and Juan Zanutto**

Rave Reviews
"Made for about seventy-five bucks . . . hilarious from start to finish."
— **Brian J. Wright, Cavalcade of Schlock (Web site)**

"Uniquely, mesmerizingly bad. . . . Highly recommended stuff!"
— **Mike Martinez, Grisly, Grimey Reviews (Web site)**

"Horrible movie, highly recommended—rife with bad acting, bad writing, bad directing, bad post-production . . . bad everything."
— **"Rob," OhTheHumanity.com**

Plot, What Plot? Okay, so it *was* filmed in, of all the appropriate places, Turkey. And yes, it predates *Jurassic Park* by about ten years, so its special effects *are* primitive. And its budget *may* have been as high, in modern funds, as about 367 euros. But even with all these provisos and excuses, *Yor, the Hunter from the Future* is still a shockingly funny, who-did-they-think-would-ever-buy-that example of a No-Budget Wonder.

With a title character who looks like a frat brat conned into an initiation stunt requiring him to wear a fur diaper and a blond Doris Day wig, *Yor* is a hoot from its nonsensical, phonetically sung opening song until its inevitably dopey happy ending. Yor is played by Reb Brown, a former USC football player who's almost the only English-speaking actor in the film . . . and his command of the language is rather limited at that. Stranded in a primitive world populated with papier-mâché dinosaurs, Styrofoam boulders, and clans of cavemen who all look like Bela Lugosi with blue faces and fake beards, Yor sets out on that most human of quests: to discover his own origins. Given his accent, anyone in the audience could tell him he's a native of L.A. but, hey, some things you've just gotta find out for Yor-self.

Joining our "star" on his journey are Ka-Laa, a deposed princess who looks amazingly like '80s TV bimbo Adrienne Barbeau, and her father, Pag, an older man in a bearskin toga with a sunken chest, a bald spot, and a dead aim with a bow and arrow. So far, everything sounds like a Turkish knockoff of *One Million B.C.* But after fighting off Cro-Magnon bad guys and plastic pterodactyls for half the film's running time, Yor suddenly finds a second person wearing the same gold medallion that's his only clue to where he's from. Her name is Roa, she looks like Charo with Brooke Shields's eyebrows, and she will lead him to an island where it turns out . . . that all of this takes place in a postapocalyptic future!

The future is in the hands of an evil scientist called the Overlord, who plans to use Yor to "inseminate" a master race of robots obedient only to Overlord himself. Can Yor, who is ill equipped for the task, outwit the Overlord? Will Ka-Laa or Yor's medallion-mate Roa win Yor's hand and heart? And why are all of Overlord's robots wearing Kmart Darth Vader costumes? These and other thrilling questions will be answered before you're through watching *Yor*. And if you're willing to take the time to find this classic, rarely seen Turkish turkey, believe us . . . *Yor* in for a treat.

Loopy Lyrics
From the thickly accented theme song "Yor's World":
"A dream so wild ant stronk can neffer fail go wronk—Yor's world!
He's born to come alife, he's born surfivor—Yor's world!
Efen his days are gone, dey say he will go on, de search goes on ant on—Yor's world!"

Special Recommendation Show this film at a "Bring *Yor* Own Booze" party, serve those dinosaur-shaped chicken nuggets from Costco, red fruit punch for dinosaur blood (reminding *Yor* guests of Yor's admonition: "Drinking the blood of *Yor* enemy makes you stronger!"): and give *Yor* guests one simple challenge: How many awful puns on "Yor" can you and *Yor* friends come up with while *Yor* watching this film?

(1974/20th Century-Fox) **DVD / VHS**

Who's to Blame CAST: **Sean Connery** (*Zed*); **Charlotte Rampling** (*Consuella*); **Sara Kestelman** (*May*); **John Alderton** (*Friend*); **Sally Anne Newton** (*Avalow*); **Niall Buggy** (*Arthur Frayne/Zardoz*); **Bosco Hogan** (*George Saden*); **Jessica Swift** (*Apathetic*); **Reginald Jarman** (*Death*)
CREW: **Written, produced, and directed by John Boorman**

Rave Reviews
"A glittering cultural trash pile—the most gloriously fatuous movie since *The Oscar*!" — *The New Yorker*

"Director Boorman . . . falls flat on his face with this pretentious piece of science fiction claptrap." — *TV Guide's Movie Guide*

"Goofy from start to finish and . . . [features] one of the lamest stunning revelations ever." — **Rob and Allan, OhTheHumanity.com**

Plot, What Plot? Whatever substance John Boorman was self-medicating with when he made this obtuse, ultra-outré, fetishistic, futuristic fantasy, you'll need a double dose of it if you actually expect to follow its "plot." But if you watch it just for laughs, you *will* get high on its hilariously pompous pretentiousness.

Starring Sean Connery, wearing a bright red diaper, hip boots, a ponytail, and not much else, *Zardoz* is so busy being "about something" that it forgets to have anything intelligible going on. When it begins, with the head of a man in a painted beard floating through a black void and speaking in riddles, you may think it's a Monty Python skit—and you wouldn't be far off. The Crayola-goatee guy's head leaves the screen after asking, "Is God in show business too?" and we are then "transported" to an unnamed countryside in the year 2293, where an entire army of men in red diapers are paying homage to a giant floating stone head. The head's echoing voice intones the first of the film's laugh-out-loud aphorisms: "The gun is good. The penis is evil. The penis shoots seeds!" Ol' Stone Head then ejaculates a giant pile of guns and ammo, and "heads" off for its next appointment. Barely five minutes in and Boorman has already established the tone for his entire film: Nothing will make sense, everyone will overact, and all the costumes and sets will look like they're from a Sonny and Cher skit based on *Logan's Run*.

About all that can be gleaned from paying attention (and we warned you already what a waste of time *that* was) is that in the future, society has done away with all individual thought and emotion, and the worst punishment of all is not dying, but growing old (wait a minute—that sounds just like modern-day Hollywood!). Since Sean, in his sexy red Depends, is still an emotional and sensual being, he becomes an object of study and fascination to his blank-faced hosts. In one especially funny sequence, Sean is shown sexually stimulating images, and everyone's eyes focus on Sean's diaper to see if they get a rise out of him. In another bizarrely comic scene, a tableful of dinner guests are asked to vote on someone's fate, and when one of them disagrees with the others, they turn on him. It's their method of doing so that's hilarious: They all face the culprit, extend their fingers in his direction, and start twiddling them toward him, ever more loudly yelling "Renegade!" in unison. Eventually, the "freethinker" goes into an eyeball-rolling fit and collapses on the tabletop.

But this twaddle-filled trip through time saves its biggest wad of twaddle for last: the revelation of what "Zardoz" means. We won't spoil it for you, but it left us wondering if Boorman was implying that the future belongs to the "Friends of Dorothy." Hoity-toity and self-important to the point of supreme silliness, *Zardoz* is an odd artifact of a time in Hollywood when moviemaking and drug-taking often intertwined, to the benefit of no one but bad movie fans like us.

Dippy Dialogue
Zed (*Sean Connery*): "Stay behind my aura!!"

Choice Chapter Stop
Chapter 11 ("The Vote"): In which a "renegade" is roundly punished by his finger-twiddling peers.

Fun Footnote
Boorman's next film was the even more ridiculous *Exorcist II: The Heretic*.

The Betsy

(1978/Allied Artists) **DVD / VHS**

Who's to Blame **CAST:** **Laurence Olivier** (*Loren Hardeman I*); **Robert Duvall** (*Loren Hardeman III*); **Katharine Ross** (*Sally Hardeman*); **Tommy Lee Jones** (*Angelo Perino*); **Jane Alexander** (*Alicia Hardeman*); **Lesley-Anne Down** (*Lady Bobby Ayres*); **Kathleen Beller** (*Betsy*)
CREW: **Directed by Daniel Petrie; Screenplay by William Bast and Walter Bernstein; From the novel by Harold Robbins**

Rave Reviews
"Entertaining trash!" — *Leonard Maltin's Video & Movie Guide*

"An incredible cast [in] an extra-long, better acted episode of *Dynasty*!" — **Abbie Bernstein, AudioRevolution.com**

"An all-star howler . . . making us wonder why America ever fretted about a gas shortage with this cast in this script!"
— **Edward Margulies and Stephen Rebello,** *Bad Movies We Love*

Plot, What Plot? What happens when a film adapted from a Harold Robbins novel actually has a cast full of competent actors as well as marquee names? *The Betsy*, in which just such a cast lend their talents to a tale of greed, lust, incest, and car manufacturing, proves that it doesn't matter who is in front of the camera, as long as Robbins and his trashy touch is behind it.

The central character in this multigenerational soap opera is Loren Hardeman the First, patriarch of the family that runs Bethlehem Motors. Played by Laurence Olivier in his "my-career-is-over-anyway-so-I-may-as-well-make-lotsa-money" mode, the character is blatantly based on Henry Ford, but with a come-and-go accent that only an actor as self-impressed as Sir Larry would dare try to get away with. It is unclear exactly where the character is supposed to be from since, in the course of the film, there are touches of southern, midwestern, and even Bronx accents flitting in and out of Larry's line readings.

Anywaze, having sired a son who marries for appearances, horny old Hardeman is caught in flagrante delicto as the wedding reception is going on downstairs. First appalled by the sight (possibly the only time Olivier ever appeared onscreen with his pants down around his ankles), his daughter-in-law Katharine Ross later decides she herself wants to experience a diddle of the delicto variety. As fate would have it, after years of exchanging the kind of smoldering, come-hither looks that only heroines in Robbins novels (and hookers in real life) ever use, Ross chooses the very night her closeted gay husband blows his brains out to consummate her passion for papa-in-law. Ross's son witnesses his father fellate a pistol, then walks in on Mommy and Grandpa in bed together. Naturally, when he grows up to be Robert Duvall, he has lots of "family issues."

Further complicating this already ludicrous plot is a secondary storyline featuring Tommy Lee Jones as a race car driver hired by Olivier to design a new, fuel-efficient "people's car," to be named after Olivier's nubile granddaughter Betsy. Played by *Dynasty*'s Kathleen Beller, Betsy is a child in a woman's body (as is amply demonstrated in a number of awkwardly staged nude scenes) who maintains a childlike crush on Jones, who meanwhile is romancing English race widow Lesley-Anne Down, who is at the same time carrying on an extramarital affair with Jane Alexander's husband... Robert Duvall. See how all these plot threads brilliantly dovetail into one crazy quilt of guilty pleasures? It's classic Razzie plotting, as only Robbins could weave it.

By film's end, Larry has paid his mobster friends to fling his son's gay lover (or at least, a dummy *dressed* like the son's lover) from a high balcony, Jones has married the headlight-heavy heiress Betsy to get control of Bethlehem Motors, and the mobsters call in their chits on both Sir Larry and Mr. Jones. All accompanied by an overly solemn John Barry musical score that, in several dramatic moments, sounds suspiciously like "How Dry I Am."

As trashy guilty pleasures go, this is one of the trashiest (and guiltiest) in the Robbins canon.

Dippy Dialogue
Sally (*Katharine Ross*) to her father-in-law (*Olivier*): "I love you, Loren, even if I have to be damned for it!"

Choice Chapter Stop
Chapter 27 ("Rough Stuff"): Ross bids Larry farewell and mobsters ask, "How much for that dummy out the window?"

Beyond the Forest

(1949/Warner Bros.) **VHS**

Who's to Blame **CAST:** **Bette Davis** (*Rosa Moline*); **Joseph Cotten** (*Dr. Lewis Moline*); **David Brian** (*Neil Latimer*); **Ruth Roman** (*Carol*); **Regis Toomey** (*Sorren*); **Minor Watson** (*Moose*)
CREW: **Directed by King Vidor; Screenplay by Lenore Coffee; Based on the novel by Stuart Engstrad**

Rave Reviews
"As hilariously overplayed as a Mexican soap opera!" — **Channel 4, Britain**

"Consistently (though inadvertently) hilarious. There's not a sane, dull scene in this peerless piece of camp." — **Pauline Kael, *The New Yorker***

"Davis overplays this so much that she appears to be a female impersonator doing Bette Davis." — ***TV Guide's Movie Guide***

Plot, What Plot? By 1949, convinced that her studio was "holding her back," Bette Davis was willing to do just about anything to get out of her long-term contract with Warner Bros. Perhaps she knew *Beyond the Forest* would be enough of a stinker to finally get her fired by Jack Warner, and the studio, in their infinite wisdom, sold this one with the inadvertently apt tagline: "No one's as good as Bette when she's bad." They were referring, of course, to the character Davis played—but they could just as easily have meant her performance.

As Rosa Moline, an egocentric, frustrated woman with delusions of grandeur—and a hideously obvious black wig that makes her look like Dracula's daughter—Davis plays this role with every one of her trademark cigarette-flicking, hips-twitching, head-bobbing trademark gestures on rampant display. As gossip columnist Dorothy Manners remarked in the *Los Angeles Examiner,* "No nightclub caricaturist has ever turned in such a cruel imitation of the Davis mannerisms as Bette turns on herself in this one!" Davis turns in such a ludicrous performance that one begins to suspect she's commenting on the idiotic dialogue by making her character even more absurd than the words in the script. Whatever Davis may have been thinking, this is one of the all-time great ridiculous acting jobs.

The absurdity is abetted, in no small part, by Lenore Coffee's screenplay, which casts bigger-than-life Bette as a half-breed bride who can't wait to escape the constraints of her doctor husband's small Wisconsin town. Things start off with a bang as Davis's very first line is one of her all-time most imitated. Frumping and hip-swishing into her cabin, Bette puts her overemphasizing all into the declaration, "What a dump!" We quickly learn that her "Rosa" will do anything—at least, anything the film censors in 1949 would allow—to escape her home and marriage.

When hubby Joseph Cotten pays her off to leave him, Rosa goes to Chicago, starts an affair, and winds up with no man—and a baby on the way. She is then forced to return home, terrified to tell her spouse what a louse she's actually been. Soon the "boyfriend" shows up, saying he's now ready to marry Rosa, and that she must get a divorce. In a perfect example of plot-driven coincidence, their conversation is overheard by a friend of Cotten's, who threatens to blackmail her about both the affair and the pregnancy. How does she plan to escape this awkward situation? Simple . . . first, kill the blackmailer and claim it was a hunting accident, then throw herself over a highway embankment to induce a miscarriage. Pretty racy stuff by 1949 standards, but hokey in the extreme today.

The baby is miscarried, but in the process Davis contracts peritonitis and, although supposedly on her deathbed, will move heaven and earth to catch the next train for Chicago. At this point, Max Steiner's inexplicably Oscar-nominated musical score *really* starts "going to town," with overuse of the old tune "Chicago (That Toddlin' Town)" fully orchestrated and thundering away under images of Bette first weakly ambling, then literally crawling, toward the train station to meet her lover. Since it *was* made in 1949, Rosa must die for her sins, and she does so just as the nine o'clock train for Chi-Town, as massive and obvious a phallic symbol as ever was seen onscreen, steams off without her. Print ads for this film's original release declared, "She was a midnight gal in a nine o'clock town." But if you ask us, Davis's performance in this film is several springs short of having a fully working clock in her belfry!

Dippy Dialogue
Title card from opening credits: "This is the story of evil. Evil is headstrong—is puffed up. For our soul's sake, it is salutory for us to view it in all its ugly nakedness once in a while. Thus may we know how those who deliver themselves over to it end up like the Scorpion, in a mad frenzy stinging themselves to eternal death."

Fun Footnote
Davis's "What a dump!" line, endlessly imitated over the years, was also spoken by Elizabeth Taylor (impersonating Bette) in Liz's Oscar-winning performance in *Who's Afraid of Virginia Woolf?*

The Conqueror

(1956/RKO Radio Pictures) **DVD / VHS**

Who's to Blame CAST: **John Wayne** (*Temujin/Genghis Khan*); **Susan Hayward** (*Bortai*); **Pedro Armendáriz** (*Jamuga*); **Agnes Moorehead** (*Hunlun*); **William Conrad** (*Kasar*); **Lee Van Cleef** (*Chepei*)
CREW: **Directed by Dick Powell; Written by Oscar Millard**

Rave Reviews

"Notoriously awful . . . a disaster for a variety of reasons, including its remarkably atrocious dialogue [and] ridiculous casting."
— *TV Guide's Movie Guide*

"Rife with stilted, unintentionally funny dialogue . . . it's surreal enough to enable viewers to approximate an out-of-body experience."
— *VideoHound's Golden Movie Retriever*

"Astoundingly ridiculous characters, bad acting and laughable writing."
— **Richard B. Jewell**, *The RKO Story*

Plot, What Plot? In the history of hilarious Hollywood miscastings, perhaps nothing ranks so high on the ha-ha scale as John Wayne playing Mongol warmonger Genghis Khan. Wearing a badly cut black wig, his eyes taped into a semblance of Mongol features, and speaking in his patented halting cowboy drawl, Wayne as an Oriental is, as the *Los Angeles Times* noted, about as convincing as Mickey Rooney playing Jesus.

Cast opposite Wayne, and wearing costumes, makeup, and hairdos more appropriate for a 1950s Oscar night than a twelfth-century desert, is Susan Hayward as Bortai, the Tartar woman whose smoldering resistance to him Wayne finds irresistible. When these two egos meet and clash, nostrils flare, slaps are exchanged, and words that only a 1950s hack screenwriter could have written flow from their mouths. Wayne forces his attentions on her, matter-of-factly declaring, "Your hatred will kindle into love . . ." To which Hayward spits back, "Before that day dawns, Mongol, the vultures will have feasted on your heart!" This is greeted with a loud *slap* from Wayne . . . and a vaguely S&M smile from Hayward.

"There is no limit to her perfidy!" warns Wayne's brother Jamuga—a name you can't help tittering over every time Wayne tries to get his mouth around it. "She is a woman, Jamuga," says Wayne in his best Mongolian monotone. "Much woman!" So much woman, in fact, that when Wayne suggests she hasn't the same "talents" as a bevy of Vegasy-looking dancing girls who perform for their pleasure, Susan grabs a pair of swords, shimmies for a moment, pulls off a few Madonna "Vogue" moves with them—then throws them right at Wayne. This proves Wayne's earlier contention that "Her nature is as ugly as her body is fair."

The battle of the sexes soon gives way to a literal battle between Wayne's Mongols and Hayward's father, Kumlek, who wears even sillier helmets than Wayne. Torn between loyalty to Daddy or loyalty to the man who essentially kidnapped and raped her on her wedding night, Hayward eventually sides with Wayne. After all, he *does* have billing above her. Given that this is a John Wayne film, you can guess who wins the final battle. As Johnny and Susan literally ride off into the hills, a narrator proclaims at the end, "For a hundred years, the children of their loins ruled half the world . . ."

In its original 1956 release, this film returned over $4.5 million to RKO's coffers. But it cost over $6 million to produce, and for years afterward was cited as a perfect example of Hollywood excess. While it's true they don't make 'em like *The Conqueror* anymore, this film also serves as a perfect argument for why they *shouldn't*.

Dippy Dialogue
Genghis Khan (*John Wayne*), eyeing Hayward: "See to the sharing of the booty . . ."

Choice Chapter Stop
Chapter 7 ("Wang Khan"): In which concubines dressed like Vegas showgirls entertain Genghis Wayne and his bride, Bortai (dance number begins at 39:45).

Fun Footnote
This film's producer, reclusive billionaire Howard Hughes, at one time owned all rights to this film. Rather than rerelease it, he decreed himself the only one allowed to see it, and ordered it shown for him privately night after night for years on end.

The Godfather: Part III

(1990/Paramount Pictures) **DVD / VHS**

Who's to Blame **CAST:** **Al Pacino** (*Michael Corleone*); **Talia Shire** (*Connie Corleone-Rizzi*); **Diane Keaton** (*Kay Adams*); **Andy Garcia** (*Vinnie Mancini*); **Eli Wallach** (*Don Altobello*); **Joe Mantegna** (*Joey Zasa*); **George Hamilton** (*B. J. Harrison*); **Sofia Coppola** 🍅🍅 (*Mary Corleone*)
CREW: **Directed by Francis Ford Coppola; Written by Mario Puzo and Coppola; Based upon characters created by Puzo**

Rave Reviews
"Sofia['s] performance here is so wooden you want to yell 'Timber!' every time she appears on screen." — **Neil Smith, BBC Films (Web site)**

"One offer director Francis Ford Coppola should have refused. It's hard to tell if this thing's serious or parody and, if it is parody, whether or not it's intentional." — **Desson Howe,** *Washington Post*

"Sofia Coppola's acting talents here are as bad as you've heard. Her scenes are laughable to the point of making any sequence in which she appears seem absurd." — **Christopher Null, FilmCritic.com**

Plot, What Plot? Anyone who doubts nepotism is alive and well in Hollywood need only see *Godfather III*. A $55 million follow-up to the only hit-and-sequel pair of films to both win Oscars as Best Picture, *GFIII* has an overly operatic plotline that hinges heavily on the character of Mary Corleone, daughter of Al Pacino and Diane Keaton. But when Winona Ryder fell ill just as production was to begin in Italy, rather than cast some other established actress, Coppola chose to grant the role to his real-life daughter, Sofia, whose only previous acting experience was playing the infant Michael Corleone in the original 1972 *Godfather*.

The result . . . made Razzie history. While most critics admitted this sixteen-years-later third film in the *Godfather* trilogy was decidedly not up to the standards of its predecessors, every single critic lambasted Sofia's astoundingly awful turn as the daughter of Pacino and Keaton, who falls in love with her first cousin Andy Garcia and unwittingly sets in motion a series of events that inevitably end in tragedy. That someone so bald-facedly untalented as an actress could be the child of two Oscar winners implies that Mary must be the milkman's or the postman's child—surely she couldn't have come from Keaton's womb or Pacino's loins. And that Coppola could be so blind to his child's shortcomings suggests a serious lapse in directorial judgment. Didn't he watch the dailies? Did he honestly think no one would notice?

Beyond Sofia's nasal, monotone/zombie performance, the film is also amusing for other choices it makes. Basically, the first two films covered anything interesting Coppola or author Puzo had to say about the Corleones, so this film had to trump up drama and excitement. When Robert Duvall asked for more than Coppola was willing to cough up to reprise his role as a lawyer, the part was rewritten and recast with Mr. Man-Tan himself, George Hamilton. Don Novello, once known as *Saturday Night Live*'s Father Guido Sarducci, shows up in a small role as a family spokesman. And Sofia isn't the only Coppola family member getting away with awful acting here. Francis's sister Talia Shire, Oscar-nominated for *Godfather II*, gives just as shrill and mechanical a performance here as she did in any *Rocky* sequel. A subplot with her character trying to off Eli Wallach with a poisoned cannoli is only one of the film's numerous ludicrous plot devices.

But whenever little Sofia is onscreen, everything grinds to a screeching halt. Rolling gnocchis and sharing nookie with Garcia in a kitchen scene, she makes us respect Garcia's professionalism for keeping a straight face while the cameras rolled. Stamping her feet and whining to Pacino, "But Dad, I love him!" she makes parents in the audience want to slap her. And when, in the film's climactic set piece, she is accidentally struck by a bullet intended for Pacino and falls stiffly to her knees, flatlining the single word "Dad?!?!" it can only be greeted by derisive laughter as the single worst death scene ever filmed. In fact, when the film was shown for Academy members on the Paramount lot, this scene was greeted by hoots and howls from the usually staid and respectful Oscar voters, who then burst into applause when her character dropped dead.

A sad and ultimately unnecessary follow-up to the far superior first two *Godfather* films, *Godfather: Part III* should never have been made. But if it hadn't been, the single worst female performance of all time would never have been captured on film. Thanks, Papa Coppola!

Dippy Dialogue
Mary Corleone (*Sofia Coppola*): "I'll always love you . . ."
Her cousin Vincent Mancini (*Andy Garcia*): "Love somebody else!"

Choice Chapter Stop
Chapter 23 ("Finale on the Steps"): Sofia proves that among the World's Worst Actresses, she's #1 . . . with a bullet.

Fun Footnote
Sofia Coppola still holds the record for the largest percentage of votes ever received by a Razzie nominee. In both categories in which she was nominated, she polled over 65 percent of all votes, in a field of five contenders. Not even Pia Zadora ever equaled those numbers!

Harum Scarum

(1965/MGM) **DVD / VHS**

Who's to Blame   CAST: Elvis Presley (*Johnny Tyronne*); **Mary Ann Mobley** (*Princess Shalimar*); **Fran Jeffries** (*Aishah*); **Michael Ansara** (*Prince Dragna*); **Jay Novello** (*Zacha*); **Billy Barty** (*Baba the Midget*)
CREW: **Directed by Gene Nelson; Screenplay by Gerald Drayson Adams**

Rave Reviews

"One can see why the younger members of the audience were apt to snigger." — **Eric Braun,** ***The Elvis Film Encyclopedia***

"With the ripest dialogue this side of *What's Up, Tiger Lily?*, the movie offers one delirious interlude after another."
— **Marshall Crenshaw, *Hollywood Rock***

"This is close to bottom of the barrel as far as Elvis movies are concerned." — **The Elvis Movie Database (Web site)**

Plot, What Plot? Trying to pick Elvis's best bad movie may, at first, seem like a fool's errand. After all, the man himself as much as admitted he made the same movie thirty-three times. The scary part is just how successful the Elvis movie formula was. Most people no longer remember that Presley was actually listed on the annual Top Ten Money-Making Stars Poll *seven* times between 1957 and 1966.

The formula was a simple and efficient one, set in cement after 1960's *Blue Hawaii* became the King's biggest box-office hit: Take Presley and one or more pretty female costars, put them in an exotic location and/or situation, then ladle eight or more songs over the top so Colonel Parker could get a tie-in soundtrack album out of each film.

The problem was that churning out about three feature-length efforts a year soon caused even Elvis himself to tire of doing these films. With titles like *Tickle Me*, *Girl Happy*, and *The Trouble with Girls (And How to Get into It)*, they were essentially innocuous imitations of one another, produced on ultra-low budgets and returning multimillion-dollar profits (most of which went directly into Parker's pocket). But by 1965, with the Beatles having replaced him as the world's most popular rock stars and his box-office status slipping, Presley abandoned even feigned interest in what he was doing—and it showed.

Shoddy even by the low standards of an Elvis film, *Harum Scarum* is easily the dumbest title among the King's three dozen Hollywood movies. This time Elvis plays an American movie star named Johnny Tyronne, who's kidnapped during a publicity tour for his latest movie and told he must kill a king to regain his freedom. It all takes place in the Middle Eastern nation of Lunarkand, located somewhere on the MGM backlot and littered with sets, props, and costumes cadged from previous pictures like *Kismet* and *Lady of the Tropics*. It includes the requisite nine songs, three of which are tossed off in the first seven minutes, and not one of which anyone but an Elvis fan would even claim to remember. One of them has a creepy Michael Jackson quality, as Presley sings a love song to a hip-jiggling, come-hither dance by a ten-year-old would-be slave girl.

Besides its borrowed props, the sets are also adorned with dozens of scantily clad harem girls lounging in the background, bopping bad guys with clay pots or joining Elvis to perform numbers like "Shake That Tambourine" (wonder what *that* could mean?). Presley's costar here is 1959's Miss America, Mary Ann Mobley, as an Arab princess with Anglo features, a never-explained Mississippi accent, and even more mascara than Elvis himself appears to be wearing. And, just for good measure, Billy Barty is thrown in for comic relief, as a midget thief who doubles as a court jester.

A jumbled mess that proved one of the most embarrassing films in one of the most embarrassing film careers in Hollywood history, *Harum Scarum* didn't even manage to turn the usual profit a 1965 Elvis title should have. But at least it came out before the Razzies existed . . . otherwise, it might have swept our 1965 Worst Achievement dis-honors.

Loopy Lyrics
Johnny Tyronne (*Elvis Presley*), singing the closing number in a Las Vegas casino, surrounded by harem girls: "If Romeo had a harem holiday, you can bet that Juliet would have never been his girl forever . . ."

Fun Footnote
An MGM executive once said about Elvis movies, "They don't need titles. They could be numbered."

The Jazz Singer

(1980/AFD) **DVD / VHS**

Who's to Blame CAST: **Neil Diamond** 👁 (*Yussel Rabinovitch*); **Laurence Olivier** 👁 (*Cantor Rabinovitch*); **Lucie Arnaz** (*Molly Bell*); **Caitlin Adams** (*Rifka Rabinovitch*); **Franklin Ajaye** (*Bubba*); **Ernie Hudson** (*Club Heckler*)
CREW: **Directed by Richard Fleischer** 👁 **and Sidney J. Furie** 👁**; Screenplay by Herbert Baker; Adapted by Stephen H. Foreman from the play** *The Day of Atonement* **by Samson Raphaelson**

Rave Reviews
"Makes Neil Diamond the champ chump . . . the pop singer who made the biggest fool of himself when he unwisely tried his hand at making movies." — **Kevin Hennessey,** *Movieline* **magazine**

"An unintentional laff riot—Olivier is so over-the-top that it's mesmerizing!" — **Ken Hanke,** *Asheville (N.C.) Mountain Express*

"BOMB: This remake may actually contain more clichés than the 1927 original!" — *Leonard Maltin's Movie & Video Guide*

Plot, What Plot? It is difficult to imagine *anyone* wanting to remake the rickety old 1927 Al Jolson vehicle *The Jazz Singer* in 1980. For one thing, the original version is remembered only for being the first hit film with sync sound. For another, it had already been remade, and not very successfully, in 1953. It also didn't help that its basic plotline, about a rabbi's son who abandons singing in the synagogue to achieve jazzy pop stardom, was hopelessly outdated. If it was going to be remade at all, it would require a major overhaul . . . unless the singer they chose to play the title role was himself hopelessly outdated. Like . . . Neil Diamond.

This problem-plagued production was conceived as a "showcase" for the presumed talents of singer/songwriter Diamond, whose albums had sold some 50 million copies and whose concerts sold out from coast to coast in the late 1970s. The only problem is, in the nonsinging sequences, Diamond would be required to *act*—something for which he had even less aptitude than fellow pop star Madonna. Along to bring class to the film (and put a fast buck in his pocket?) is Laurence Olivier as Diamond's rabbi dad. You haven't *seen* overacting till you've witnessed Ol' Larry literally tearing at his clothes and doing a giddily over-the-top Yiddish accent as he tries to guilt his onscreen son into giving up his dreams of stardom. "Eet's not tuff enuff beink a Chew?" Olivier intones as he bails Diamond out of jail for inciting a riot at a black nightclub by singing in blackface. Yes, believe it or not, this film's makers were *so* out of the loop that, in 1980, they actually retained the blackface element from Jolson's 1927 version. The ditty Diamond tries to perform for the black audience is the utterly whitebread Worst Song nominee "You, Baby, Baby," a tune so lazy Diamond probably wrote it in less time than it takes to sing it. When the club audience riots at the end of the song, they could be objecting to both Neil's being in blackface, and to his having the balls to perform such a lame-o tune . . .

Once out on bail, Neil explains to hammy Larry that he plans to head to L.A. and break into pop music, even though his sound is more suited to an elevator than to any hip club in California. Once he reaches the Left Coast, Diamond hooks up with Lucie Arnaz as his promoter-cum-live-in-lover, and when Larry once again shows up and discovers that his still married son is cohabiting with a shiksa—Oy! Such mishegas and misbegotten acting you could die from!

All ends happily, though, as everyone is reconciled for a finale concert featuring Diamond in sequins and helmet hair performing the applause-baiting tune "They're Coming to America." Both Arnaz and Olivier are seen smiling and applauding wildly backstage. But almost no one in the movie's audience applauded. This film's dismal box office, along with that of *Saturn 3* and the Village People's Allan Carr fiasco *Can't Stop the Music,* helped sink the company that made all three. AFD was supposed to stand for Associated Film Distribution, but after that string of turkeys, it could instead have stood for Another Freakin' Dud.

Fun Footnote
Before *Jazz Singer* opened, the *New York Daily News* reported overhearing Olivier denigrating the film at a restaurant. His supposed comment: "This piss is shit!"

(1956/MGM) **VHS**

Who's to Blame CAST: **Doris Day** (*Julie Benton*); **Louis Jourdan** (*Lyle Benton*); **Barry Sullivan** (*Cliff Henderson*); **Frank Lovejoy** (*Detective Pringle*); **Jack Kruschen** (*Detective Mace*); **Jack Kelly** (*Copilot*)
CREW: **Directed by Andrew L. Stone; Screenplay** *O* **by Stone**

Rave Reviews
"From the opening strains of its Oscar-nominated title tune to the finale... *Julie* hits and sustains a pitch of all-out nuttiness."
— **Edward Margulies and Stephen Rebello,** *Bad Movies We Love*

"It's seven parts melodrama and three parts *Perils of Pauline*... colorful, lurid, and overwrought." — *Motion Picture Herald*

"The melodramatics are absurd, none more so than the final sequence in which Doris flies a pilotless airliner to a safe landing... with her eyes shut!" — **Jesse Zunser,** *Cue* **magazine**

Plot, What Plot? Cross-eyed Karen Black in *Airport 1975* wasn't the first movie stewardess to land a jumbo jet via headphones—that distinction belongs to Doris Day in one of the most purply titles in the pretty-girl-in-peril genre, *Julie*. Inexplicably Oscar-nominated as Best "Original" Screenplay for Andrew L. Stone's shrill, tone-deaf, and utterly unoriginal work, *Julie* is the story of a woman terrorized by a seventy-two-inch "pianist." Louis Jourdan, dark-eyed and demi-unintelligible as Day's pathologically jealous soon-to-be-ex-husband, relentlessly stalks Miss Happy-Go-Sunshine throughout the film, at one point terrifying her by playing an audiotape of one of his piano concerts—enough to frighten any fan out of their wits!

Unaware that loony Louis murdered her first husband, Doris begins to suspect something must be amiss when Jourdan slams her foot down on the gas pedal of their convertible and very nearly forces them to reenact Princess Grace's final moments. But it's not until he flat out tells her, "You can't get away from me—you're going to die, Julie," that Day realizes she's made a poor choice of spouse. And an even worse choice in footwear: When she decides to flee their cliffside home in Carmel, Doris does so in high heels, lugging a suitcase full of designer gowns.

Even more incoherently hysterical than she was in Hitchcock's *The Man Who Knew Too Much,* Doris seeks solace from friendly cop Frank Lovejoy, who basically tells her that until Jourdan actually strikes, there's little the police can do. Trying to get her mind off her personal problems, Day naturally goes back to work as a stewardess . . . only to discover that one of the passengers on her flight is Mr. Piano Man himself. Gunplay ensues, the entire crew except Our Plucky Star is killed or wounded . . . and it's up to Calamity Jane to land the plane, as instructed via headset by the San Francisco control tower. To help keep this perky but inexperienced pilot from panicking, the control tower offers her helpful hints like, "Don't let that meter get under 120—you'll crash if you do!" Tears streaming down her face, and with both eyes shut (!), Doris manages the incredible feat of bringing in what's left of the passengers and crew safely. Which just goes to show you: If you're going to pick on someone, for goodness sakes, *don't* pick on the Girl Next Door!

Dippy Dialogue
Julie's roommate (*Aline Towne*): "Let's face it, honey, you've been jittery as all get-out ever since we landed . . . What gives?!?!"

Fun Footnote
Among film flub aficionados, *Julie* is notorious for how many times the boom mike, or its shadow, appears in frame. See how many times you can spot them.

Rambo: First Blood Part II

(1985/TriStar Pictures) **DVD / VHS**

Who's to Blame   CAST: **Sylvester Stallone** (*John Rambo*); **Richard Crenna** (*Col. Trautman*); **Charles Napier** (*Marshall Murdock*); **Steven Berkoff** (*Lt. Col. Podovsky*); **Julia Nickson** (*Co Bao*); **Don Collins** (*POW #1*)
CREW: **Directed by George P. Cosmatos**; **Screenplay** by Sylvester Stallone and James Cameron; Story by Kevin Jarre; Based on characters created by David Morrell

Rave Reviews
"Absurdly overwrought comic book action."
— *Halliwell's Film & Video Guide*

"Incredibly dumb." — *Leonard Maltin's Movie & Video Guide*

"Stupid slaughter . . . the Bernie Goetz of Vietnam movies."
— **Jeremiah Kipp, FilmCritic.com**

Plot, What Plot? If an eight-year-old boy were given millions of dollars to make a movie starring his G.I. Joe dolls (sorry, "action figures"), the result would probably be eerily similar to Sylvester Stallone's most successful film, which is also one of the biggest-grossing Worst Picture "winners" in Razzie history: *Rambo: First Blood Part II.*

    Completely ignoring the premise of the first *First Blood*, *Part II* turns deeply damaged war hero John Rambo from a psychologically scarred veteran into an overly muscled, well-armed killing machine, who almost single-handedly sees to it that in his search for Vietnam-era POWs, "we get to win this time." Putting the simplemindedness of the film's premise aside, *Rambo II* has little or no dramatic tension, since, from the minute it begins, we instinctively know Rambo will survive, no matter how many enemy guns, tanks, grenades, and other armaments are aimed at his big, fat, red-bandanna-wrapped head. The "fun" is supposed to be in seeing how many "Cong" and other Commies Rambo can kill, and how many fireballs he can make by "blowing stuff up real good." The body count for this film has been estimated at over seventy-five onscreen deaths, the highest of the three *Rambo* movies and a number that, considering the film is barely 95 minutes long, averages almost one victim per minute.

While the idea of using America's anguish over its Vietnam POWs as a device to sell movie tickets is inherently offensive, the filmmakers' execution of their premise—and especially Stallone's steroid-driven star turn in the title role—is often laugh-out-loud funny. Grimacing, grunting, and flexing his chest muscles like Steve Reeves playing Hercules, Sly never slows for a minute in pursuing his self-righteous slaughter of what he considers "the bad guys." When it finally dawns on him near the film's end that the American government itself is among the bad guys, his answer is to unload an entire ammo belt from his machine gun into the Army's computers while unleashing a guttural, 30-second-long grunt at the top of his lungs. Aside from the sexually impotent implications of the image, the look on Stallone's face in this scene sums up what Rambo is really about: blind rage more appropriate to a sleep-deprived toddler than a decorated war hero. He then follows this up with a flag-waving, jingoistic final speech (see Dippy Dialogue below) that is both shameless in its pandering and hilarious in its melodramatic overintensity. But wait, the lunacy isn't over yet: Under the end titles, Sly's little brother, Frank, provides a song so out of whack with the rest of the film that your jaw may drop to the floor. It's entitled "Peace in Our Life," and it deservedly "won" our Worst "Original" Song Razzie.

The idea that millions of Americans embraced this film (while failing to question its worldview) is in many ways disturbing. But if you can get past that, Stallone gives one of his most audaciously, amusingly over-the-top performances. And that's without even addressing the homoerotic implications of the material . . .

Dippy Dialogue
Colonel Trautman (*Richard Crenna*): "What *do* you want . . . ?"
John Rambo (*Sylvester Stallone*), after a deep breath and a dramatic pause: "I want . . . what they want . . . and every other guy who

came over here and spilt his guts and gave everything he had wants . . . For our country to love us as much as we love it. *That's* what I want!" (*After pausing again for audience applause, Rambo walks off.*)

Choice Chapter Stop
Chapter 34 ("Destruction"): In which hambo Rambo lets loose a load of Freudian "bullets" into the Army's computers.

Fun Footnote
When *Rambo II* and *Rocky IV* between them took sixteen nominations, then "won" eight dis-honors, the headline on our "winners" press release read "Sly and the Family Stallone Dominate 6th Annual Razzie Awards."

(1935/RKO Radio Pictures) **DVD / VHS**

Who's to Blame   CAST: **Helen Gahagan** (*She Who Must Be Obeyed*); **Randolph Scott** (*Leo Vincey*); **Helen Mack** (*Tanya Dugmore*); **Nigel Bruce** (*Horace Holly*); **Gustav von Seyffertitz** (*High Priest*)
CREW: **Directed by Irving Pichel and Lansing C. Holden; Screenplay by Ruth Rose; Additional dialogue by Dudley Nichols; From the novel by H. Rider Haggard**

Rave Reviews
"Hilarious, terrible, essential. . . . Camp like this is a rarity!"
— **Pauline Kael,** *5001 Nights at the Movies*

"Plot and acting are sheer hokum and there's much unintentional humour." — **Channel 4 (Britain)**

"There are scenes that skirt the twilight zone of the horse laugh."
— *Variety*

Plot, What Plot? When 1933's *King Kong* proved to be one of their most profitable pictures ever, RKO decided to roll the dice again two years later with what they thought was a similar enough project to be a shoo-in: a third version of H. Ryder Haggard's novel *She*. They sank a fortune into the film . . . and wound up losing $180,000, back when $180,000 was a fortune in itself.

    Their first mistake was one of casting. For the title role of the ageless beauty "She Who Must Be Obeyed," they needed someone so alluring that a mere mortal would willingly follow her into the Flame of Eternal Life. Instead, they cast Helen Gahagan, a Broadway actress and former opera singer whose performance here was so stilted and unappealing that she never made another film. It didn't help matters that she looked like a female impersonator made up to be Katharine Hepburn, was frequently frocked in gowns that resembled those of the Wicked Queen from *Snow White,* and spoke nearly every line in a whispery, otherworldly way that left audiences questioning not only her character's beauty, but her sanity as well.

Surrounding this stupendously silly central casting choice is a film that's a monument to 1930s art deco excess. One enters the Kingdom of Kor through giant white gates (which you may recognize as the same gates through which Fay Wray was dragged in *Kong*, simply whitewashed) and from there proceeds to a throne room that looks like a broken-down Macy's escalator. "She" rules her kingdom from a throne that looks like an oversized commode at Grauman's Chinese. And the setting for the film's centerpiece, and most stupendously campy sequence, is a gargantuan chamber with fifty-foot figures lining its walls, all of which look like they've squatted to take a dump in the woods.

Into this fantasy world, which purports to hold the secret of Eternal Life, come three explorers: blustery Nigel Bruce, mealy-mouthed Helen Mack, and stalwart Randolph Scott. It turns out Scott is a near Xerox of John Vincey, with whom "She" had fallen in love five centuries earlier, and a rivalry arises between Gahagan and Mack for Scott's affections (lucky him!). Everything culminates in a sacrificial ritual where Mack's face is shrouded and she is to be tossed into a flaming pit while Scott unknowingly witnesses her death. It's the ritual itself, though, that's truly flaming: a hilariously costumed, clumsily choreographed ten-minute sequence that features hand moves you may recognize from Olympic synchronized swimming competitions, gyrations and hip-hops right out of a Janet Jackson music video, and everybody dressed like it's Halloween in West Hollywood.

Getting to this point in *She* can be a real slog, so you may want to skip all the hokey, dragged-out setup stuff and go right for the film's final half hour. That way you'll miss some of the reasons Gahagan "retired from the screen" after just this one legendarily awful performance, but you will see not only the Sacrifice ritual, but also the film's other great highlight, Gahagan trying to lure Scott into the Flame of Eternal Life. As the flames rise around her, and wind blows up her backside, "She" discovers to her horror (and our snickering delight) that something's gone terribly wrong. Instead of rejuvenating her youth and "beauty," "She" is rapidly aged every one of her five hundred years, and winds up looking like *Snow White*'s Wicked Queen when she showed up with the poisoned apple. Yes, the hokum factor in *She* is in some ways intentional—but that doesn't make it any less fun to laugh at.

Dippy Dialogue
She (*Helen Gahagan*), introducing herself: "I am yesterday, and today, and tomorrow. I am sorrow and longing and hope unfulfilled. I am . . . She Who Must Be Obeyed!"

Choice Chapter Stop
("Sacrifice of Gratitude"): She Who Must Be Obeyed nearly gets away with her big Mack attack, and the Dancers of Kor put on a supremely silly show.

Fun Footnote
Believe it or not, *She* was actually Oscar-nominated in the now defunct category of Best Dance Direction . . .

(1964/Columbia Pictures) **DVD / VHS**

Who's to Blame CAST: **Joan Crawford** (*Lucy Harbin*); **Diane Baker** (*Carol Harbin*); **Leif Erickson** (*Bill Cutler*); **George Kennedy** (*The Farmhand*); **Lee Majors** (*The Decapitated First Husband*)
CREW: **Directed by William Castle; Written by Robert Bloch**

Rave Reviews
"Cheap-jack production, inept supporting players and direction better suited to the mist-and-cobweb idiocies of the Karloff school of suspense." — **Judith Crist, *New York Herald Tribune***

"Serves up so many horror (and horrible) clichés with numerous disembodied noggins that the result is an unintentional comedy."
— **Margaret Hartford, *Los Angeles Times***

"Crawford tears into her role with all the vigor her camp devotees would expect... [which] will delight anyone who can appreciate chills of the campiest variety." — **Donald Guarisco, *All Movie Guide***

Plot, What Plot? Unlike Bette Davis, who parlayed her appearance in the box-office smash *What Ever Happened to Baby Jane?* into an eleventh Oscar nomination and a long-lasting career revival, Bette's costar Joan Crawford found her post–*Baby Jane* career spiraling ever downward in a series of increasingly shoddier horror pictures, culminating in her final embarrassment, 1970's *Trog*. Among the more amusing rungs on Crawford's career down-alator is her appearance in schlocky shockmeister William Castle's *Strait-Jacket*. Apparently working on the assumption that she was not Oscar-nominated for *Baby Jane* because she didn't overact enough, Joan pulls out all the stops for this performance... and it's an amazing sight to see.

We first see her as a "young wife" getting off a train. With a loud polka-dot dress, even louder jangling jewelry, a wildly obvious dark wig, and her face pulled back just enough to make her look ridiculous but not enough to make her look "young," Crawford sashays through billowing steam, supposedly anxious to get home to her loving hubby, looking like a too-long-in-the-tooth trick-turner. When she arrives at her wrong-side-of-the-tracks shack of a home, Joan sees "hubby" in bed with another woman. And, like any reasonable "young wife," she grabs a nearby axe, and hacks the two lovers' heads off—right in front of her toddler daughter.

Flash forward twenty years: Joan is being released from the slammer, and now looks almost her true age. She's been invited to come stay with her brother, his wife, and the daughter who witnessed the axe murder all those years ago. Soon "little signs" start turning up that maybe jittery Joan *isn't* what you'd call "balanced": heads cut off of photos in the family album, knives stabbed through sculptures, severed heads showing up in Joan's bed—like we said, "little signs." But Diane Baker, in a performance that could seem restrained only next to Crawford's, plays a loving daughter who encourages her formerly axe-wielding Mommie Dearest to enjoy her new freedom. So the two "gals" go shopping, and buy Joan a near-exact replica of the outfit she wore the night of the murder—right down to the jangling jewelry and the blatant black wig. While shopping, Joan (but inexplicably no one else) hears a group of jump-roping children taunting her with a variation on the old "Lizzie Borden took an axe" bit. And in a bit of acting subtlety for the ages, Crawford doesn't take it very well.

Proud of her beau, Baker naturally wants Mommie to meet him. And in one of the film's most hilarious scenes, Joan comes on to the boyfriend so overtly that both Baker and the audience are mortified. Then Crawford's prison psychiatrist shows up, "just to check on her." He becomes the first of several fresh victims, and his frumpy old Ford sedan is then commandeered by George Kennedy, playing a slow-witted farmhand. We know he's slow-witted because he stupidly taunts the fresh-from-prison Crawford, and thus becomes (go on, guess!) the next victim.

As the murder spree progresses, so do Baker's plans for introducing Joan back into family life, so Mommie is now invited to meet her future in-laws. But Joan once again makes one of those faux pas to which she's so prone. Instead of going in her most staid, age-appropriate outfit, she puts on the full wig and harness, showing up at her future in-laws' looking like a hooker seeking sailors to "entertain." It is, of course, only a matter of time before the axe comes out again, the in-laws look like the next potential victims, and the "real murderer" is revealed. Suffice it to say, the denouement is so dubious that you'll think nothing dumber could possibly follow. But you'd be wrong, because the screenwriter for *Strait-Jacket* was Robert Bloch, creator of *Psycho* . . . So naturally, we *have* to end with a psychiatric "explanation" for all those in the audience too dense to understand exactly what went on.

With every ounce of "sincerity" she can muster (and that's a vodka-bottle-full at least!), Crawford takes us on a tour of the clues, "explaining" and "figuring out" how the killer set it up to look like Joan was back to her old axe-wielding ways. We're not going to tell you who *really* killed the second set of corpses, but if you axe me, you ought to be able to "figure it out"—with no help from Doctor Dearest.

But don't stop your video player just yet—the only intentional humor in the whole film comes literally at the very end: As Joan sashays off once more to "be with" her daughter, we fade out—then fade up on the Columbia Pictures logo . . . with Lady Liberty's severed head sitting at her feet!

Dippy Dialogue
Lucy (*Joan Crawford*), looking like a hundred-year-old hooker: "Are you sure I look okay?!?!"

Choice Chapter Stops
Chapter 11 ("Drinks with Mother"): Joan puts the moves on Baker's beau.
Chapter 28 ("Explanations"): Crawford "assists" the mystery-impaired, and Lady Liberty loses her head.

Fun Footnote
When *Mommie Dearest* became an instant camp classic in 1981, T-shirts were created using the image of Crawford wielding an axe from *Strait-Jacket,* subtitled, "Joan Crawford Daycare Center."

Beyond the Valley of the Dolls
(1970/20th Century-Fox) **VHS**

Who's to Blame   CAST: **Dolly Read** *(Kelly)*; **Cynthia Myers** *(Casey)*; **Marcia McBroom** *(Pet)*; **John LaZar** *("Z-Man" Barzell)*; **Michael Blodgett** *(Lance Rocke)*; **David Gurian** *(Harris)*; **Duncan McLeod** *(Porter Hall)*; **Charles Napier** *(Baxter Wolfe)*; **Edy Williams** *(Ashley St. Ives)*
CREW: **Directed by Russ Meyer; Screenplay by Roger Ebert; Story by Meyer and Ebert** (Yes, *that* Roger Ebert!)

Rave Reviews
"Weirdly funny and a real curio—rather like a Grandma Moses illustration for a work by the Marquis de Sade."
           — **John Simon,** *The New Yorker*

"A psychedelic wow that serves up the free love, plunging necklines, androgynous boys, and lusty lezzies of the era with a narcotized abandon." — **Michael Musto,** *Village Voice*

"If you're going to watch it, invite a group of people (at least five) both men and women, grab the popcorn and laugh your head off with this cult classic." — **Patrick Brogan, BadMovieNight.com**

Plot, What Plot? One of the hardest things to do well is an "intentional" bad film. If you can pull off being deliberately tasteless, clueless, *and* funny all at once, you're a master. The most often-cited example of this extremely select genre is *Attack of the Killer Tomatoes*, which, despite its killer title, is actually just a bad movie. The true best of this genre, complete with nudity, violence, kinky sex, oddball characters, and dippy dialogue to spare, is breast-obsessed director Russ Meyer's 1970 "sequel" *Beyond the Valley of the Dolls*. As a lawsuit by Jacqueline Susann forced the film's print ads to declare, "This is *not* a sequel—there has never been anything like it!"
 Riffing on the three-young-chicks-trying-to-make-it-in-Tinseltown

premise of Susann's original *Dolls*, Meyer's film focuses on a three-girl rock band called the Carrie Nations, who hit Hollywood at its hedonistic, head-tripping peak: the end of the Swingin' '60s. Almost everyone in this film was either making their screen debut, or would never be seen again in any mainstream movie, or both. And every actor's rank amateurishness only contributes to it being the wild joyride of a movie that it is. Psychedelic in the extreme, *Beyond* was written for Meyer by, of all people, now respected film critic Roger Ebert. Together, Meyer and Ebert manage to get into their film elements of almost every movie genre there is, spoofing them all in a way that leaves the audience certain they were in on the joke. This one's so out there it *has* to be bad on purpose.

The Carrie Nations consist of Kelly (Dolly Read), Casey (Cynthia Myers), and Pet (Marcia McBroom), two white babes and one black chick, whose music catches the ear of rock impresario (and weirdo extraordinaire) Z-Man Barzell. Before you can say "orgy," these three young innocents find themselves sucked into the sleazy sex-and-drugs scene of the time—lusted after by lesbians, dirty-old-man lawyers, and just about everyone they meet. The band's manager, Harris (David Gurian) has an affair on the side with porn star Ashley St. Ives (Edy Williams), and everything ends in near-tragedy as he plummets to the stage from the rafters during a TV appearance by the Carrie Nations. This particular scene, with its deliberately melodramatic setup and payoff (and its brilliantly snide use of sound effects), summarizes what's so wonderful about *Beyond*. Beyond mere trash, this film exists on a level of social commentary and self-awareness all too rare in mainstream Hollywood moviemaking. As Ebert called it on the film's tenth anniversary, *Beyond* is "a movie that got made by accident when the lunatics took over the asylum." Sadly, many of the truths it reveals are still true in Hollywood. For a movie that set out to be trashy from the git-go, *Beyond* is head-and-bazooms above and beyond any other film like it . . . but then, there really *is* no other film quite like it!

Dippy Dialogue
Z-Man *(John LaZar)*, surveying the wild Hollywood party he's hosting: "This is *my* happening, and it freaks me out!"

The Carpetbaggers

(1964/Paramount Pictures) **DVD / VHS**

Who's to Blame CAST: **George Peppard** *(Jonas Cord Jr.)*; **Carroll Baker** *(Rina Marlowe)*; **Alan Ladd** *(Nevada Smith)*; **Bob Cummings** *(Dan Pierce)*; **Elizabeth Ashley** *(Monica Winthrop)*; **Martha Hyer** *(Jennie Denton)*
CREW: **Directed by Edward Dmytryk; Screenplay by John Michael Hayes; Based on the novel by Harold Robbins**

Rave Reviews
"Big, fat, supremely silly soap opera."
— **Edward Margulies and Stephen Rebello,** *Bad Movies We Love*

"A high point in the long history of clumsy-sexpot kitsch that deserves mention alongside . . . Paul Verhoeven's *Showgirls*."
— **Eric Henderson,** *Slant* **magazine**

"*The Carpetbaggers* is first-rate trash—and trash of so high a caliber is not easy to find." — *TV Guide's Movie Guide*

Plot, What Plot? One of the parlor games that helped make Harold Robbins's ribald novels must-reads in their time was trying to guess which famous celebrity each of his hedonistic, hard-drinking, whore-humping main characters was based on. In *The Carpetbaggers*, we get obvious knockoffs of both Jean Harlow (Carroll Baker as "Rina Marlowe") and John Wayne (Alan Ladd as "Nevada Smith"), but its central character may be harder for today's moviegoers to place. Played by George Peppard with a glint in his eyes and a fuse shorter than a munchkin's, Jonas Cord is an aerospace heir turned movie mogul who finds he can be attracted only to trampy women, but puts the moves on everything in skirts anyway. While Robbins and Paramount could have been sued for admitting it at the time, Cord is clearly based on reclusive, reputedly abusive billionaire Howard Hughes. But if the real Hughes had lived as debauched a life as

Peppard does here, he'd have died of syphilis by the age of nineteen.

We open with the death of Jonas Cord's father, a blustery lush who dies from a stroke (or is it Overactor's Disease?) when Junior calls him a "dried-up, impotent old man." To console Dad's buxom blonde widow, Rina, Junior forces himself on her that very afternoon, then dumps her to pursue other women. But for the rest of the film, it's Miss Marlowe he can't forget. On a dare, he marries Elizabeth Ashley, who tells him what she most wants to see on their honeymoon is "Lots of lovely ceilings!" He finagles his way into ownership of a movie studio, turns trashy Rina into a sexy screen siren, then figures she ought to express her "gratitude" with that body she earlier insisted "speaks several languages fluently." Their impassioned, purplish consummation of their mutual lust and loathing for each other (see Dippy Dialogue) is one of the film's many campy climaxes. Ashley miraculously gives birth to a daughter (even though it's laboriously established that she and Peppard haven't so much as touched each other for years) but he's such a heel he divorces her anyway. Rina proceeds to become Hollywood's sexiest star, easiest lay . . . and biggest lush. When we see her leading a police car on a midnight chase, we can practically count out the beats until she loses control of her roadster and "dies tragically" in a car wreck.

Peppard wastes no time grieving, and quickly finds another busty blonde to take Rina's place—apparently not realizing that Jennie Denton (Martha Hyer) was once a professional hooker. When he proposes marriage, and admits he not only knew she was a tramp but has seen her stag reel twice, she goes ballistic and calls him "crazy." Turns out saying so is the one way to prove Peppard is a nutcase, and he and Ladd wind up in a knock-down, drag-out fistfight during which we learn Jonas's "awful secret" (yes, like every character in a Robbins or Susann story, he's hiding the requisite "awful secret"): Jonas had a twin brother who lived only to the age of nine, and died "incurably insane." So all of Jonas's womanizing, corporate gobbling, and spouting of deliriously over-the-top dialogue can be traced to his fears that he too may be crazy.

The Carpetbaggers is trash . . . trash, I tell ya! Right down to its wonderfully overblown Elmer Bernstein musical score and stentorian narration by Paul Frees, who did the host's voice for Disneyland's Haunted Mansion ride in the same style he uses here. If *Carpetbaggers* can't get you laughing, you must have some "awful secret" of your own. But whatever it is, don't bring it up until five minutes before the end titles roll. Otherwise, it'd spoil all the fun of getting to it . . .

Dippy Dialogue
Rina Marlowe *(Carroll Baker)*, **to Jonas Cord** *(George Peppard):* "You really are completely no good!"
Jonas: "But that's what's always excited you about me. You can't make love to anyone you like . . . we've both always known that, haven't we?"
Rina *(kissing him violently***):** "Yes . . . yes . . . oh, dammit . . . *Yes!!!*"

Choice Chapter Stop
Chapter 5 ("Cornering the World"): Jonas buys up companies like they're snack crackers, Nevada winds up in Tinseltown, and Rina does a striptease atop a crystal chandelier that crashes to the floor.

Fun Footnote
Originally considered too sleazy to be shown on network TV without being cut to shreds, *Carpetbaggers* was "restored" to its original theatrical version for its recent DVD release, and was found sexy enough by the MPAA to be rated . . . PG.

The Greatest Show on Earth O

(1952/Paramount Pictures) **DVD / VHS**

Who's to Blame **CAST:** **Betty Hutton** *(Holly)*; **Cornel Wilde** *(The Great Sebastian)*; **Charlton Heston** *("Brad" Braden)*; **Dorothy Lamour** *(Phyllis)*; **Gloria Grahame** *(Angel)*; **James Stewart** *(Buttons, a clown)*
CREW: **Directed by Cecil B. DeMille** O; **Screenplay by Frederic M. Frank, Barré Lyndon, and Theodore St. John; From a story** O **by Frank, St. John, and Frank Cavett**

Rave Reviews
"The all-time weirdest, screwiest, funniest Best Picture Oscar winner.... A three-ring hootfest!"
— Edward Margulies and Stephen Rebello, *Bad Movies We Love*

"A huge, mawkish, trite circus movie ... [a] cornball enterprise."
— Pauline Kael, *The New Yorker*

"The worst film ever to win Best Picture ... hammy performances ... overheated narration ... cheesy special effects [and] a hokey script!"
— Brian Koller, e-Opinions.com

Plot, What Plot? A master at putting together all-star extravaganzas that played off religion, Americana, or both, Cecil B. DeMille was Hollywood's consummate showman from the silent era through his death in 1959. This luridly colorful, shamelessly overacted circus spectacle, which actually beat out *High Noon, Ivanhoe, The Quiet Man*, and John Huston's *Moulin Rouge* to win 1952's Best Picture Oscar, is often cited as the worst movie ever to win that coveted award. It was also one of DeMille's biggest successes.

Elephantine in its scope, and minuscule in its efforts to be about anything more than exploiting its circus setting to milk countless moments of pathos, *Greatest Show* has among its cast some of the most respected names in movies at the time. James Stewart spends most of the film behind hokey clown makeup, hiding a "desperate secret." Brassy Betty Hutton is an aerialist with designs on fellow high-wire risk-taker Cornel Wilde. Dorothy Lamour, Gloria Grahame, and Henry Wilcoxon, among others, are also members of the circus troupe, and stalwart, stodgy Charlton Heston is in charge of it all. Almost from the moment the film begins, the hokum sets in—and doesn't let up until the big train-wreck climax. Essentially a big-budget soap opera, this is what passed for mainstream entertainment back in the days when TV first began encroaching on movie ticket sales.

"You don't have anything but sawdust in your veins!" angry Hutton tells huffy Heston when he informs her that she's lost the center ring to newly hired aerialist Cornel Wilde. Before anyone can say "elephant pucky," Wilde makes his big entrance accompanied by cop cars, vainly checking out his appearance in his sports car's rearview mirror. "He may be a god in the air, but he's a devil on the ground," Heston warns Hutton. She, being the mature adult that she is, immediately decides to play off Wilde against Heston, just to see what happens.

The consummate "ladies' man," Wilde agrees to a friendly rivalry with Hutton to stir up business, then tries to bed her down besides. While cavorting with Hutton atop a bale of hay, and comparing her to champagne bubbles, Wilde is interrupted by one of Gloria Grahame's performing elephants, which rescues Betty from a fate worst than death. But fate is stalking this circus nonetheless, as Wilde takes his midair antics to a new level, attempting to dive through a flaming, streamer-strewn hoop 100 feet in the air, without a net. As a horrified audience watches, Cornel's stunt backfires, and he plummets to the sawdust below, mangling one of his arms in the process.

As Wilde tries to tell Hutton the good news that he may regain the use of his crippled hand, the train on which the circus is traveling (apparently made by Lionel Toys) collides with a car on the tracks. A spectacular wreck ensues, with circus folks tossed every which way, escapes by lions and tigers and bears (oh, my!), and Heston pinned under the wreckage. Turns out Wilde is the only blood donor who can offer Heston a blood transfusion, Stewart (still in clown makeup) is the only doctor who can save Chuck, and Betty's pluck and determination are the only thing that can rally the circus folks to give an open-air performance in a field to create a big finale.

Filmed in now lurid-looking Technicolor, peopled with characters who speak like stick figures in dime-store novels, and utterly predictable from start to finish, *Greatest Show* is perhaps the greatest example of just how gullible audiences were half a century ago. It not only won 1952's Best Picture Academy Award, it was crowned the year's box-office champion as well, hauling in over $14 million for Paramount, back when many theatres were charging less than 25 cents for admission. As P. T. Barnum once observed, "There's a sucker born every minute!"

Dippy Dialogue
DeMille's voice-over, describing the circus parade following the train wreck: "Scars covered by greasepaint, bandages hidden by funny wigs, the spangled Pied Piper limps into town."

Choice Chapter Stop
Chapter 10 ("On the Ground"): In which Hutton's "purity" is preserved by a circus elephant with excellent timing.

Fun Footnote
Greatest Show won its Best Picture statuette during the 1953 Oscars—the first ever seen on live TV.

The Legend of Lylah Clare

(1968/MGM)

Who's to Blame CAST: **Kim Novak** *(Else Brinkmann/Lylah Clare)*; **Peter Finch** *(Lewis Zarkin)*; **Ernest Borgnine** *(Barney Sheehan)*; **Rosella Falk** *(Rosella)*; **Valentina Cortese** *(Countess Bozo Bedoni)*; **Coral Browne** *(Molly Luther)*
CREW: **Directed by Robert Aldrich; Written by Hugo Butler and Jean Rouveral; From a teleplay by Robert Thom and Edward De Blasio**

Rave Reviews
"Not merely awful; it is grandly, toweringly, amazingly so. . . . I laughed myself silly at *Lylah Clare*, and if you're in just the right mood, you may too." — **Richard Schickel,** *Life* **magazine**

"So splendidly, memorably, unforgettably awful that you begin to wonder why it's not more well-known. Do whatever you have to to see it. It's worth it!" — **"Mike," ProgBearCinema.com**

"A laugh-till-you-ache classic . . . directed by Robert ('Over the top? Never heard of it!') Aldrich."
— **Edward Margulies and Stephen Rebello,** *Bad Movies We Love*

Plot, What Plot? As laughably awful as *The Oscar* was, at least it has shown up on video over the years. *The Legend of Lylah Clare*, on the other hand, is still an undiscovered gem of Hollywood hash-making, glomming together elements of not only *The Oscar* but also *Sunset Blvd., Vertigo, Frankenstein, What Ever Happened to Baby Jane?* and just about any movie you can name. Though highly revered among the Crap Cinema Cognoscenti, *Lylah* has remained unsung among mainstream movie historians.

Taking the basic plot device of *Vertigo*, *Lylah* is a fictitious story about a near-death filmmaker finally getting the go-ahead to make a movie based on his late sex symbol wife's tragic life. The "legend" of

Lylah Clare says that she was killed falling from atop the staircase of her Beverly Hills mansion during a knife fight with a burglar. But as we'll soon see, legend and truth rarely intersect in Hollywood.

Populated almost exclusively by sycophants, media snakes, opportunists, and other varieties of Tinseltown reptiles, *Lylah* is meant as an indictment of an industry built on fantasy, wet dreams, and outright lies. But in the course of making its case against Hollywood's reliance on clichés, *Lylah Clare* voraciously unearths just about every Hollywood cliché imaginable.

Under the main titles, we follow an undiscovered starlet down Hollywood Boulevard, as she tries her feet in the stars' footprints at Grauman's, checks out the names in terrazzo tile along the Walk of Fame, and basically gambols down memory lane through every newcomer-in-Hollywood platitude ever invented. The "girl" is Elsa Brinkmann, struggling to make it in the Big City with No Heart, determined to grasp every tiny break fate decides to hand her . . .

Her big chance comes in the form of a casting call for a movie about the life, and death, of the late lamented legendary love goddess Lylah Clare. Relying on the oldest and hoariest of all clichés, the mousy girl who becomes sexy just by taking off her glasses, Elsa is brought to the home of Lylah's widower, director Lewis Zarkin, who makes von Stroheim's Max in *Sunset Blvd.* seem laid-back. At the "audition," Elsa is asked to emulate Lylah coming down the very stairs where Lylah died. Gliding awkwardly toward Zarkin, Elsa is told she's "moving like a deeply offended Tibetan yak!" It is only the first of a string of over-the-top put-downs and one-liners that clutter this film like clumps in a cat litter box.

Just like Norma Desmond did in *Sunset*, Elsa must undergo extreme preparations to play this coveted role. But as the project progresses, she finds her voice falling into the guttural tones of Lylah's Germanic accent even when she's not rehearsing. And when dressed in full costume as Lylah, Elsa so resembles the late actress that both Zarkin and Lylah's lesbian voice coach find her irresistible.

The centerpiece of this tiara-cum-turd is the scene where Elsa makes her debut at a press conference, posing on those stairs again, this time dressed exactly like the painting of Lylah that hangs behind her. In one of the filmmakers' few savvy decisions, most of the Hollywood press corps in the film are played by actual members of the Hollywood press corps, thus assuring coverage for *Lylah* in every gossip rag cranked out at the time. The one fictitious film journalist in attendance is Molly Luther, played by Coral Browne as a dikey, crippled old broad who could be the love child of Louella Parsons and Boris Karloff. Our first impression of this gruesome gal is of her leg brace, into which has been placed a single red rose. Barking orders at Elsa, poking her with her cane, and generally testing the girl's mettle, Molly is met with a rebuke spoken in full Lylah voice, calling Luther "The Wicked Witch of the West—throw water on her and she shrivels, she melts!"

Having established that press conferences may not be the best way to promote their potential new star, Zarkin and studio head Ernest Borgnine (the only actor who has the dis-stink-tion of being in both this film and *The Oscar*) decide to shoot on a closed set. But Elsa becomes ever more Lylah-like as shooting goes on, and by the end of the production, she's gone completely bonkers. The scene they're shooting last is Lylah's death. By now we've learned that her "tragic" fall didn't involve a burglar, but rather a "lady friend" dressed as a man who pulled a shiv on Lylah, and was attacked by the lesbian vocal coach. As Lylah watched her assailant tumble down the marble steps, Zarkin, knowing she suffered from vertigo (that word again!), prompted her to look down at the dead body, and, growing dizzy, she fell to her fate.

For some unexplained reason, the death scene in Zarkin's movie takes place on a high trapeze, with Novak dressed in tights and spangles, and loudly declaring as she exits her dressing room, "Tell them Lylah's coming—as soon as she can get her harness on!" As any student of B moviemaking knew it would, *Lylah* ends with the death of Lylah's ersatz stand-in, toppling from her trapeze as Zarkin zooms in for one last close-up, planning to use the real death as the end of his film.

At the premiere of Zarkin's masterpiece—well, piece of *something*—the audience goes wild as Elsa/Lylah expires and the words "The End" write across her peaceful face. Outside, the TV announcer covering the premiere intros a dog food commercial, which freeze-frames with two curs going at it . . . then launches into an end title song by Frank De Vol that's almost indescribable in its laughableness. Set to a mambo beat, it endlessly repeats the same several notes, interspersed with a breathy woman's voice intoning "Cha! Cha! Cha!" every now and then.

Legendary in Bad Movie Maven circles, *Lylah Clare* will be hard to get your hands on. But if you wanna become a Serious Student of Sucky Cinema, you simply *must* see this one!

Dippy Dialogue
Crotchety gossip maven Molly Luther *(Coral Browne)*: "Aren't you borrowing rather heavily from *Sunset Blvd.*?"

Availability
Legend of Lylah Clare is *so* good, it's never been on video. It can be seen only on cable TV, and shows up about once a year or so on TCM. If you have TiVo, put it on your Wish List *now*!

Fun Footnote
Realizing they had a less-than-stellar film on their hands, MGM decided just before releasing *Lylah Clare* to play up its campiness. Even this ploy didn't help, and Lylah died all over again at the box office.

The Love Machine

(1971/Columbia Pictures) **VHS**

Who's to Blame CAST: **John Phillip Law** *(Robin Stone)*; **Dyan Cannon** *(Judith Austin)*; **Robert Ryan** *(Gregory Austin)*; **David Hemmings** *(Jerry Nelson)*; **Jodi Wexler** *(Amanda)*; **Jackie Cooper** *(Danton Miller)*; **Shecky Greene** *(Christie Lane)*; **Eve Bruce** *(Amazon Woman)*
CREW: **Directed by Jack Haley Jr.; Screenplay by Samuel Taylor; Based on the novel by Jacqueline Susann**

Rave Reviews
"A bomb-of-all-bombs."
— **Harry and Michael Medved,** *The Golden Turkey Awards*

"Ridiculous screen version of Jacqueline Susann's best-seller."
— *Leonard Maltin's Movie & Video Guide*

"Indescribably tacky."
— **Edward Margulies and Stephen Rebello,** *Bad Movies We Love*

Plot, What Plot? 1967's *Valley of the Dolls* may be the most successful, best-remembered trashy movie made from a tacky Jackie Susann novel, but 1971's *The Love Machine* manages the impossible feat of being even trashier than *Dolls*. Set in the world of television programming, it follows the exploits of sex-obsessed TV executive Robin Stone, played by stone-faced John Phillip Law, whose meteoric rise is tied into the numerous women he uses on his way up.

Clearly patterned after *Dolls*, *Machine* even opens with a generic theme song performed by Dionne Warwick, heard over a quick-cut, hokey montage of local reporter Stone working his New York beat. As the song and main titles end, we see Dyan Cannon, looking eerily like an anorexic Miss Piggy, watching Stone on TV. Dyan is not only a sleep-about sleaze, but also the wife of "IBC" network chief Robert Ryan. "He's the best thing on your network," Dyan tells Bob, as

Robin's report launches into a pricelessly outdated fashion montage featuring lots of feathers, sequins, and shiny red vinyl. Thus begins Robin's climb to the top.

At the fashion shoot, Robin meets a blonde, mindless model who introduces herself as "Amanda. Just Amanda, that's all there is." Taking the bait, and setting the standard for what passes for witty repartee in this film, Stone replies, "Well, that's all you need." The line apparently works, because moments later we see Amanda peeling off her top at Stone's bedside and warning him, "You don't know about models, do you? Without our clothes on, we look like little boys." Her observation proves a turn-on for Robin, for reasons we're not supposed to guess yet, but when the director, screenwriter, and stars are as slow on the uptake as everyone involved in this film, you can't help but get ahead of the so-called plot.

Stone's next big conquest is Cannon herself, who jumps under the covers with him so fast you'd think she ordered silk sheets from the waiter at their first lunch. While Cannon and Law mutually adjust each other's horizontal holds, Ryan suffers a massive heart attack and, barely twenty minutes into the film, Stone is appointed by Cannon, using her hubby's "proxy," to be the new president of IBC.

Meanwhile, Amanda, who speaks every line as though she's reading it for the first time (and with the reading skills of a slow kindergartner), has been shunted aside by Stone, and doesn't take it well. When we hear a reprise of Amanda's theme song, we know something tragic is about to happen. Sure enough, Amanda swallows enough sleeping pills to kill all three stars of *Dolls*, and is found "too late" by fey photographer David Hemmings.

The loss of Amanda devastates Stone—so much that he goes to Times Square and hires an eight-foot-tall hooker, who he beats the bejesus out of for calling him "a faggot." As an alibi in case the whore (billed in the end credits as "Amazon Woman") dies, Robin asks Hemmings to say they were together "all evening, sharing drinks." For this favor, Robin's fey "friend" gets to buy himself a slave bracelet and have it inscribed as being from Stone. Will that bracelet become a plot device by film's end? Could be . . .

When Ryan and Cannon return from "recuperating" in Europe, Robin makes the classic mistake of ignoring Dyan's insistent requests that they "get together." So Dyan does the sensible thing: Using her key to sneak into Stone's apartment and catching him in the shower with two *other* sleazy sleep-abouts, she sets Stone's bed afire with vodka and a book of matches.

Having established that fire safety is not her forte, Cannon is ready to show Law how flaming her rage can be. Suddenly she's bad-mouthing him to her hubby, setting up a battle royal that can only end with one of them being ousted, while drawing the line at believing accusations that her lover is "AC/DC." "Since when is it against the rules," she asks Ryan in one of the film's most memorably clueless lines, "to buy a show from a fag?" Cannon then winds up at a Hollywood party with Law, Hemmings, and "a well-known British actor" we know is gay, because he wears pink shirts and purple ascots. When Cannon finds that slave bracelet (see how neatly everything ties together?) the festivities degenerate into a free-for-all in which Hemmings slaps Cannon, she retaliates by bopping him on the head with the actor's imitation Oscar, and the resulting scandal leaves Stone wandering the streets of Beverly Hills alone, as his theme song is reprised on the soundtrack and the end titles come up.

What life lessons do we learn from *The Love Machine*? That everyone involved in TV is sleazy, easy, and dresses very cheesy. That using people to get ahead, while it may be a great device for writing a trashy novel, *isn't* an acceptable lifestyle. And that if you're a character created by Susann, even if you *do* have your own personal theme song cued to swell up on the soundtrack at every life crisis, the chances you'll survive are still only 50/50 . . .

Dippy Dialogue
IBC publicist Ethel Evans *(Maureen Arthur)* defending her "honor":
"When I ball a guy, it's cause I dig him . . ."

Fun Footnote
Susann apparently had a clause whenever she sold a book to be made into a film, requiring her to be given a cameo role. In *Love Machine*, she's one of the TV anchors reporting Amanda's tragic end, reading a line that could easily have applied to herself: "Without a message or a clue, she stepped out of life . . ."

Valentino

(1977/United Artists)   **VHS**

Who's to Blame   CAST: **Rudolf Nureyev** *(Rudolph Valentino);* **Leslie Caron** *(Alla Nazimova);* **Michelle Phillips** *(Natasha Rambova);* **Felicity Kendal** *(June Mathis);* **June Bolton** *(Bianca de Saulles);* **Huntz Hall** *(Jesse Lasky);* **Carol Kane** *(Fatty Arbuckle's Girlfriend)*
CREW: **Directed by Ken Russell; Written by Russell and Mardik Martin; Based on the book** *An Intimate Exposé of the Sheik* **by Brad Steiger and Chaw Mank**

Rave Reviews
"Ken Russell's *Valentino* is so embarrassingly and extensively bad that it achieves a kind of excruciating consistency with the rest of his career." — ***Village Voice***

"Failed folly . . . diversity run amok . . . superficial and silly."
— Charles Champlin, *Los Angeles Times*

"Camp at its best." — **Brant Mewborn,** *After Dark* **magazine**

Plot, What Plot? Ken Russell is one director who can always be counted on to go "over the top." Whether it's full-frontal male-on-male nude wrestling in *Women in Love*, or nuns participating in S&M orgies in *The Devils*, Russell seems to look at every filmmaking venture as a chance to share more of his twisted personal perspective than most of us really want to know. And *Valentino*, Russell's 1977 rumination on the life and career of silent film legend Rudolph Valentino, is perhaps the most moist of Bad Kenny's many wallows in the land of wet dreams.

Valentino's sole nod to commercialism is the casting of former Kirov Ballet primo ballerino Rudolf Nureyev in the film's title role. It is at once a bold and bald-facedly misguided gimmick. Although both Rudys *were* famous dancers, Nureyev not only looks nothing like Latin lover Valentino, but when the modern Rudy attempts to wrap his often unintelligible Russian accent around the Italian-American cadences of the 1920s Rudy, we defy anyone to understand a single word he's saying!

The other major problem with *Valentino* is that it plays so fast and loose with facts that it's surprising Russell wasn't sued for libel. The whole thing opens with a main title sequence depicting the real-life rioting-in-the-streets reaction to Rudy's death in 1926, played out under one of the biggest song hits of 1926, "There's a New Star in Heaven Tonight," a ballad bemoaning Valentino's death. The complete lack of subtlety established in these first five minutes will, in the course of the film, be topped again and again . . . and yet again.

In its one and only similarity to *Citizen Kane*, *Valentino* is told almost entirely in flashback, as various acquaintances of Rudy's make more and more outrageous entrances into the funeral home where Valentino's rouged corpse lies in state. Each mourner is accosted by paparazzi who make the reporters in Fellini's *La Dolce Vita* seem low-key, and is then prompted to share memories of the Great Lover. Several people's actual names are used, yet almost nothing that takes place in this film bears even a passing resemblance to either truth . . . or reality as most of us mere mortals know it.

First to arrive for the funeral is June Bolton as Bianca de Saulles, a fictional character, and a wealthy patron of taxi dancer Rudy. Even though Bolton's entire performance is dubbed, when she and Nureyev converse, you'll wish the video were closed captioned, just so you could follow what on earth they're saying. De Saulles supposedly has a torrid affair with Rudy. Tepid is more like it, but eventually, Bianca blows away her rich husband, and Rudy blows town to head for Hollywood.

The next funeral attendee is screenwriter June Mathis, who (according to Russell) "discovered" Rudy while he was dancing a tango at a party for Fatty Arbuckle, then launched him to "instant stardom" in *The Four Horsemen of the Apocalypse*. Dramatically filling her hankie with snot and tears, Mathis has the film's most apropos line: "Every day is Halloween in Tinseltown!"

Next, as if to prove Mathis's point, Leslie Caron shows up as Alla Nazimova, a flamboyant "artiste" who costarred with Valentino in *Camille*. Outrageous makeup, music, costuming, and coiffure combine for Caron's "grand entrance," one of the film's high points of campiness. Caron then swoons beside the bier for photographers, and proceeds to recall her role in Rudy's sad but cataclysmically colorful life: It was she who introduced the soon-to-be-Sheik to his second wife, Natasha Rambova.

At this point, you're convinced that no one could possibly top the low bar for bad acting already set by this film. But Rambova is played by Michelle Phillips, formerly lead singer for the Mamas and the Papas, who gives splinter-inducing new meaning to the term "wooden." She has nearly as much dubbed dialogue as Bolton does, but in her case, it's not the accent that's the problem—it's her utter lack of acting chops. In fact, Phillips's atonal, nasal delivery of line after line is so atrocious that even when she appears nude in a restaging of the famous "rape" scene from *The Sheik*, you pay more attention to her asinine acting than to her bare assets.

Soon Natasha has Rudy wearing a "slave bracelet," playing French fops onscreen and joining him in consulting a collection of mystical bones she calls "Meselope," which she's constantly tossing on the ground to determine their life choices. In the film's choicest example of dramatics so over-the-top they're painfully funny, Nureyev and Phillips throw Meselope's bones on their living room floor, then Rudy jumps Michelle's bones as a throng of fans on their front lawn orgiastically recite a love poem written by the real Valentino. Her face distorted through a crystal ball, Phillips rants and raves as Nureyev flops atop her, intercut with zoom-in close-ups of the fan club's dowdy leader, ever more loudly shrieking the single word "YOU!" We guarantee, once you've seen this scene, YOU will never forget it.

As Rudy's career progresses, and Russell digresses into more and more fantastical fever-dreaming about Valentino, we are endlessly reminded of the sex symbol's secret desire: to use his agricultural degree from Italy to start his own orange grove and live the simple life of a farmer. After an implied jailhouse rape, a faux lesbian wedding tableau featuring Caron and Phillips at the funeral home, and a boxing match as bogus as that in any *Rocky* sequel, Rudy's life ends as he falls to the floor, reaching for an elusive orange, just out of his reach. And you'll find yourself reaching for new sub-parlatives if you can get your hands on this superlative example of how Hollywood loves to devour its own idols.

Dippy Dialogue
Billy Streeter *(Linda Thorson)*, **describing Valentino's tango with Nijinsky:** "Talk about the dance of the sugar-plum fairy!"

Fun Footnote
If Nureyev and Phillips's "romantic vibes" in this film seem nonexistent, it may be because off camera they loathed one another, so much that at one point they engaged in an on-set slapping match.

Valley of the Dolls

(1967/20th Century-Fox) **VHS**

Who's to Blame   **CAST: Patty Duke** *(Neely O'Hara);* **Barbara Parkins** *(Anne Welles);* **Sharon Tate** *(Jennifer North);* **Susan Hayward** *(Helen Lawson);* **Paul Burke** *(Lyon);* **Tony Scotti** *(Tony Polar);* **Martin Milner** *(Mel);* **Joey Bishop** *(Telethon MC);* **George Jessel** *(Grammy Awards MC)*

CREW: Directed by Mark Robson; Screenplay by Helen Deutsch and Dorothy Kingsley; Based on the novel by Jacqueline Susann

Rave Reviews
"The definitive camp classic. . . . *Valley of the Dolls* is a great movie in the very same way that *Showgirls* is a great movie. Rent it and howl!"
— Stephen M. Moser, *Austin Chronicle*

"One of the most stupefyingly clumsy films ever made by alleged professionals." — Joe Morgenstern, *Newsweek*

"Pure trash, based on a trashy book, filled to the brim with trashy performances." — *TV Guide's Movie Guide*

Plot, What Plot? At one time, Jacqueline Susann's novel *Valley of the Dolls* was one of the best-selling books ever published, second in sales only to the Bible. So naturally, Hollywood *had* to make a movie of it. But in still staid 1967, how on earth could this novel be made into a movie? By hiring the Oscar-nominated director of the similarly trashy *Peyton Place* to supervise it, hiring two Oscar-nominated screenwriters to adapt Susann's novel to the screen, and casting "respectable" actresses as the three leading female characters.

    And by the time they were finished, the brainiacs at 20th Century-Fox had taken a sleazy, crowd-pleasing novel and turned it into . . . a sleazy, crowd-pleasing modern classic of camp. Although crowds flocked to it, making it Fox's biggest moneymaker in years, the years since *Dolls* was released have not been kind to it. Its reputation as one of Tinseltown's tackiest titter-fests has grown steadily over the last three decades, and now no Best of the Worst list is considered complete without including it.

The storyline follows three innocent young girls who must find their way through a maze of booze, sex, and dope to achieve show-biz success. As Barbara Parkins, the "Nice Girl," puts it in opening voice-over narration, "You've got to climb Mount Everest to reach the Valley of the Dolls." Joining Parkins on this Cook's Tour through perseverance and perversion are Sharon Tate as Jennifer North, a sex symbol who doesn't survive, and Oscar winner Patty Duke as Neely O'Hara, a boozehound who technically survives till the end, but is ruined by her own ego.

Along the way, *Dolls* features some of the most incredibly inept dialogue, costuming, and musical numbers ever concocted for a big-budget film. Tate, speaking in a monotone on the telephone, gets to declare, "Mother, I know I don't have any talent, and I know all I have is a body, and I am doing my bust exercises!" Parkins, who inexplicably becomes a high-fashion model, gets featured in an almost surreally campy "fashion show" montage. And poor old Patty Duke is called upon to scream, rant, and rave, as well as sing (!) several of those liltingly lame ditties we mentioned. Her best moment, and perhaps the high point of the film, comes when Duke is locked away in a booby hatch and recognizes Tate's now vegetative husband. With just a song, she breaks through and "reaches" him as her fellow drooling, glassy-eyed inmates applaud wildly. But by far the funniest, frumpiest production number is Susan Hayward (with the voice of Margaret Whiting) performing "I'll Plant My Own Tree" on opening night of a big Broadway musical. "It's my yard, so I will try hard to welcome friends I have yet to know!" her raspy, barely in-sync baritone intones as she stumbles among flying colored panels, struggling with a dress and wig that make her look like a drag queen doing Susan Hayward. Naturally she too is rewarded by wildly ecstatic applause. In fact, anytime anyone in this film does anything, it's treated as earth-shattering in its greatness, even though anyone with taste would cringe at 97 percent of what goes on here.

A favorite of Bad Movie Cultists for years, *Valley of the Dolls* is one of those rare Hollywood success/fiascos that even its participants have eventually admitted stunk. Speaking of *Dolls*'s 1967 premiere aboard an ocean liner, Patty Duke recently told AMC that "there were only two problems. One, the ship's generator kept slowing down then speeding up the film. And, two . . . they showed the movie!"

Dippy Dialogue
Neely O'Hara *(Patty Duke)*: "Boobies, boobies, boobies! Nothin' but boobies. Who needs 'em?"

The Wild Wild World of Jayne Mansfield

(1968/Blue Ribbon Pictures) **DVD / VHS**

Who's to Blame   CAST: **Jayne Mansfield** *(as Herself and "Narrator")*; **Mickey Hargitay** *(as Himself)*; **Rocky Roberts and the Airdales** *(Themselves)*; **The Ladybirds** *(Topless Quintet/Themselves)*; **International Transvestite Contest Winners**
CREW: **Directed by Arthur Knight, Joel Holt, and Charles W. Broun Jr.; Script by Charles Ross**

Rave Reviews

"A grotesquely enjoyable turn through the pulp-cinema wringer."
— **Nick Rutigliano,** *Village Voice*

"Tacky exploitation flick combining footage shot during the actress's career with coy shots of 'shocking' material (stripteases, drag queens) and a mini-documentary about the car crash that ended her life." — **David Sterritt,** *Christian Science Monitor*

"Wonderfully trashy fun! Tasteless? You bet, but that's exploitation!"
— **Ken Fox,** *TV Guide's Movie Guide*

Plot, What Plot? As witnessed by this mondo-trashy docudrama, the exploitation of Jayne Mansfield didn't end with her death in a 1967 car crash. Begun in 1964, and apparently plagued by endless funding problems, this definitively tasteless tour of the world's top topless spots, "hosted" by Jayne (with voice-over provided posthumously by a breathy "soundalike"), was rushed into release in 1968 to capitalize on the notoriety of the dumb blonde's decapitation. Anyone doubting just *how* low Mansfield had sunk by the time of her demise need only view this film: After an hour of footage following the ultimate bimbo to every sleazy strip joint on earth, it ends with graphically grisly photos of the famous fatal car wreck (including images of the sex symbol's dead poodle Choo-Choo), then takes us on a tour of Jayne and Mickey Hargitay's Beverly Hills mansion, dubbed the "Pink Palace."

With three different directors listed in the main credits, it's hard to know who's to blame for what. But since onetime *Playboy* film critic Arthur Knight is also credited with directing 1961's *Around the World with Nothing On*, he seems the logical culprit for what has to be the most astoundingly asinine documentary ever assembled. Much of the film finds Jayne merely wandering through European capitals, shot "MOS" (Mit Out Sound), flouncing and bouncing her assets in the eyes of passersby. Jayne repeatedly oohs and aahs about the sights, blows kisses from various hilltops, or makes such earth-shattering observations as, "The Fountain of Trevi . . . the most famous fountain in Europe—in the world, even!"

Then, in each of the cities she "visits," Jayne goes out after dark looking for "where the action is." And boy, does she find it: everything from an Italian nudist colony to a Parisian gay bar, and from a New York transvestite competition to a Most Beautiful Breasts in the World contest, in which entrants show only their relevant assets peeking through a chest-high curtain. Throughout, the ersatz voice of Jayne continues to share her "thoughts," such as they are. Referring to the guys-dressed-as-gals competitors at the transvestite contest, "Jayne" declares, "Gosh! I'd seen some strange things in Europe, but this took all the cakes *ever* made! . . . Sure is a mixed-up world!"

As the film progresses, you begin to notice how little actual footage of Mansfield the filmmakers had to work with. Certain shots (especially audience cutaways of Jayne watching various sex shows with Choo-Choo in her lap) are repeated several times. Not even Ed Wood's three shots of Bela Lugosi for *Plan 9* were that overused. You also begin to suspect at least a modicum of satirical intent—surely *someone* realized that having comments like, "That dog was eyeing my Choo-Choo!" would elicit derisive laughter. But the whole thing seems to be aiming for a tone more risqué than risible. And since it was shot almost forty years ago, the risqué element has now careened overboard into campiness, while the risibility quotient has gone off the scale.

If you've any doubt whether the filmmakers made *Wild World* with a straight face, you need only hear the male narrator's final comment: "Jayne's IQ was . . . among the top 5 percent in the country . . . yet she chose show business as a career instead of her original goal to be a scientist!" We dare you, after seeing all that's preceded it, to hear that line and *not* fall off your couch laughing!

Dippy Dialogue
"Jayne" *(Fake Narrator)*: "After all, there are only two sexes . . . well, more or less!"

Choice Chapter Stop
Chapter 22 ("The House That Love Built"): A tour of Jayne and Mickey's "Pink Palace" in Hollywood, turned into a combo museum/mausoleum after her death.

The Astounding She-Monster

(1958/Hollywood International Pictures)   **DVD / VHS**

Who's to Blame   CAST: **Robert Clark** *(Dick Cutler)*; **Kenne Duncan** *(Nat Burdell)*; **Marilyn Harvey** *(Margaret Chaffey)*; **Shirley Kilpatrick** *(The She-Monster)*; **Scott Douglas** *(The Narrator)*
CREW: **Directed by Ronnie Ashcroft; Screenplay by Frank Hall**

Rave Reviews
"Awesomely cheap little film . . . has developed a kind of perverse fan following." — *Leonard Maltin's Movie & Video Guide*

"How can you not love a movie with a title like this. . . . For connoisseurs of truly bad movies!" — *VideoHound's Golden Movie Retriever*

"One of the Grade Z sci-fi classics of the 1950s, right up there with . . . the works of Ed Wood, Junior" — **Richard Scheib, Science Fiction, Horror and Fantasy Film Review (Web site)**

Plot, What Plot? From its beginning narration, spoken stentorially over a globe spinning on a wire, you suspect that Ed Wood *must* have had some connection to *The Astounding She-Monster*, and in a sense you'd be right. Director Ronnie Ashcroft was once Wood's assistant, and it's obvious that he learned a penny-pinching lesson or two from the master.

Like Wood, Ashcroft is a big fan of hokey voice-overs, since they let you shoot on location without sound, letting the disembodied voice explain things your shooting script is too poorly written to convey. Like Ed Junior, Ashcroft knows the cheapest optical houses in Hollywood, who can make a "special effect" look special for about five bucks a pop: Whenever we see the She-Monster, she is supposed to be glowing and rippling before our eyes, giving off radiation of some kind. But the optical Ashcroft opted for instead makes it look like we're seeing the creature through a dirty aquarium. And, like the man who planned *Plan 9*, Ronnie knows how to get his money's worth: There's one shot of the glowing She-Creature walking down a dirt road that

Ashcroft uses (sometimes running it backwards to throw us off) a dozen times or more. And, like Wood, Ashcroft can't create a convincing character, situation, or setting to save his life.

Astounding She-Monster features other Wood-ian touches like "day for night" shooting that looks like it was done at straight-up noon, costumes and makeup worthy of women wrestlers and Hollywood hookers, and a premise that's so clichéd it's a wonder Ashcroft could get anyone to put up the 23,000 bucks it looks like this film cost to make.

Our principal earthling characters are a gang of hoods who kidnap an heiress in broad daylight, then blow out their getaway car's tire on a mountain road. The only cabin they can find to hole up in belongs to a hermit geologist, who's fixated on a meteor he saw crash nearby. Naturally, the geologist takes a liking to the heiress, and of course the "meteor" turns out to be a spaceship that has sent the She-Monster to Earth. Everything she touches dies immediately from radium poisoning: a collie, a big black bear, and, when she touches his tush, the gang's leader.

Only the geologist and the heiress survive, and they devise a plan to do in this strange creature. It's only when they've destroyed her that they find a note (conveniently written in English) explaining that she was sent to Earth by an intergalactic Council of Planets on a goodwill mission. After reading the note, the geologist wonders, "You think they might send another emissary? But would it come to bring us goodwill . . . or simply to . . . avenge her death?" As the camera pans to a window with a painted panorama of the night sky, a loud music sting hits and the words "The End" zoom up.

Blatantly cheap, ineptly paced, and "Woodenly" acted, *The Astounding She-Monster* is one No-Budget Wonder that truly *is* astounding . . . but *not* in any way that reflects favorably on anyone involved in it.

Dippy Dialogue
Narrator *(Scott Douglas)*: "Being kidnapped could be termed almost normal for a wealthy socialite—and you *are* being kidnapped. In fact, you're *all* being taken to a rendezvous . . . with fate."

Choice Chapter Stop
Chapter 10 ("Monster vs. Monster"): Does a bear take on a She-Creature in the woods?

(1968/Paramount Pictures)   **DVD / VHS**

Who's to Blame   CAST: **Jane Fonda** *(Barbarella)*; **John Phillip Law** *(Pygar, the Blind Angel)*; **Marcel Marceau** *(Professor Ping)*; **Milo O'Shea** *(Duran Duran)*; **David Hemmings** *(Dildano)*; **Ugo Tognazzi** *(Mark Hand)*; **Claude Dauphin** *(President of Earth)*
CREW: **Directed by Roger Vadim; Screenplay by Terry Southern and Roger Vadim, in collaboration with Claude Brule, Vittorio Bonicelli, Clement Biddle Wood, Brian Degas, Tudor Gates, and Jeane Claude Forest. Based on the "adult comic strip" by Forest**

Rave Reviews
"So ludicrous it really is brilliant . . . anyone can make a bad movie: A flick this sincerely bad, though, requires genius." — **Ernest Hardy, *L.A. Weekly***

"A whacked-out romp in the 41st century, an acid-trip light show. . . . Ultra groovy!" — ***American Cinematheque* magazine**

"The highest high camp has ever been . . . seems to have been co-authored by Jules Verne and the Marquis de Sade . . . *2002: A Space Idiocy*." — **Charles Champlin, *Los Angeles Times***

Plot, What Plot? In the Swingin' '60s it was not uncommon for movies to be made for the express purpose of being watched by audiences stoned off their gourds. One of the better-known examples of this genre stars Jane Fonda in her then husband's supreme achievement in softcore sci-fi silliness. It is clear from the moment Roger Vadim's *Barbarella* begins, with Fonda floating in midair doing a slo-mo striptease in a space suit, that this film has no intention of being taken seriously. But the level of goofiness *Barbarella* achieves is nevertheless amazing: The spaceship in which Fonda gets nekkid during the main titles is entirely lined in late-'60s Day-Glo orange shag carpet; the computer that plots

Barbarella's course to Delphi Ceti speaks with a mincing lisp; and every one of Jane's dozens of exotic/erotic costumes looks like it resulted from a collaboration between Bob Mackie and Hugh Hefner.

Sent from Earth in the year 40,000, Jane is assigned to rescue a missing soldier named Duran Duran. But Fonda instead crash-lands on the ice planet Lythion (which looks suspiciously like the dry-ice-and-fog-infested soundstage where Sonja Henie once skated to screen fame). She is greeted by small children with slightly askew ratty wigs plopped on their heads, speaking angry-sounding gibberish. These Children of the Darned attempt to dispatch our heroine using steel-toothed killer dolls. And just when you're thinking, "What the?!?!" the first of Barbarella's rescuers comes to her aid: a horribly dubbed Ugo Tognazzi, who asks in return for saving Jane's life that they "make love the old-fashioned way." If you're not following this so far, you must not have toked deeply enough before the film started.

Encased in excessive '60s facial makeup that almost prevents her from expressing any emotion, Fonda is quintessentially vacuous throughout as she traipses through a series of intergalactic escapades. They include flying in the arms of blind angel John Phillip Law, sharing hand-to-hand sex "the modern way" with a codpiece-clad David Hemmings, and trying to deflect the advances of both the aggressively amorous Black Queen and the missing mad genius Duran Duran, whose orgasmic Music Machine is one of the film's hootiest highlights.

A piece of intentional over-the-top campiness that has aged so poorly it perhaps belongs in a time capsule, *Barbarella* has been a source of amusement to lovers of bad movies for over thirty-five years—and a continuous source of embarrassment to Jane Fonda, whose serious Women's Lib attitudes later in life were clearly undermined by this bare-bosomed performance. Asked years later "where her head was at" when she made this, Jane replied, "I don't know—up my armpit, I guess!" An armpit liberally sprinkled, it appears, with a potent mix of psychedelic '60s drugs.

Dippy Dialogue
Pygar *(John Phillip Law)*: "An angel doesn't *make* love ... an angel *is* love ... "
Black Queen *(Anita Pallenberg)*: "Then you're a dead duck!"

Choice Chapter Stop
Chapter 16 ("Dr. Duran's Music Machine"): A nude Fonda is "orchestrated" to a musical "climax" by Duran Duran.

The Creeping Terror

(1964/Metropolitan International Pictures)   **DVD / VHS**

Who's to Blame   CAST: **Vic Savage** *(a.k.a. Director Argyle Nelson) (Martin Gordon)*; **Shannon O'Neil** *(Brett Gordon)*; **William Thourlby** *(Dr. Bradford)*; **John Caresio** *(Colonel Caldwell)*; **Larry Burrell** *(Narrator)*
CREW: **Produced, edited, and directed by A. J. Nelson; Written by Arthur Ross and Robert Silliphant (No screenplay credited in main titles!)**

Rave Reviews
"Lame. . . . Undoubtedly one of the top five worst movies of all time."
— **Michael Weldon,** *The Psychotronic Encyclopedia of Film*

"Lots of bad acting, a worse script, laughable sets and a ridiculous monster." — *VideoHound's Golden Movie Retriever*

"Reputedly the worst film of all time . . . an example of superior ineptitude." — **John Stanley,** *Creature Features Movie Guide Strikes Again*

Plot, What Plot? This is the legendary low-budget feature to which the production crew "misplaced" the entire audio track, couldn't afford to replace it, and so resorted to the kind of hokey voice-over narration in which Ed Wood's films specialized. Add to that the fact that in postproduction the filmmakers inserted random, often badly out-of-sync dubbed "dialogue" and phony, prefab sound effects, then slathered the whole thing with a $1.98 music score, and you have the makings of a Classic of Ineptitude.

When you first glimpse the "monster from space" that is the film's main source of "terror," you're in for a unique bad-movie-watching treat. Moving like Ethel Merman with her girdle down around her ankles, and apparently made from carpet remnants cadged from a Dumpster, the film's monster seems to be an ambulatory cow pie with a giant pinecone for a head. Stumbling through forests and fields at the pace of a snail on Sudafed, this "beast from another planet" requires its victims to literally feed themselves into its maw, their flailing feet the last thing the creature "swallows."

After our Big Bad Beastie lumbers away from camera the first time, we discover that it has a soul mate still strapped in the spaceship from which it came. Soldiers, scientists, and the local sheriff all climb into the ship to get a gander at this ghastly creature, which consists of squirming vacuum cleaner hoses and a body that resembles a wad of ABC (already been chewed) chewing gum. In a totally *un*-special "special effect," everyone who sees this monster is shown with a flashlight held below camera and "eerily" turned on and off.

The horror mounts as the escaped beast heads first for Lover's Lane (where it overturns a hot rod and sucks its occupants from the car), then to a nearby "hootenanny," and finally to that popular teen hangout, the local "dance hall." Several minutes of footage is shown of town teens "twisting" up a storm, some of them writhing in ways that telegraph the "terrors" to come. Since the creature moves so slowly, it *does* take several reels for it to reach the dance floor, but when it does, its people-eating movements are actually more in sync with the rock music than the dancers' ever were.

Having snacked on dozens of local denizens, the creature must somehow be stopped. What sophisticated weapon do the Earth folk use to dispatch this dust bunny from another world? A simple hand grenade, thrown into its mouth. Its evil twin is then destroyed using a 1956 Ford sedan—don't ask! And whatever you do, don't miss this world-class example of how *not* to strike terror into the hearts of movie audiences. Sure, you *will* be screaming, but it'll be with uncontrollable laughter.

Dippy Dialogue
Narrator *(Larry Burrell)*: "Life has its way of making boys grow up. And with marriage, Martin's time had come..."

Choice Chapter Stop
Chapter 8 ("At the Dance Hall"): The Carpet Creature cuts in on some twisting teens.

Devil Girl from Mars

(1954/British Lion Films) **DVD / VHS**

Who's to Blame   CAST: **Patricia Laffan** *(Nyah, the Devil Girl)*; **Hazel Court** *(Ellen Prestwick)*; **Hugh McDermott** *(Michael Carter)*; **Peter Reynolds** *(Robert/Albert)*; **Adrienne Corri** *(Doris)*; **Joseph Tomelty** *(Prof Hennessey)*
CREW: **Directed by David MacDonald; Screenplay by James Eastwood; From a play by John C. Mather**

Rave Reviews
"Hilariously solemn, high-camp British imitation of U.S. cheapies."
— ***Leonard Maltin's Movie & Video Guide***

"A delightfully bad movie that is based upon what must have been a gloriously bad stage play." — **Doug Pratt, DVDLaser.com**

"This primitive British effort at science fiction is quite enjoyably ludicrous." — ***Monthly Film Bulletin*** **(United Kingdom)**

Plot, What Plot? Leave it to the British, the only people even more sexually repressed than Americans, to make a movie about a creature from Mars seeking to mate with earthlings that's less sexy than a science lecture on the periodic table of elements. Throw in acting below the standards of rural community theatre, plus "Martian" props and costumes already outdated when they were created in 1954, and you have all the ingredients of *Devil Girl from Mars*, a rare English entry into the "They Came from Another Planet" genre of 1950s sci-fi.

Staged like a low-budget theatre production of the play on which it's based (you may find yourself looking for the stage manager lurking behind the window curtains), *Devil Girl* centers on Nyah, a creature from Mars who looks amazingly like a '50s version of a '60s go-go dancer, clad in black leather boots, a formfitting miniskirted outfit with a shiny monk-like skull cap, and a cape made of crinkly fabric that rustles as loudly as Jean Hagen's petticoats in *Singin' in the Rain*. Mars, intellectually superior though it may be, needs Earth males to breed with in order to propagate its species. About the time we begin to wonder why, unless they're seeking sexual partners with bad teeth and awful taste in clothes and food, Martians would pick an English country inn as the starting point of their invasion, Nyah explains that the gyro-whatzit on her spaceship fell off and they crash-landed. Since her ship looks like an oversized, motorized salad spinner, and her clothes are barely a decade ahead of 1954 Earth fashion, you may find yourself joining with the guests at the inn in questioning Martian peoples' avowed superiority. But Nyah soon puts those questions to rest by demonstrating her awesome robot "Chani," which looks like a 1937 Kelvinator refrigerator with mechanical cow legs whose "death ray" is capable of vaporizing tiny trees, toy trucks, and miniature barns.

Suitably terrified (and overacting their terror to the hilt) the earthlings struggle to figure out some way to overtake Nyah before she can get to London and pursue her evil plans. Meanwhile, the inn's barmaid is reunited with her escaped convict fiancé, and a newspaper reporter finds himself irresistibly drawn to a jaded fashion model who says she's twenty-six, but looks thirty-six. These backstories of love blooming in the face of oblivion provide some of the film's funniest dialogue moments, and the repeated "impassioned kisses" shared by these couples make Nyah's lack of emotion seem torrid by comparison. When Nyah makes the mistake of showing the Professor how her ship's "perpetual motion" mechanism works, a plan is hatched: One of the men will agree to join Nyah in the ship, and sacrifice his own life to save the future of Earth.

But which man? The innkeeper's horny old sot of a husband? The Professor (whom Nyah has already dismissed as "a puny specimen")? The blowhard reporter, who volunteers first? Or the escaped convict who has nothing to lose? If you've seen enough of these kinds of movies, you should be able to guess who goes off with Nyah in the Giant Motorized Salad Spinner at the end, and whether or not the plan succeeds. But it's the process of getting to that moment that makes the film so inadvertently enjoyable.

If only Image Entertainment had thought to have their DVD version of *Devil Girl from Mars* hosted by Dan Aykroyd as Leonard Pinth-Garnell of *Saturday Night Live*'s "Bad Playhouse," the experience could have been complete. *Devil Girl* is so stodgy, stagy, and sexless that it cries out for that one extra touch to elevate it from the amusingly bad to the astoundingly awful.

Dippy Dialogue
Nyah *(Patricia Laffan)*, dismissing Earth weaponry like one of the aliens in *Plan 9*: "You poor, demented humans—to imagine you can destroy me with your old-fashioned toy!"

Choice Chapter Stop
Chapter 7 ("Robot of Death"): In which nattily clad Nyah demonstrates her people's "superior intelligence" by showing off that "terrifying" robot.

The Green Slime

(1969/Toei/MGM) **VHS**

Who's to Blame   CAST: **Robert Horton** *(Jack Rankin)*; **Luciana Paluzzi** *(Lisa Benson)*; **Richard Jaeckel** *(Vince Elliott)*; **Bud Widom** *(Thompson)*; **Robert Dunham** *(Captain Martin)*
CREW: **Directed by Kinji Fukasaku; Screenplay by Charles Sinclair, William Finger, and Tom Rowe; Based on a story by Ivan Reiner**

Rave Reviews
"The most laughably unconvincing monsters of any Japanese production in years."
— **Michael Weldon,** *The Psychotronic Encyclopedia of Film*

"Some of the worst American actors meet some of the worst Japanese special effects in this multinational fiasco."
— **Harry and Michael Medved,** *Son of Golden Turkey Awards*

"One of the funniest made-in-Japan Sci Fi monster movies ever."
— *Los Angeles Times*

Plot, What Plot? Some bad movies are *so* amusingly bad, they're still memorable thirty-five years later—even if you were bombed off your butt when you first saw them. *Green Slime*, with its ridiculous dubbing, ludicrous creatures, and curvaceous female lead Luciana Paluzzi, is one of those films.

It opens with a classically schlocky rock 'n' roll theme song, with lyrics like, "Is this just something in your head? Will you believe it when you're dead? Green Slime!" Our plot is then set in motion when scientists on Space Station Gamma 3 (which looks a lot like those balloon animals hired clowns whip up at kids' birthday parties) find out that a giant asteroid (a megaton orange crumb donut floating through space) is on a collision course with Earth, and will impact in a matter of hours. With no time to lose (and no budget either) they call in retired astronaut and Clutch Cargo lookalike Jack Rankin to blow the

THEY CAME FROM PLANET RAZZIE

bugger up. His hair dyed a bright, phony-looking orange, his face pulled back into a permanently sardonic expression, and his stony features rarely moved by any emotion, Rankin is played by *Wagon Train* veteran Robert Horton.

Drat the luck, both Rankin's ex-fiancée and her current beau are working on Gamma 3, so things could get tricky. But first things first—Rankin and a small crew land a rocket ship on the asteroid and implant detonators into it. While there, one of them collects a sample of something that looks like your aunt Helen's green Jell-O-and-fruit salad, except that it pulsates and is capable of oozing upward. Rankin tosses the jar of Jell-O from Jupiter against a rock. It shatters, and a loogie-like clump of green goo sticks to one of the astronaut's pant legs.

The crew achieve their mission and save Earth by blowing it out their asteroid, and back on Gamma 3 champagne corks pop, '60s Day-Glo miniskirts dominate the dance floor, and Rankin and the new beau, played by the even-stonier-faced Richard Jaeckel, exchange loaded glances as each boogies with Paluzzi. Suddenly a scream is heard over the PA, the lights go out—and the party's over. What started off as a loogie on someone's leg has now grown to the size of an eight-year-old dressed in a giant pickle suit, complete with tentacles and a glowing red eye—in its mouth.

One of the scientists figures out that these "creatures" thrive on energy, grow at an alarming rate (duh!), and that even one drop of their green blood can grow into a complete new "creature." In other words, everybody on Gamma 3 is doomed. Panic sets in, and soldiers with only motorcycle helmets for protective gear start whizzing all over the space station on miniature Zamboni machines, looking for new "creatures" in every nook and cranny. As the head of the station's infirmary, Paluzzi is entrusted with diagnosing and caring for the wounded. Her expertise is brought to bear when, taking the pulse of an obviously deep-fried victim of El Green-O, she concludes: "He's . . . dead!"

Eventually it becomes clear that the only way to completely destroy the Slime is to completely destroy the entire space station. Naturally, both Jaeckel and Horton volunteer to be the last one off after the crew has been evacuated. And of course, Luciana faces a choice as to which of them she hopes survives. We won't give away the ending, but here's a hint: Paluzzi's puppies will definitely have phony-looking red hair.

Hailed in 1969 as a camp classic, *Green Slime* is today a time-capsule piece, reminding us of an era when a gimmick as simple as running newspaper ads using green ink could draw crowds to theatres. In fact, *Slime* was so successful on the drive-in circuit that it became a reissue staple as filler on double bills for many years after its original release.

Dippy Dialogue
Captain Martin *(Robert Dunham)*: "Space Center reports our power output has dropped so low, they can't activate guidance by remote control!"
Lisa Benson *(Luciana Paluzzi)*: "What does that mean??"

Fun Footnote
Literally translated, this film's original Japanese title means, "After the Destruction of Space Station Gamma: Big Military Operation."

Mac and Me

(1988/Orion Pictures) **VHS**

Who's to Blame CAST: **Christine Ebersole** *(Janet)*; **Jade Calegory** *(Eric)*; **Jonathan Ward** *(Michael)*; **Lauren Stanley** *(Debbie)*; **Katrina Caspary** *(Courtney)*; **Ronald McDonald** 🍔 *(As Himself)*
CREW: **Directed by Stewart Raffill** 🍔 ; **Screenplay** 🍔 **by Raffill and Steve Feke**

Rave Reviews
"It is incredibly stupid, exists only for the product placement it utilizes, and . . . is more unintentionally hilarious than any other kiddie movie I have ever seen." — **Jason Coffman, BadMovieNight.com**

"I'm not sure I've ever seen a movie that is as crass a 90-minute commercial as *Mac and Me* . . . perhaps the most blatant *E.T.* ripoff ever."
— **Chris Hicks,** *Deseret News* **(Salt Lake City)**

"Forget about calling home; E.T., call lawyer."
— **Richard Harrington,** *Washington Post*

Plot, What Plot? Product placement, the practice of plugging a product by placing it onscreen, may have first reared its ugly head some ninety years ago, when the Keystone Kops cavorted across the screen in a Tin Lizzie with the Ford logo clearly visible on its radiator. But its head was never uglier—nor farther up its own rear—than in 1988 Worst Picture nominee *Mac and Me*.

The story of a young boy who befriends a small alien by luring it into his house with sweets, shares his secret with an older brother and a little girl, draws the ire of the Space Administration when they discover he's harboring the creature, then ends with a big police chase through a suburban community, *Mac and Me* goes beyond being a mere knockoff of *E.T.* In its slavish devotion to imitating almost every moment from the earlier film, *Mac and Me* achieves a degree of duplication that could have left it open to copyright infringement claims by both Spielberg *and* Xerox. The one "original" element in *Mac* is that the young boy is wheelchair-bound. The only reason the filmmakers don't show him gliding across the moon in his wheelchair is that their incredibly low budget wouldn't allow it.

Unlike *E.T.*, the space creatures here are wholly unbelievable. Their skin has the texture of those joke rubber chickens sold in novelty stores, their oversized eyes are glassy and expressionless, and their legs move like those wind-up toys that place one motorized foot in front of the other. In a couple of scenes where they are required to move quickly, it actually looks like the rubber alien suits were literally thrown across frame. We first see them on their native planet, where a gawky dad, a slender mom, a young daughter, and what appears to be a baby are all sucked into a space probe, which returns to Earth under the main titles. Once here, they escape and their baby winds up in the back of a family van on its way to the San Fernando Valley.

Where *E.T.* was charming in both its originality and its references to previous movies, *Mac and Me* hasn't a single frame with an ounce of charm in it. The wheelchair-bound boy is so grating that when he careens out of control and over a cliff into a lake—a moment meant to have great dramatic impact—you are torn between applauding or laughing at his predicament. And when, near the film's end, we are told that little Eric has died trying to rescue the alien family, we know perfectly well that by some bogus device, he will wind up resurrected.

But the most irksome element in *Mac and Me* is the incessant, insistent, and inexcusable product placement. The "sweets" used to lure the creature are cans of Coca-Cola, carefully placed in their holders' hands with the logo aimed at the camera whenever they're seen. The mom works at Sears, and on her first day at work the logo on the store is almost lovingly focused on. But the most shameless plug of all is for McDonald's. One of the characters works at a Mickey D's, another holds her birthday party there, and Ronald McDonald "himself" is prominently featured during the party scene. Even the creature's nickname, Mac, although explained as an acronym for "Mysterious Alien Creature," seems like a subliminal plug for Big Mac sandwiches.

All this greed and avarice aimed at impressionable child moviegoers proved to be an utter failure. Other than whatever notoriety it generated as a Worst Picture Razzie nominee, *Mac and Me* was barely noticed by the public, grossing a paltry $6.4 million compared to *E.T.*'s

$435 million. In fact, it bombed so badly that when it ends with a title promising "We'll Be Back!" you breathe a sigh of relief knowing no sequel was ever made. Just as most sequels can't achieve the quality of their predecessors, no sequel could ever be the incompetent equal of *Mac and Me*. So order in some Happy Meals, get a six-pack of Cokes, and check out *E.T.*'s ugly second cousin. And while you're watching, remember: Never let your hands get in the way of the logos on those Cokes and McDLTs . . .

Loopy Lyrics
From the sugar-coated end title song:
"Here in the heart, we're not two worlds apart,
the same dream we've both seen . . .
Reach for that star, no matter where you are,
it will be—just believe in you and me . . ."

Robot Monster

(1953/Astor Pictures) **DVD / VHS**

Who's to Blame **CAST:** **George Nader** *(Roy)*; **Claudia Barrett** *(Alice)*; **Selena Royle** *(Mother)*; **John Mylong** *(The Professor)*; **Gregory Moffett** *(Johnny)*; **George Barrows** *(Ro-Man and Great Guidance)*; **John Brown** *(Voice of Ro-Man)*
CREW: **Directed by Phil Tucker; Written by Wyott Ordung**

Rave Reviews
"One of the genuine legends of Hollywood: embarrassingly, hilariously awful!" — *Leonard Maltin's Movie & Video Guide*

"Belly laughs meet stark terror . . . movies don't come any better!"
— Charles Beesley, *The Psychotronic Encyclopedia of Film*

"[The creature] looks like a gorilla wearing a diving helmet. . . . When the critics reviewed this, the director had a nervous breakdown!"
— **Joe Bob Briggs,** *Joe Bob Goes to the Drive-In*

Plot, What Plot? Okay, when it comes to low-end moviemaking, there's small-budget . . . low-budget . . . and *no*-budget. A perfect example of how *not* to get around the problem of having no budget, *Robot Monster* purports to tell the tale of Earth's last days, when a creature from a distant planet has killed all but half a dozen earthlings. Looking worse than Earth's chances for survival, though, is this film's "creature from a distant planet." Basically yet another guy in a monkey suit, but this time with the added touch of a silver-spray-painted diving helmet, topped with a sagging TV antenna, Ro-Man is certainly a finalist in the Worst Movie Monster of All Time sweepstakes. Among this fearsome conqueror's weapons is an eternally running bubble machine (like on the old *Lawrence Welk Show*) whose stream of tiny bubbles continuously float toward the camera lens. And, oh yes, while here on Earth, Ro-Man often communicates (through what looks like a bedroom mirror covered with tinfoil) with Great Guidance, his superior on his home planet. When you first see Great Guidance, you'll think you're seeing double, until you realize GG is . . . the *same* actor in the same monkey suit and diving helmet as Ro-Man!

Among the half dozen surviving earthlings who represent Our Only Hope are B-movie beefcake staple George Nader as Roy, the burly boyfriend of Alice, played by Claudia Barrett in a bra and girdle that make her torso look like it could poke someone's eye out. Alice's parents, "Mother" and "The Professor," are sure there is some way to conquer Ro-Man and make the world safe again. Roy and Alice, when not hunting Ro-Man, are constantly doing all they can to help repopulate the planet, strenuously working on that project in canyons, behind bushes, and wherever they think they're out of sight of "Mother" and "The Professor."

Ordered by Great Guidance, through the wonders of the Bedroom-Mirror-Covered-With-Tinfoil Scope, to collect live human specimens for study, Ro-Man kidnaps Alice's little sister, then strangles her. This scene is witnessed by one of the most obnoxious child actors of all time, Gregory Moffett playing little Johnny. Undaunted by Ro-Man's clearly superior intellect, Johnny taunts the invader with the lamest put-down ever uttered onscreen: "You look like a pooped-out pinwheel!"

After killing the girl, Ro-Man decides that his next specimen should be buxom Alice, who resists him with the usual flailing feet and fisticuffs of B-movie Damsels in Distress, but winds up in his cave anyway. Just before Ro-Man "has his way" with Alice (but not till after he's pulled her blouse down) little Johnny distracts him with a toy ray gun, allowing "Mother" and "The Professor" to rescue Alice. Finally realizing that Ro-Man is the only creature in the universe more inept than *Robot Monster*'s creators, Great Guidance sends down a bolt of lightning from space, killing his protégé as his booming voice declares, "You wish to be a Hu-Man? Good, you can *die* a Hu-Man!" The picture flashes from positive to negative to positive (a 99-cent "special" effect) and the silver-spray-painted diving helmet then hits the dirt one final time. But Great Guidance has one last trick up the sleeve of his monkey suit—he unleashes his Cosmic Tube Ray, which begets prehistoric reptiles (actually claymation figurines) and earthquakes (seen in cheesy stock footage). Suddenly Nader returns carrying little Johnny, who declares in his best monotone, "Boy! Was that a dream, or what?" As the happily reunited family exits the screen to peppy,

1950s-sitcom-style music, the tone suddenly shifts ominously and, coming from the cave, heading right at the camera, we see ... Ro-Man. Not just once, not just twice ... but *three times* (!), and it's finally time for the audience to go home.

Told in an economical (but still poorly paced) 64 minutes, *Robot Monster* has long been a favorite of many Razzie members. One look at the cover of the video box and you'll know why ...

Dippy Dialogue
Ro-Man *(voice of John Brown)* debating with himself, and losing: "I cannot—yet I must. How do you calculate that? At what point on the graph do 'must' and 'cannot' meet? Yet I must—but I cannot!"

Choice Chapter Stop
Chapter 10 (*"Becoming Human"*): Great Guidance destroys Ro-Man with his stock footage lightning bolts.

Fun Footnote
Robot Monster was originally released in 3-D, which may explain all those bubbles constantly coming toward the camera.

Santa Claus Conquers the Martians

(1964/Embassy Pictures)   **DVD / VHS**

Who's to Blame   CAST: **John Call** *(Santa Claus)*; **Leonard Hicks** *(Kimar)*; **Vincent Beck** *(Voldar)*; **Bill McCutcheon** *(Dropo)*; **Victor Stiles** *(Billy)*; **Donna Conforti** *(Betty)*; **Chris Month** *(Bomar)*; **Pia Zadora** *(Girmar, a Martian Girl)*

CREW: **Directed by Nicholas Webster; Screenplay by Glenville Mareth; Based on a story by Paul L. Jacobson**

Rave Reviews
"The sets, props and acting are all bottom-of-the-budget-barrel. One of the worst movies of any kind ever made!"
— **Michael Weldon,** *The Psychotronic Encyclopedia of Film*

"The acting in this film has to be seen to be believed: it would embarrass even the players in a sixth-grade Christmas pageant." — **Harry Medved and Randy Dreyfuss,** *The Fifty Worst Films of All Time*

"Supplies humor not quite attuned to this planet."
— **Howard Thompson,** *New York Times*

Plot, What Plot? Long before she became our Razzie poster child in the 1980s, Pia Zadora was a child actress with varied stage and screen "credits" to her name, the best remembered of which is her appearance in the ultra-low-budget kiddie Christmas flick *Santa Claus Conquers the Martians*. Cast as a green-faced little Martian girl who convinces her father to kidnap Santa and bring him to the Red Planet, Pia proves her wooden acting style was set in cement by the time she was nine years old.

Produced on such a shoestring budget that Mars and the North Pole appear to be the same sets simply spray-painted different colors, *Martians* is a delight in ways its makers could never have imagined. Besides the cheap-jack sets, which have that space-age look of early-'60s "modernism," it features "Martians" whose faces are sometimes dark green, sometimes a greasy light green, and often not tinted at all. Its vision of Martian attire includes poorly fitting light green leotards, badly hand-sewn dark green capes and copper plumber's tubing, upside-down snorkeling masks, and deely-bopper antennae atop their heads.

Further contributing to the film's wildly funny woes is the fact that not one actor in it gives a credible performance. As Santa Claus, John Call consistently chortles and snorts instead of Ho! Ho! Ho-ing, tells truly atrocious jokes to cheer up the kids kidnapped along with him, and is generally as unpleasant a Kris Kringle as the kid-kicking Santa in *A Christmas Story*. Martian "leader" Kimar, played by Leonard Hicks, often appears embarrassed by his lines and his costumes. But most awful of all are the child "actors," a group of saccharine little zombies led by Zadora. Whether laughing heartily, cowering in fear, or defying their captors, Victor Stiles, Donna Conforti, Chris Month, and precious little Pia all sound like they're reading from Dick & Jane primers while overdosed on Prozac.

The storyline focuses on the need for "joy" in the lives of Mars's children, who watch Earth TV via satellite and are becoming, according to the only sane man on Mars, "nincompoops." Naturally, the lone speaker of truth in this logic-challenged melange of clichés and klutzy comic efforts is the villain. Once convinced by a Martian elder that what Mars needs is Santa Claus, they set out in a "spaceship" whose rocket tail flames look suspiciously like toilet tissue blowing in the wind to kidnap the Jolly Old Elf himself. Along with Saint Nick, they capture Billy and Betty as guides to the North Pole, then bring them to Mars to befriend Girmar and Bomar. All ends happily when Santa and the Earth kids are returned to our planet and lame-o laughing gas abuser Dropo is appointed Mars's new King of Christmas.

But don't turn off your video player yet, since after the end credits, you'll get a chance to read and sing along with the film's insistently insufferable theme song, "Hooray for Santa Claus!" With lyrics like, "He's fat and round but, jumpin' jiminy, he can climb down any chim-o-ney," it's a holiday classic of the fingernails-on-the-blackboard variety.

Produced for a minuscule $200,000 in a New York film studio, *Santa Claus Conquers the Martians* was admittedly aimed at children who might not realize just how awful it was. But any child over the age of five who doesn't spot its inherent tackiness should have his or her IQ tested immediately . . . or be punished with a lump of coal and a DVD of this film in their Christmas stocking.

Dippy Dialogue
Kimar *(Leonard Hicks)*: "Chochem is 800 years old—you can't dismiss the wisdom of centuries!"
Voldar *(Vincent Beck)*: "I can!!"

Choice Chapter Stop/Availability
As a "public domain" title, *Santa Claus Conquers the Martians* is available on DVD and VHS from various video companies, each with different chapter stops. Since it's barely 80 minutes long, we suggest you watch the entire thing.

Supergirl

(1984/TriStar Pictures)   **DVD / VHS**

Who's to Blame   CAST: **Helen Slater** *(Kara/Supergirl/Linda Lee)*; **Faye Dunaway** ☉ *(Selena)*; **Peter O'Toole** ☉ *(Zaltar)*; **Hart Bochner** *(Ethan)*; **Peter Cook** *(Nigel)*; **Mia Farrow** *(Alura)*; **Brenda Vaccaro** *(Bianca)*; **Simon Ward** *(Zor-El)*
   CREW: **Directed by Jeannot Szwarc; Screenplay by David Odell**

Rave Reviews
"A juvenile script anchored to questionable special effects... blockbuster-striving '80s film excess at its tackiest, although it works as Superkitsch." — **Kevin Phipps, TheOnionAVClub.com**

"Big-budget bomb in which Helen Slater made her debut and nearly killed her career, with the help of... a magic paperweight."
— *VideoHound's Golden Movie Retriever*

"Faye Dunaway in a nostril-flaring performance that suggests she was still possessed by the spirit of *Mommie Dearest*."
— **Michael Sauter**, *The Worst Movies of All Time*

Plot, What Plot? The Anchor Bay DVD of *Supergirl* proudly boasts on its cover that it's the "European" version of the film, containing some ten minutes of additional footage "not seen in the U.S." But in this case, more is simply... more. More of the hokum, more of the hammy overacting, and more of the horribly executed special effects that made *Supergirl* a box-office bomb both in America and abroad.

   The fourth entry in the *Superman* franchise, *Supergirl* was a desperate attempt to breathe new life into the series by branching out with the Man of Steel's female cousin as the protagonist. Although Helen Slater has a charming screen presence as Kara, a.k.a. Supergirl, a.k.a. Linda Lee, the screenwriter and director repeatedly put her into situations that are so poorly written and staged that one is left to wonder if they were meant to be funny, or just failed so miserably that they're laughable. At one point, when she falls asleep in the forest her first morning on Earth, Slater actually wakes up to a fluffy bunny nuzzling her cape, an apparent homage to Disney's *Snow White*. But we've just seen her threatened by two would-be rapists, so the innocent tone rings hollow.

Speaking of hollow, Dunaway's turn as Selena, the silliest of supervillains, is in the same vein—and delivered at the same volume—as Faye's famously over-the-top, Razzie-"winning" impersonation of Joan Crawford. Bedecked in garish flowing robes and a bright red fright wig that falls off her shoulders like it's trying to escape from her head, Dunaway is clearly overacting on purpose here. But putting an intentionally arch tone into lines like, "Such a pretty world. I can't wait until it's all mine," doesn't serve to make them any less lame, it only points up how hard up Faye must have been to accept this role.

Our story starts in Argo City, which looks like one of those all-pastel supermalls built in the 1970s. The first character we meet is Peter O'Toole as Zaltar. O'Toole is uninterested enough in giving an actual performance here that he reads each line with ever more bloviating bombast. Supposedly a brilliant scientist, he's dumb enough to let teenaged Kara "play" with two devices that bring about the destruction of Argo City. One of them is the film's "MacGuffin," the ridiculously named Omegahedron. A swirling, glowing, billiard-sized marble ball that is supposedly the source of Argo City's energy, it is also supposed to be a source of wonderment throughout the film. But it couldn't look phonier if the filmmakers had actually shown the wires we all know are running up the back of every actor's hand that handles it.

When Kara accidentally tears a hole in the protective outer shell of Argo City, we realize that someone must have thought they could keep all these hammy actors fresh by wrapping them in Saran—and the all-powerful Omegahedron is sent sailing through space. When it lands in sorceress Dunaway's cheese dip (!), she immediately realizes it's no ordinary glowing, spinning, billiard-sized marble ball, and begins plotting world domination. She starts out small, levitating irritating guests at a dinner party and lighting people's cigarettes with her fingernails. But when a love spell she casts to make a hunky gardener fall for her makes him fall for Supergirl instead, Selena will resort to anything, including threatening Earth's very existence, for revenge.

Besides its cartoonish characters and clunky visual effects, *Supergirl*'s biggest bad movie asset is an eclectic cast of arguably reputable actors, many in cameos less than two minutes long, all of whom give the impression they'd be more excited to participate in a high school cheerleaders' fund-raiser car wash than be seen in this film. Lending their names, but not their so-called talents, to this film are such diverse "actors" as Mia Farrow, Brenda Vaccaro, Hart Bochner, Simon Ward, and, saddest of all, the formerly funny Peter Cook as Dunaway's fussy sidekick.

A less than shining example of a movie franchise carried two sequels too far, *Supergirl* proved not to be the nadir of the *Superman* films. That would be Cannon Films's incredibly inept *Superman IV: The Quest for Peace*. But *Supergirl is* the funniest of the five Man of Steel movies—whether it's meant to be or not.

Dippy Dialogue
Kara *(Helen Slater)*, questioning Zaltar's escape plan: "The binary shoot? But you could never survive the pressure!"
Zaltar *(Peter O'Toole)*, overacting like mad: "That I can—ZIP! ZAP! And I'm GONE!!"

Choice Chapter Stop
Chapter 22 ("Final Confrontation"): Selena uses her feathered "Berendy Wand" (don't ask!) to conjure up a Giant Horned Possum from Hell.

Barb Wire

(1996/PolyGram Filmed Entertainment)   **DVD / VHS**

Who's to Blame   CAST: **Pamela Anderson** 👁 *(Barb Wire)*; **Temuera Morrison** *(Axel Hood)*; **Steve Railsback** *(Col. Pryzer)*; **Udo Kier** *(Curly)*; **Xander Berkeley** *(Alexander Willis)*; **Clint Howard** *(Schmitz)*
CREW: **Directed by David Hogan; Screenplay** 👁 **by Chuck Pfarrer and Ilene Chaiken; Story by Chaiken; Based on a comic strip by Chris Warner**

Rave Reviews
"Bad Movie manna for fans of deliriously cheesy sci-fi thrillers set in the near future." — **Edward Margulies,** *Movieline* **magazine**

"A trashy, violent action film that will appeal to comic readers, curiosity seekers and prison inmates throughout the land."
— **Janet Maslin,** *New York Times*

"There's a reason music videos don't last 99 minutes, and should *Barb Wire* cross your path, you'll know what it is."
— **Kenneth Turan,** *Los Angeles Times*

Plot, What Plot? If the plot of *Barb Wire* seems overly familiar, that's because it was lifted—one might even say "ripped off"—from, of all things, *Casablanca*. Imagine the pitch meeting where the screenwriters suggested remaking the Humphrey Bogart classic, and replacing Bogie . . . with the bodacious (but talent-challenged) Pamela Anderson. Then imagine that no one involved in the project intended it as a comedy. The resultant film is a truly oddball combination of one part noble sacrifice, one part splatter film, one part soft-core porn, and two oversized parts T&A. Note to the filmmakers: When a noble sacrifice is made by a star clad not in a trench coat and fedora, but in stiletto heels and a bosom-boosting bustier, it loses at least a skosh of its nobility.

Barb Wire, a.k.a. Pamela, is a take-no-guff kinda gal who runs a dive bar in post-Apocalypse 2017. Like Bogie in *Casablanca*, she has run-ins with local Nazi types, still pines for an ex-love she'd do anything for, and when the chips are down she can be counted on to be on the side of the underdog. What she doesn't have that Bogart did is the trench coat, a black piano player to tinkle "As Time Goes By," memories of Paris . . . or any discernible acting ability. What she *has* got that Bogart didn't are the assets nature (and a surgeon or two?) gave her. And since *Barb Wire* is blatantly an exploitation film, those assets are front-and-center throughout. In fact, the film opens on an extensive, slo-mo striptease with Anderson thrusting her bazooms at the camera in such a way that, if the film were in 3-D, audience members' eyes might get put out. Unfortunately for those drawn to this film by the chance to ogle Anderson's ta-tas, they're mostly contained for the rest of the film, though just barely. Halfway through she takes a bubble bath à la Jayne Mansfield, and in the big chase finale, her bustier threatens once again to unload its contents . . . but doesn't.

The object of the film's plot, other than Anderson's physical assets, is a pair of contact lenses that will permit anyone wearing them to exit the police state in which this film's characters all live—the 1990s equivalent of the exit letter Bergman sought from Bogart in *Casablanca*. Like Bogie, Pamela stands up to the "Nazis" who are after her old flame, and, like Rick, Barb makes the same sacrificial choice at the end. But in this ribald, risible, and decidedly Razz-able remake, the proverbial "hill of beans" is a *pair* of hills . . . and the film itself is full of beans.

Dippy Dialogue
Barb Wire *(Pamela Anderson)*, impaling a patron with her stiletto heel for calling her by the nickname she hates: "If one more person calls me 'Babe'!"

Razzie Credentials
Barb Wire was nominated for six 1996 awards, including Pamela's "Impressive Enhancements" as Worst Screen Couple. It was "shut out" by Demi Moore's similarly sleazy *Striptease*, and "won" only one award: Anderson as Worst New Star.

Choice Chapter Stop
Chapter 1 ("Opening Credits"): Pamela does the slo-mo, firehosed-down striptease that "establishes her character."

The Blue Lagoon

(1980/Columbia Pictures)　**DVD / VHS**

Who's to Blame　CAST:　**Brooke Shields** *(Emmeline)*; **Christopher Atkins** *(Richard)*; **Leo McKern** *(Paddy Button)*; **William Daniels** *(Arthur Lestrange)*; **Alan Hopgood** *(Captain)*
CREW: **Directed by Randal Kleiser; Screenplay by Douglas Day Stewart; Based on the novel by Henry De Vere Stacpoole**

Rave Reviews
"As hygienically sanitized as a Hilton Hotel toilet seat . . . makes Adam and Eve seem like hard porn." — ***Sunday Times* (London)**

"All we have to look forward to is: When will these two discover fornication. . . . It's Disney nature porn." — **Pauline Kael, *The New Yorker***

"An exploitation film whose core is so soft it's turned into an overripe mango. . . . Pornographicus interruptus." — **Jack Kroll, *Newsweek***

Plot, What Plot? In 1980, Brooke Shields was one of the highest-paid models in the world ("Nothing comes between me and my Calvins"), with a few low-budget film roles to her credit. All of that changed with her first successful starring role, as shipwrecked Emmeline, stranded on a desert island, forced to wear her hair glued strategically to her chest, and discovering the joys of sex with equally vapid costar Christopher Atkins in *The Blue Lagoon*. This film was so successful that its director, Randal Kleiser, essentially remade it as a ménage à trois a few years later, entitled *Summer Lovers*. *Lagoon* was also the first film ever to "win" Worst Actress, starting Shields off on her long and ill-lustrious career as a Razzie Repeat Offender.

Based on a 1903 novel by Henry De Vere Stacpoole, Douglas Day Stewart's screenplay pared away almost every distracting element of Stacpoole's *Gilligan*-like novel—things like character development, motivation, and plot—and honed in on the two shipwrecked children's idyllic, isolated existence, which could naturally lead to only one conclusion. Stunningly photographed, laconically paced, and laden with innuendo, *Blue Lagoon* is like a combined photo shoot for *Playboy* and *Playgirl*, shot on a gorgeous, clothing-optional desert island where the sun tans but never burns, ample food is found in every pond and on every tree, and worldly worries are left behind. Club Med . . . with sex ed.

Much was made at the time of the film's release about Shields's use of body doubles for all scenes involving nudity. Too bad she couldn't get an acting double for scenes involving emotions. Beautiful to look at, but hopeless as an actress, Shields is so incapable of expressing human feelings that one begins to wonder if sunstroke may be her problem. Her costar, clad in a gauze diaper, a seashell necklace, and nothing else, is her equal in the acting sweepstakes. But at least Atkins had the excuse that he was "discovered" for this film and had never appeared in front of a camera before. Since he followed this up with roles in *The Pirate Movie* and *A Night in Heaven*, it's a gift from the Bad Movie Gods that he passed the audition for this role.

If you were expecting a storyline here, you must be one of the few who didn't come seeking soft-core kiddie porn, since that is what this film boils down to. We follow the youngsters as they grow to "physical maturity," then are asked to wait patiently as they sunbathe, skinny-dip, build a bamboo condo, and otherwise frolic in their innocence, awaiting that moment when they finally figure out "the mysteries of life." It takes about half the film's 105-minute running time, and when it does arrive, the idiocy of *Blue Lagoon* shifts into overdrive.

The banality of the two young stars' performances is matched by the dialogue they're asked to speak. In one argument, Brooke accuses Chris of "always staring at my buppies," to which Atkins retorts that her "hoochy-coochies" always "jiggle"—and she bops him with a coconut in response. Clearly, these two are made for each other . . . and made to make beautiful babies. If the scene we just described strikes you as ludicrous, wait'll you see Shields squatting to give birth, grunting and screaming like a seriously constipated elephant, until the poorly dubbed sound effect of a baby's cry is heard on the sound-track. Now that they're parents, the two decide to sail off from their paradise and find a bigger condo on the mainland.

Juvenile, jugheaded, and jerky in the extreme, *Blue Lagoon* is both a bad movie wallow and a wet dream worthy of the most ardent child molester. Fortunately for anyone choosing to spend a chunk of eternity on that island with Shields and Atkins, it's also one of the funniest "romances" ever filmed.

And please, stop staring at my buppies!

Dippy Dialogue
Richard *(Christopher Atkins)*, after sucking on a juicy mango: "Kiss me . . ."
Emmeline *(Brooke Shields)*: "You're all . . . sticky . . ."
Richard: "So what—kiss me!"
(Emmeline smiles stupidly, and leans in for a lip-lock . . .)

Razzie Credential
In addition to "winning" our first ever Worst Actress award for Brooke Shields, *Blue Lagoon* was also cited when Brooke was nominated as Worst Actress of the Century at our 20th Annual Razzie Awards.

Choice Chapter Stop
Chapter 22 ("In Labor"): In which baby Brookie has a baby herself.

Duel in the Sun

(1946/Selznick International)   **DVD / VHS**

Who's to Blame   CAST: **Jennifer Jones** O *(Pearl Chavez)*; **Gregory Peck** *(Lewt McCanles)*; **Joseph Cotten** *(Jesse McCanles)*; **Lionel Barrymore** *(Sen. McCanles)*; **Lillian Gish** O *(Laura Belle McCanles)*; **Herbert Marshall** *(Scott Chavez)*; **Walter Huston** *("The Sin Killer")*; **Butterfly McQueen** *(Vashti)*
CREW: **Directed by King Vidor; Screenplay by Oliver H. P. Garrett and David O. Selznick; From the novel by Niven Busch**

Rave Reviews
"Hilariously florid . . . a sensual spectacle, so heightened it becomes a cartoon of passion." — **Pauline Kael,** *The New Yorker*

"Big, brawling, often stupid sex-Western with an unexpectedly bizarre finale." — ***Leonard Maltin's Movie & Video Guide***

"We who love bad movies positively worship David Selznick's over-produced, overwritten, overwrought *Duel in the Sun*."
   — **Edward Margulies and Stephen Rebello,** *Bad Movies We Love*

Plot, What Plot? Poor David O. Selznick—he had the misfortune of producing one of the biggest hit movies of all time, *Gone with the Wind*. He was a mere thirty-seven years old when *Wind* broke in theatres to record-breaking box office, then spent the next twenty-six years of his life feebly trying to top it. One of his most financially successful and entertainingly overripe post-*Wind* efforts was *Duel in the Sun*. The fact that it starred Selznick's then paramour Jennifer Jones only served to further cloud the great showman's vision.
   Stories about the erratic making of this supposedly erotic western are Hollywood folklore: No fewer than seven directors were said to have had a hand in it, among them Selznick himself. Lord only knows how many screenwriters were gone through looking for "just the right

tone," but Ben Hecht (*Notorious*) is rumored to be among the dozens who tried their hands at adapting Busch's novel for the screen. Stops, shutdowns, delays, and reshoots plagued the $6 million, two-year production, much as they would *Heaven's Gate* nearly four decades later. But when all was said and done, *Duel in the Sun* wound up the top moneymaking film of 1946, tying with that year's Best Picture Oscar winner *The Best Years of Our Lives*. It grossed a staggering $11.3 million, back when movie admission was 25 cents.

While millions flocked to see the film (some lured by the Catholic Legion of Decency's condemning its "overt sexuality"), critics had a field day poking fun at its lurid, ludicrous script and lascivious performances. It was quickly redubbed *Lust in the Dust* by wags, and that title has clung to it ever since.

Duel is basically the old two-guys-in-love-with-the-same-gal plot, the "gal" in this case being fiery-tempered "half-breed" Pearl Chavez, played with a bland-as-oatmeal, cotton-in-her-mouth corniness by Oscar winner Jones, who would inexplicably receive her fourth Best Actress nomination for this performance. Spray-painted brownish orange and bedecked in a long black wig, Jennifer plays this little "spitfire" with only a tad more sexuality than she brought to playing a saint in *The Song of Bernadette*. Watching the film, one has no idea why Selznick crashed his long-term marriage to Louis B. Mayer's daughter Irene to be with this woman. But it is clear, from how she's costumed, lit, and photographed, that the producer is besotted with his star.

Also besotted themselves over Jones are drawling Joseph Cotten as "the good brother" Jesse McCanles and Gregory Peck, in one of his few unsympathetic roles, playing "the bad brother," Lewt. And yes, the hokey character names *are* indicative of the tone of the film. Jesse and Lewt are "begat" of Senator McCanles (Lionel Barrymore in an even less subtle portrayal than he gave as Mr. Potter in *It's a Wonderful Life*). Their ever-patient, ever-suffering mother, Laura Belle, is played by silent film star Lillian Gish, who brings to the film its only smidgen of class, and was also Oscar-nominated for *Duel*.

Much hootin', hollerin', and how-de-doo, narrated by a so-super-serious-it's-silly Orson Welles, precedes the eventual meeting of the three principals. It's immediately clear that Jesse wants to turn Pearl into a lady, while Lewt just wants to lay her. And anyone who recognizes film clichés will know immediately which of the two brothers Pearl *should* choose . . . and which of them she *will* choose.

A range war, an attempt by preacher Walter Huston to "kill Pearl's sin," and other supposed highlights occur before the now famous denouement, in which Peck and Jones profess their unbridled love for one another while crawling up a mountainside and shooting each other to death. No written description of this purply impassioned "climax" can do it justice. As hard as it is to believe today, many audiences in 1946 not only sat through *Duel* with a straight face, but considered it a new high in screen "romance."

Ever a clever marketing maven, Selznick turned the fact that his film was banned in many major cities to his advantage, sold it as the sex-obsessed soap opera it actually was, and mistakenly thought he had successfully turned Jones into a sex symbol. After Selznick and Jones married in 1949, he devoted the rest of his career to nurturing and supervising hers, repeatedly casting her in roles for which she was embarrassingly unsuited (not unlike John Derek did for Bo). Except in Jones's case, with an impressive career total of five Best Actress Oscar nominations, many people actually believed she had talent. That hat trick Selznick *was* able to pull off.

Dippy Dialogue
Pearl *(Jennifer Jones)*: "I'm trash, I tellya—trash!"

Choice Chapter Stop
Chapter 26 ("The Duel"): The film's most famous "sexy" sequence has Jones and Peck declaring their love in a duel to the death.

Ghosts Can't Do It

(1990/Triumph Releasing) **VHS**

Who's to Blame CAST: **Bo Derek** ● *(Katie O'Dare Scott)*; **Anthony Quinn** *(Scotty)*; **Don Murray** *(Winston)*; **Leo Damian** ◐ *(Fausto)*; **Julie Newmar** ◐ *(Angel of Death)*; **Donald Trump** ● *(Cameo as Himself)*

CREW: **Directed by John Derek** ●; **Screenplay** ◐ **by Derek**

Rave Reviews
"The worst movie ever from John & Bo . . . highly recommended for Bad Movie Buffs!" — *TV Guide's Movie Guide*

"The finest collaboration between a husband and wife team since Ferdinand and Imelda discovered Geneva bank accounts."
  — **Joe Bob Briggs, Drive-In Movie Reviews (Web site)**

"Ratcheting the film into so-bad-it's-good territory are supporting turns by Julie Newmar, Don Murray, and, yes, Donald Trump as Himself."
  — **Jack Purdy,** *Baltimore Citypaper*

Plot, What Plot? *Ghosts Can't Do It* is the third entry in John and Bo Derek's "Trilogy of Terror," following on the heels of previous Razzie champions *Tarzan, the Ape Man* and *Bolero*. *Tarzan* took the classic Burroughs novel and went way beyond the "me Tarzan, you Jane" element of the characters' "relationship," yet managed to be sex-laden and slow at the same time—you might say half-fast. *Bolero*, while equally sex-obsessed, was simply half-assed—a feature-length rumination on Bo's process of "losing her virginity." Of the three, *Ghosts* comes closest to giving us a peek behind the curtain of John and Bo's off-screen life. And what a creepy peek it is.

Just like in real life, Bo's character is married to a macho, demanding older man whose age is about to catch up with him. Presumably like in real life, Bo's character refers to her heart-challenged hubby as "Great One." And in a running device, probably taken from John and

Bo's private predilections, Bo and her onscreen beau share a "special smooch" that involves her sticking out her lower lip so he can bite it. It's during one of these "bite me" moments that ancient Anthony Quinn as the husband suffers his first heart attack. Even though he tells us he's a billionaire ("I'm worth two billion dollars!" he declares in what passes for exposition in a John Derek script), Quinn is told he's "too old" to be a candidate for a heart transplant. So, despondent that he can no longer "do it" with Bo, Tony opts to blow his brains out. Smart move, you're thinking, now he won't have to be seen in the rest of the film, and we won't have to watch him shamelessly overact with his hands and eyebrows, desperately trying to make John Derek's dialogue seem like it's about something . . .

But while the "do it" part of *Ghosts Can't Do It* has now been explained, you're forgetting the "ghosts" part. Yep, Anthony may be dead but, darnit, he's not gone. During his funeral, he returns in "spirit form" (actually an awful optical that makes Quinn look like he's being filmed through wiggling pantyhose) and makes a preposterous posthumous proposal to his widow. Together, they will "shop" for a new body his spirit can inhabit so they can once again "do it." Idiotic, you say? How about so dumb it's downright laughable?

As in every "Bo peep" film he made, director/screenwriter John takes every opportunity to get his wife naked—preferably wet and naked. To John's repertoire of nudie cutie shots, *Ghosts* adds a new, uncomfortable one when Bo strips down on the beach while talking to Quinn's ghost. Bo then sits down, and when she stands up, her nether regions are covered with gritty sand . . . wow, ain't *that* sexy? But the most entertaining new element John and Bo together bring to *Ghosts* is . . . her hats. That's right, throughout the film Bo has such a gripping screen presence that you'll find yourself more focused on her headwear than her beautiful but blank face. One hat looks like a baby wolf climbed up on her skull and died. Another looks like a piece of cracked Native American crockery fell on her head and she didn't notice. And for Anthony's funeral, she wears a black yak-fur get-up that looks like she's being swallowed by the Creeping Terror. Almost every time the film's pace hits a snag, out comes another chuckle-worthy chapeau. How does it all turn out—and what hat does Bo wear for the finale? We're not telling . . .

The films of Mrs. and Mr. Bo Derek are the cinematic equivalent of a *Hustler* photo shoot. But *Ghosts Can't Do It* came along at the point where nobody but the immediate Derek family and Razzie members still had any interest in them, and it's their muddle-headed masterpiece: a never-to-be-forgotten hat trick of horrible moviemaking.

Dippy Dialogue
Katie *(Bo Derek)*: "You have my heart—how can I live without my heart?!?"

Razzie Credential
Ghosts Can't Do It didn't "win" Worst Picture of 1990 outright . . . it tied with Andrew Dice Clay's stunningly smug screen debut *The Adventures of Ford Fairlane*.

Kitten with a Whip

(1964/Universal Pictures) **VHS**

Who's to Blame CAST: **Ann-Margret** *(Jody Dvorak)*; **John Forsythe** *(David Stratten)*; **Peter Brown** *(Ron)*; **Patricia Barry** *(Vera)*; **Richard Anderson** *(Grant)*; **Ann Doran** *(Mavis Varden)*
CREW: **Written and directed by Douglas Heyes; Based on the book by Wade Miller**

Rave Reviews
"Inept direction and ludicrous dialogue.... One of the most inane pieces of black-and-white screenfare to emerge from a major studio in a long, long time." — **Nadine Edwards, *Hollywood Citizen-News***

"Misses because of a poor script and frequently inept acting."
— **William Wolf, *Cue* magazine**

"A trashy movie ... about a fairly stupid man and a savvy little juvenile delinquent." — **"Mae Tinee," *Chicago American***

Plot, What Plot? When Hollywood finally figured out that the customers at most of the nation's drive-ins week after week were teenagers, a whole rash of teen-oriented films resulted. And few of them were as hilariously "hip" and hopelessly hokey as 1964's *Kitten with a Whip*, starring "sex kitten" Ann-Margret as a juicy juvie on the run.

From the git-go, when we hear the first strains of the insistently sleazy theme music (and notice that the basic graphic gimmick of the film's main title sequence is ripped off from *Psycho*), *Kitten with a Whip* runs roughshod over all logic and good taste. In fact, taken in toto, it would be perfectly described by using one of the favorite "hip" phrases of its teen tough guys: "Cheezoid!"

Clad only in a filmy nightie, babydoll blonde Jody (Ann-Margret) has broken out of juvenile hall and broken into super-square senatorial candidate David Stratten's house. As soon as Jody has made herself at home and fallen asleep, we quick-cut from the wide-open eyes of a toy monkey in her arms to the headlights of Stratten's limo, arriving home after a fund-raiser. *Kitten* is literally littered with this kind of "lookit-me-I'm-a-fillum-maker" touches, made all the more ludicrous by writer/director Douglas Heyes's overheated dialogue and situations.

When Stratten (John Forsythe) discovers Jody's been sleeping in his daughter's bed, she convinces him that he's the one in a situation, and he'd better "cool it" unless he wants Jody going to the press. Trying to take the edge off things, he offers his sympathy for the mess Jody's gotten into, and she flatly replies, "That's me, the Jody doll—wind me up and no matter which way you point me, I wind up lousy!" As we can already tell, this entire film will be lousy with hilariously "hard-edged" dialogue.

Figuring she's in the catbird seat, Jody decides to invite three of her "friends" over to Stratten's to party. It turns out that these three have an even greater mastery of juvenile mumbo-jumbo than Jody does. A brief list of their countless unintentionally comic comments: "Don't hot up, man, hot down!" "What a brain-bucket!" "Cork it up, you're beginning to bug me!" and "Cool it, you creep, and coexist!"

Jody's quick-witted quartet soon coerce Stratten into driving them down to Tijuana to see a striptease show featuring "Patricia Tiara." There, things progressively unravel, ending up in a car chase in which Stratten's brand-new white 1964 Chrysler Imperial crashes, and inexplicably turns into a 1956 Plymouth as it sails through the guardrail and explodes. Only Forsythe survives.

Even funnier than the film itself was the way Universal sold it. The ad copy: "This is Jody's story. The kicks she digs. The swingers she runs with. And the special kind of hell she can make for a man." Funnier still—it worked. In 1964, Ann-Margret was Hollywood's eighth-biggest box-office draw.

Dippy Dialogue
Jody *(Ann-Margret)* reveling in her newfound surroundings: "Everything is so creamy! Oh, kill me quick—I never had it so good!"

Love Crimes

(1992/Miramax Films)   **VHS**

Who's to Blame   CAST: **Sean Young** ☉ *(Dana Greenway)*; **Patrick Bergin** *(David Hanover)*; **Arnetia Walker** *(Maria)*; **James Read** *(Stanton)*; **Ron Orbach** *(Detective Tully)*
CREW: **Directed by Lizzie Borden; Screenplay by Allan Moyle and Laurie Frank; Story by Moyle**

Rave Reviews

"Hilariously unspeakable depravities . . . some of the hootiest dialogue ever." — **Edward Margulies and Stephen Rebello,** *Bad Movies We Love*

"Astonishingly inept, confusing 'thriller.'"
— *Leonard Maltin's Movie & Video Guide*

"Implausible and sleazy." — *VideoHound's Golden Movie Retriever*

Plot, What Plot? When making a thriller, it always helps to have it be at least somewhat "thrilling." And if it's going to be a mystery, it's lethal if the audience can stand back and analyze the film while they're watching it and decide that the main mystery is the film's lack of logic. These two large problems, along with a laughably laconic-yet-manic lead performance by Sean Young, manage to kill any chance *Love Crimes* has of being taken seriously at all. Garbled, trashy, and littered with dialogue and situations that cross the line from sexy to outright silly, *Crimes* probably played a bigger role in ruining Young's career than did her precedent-setting double Razzie "win" as both Worst Actress and Worst Supporting Actress for playing twins in 1991's *A Kiss Before Dying*.

With her hair slicked close to her head, leaving her ears sticking out like the handles on a sugar bowl, and costumed in mannish outfits that make her figure look anorexic and boyish, Young resembles the homely younger brother of Keanu Reeves. She's supposed to be a crackerjack assistant DA from Atlanta who goes hell-bent-for-leather after a serial abuser of women who makes sexual advances to strangers in bars, uses the name of a famous photographer, then humiliates the women by taking nude Polaroids and "raping" them. But if the women enjoy their encounters with perpetrator Patrick Bergin, is it really rape? And if none of the dozen or more women he's assaulted want to press charges, why does Young even bother to pursue this case? Simple: If she didn't become obsessed with it, there would be no movie.

That kind of stuff-happens-because-we-need-it-to-happen-for-plot-reasons "logic" pervades the entire film. Tracking Bergin to backwoods Georgia, Young spends a bizarre weekend with him at a cabin, where he handcuffs her to a sofa, cuts off her clothes with scissors, then gives her a hand bath while telling her exactly what we've *all* been thinking: "You look like shit!" With that kind of come-on, and hokey flashbacks to seeing her own parents doing the sign of the humpbacked whale as a child playing in her head, how can Young *not* fall for this pervert? Just to show how much she loves him, she rips open her blouse by a campfire, smears fish blood all over her face, and yells, "Are you happy now? Am I fucked up enough for you?" But before we can answer that she was *way* beyond fucked up three or four reels ago, she suddenly has a mood swing, pulls out her gun, and has Bergin handcuff himself into the stolen car he keeps parked by his cabin. Being a great legal mind, she naturally leaves him alone in the car while she tries to call local police from a pay phone and . . . damn it if he doesn't escape.

Their game of cat and mouse (tit for tat? sexual cum-uppance?) "climaxes" with Bergin showing up at Young's apartment, and all those childhood flashbacks finally paying off. How he knew her home address is never explained. Anywaze, thanks to a glass fruit bowl conveniently placed next to her exercise machine, Young fends off Bergin in this final showdown.

But was their relationship one of abuse . . . attraction . . . or just a case of two bad actors drawn together by a mutual need to make a sexy thriller none of its makers could logically explain? *Love Crimes* is something only a Bad Movie Lover could truly love. And it's criminally funny to boot. So get out your handcuffs, a fistful of fish blood, and the strongest hair gel you can find, and join Sean Young on her shocking sexual journey . . . to laughter.

Dippy Dialogue
David Hanover *(Patrick Bergin)*, after locking Dana Greenway *(Sean Young)* in a closet: "Does this give you a little thrill? Did you wet your panties just a little?"

Availability
Love Crimes is available on VHS in both its original theatrical version and an unrated "director's cut," which runs 12 minutes longer. Neither makes even a lick of sense, but we recommend the "unrated" one.

The Naked Kiss

(1964/Allied Artists)   **DVD / VHS**

Who's to Blame   CAST: **Constance Towers** *(Kelly)*; **Anthony Eisley** *(Capt. Griff)*; **Michael Dante** *(J. L. Grant)*; **Virginia Grey** *(Candy)*; **Patsy Kelly** *(Mac)*; **Betty Bronson** *(Miss Josephine)*; **Edy Williams** *(Hatrack, the Bon-Bon Girl)*
                  CREW: **Written, produced, and directed by Samuel Fuller**

Rave Reviews

"Downright ridiculous . . . patently absurd."
— **Eugene Archer,** *New York Times*

"How they must have hooted while filming this turkey! Cannot be ignored as the worst film of the year!" — ***Cosmopolitan***

"Sam Fuller has come up with another meatball . . . a mess of pretentious insanity." — **Robert Salmaggi,** *New York Herald Tribune*

Plot, What Plot? In 1964, *The Naked Kiss* was a hard-edged, hard-boiled look at prostitution and child molestation, two very verboten subjects under the old Hollywood Production Code. Today it serves as a ridiculously over-the-top example of the extremes filmmakers had to go to in order to skirt the Code.

Writer/director Sam Fuller once said, "Film is a battleground. Love, hate, violence, action, death. . . . In a word, emotion!" He certainly proved all of that (and more) with *Naked Kiss*. The film opens with an angry prostitute beating the bejeezus out of a customer with her high heel. In the course of flailing away at him, the hooker's wig falls to the floor, revealing that she is bald-headed. She then spritzes him with a seltzer bottle, rifles his pockets for the $75 he owes her, puts her wig back on, and exits. In the first of this film's innumerable "helpful hints for the plot impaired," the drunken john awakens, looks down, and we zoom in on a calendar reading July 4, 1961.

Cut to a banner hung over a generic street, reading August 12, 1963.

Apparently, it's over two years later, as our prostitute Kelly gets off a Greyhound bus in the small town of Grantville, located somewhere on the Universal Studios backlot. Here, Kelly plans to start her life over, although the first words from her mouth as she's ogled getting off the Greyhound are, "Please check my trunk!" Since this sequence is accompanied by an innuendo-laden saxophone solo, we're unclear: Has Kelly gone into some new line of business . . . or stuck with the world's oldest profession?

We soon have our answer as a local policeman queries of Kelly on a park bench, "Traveling saleslady?" Indeed, Kelly is still selling, but now it's champagne, libidinously labeled "Angel Foam." When the cop asks for a "free sample," Kelly snaps her briefcase shut and declares, "No free sips! Angel Foam goes down like liquid gold . . ." Wait a minute . . . what exactly *is* Kelly selling here? Dissolve to Kelly and the cop, sprawled out across his couch "after" she's made her sales pitch . . . which must not have worked, as the cop tells Kelly, "You and I will get along like noise and a hangover if you try to set up shop in this town!" Her retort is to quote "Go-Thuh the poet" (Goethe) about ignorance, a subject everyone involved in this film is intimately acquainted with. Forbidden from plying her former trade, Kelly decides to find legitimate employment, and winds up . . . a nurse at a local hospital for handicapped children, all with ridiculous names like Kip, Peanuts, and Angel Face. Later she helps stage the most shamelessly manipulative children's musical performance since Jerry Lewis began hosting telethons.

Meanwhile, the cop has sniffed out Kelly's new job: "That's a new low, using crippled kids to front your trade! You'll have a problem, breaking in those little girls to walk the streets on crutches!" This is greeted by a slap from Kelly, who really *wants* to go legit, even if that darned sax solo accompanies her every time she enters a room. Enter the town's richest bachelor, one of the Grants for whom Grantville is named. From the way he eyes Kelly when he first gets a glimpse of her "sax appeal," he could be her ticket to going legit for good.

But Grant has a terrible secret, and Kelly won't find out till it's almost too late—after she's already picked out her wedding gown, and headed over to Grant's to give him a peek at it. Instead, in one of the film's most obtuse illustrations of what could and could not be shown onscreen in 1964, Kelly gets a peek at Grant's secret vice. The way it's shown, we are left to conjecture exactly *what* he was doing with a seven-year-old named Bunny, who looks startled and runs from the house. "Now you know why I could never marry a normal woman," Grant pleads in desperation, while we're still pondering what happened. "Our marriage will be a paradise," he adds, just about the time we're thinking *yuck*, "because we're both abnormal!" Kelly instinctively grabs for the phone receiver (instead of her high heel) and bops Grant. The wedding veil falls over his dead face, and we launch into the most blatant of those "helpful hints for the plot impaired": Over a series of townspeople's faces reading their morning papers, we see a headline pop onscreen one word at a time: "GRANT...IS...DEAD...SLAIN...BY...PROSTITUTE!" Locked in a jail cell, poor Kelly is doomed to hear her crippled kids endlessly sing their awful song in her head until she can identify Bunny and exonerate herself.

Since this was made in 1964, most of what it's actually about is only hinted at—albeit, with all the subtlety of a frying pan to the head. Interestingly, there are those who hail this film as a breakthrough in the treatment of adult themes by Hollywood. But to those of us who appreciate the bawdy, the gaudy, and the tawdry, *Naked Kiss* equals True Bad Movie Bliss.

Dippy Dialogue
Kelly *(Constance Towers)*, appraising her future: "I saw a broken-down piece of machinery. Nothing but the buck, the bed, and the bottle for the rest of my life!"

Choice Chapter Stop
Chapter 14 ("Mommie Dear"): Kelly rehearses the crippled kids for their musical debut.

A Night in Heaven

(1983/20th Century-Fox) **VHS**

Who's to Blame CAST: **Christopher Atkins** 😊 *(Rick Monroe, a.k.a. Ricky the Rocket)*; **Lesley Ann Warren** *(Faye Hanlon)*; **Robert Logan** *(Whitney Hanlon)*; **Deborah Rush** *(Patsy)*; **Deney Terrio** *(Tony)*; **Carrie Snodgress** *(Mrs. Johnson)*; **Sandra Beau** *(Slick)*
CREW: **Directed by John G. Avildsen; Written by Joan Tewkesbury**

Rave Reviews
"[A] student-by-day, male-stripper-by-night howler that sent Atkins into instant bimbo oblivion."
— **Edward Margulies and Stephen Rebello,** *Bad Movies We Love*

"A disaster. It's silly, poorly done and unbearably condescending."
— **Linda Gross,** *Los Angeles Times*

"Sleazy, crude and embarrassing . . . It's been rated R for very good reasons." — **Jimmy Summers,** *Box Office* **magazine**

Plot, What Plot? One of my associates in the promo business said to me at the premiere of *Blue Lagoon*, "Poor Chris Atkins. He thinks this role will bring an endless stream of sexy young starlets to his door, when in reality, it'll be an endless stream of middle-aged men." Whoever wound up at Atkins's door, Christopher himself never came closer to unintentional self-parody than in his role as a supposedly studly junior college student romancing his married public speaking teacher while moonlighting as male stripper "Ricky the Rocket" in *A Night in Heaven*.

You may be surprised to find out this film was written by the award-winning screenwriter of *Nashville*, and directed by John G. Avildsen, who won a Best Director Oscar for the original *Rocky*. But don't let their credentials fool you into thinking this will be a serious look at marital infidelity. Made during the era of Chippendale's, and leaning far too heavily on Atkins's presumed charms to be taken seriously, *Heaven*

WELL, *SOMEONE* THOUGHT IT WAS SEXY!

is exploitation all the way. In fact, it's shockingly shoddy, and gives every indication that its makers had to scramble to cobble together even the brief 80 minutes of material that made it to the screen.

Atkins plays Rick Monroe, a college student with aspirations (and suggestive gyrations) to spare. On the very day Mrs. Hanlon flunks him for an incredibly lame classroom presentation, her spunky sister takes her to a tacky male strip joint called Heaven. There, she is shocked to learn that Rick, performing in his formfitting, tearaway silver jumpsuit as "Ricky the Rocket," has talents she never dreamed of. Moving awkwardly to the classic dippy disco ditty "You Are My Obsession" (occasionally looking like he's reacting to an especially painful case of jock itch), Atkins spots his professor in the audience, and audaciously decides to dance just for her. By the song's end, he's climbed onto her chair and is undulating and thrusting his crotch three inches from her face, like a deranged lab monkey in heat. Since teacher's played by Lesley Ann Warren, how can she resist?

Student and teacher wind up "switching roles," as Rick/Ricky introduces Mrs. H to the joys of cheating on your husband in a sleazy motel room. Torn by guilt—and repulsed upon coming back for seconds and discovering Atkins using the remainder of their room rental time to tryst with some *other* cheap chick—Warren must decide if she's going to tell her unemployed (read: emasculated) husband that he's been cuckolded.

When hubby figures out what happened, and with whom, he resorts to one of the funniest revenge fantasies ever. Mr. Hanlon kidnaps Atkins at gunpoint, rows him in a canoe to the middle of a dark, possibly gator-infested bayou . . . then forces him to strip and "dance" for him right there in the canoe. Atkins's whimpering performance in this scene, meant to elicit sympathy, is instead so inane it could get those gators giggling. All ends happily, with Warren and hubby reunited, and Atkins having learned to be more selective about whose face he grinds his groin into while "performing" in Heaven.

The makers of *A Night in Heaven* clearly thought they'd come up with a "winner," and they were right in one sense: This role wound up "winning" Atkins our Worst Actor Razzie for 1983.

Dippy Dialogue
Mrs. Hanlon *(Lesley Ann Warren)*, as Ricky the Rocket *(Christopher Atkins)* removes his helmet: "Oh my God—I just flunked that kid in my class!"
Shirley *(Alix Elias)*, yelling to be heard over the music: "*What?* You did *what* in his ass?"

Orgy of the Dead

(1965/Crown International Pictures) **DVD / VHS**

Who's to Blame CAST: **Criswell** *(The Emperor)*; **Fawn Silver** *("Ghoulita")*; **Pat Barrington** *(Shirley and the Gold Girl)*; **William Bates** *(Bob)*; **Barbara Nordin** *(Skeleton Dancer)*; **Dene Starnes** *(Zombie Dancer)*; **Louis Ojena** *(The Mummy)*; **John Andrews** *(The Wolfman)*

CREW: **Directed by "A. C. Stephens"** (Stephen C. Apostolof); **Written by Edward D. Wood Jr.**

Rave Reviews
"Imagine, if you can, a film that combines 32 minutes of Ed Wood Jr's inane dialogue with 60 minutes of topless titty dancers. . . . Pure Wood camp!" — **FileThirteen.com**

"The dialogue is hilarious, and the acting is horrible, but what would you expect . . . from a script by Ed Wood, based on a novel by him."
— **Dave Sindelar, Sci-Film.org**

"The one film that could have benefited from the direction of Ed Wood!" — **Nate Yapp, Classic-Horror.com**

Plot, What Plot? By the mid-1960s, American sexual hedonism had almost caught up with the fevered wet dreams that were Ed Wood's specialty in the 1950s. But by the mid-'60s, Wood had produced a string of some of the most embarrassing movies ever made (and was reputedly a lush as well). So backers no longer allowed Ed to direct. Toward the end of his so-called career, he had to settle for mere screenwriting credits on a string of ever-more-hard-core porno films. Not to worry, though: Ed still retained his mastery of otherworldly characters, silly situations, and idiotic dialogue, all of which are on naked display (literally!) in 1965's *Orgy of the Dead*.

   A bargain-basement striptease show masquerading as a movie, *Orgy* is set in a cemetery even less convincing than the one in Wood's classic *Plan 9 from Outer Space*. The film opens with a plywood crypt, inside of which is a Styrofoam coffin. Up from the casket sits Wood's favorite occult oddball Criswell to intone (as only *he* can), "For years, I have told the almost unbelievable, and showed it to be more than a fact! Now I tell a tale so astounding that some of you may faint!" It seems that Ol' Crizzy is the Emperor of the Night, about to preside over the Eternal Judgment of a bevy of back-from-the-dead, bare-breasted bar-top dancers. His sidekick, Ghoulita, is—if possible—an even less credible actor than Criswell himself.

Their cemetery is soon stumbled upon by a bickering couple, first seen driving down a canyon road in broad daylight. Inexplicably, every time we cut to an angle inside the car, it's pitch-black nighttime. Turns out she's a redheaded shrew, and he's a failed author trying to find a cemetery to inspire his latest "monster story." The couple has a typically unconvincing Wood-style car wreck, and, thrown from the car we never see crash, they witness the awesome spectacle about to unfold in the cardboard cemetery.

In a touch that only Wood would find necessary in a soft-core film, each of the topless dancers has a backstory: One died by fire, and so dances with flames in the foreground; one worshipped gold, and so dies covered in gold spray paint; another is a slave girl who dances for Criswell and Ghoulita's pleasure with her hands bound and her breasts flailing. But the best of these Beyond Dead Bimbos are the "Cat" Girl, who wears a black-and-white catsuit with both its bottom and breast areas snipped out (the better to see both sets of assets bobble and bounce about as she spasms like a household pet hawking up a hairball), and the Skeleton's Bride (complete with wedding veil and a skeleton "groom," controlled by visible strings) as her dance partner.

A "missing link" in Wood's career that was until only recently available on grainy VHS, *Orgy* has now been restored by Rhino Video to its rightful place in the Bad Movie Pantheon with a feature-laden, pristine new DVD transfer, including a commentary track by director A. C. Stephens. If you're gonna go for dreck, always go for dreck with all the extras!

Dippy Dialogue
The Emperor of the Night *(Criswell)*: "Torture! Torture! It pleasures me!!"

The Scarlet Letter

(1995/Hollywood Pictures) **DVD / VHS**

Who's to Blame CAST: **Demi Moore** ☉ *(Hester Prynne)*; **Gary Oldman** ☉ *(Rev. Dimmesdale)*; **Robert Duvall** ☉ *(Roger Prynne)*; **Lisa Joliffe-Andoh** *(Mituba)*; **Robert Prosky** *(Horace Stonewall)*; **Joan Plowright** *(Harriet Hibbons)*

CREW: **Directed by Roland Joffe** ☉; **Screenplay** ☉ **by Douglas Day Stewart ("Freely Adapted" from the novel by Nathaniel Hawthorne)**

Rave Reviews
"Imagines all of the events leading up to the adultery, photographed in the style of those *Playboy Fantasy* videos."
— **Roger Ebert**, *Chicago Sun-Times*

"Dumbed-down adaptation of Nathaniel Hawthorne's tale . . . does everything but paint 'The Scarlet Letter' hot pink . . . give them *Moby Dick* and they'd make *Free Willy*." — **Rita Kempley**, *Washington Post*

"The script takes more liberties with [Hawthorne's] text than Elizabeth Berkley did with that pole in *Showgirls*."
— **Susan Wloszczyna**, *USA Today*

Plot, What Plot? If you're going to make a modern date movie out of a classic novel that everyone was forced to read in high school, *The Scarlet Letter* should not be your first choice of source material. For one thing, Hawthorne's tale of repression and sexual hypocrisy in the seventeenth century is itself quite repressed: All of the "action" in the book occurs after Hester Prynne and Reverend Dimmesdale have already committed the act of adultery for which they both pay dearly. For another thing, no matter how much you may "jazz up" the storyline by adding hot tubs, Indian attacks, and "sexual symbolism" an eight-year-old would find too obvious, you're still stuck with all those

WELL, *SOMEONE* THOUGHT IT WAS SEXY!

"thees" and "thous" that make its period dialogue seem either biblical, blustery, or both.

But leave it to Hollywood Pictures (the people who made *Color of Night*) and Demi Moore (the female equivalent of Sylvester Stallone in terms of self-adoration and exhibitionism) to turn Hawthorne's book into a brainless recruiting poster for "free love." They even go so far as to give the decidedly sober story a "Hollywood happy ending" in which you may think you actually see John Wayne riding to the rescue.

In interviews promoting this film, Moore was quizzed about just how "freely adapted" this version of *Scarlet Letter* was. Demi replied, "Not many people have read the book." In which case, why make a movie of it in the first place? And a movie which so violates the tone and intent of the original work that it's like Hugh Hefner remaking Disney's *Bambi* with Thumper played by a Playboy Bunny?

Starting with the premise that Hester Prynne, as played by Demi, is a circa 1666 "babe" just itching to be deflowered, this film's makers do achieve one thing none of the other nine film versions of *Scarlet Letter* managed: They turn it into a laugh riot. "Pleasuring herself" in her hot tub while recalling Dimmesdale's bare white buns, flaunting her unconventional ideas around town, and basically acting like the same character she played in *Striptease* sent through a time warp to the seventeenth century, Moore gives her most ridiculous performance here—topping even her teary-eyed Dopey-like turn in *Indecent Proposal*. "I wonder if existence as a woman is worthwhile at all," she ponders at one point, prompting many in the audience to offer up any implement of suicide they can find, just to put her—and us—out of our misery.

Costarring with dummy Demi in *Letter* are two arguably reputable actors: Englishman Gary Oldman as the skinny-dipping Dimmesdale, and Oscar winner Robert Duvall as Hester's long-gone husband, who returns too late to prevent his wife's adultery, but not too late to commit acting sins of his own. A fireside scene in which Duvall dons a dead deer carcass atop his head is one clip they *won't* be showing when it comes time to do Duvall's TV obits.

Widely lambasted by critics at the time it was released, and a box-office bomb to boot, *Scarlet Letter* earned back less than 25 percent of its production costs in ticket sales, and proved to be one of the bigger nails in Demi's career coffin before she "retired early" from the screen in the late 1990s. Unfortunately for those of us who enjoy hilariously hideous adaptations of great novels, Moore left before she got the chance to "freely adapt" *Wuthering Heights*. Methinks she'd have relocated it from the English moors . . . to Jamaica, and mayhaps with Heathcliff portrayed by . . . Sylvester Stallone?

Dippy Dialogue
Hester's husband *(Robert Duvall)*: "Has this New World turned thee into a heathen?"

Razzie Credential
Scarlet Letter was nominated for seven 1995 awards, but Hester's tale went up against Nomi's tail in *Showgirls*, and *Letter* got burned at the stake only in one category: Worst Remake or Sequel.

Choice Chapter Stop
Chapter 2 ("Forbidden Love"): Hester follows the Little Red Bird of Sin to Ye Olde Swimmin' Hole, and sees the Reverend's buns 'n' dangly bits . . .

Fun Footnote
In an oversight for which he is probably eternally grateful, original author Nathaniel Hawthorne is not mentioned *anywhere* in this film's main or end titles.

Sextette

(1978/Crown International Pictures) **DVD / VHS**

Who's to Blame CAST: **Mae West** *(Marlo Manners)*; **Timothy Dalton** *(Sir Barrington)*; **Ringo Starr** *(Laslo)*; **Tony Curtis** *("Sexy Lexi")*; **George Hamilton** *(Vance)*; **Dom DeLuise** *(Dan Turner)*; **Featuring cameos by Rona Barrett, Alice Cooper, Keith Moon, Regis Philbin, Walter Pidgeon, and George Raft**
CREW: **Directed by Ken Hughes; Screenplay by Herbert Baker; Based on the play** *Sex* **by Mae West**

Rave Reviews
"Directed with all the subtlety of a Super Bowl halftime program."
— **Steven Puchalski,** *Shock Cinema* **magazine**

"Astonishing is the only word for . . . octogenarian West still strutting her stuff." — *Leonard Maltin's Movie & Video Guide*

"The good news: This is one of the most frightening horror movies ever made. . . . The bad news: It was supposed to be a musical comedy!"
— **Robert Firsching, The Amazing World of Cult Movies (Web site)**

Plot, What Plot? Imagine an eighty-five-year-old Mae West flashing her varicose cleavage while lusting after the U.S. Olympic weightlifting team. Imagine Mae lip-syncing a duet of "Love Will Keep Us Together" with Timothy (James Bond) Dalton. Imagine Alice Cooper, Tony Curtis, Keith Moon, George Hamilton, Ringo Starr, and Regis Philbin all appearing in the same movie, and all helplessly attracted to the Queen of the Convalescent Home Circuit. Now imagine . . . you're *not* imagining.

Sextette was West's final screen appearance, a long-delayed follow-up to her "triumphal return" in the 1970 box-office bomb *Myra Breckinridge*. But in the eight years between these two films, the already decrepit West went from in-joke to geriatric basket case. About all that remained intact was Mae's own deluded image of herself as irresistible man-bait. Think of Barbara Bush posing for a Victoria's Secret catalog, and you'll have some idea of what's so ridiculous about this film.

Based on West's own 1926 play, *Sex, Sextette* tells the story of screen legend Marlo Manners, who on her sixth wedding night is accosted by still besotted ex-husbands, nervous diplomats, and fawning hotel employees while simultaneously trying to write her memoirs and struggling to consummate her latest nuptials. It all plays like a long-drawn-out skit on the old *Carol Burnett Show*, but West inadvertently parodies herself way more laughably than Burnett ever did. The double entendres are still there, of course, but by now they're so worn out that they're *single* entendres. Her famous sashaying walk is once again attempted, but doddering Mae can only manage a step or two before cutaways have to be used to disguise her feebleness. And "The Face That Launched a Thousand Quips" is now so surgically pulled back and strung up that West looks eerily like the singing cartoon Pekinese that imitated her in Disney's *Lady and the Tramp*.

It would all be terribly, terribly sad . . . if it didn't also happen to be horrifically hilarious. Catch *Sextette*, and we bet you'll laugh way more than you cringe.

Dippy Dialogue
Marlo Manners *(Mae West)* to reporters: "I'm the girl who works at Paramount all day . . . and Fox all night!"

Choice Chapter Stop
Chapter 4 ("Song of Love"): In which Mae and Mr. Dalton duet on "Love Will Keep Us Together." (Song begins at 27:00.)

Fun Footnote
While making *Sextette*, West was reputedly so addled she had to be fed her lines through an earpiece. Told to repeat whatever she heard, Mae supposedly stood atop a marble staircase in one take and, mustering all the innuendo the line deserved, announced, "There's an accident on the 405 freeway!"

Sheena

(1984/Columbia Pictures) **DVD / VHS**

Who's to Blame CAST: **Tanya Roberts** ☉ *(Sheena)*; **Ted Wass** *(Vic Casey)*; **Donovan Scott** *(Fletcher)*; **Trevor Thomas** *(Prince Otwani)*; **France Zobda** *(Countess Zanda)*; **Elizabeth of Toro** *(Old Shaman Woman)*
CREW: **Directed by John Guillermin** ☉ **Screenplay**☉ **by David Newman and Lorenzo Semple Jr.; Story by Newman and Leslie Stevens; Based on the comic strip *Sheena* by S. M. Eiger and Will Eisner**

Rave Reviews
"There are plenty of laughs to be had in *Sheena*, but it's quite impossible to tell how many of them were intentional." — ***Variety***

"Tanya looks great as the queen of jungle jiggle, but Mother Nature forgot to endow her with a script!"
— ***Leonard Maltin's Movie & Video Guide***

"A mess at every turn . . . yet [it] retains that certain appeal that only a truly awful cheesefest can provide." — **Erik Harper, DVDVerdict.com**

Plot, What Plot? Left to her own devices when her Caucasian parents are killed on safari, blonde toddler Sheena must learn the ways of the jungle. Adopted by an old shaman woman, Sheena learns such valuable lessons as how to create formfitting, flattering outfits from animal skins, how to wash her hair with zam-zam berries, and how to spray-paint a white horse so it looks kind of like a zebra. But then things go terribly wrong—Sheena grows up to be Worst Actress nominee (and former Charlie's Angel) Tanya Roberts. And once that happens, all hope of taking her story seriously is lost.

Made with tongue occasionally in cheek, the 1984 version of *Sheena* is an odd duck indeed. From the director of both of Dino De Laurentiis's awful *King Kong* films, it sometimes reaches for laughs and falls flat.

More often than not, it isn't going for guffaws, but gets them anyway. Whatever its intentions, this *Sheena* is a surefire comedy classic.

When the grown-up Sheena is first seen by TV reporter Vic Casey, she's supervising a night raid to release captive animals, using her "telepathic" powers to enlist the aid of elephants, monkeys, and other wild creatures. Impressed with both her leadership abilities and her ability to find Maybelline eyeliner in the middle of the jungle, Casey decides to find out more about this amazing Amazon. Soon, they are in love, exchanging the kind of sweet nothings that only comic book characters could be expected to utter. "Mouths were given us to eat with," Sheena tells Vic after their first kiss. "Why did you touch yours to mine?" After sharing a face-sucking session that scares off a whole flock of flamingos, Vic declares, "I love you . . . so much it busts my heart!"

Together, Sheena and Casey decide to help the Zambuli tribe resist takeover by an evil prince and his white compatriots. Using every power at their disposal (an arsenal that includes everything but mental prowess), they foil the dastardly plot, but only after Sheena has been taken captive in a helicopter. With the help of that same flock of flamingos she terrified by kissing Casey (many of which look suspiciously like plastic lawn ornaments being wielded by off-camera production assistants), Sheena leaps from the sky just in time to win the last big battle.

Pricelessly pudding-headed, *Sheena* has everything going for it. Awful acting, trite, tripe-laden dialogue, and even a Razzie-nominated musical score that blatantly rips off *Chariots of Fire*. If you're seeking something sexy, funny, and stupid all at once, make Sheena the queena your video shelf.

Dippy Dialogue
Vic Casey *(Ted Wass)*, after suffering severe burns in a Jeep crash: "I've had it, baby, and all I can think of to say is . . . *shit*!"

Choice Chapter Stop
Chapter 25 ("Zandra's Airshow"): In which a flock of flamingo lawn ornaments rescues Sheena from a crashing helicopter.

Fun Footnote
Sheena won a "Drive-In Academy Award" from redneck critic Joe Bob Briggs as 1984's "Best Attack-of-the-Stupid-White-People Flick."

Where Love Has Gone

(1964/Paramount Pictures) **VHS**

Who's to Blame **CAST: Susan Hayward** *(Valerie Hayden)*; **Bette Davis** *(Mrs. Gerald Hayden)*; **Joey Heatherton** *(Danny Miller)*; **Mike Connors** *(Luke Miller)*; **Jane Greer** *(Mrs. Spicer)*; **DeForest Kelley** *(Sam Corwin)*; **Ann Doran** *(Mrs. Geraghty)*; **Whit Bissell** *(Professor Bell)*
CREW: **Directed by Edward Dmytryk; Screenplay by John Michael Hayes; Based on the novel by Harold Robbins**

Rave Reviews
"Manages to make every dramatic line, particularly when uttered by Susan Hayward, sound like a caption from a *New Yorker* cartoon."
— Arthur Knight, *Saturday Review*

"A typical Harold Robbins pastiche of newspaper clippings, liberally shellacked with sentiment and glued with sex." — *Newsweek*

"Stupid, glossy pulp fiction, lightly based on the Lana Turner case."
— *Halliwell's Film & Video Guide*

Plot, What Plot? On Oscar night 1958, Lana Turner lost Best Actress to Joanne Woodward in *The Three Faces of Eve*, then headed home to her Beverly Hills mansion, where her teenaged daughter stabbed Lana's gang-connected paramour to death with a kitchen knife. One of Tinseltown's juiciest scandals, this case not only served to hype newspaper sales at the time, it later served as the basis for a sordid novel, as only Harold Robbins could write it. And since Robbins' particular brand of trash was big box office in the early '60s, it was only a matter of time before his cheesebag novel became a cheesebag movie.

What's surprising is the level of talent involved in making such a lowbrow effort. Susan Hayward, who *won* an Oscar, plays the Lana Turner role, here a sculptress instead of an actress (was Lana herself unavailable, or uncharacteristically classy in turning down this role?). Hollywood grand dame and *two*-time Oscar winner Bette Davis, bedecked in a white wig and sporting facial expressions that look like she's sucked on too many lemons, plays Hayward's hatefully unforgiving mother—even though in real life, she's barely ten years older than Ms. Hayward. Twenty-year-old nymphet Joey Heatherton competes for screen gravitas with Hayward and Davis, playing the fifteen-year-old daughter who takes the blame for the dirty deed. Her performance basically consists of finding about 57 different ways to whine, "Daddy!" Mike Connors, later to play TV's Mannix, is cast as Hayward's ex and Heatherton's father, and brings to this role all the subtlety one would expect from a former football player making his screen debut.

Immediately after the opening titles (and the wonderfully hokey Oscar-nominated title tune) we hear a piercing woman's scream, someone loudly yells, "No!" and a bloody sculptor's chisel falls to the floor. Just when a fever-pitched pace of hysteria has been established, we're suddenly sitting in a city council meeting in Arizona ... and beginning to wonder if a reel from some other film is being shown by mistake. Then the meeting is interrupted by an "urgent" phone call for Connors, establishing his devotion as a dad: He's willing to blow off the big deal he's nearly sealed, merely to rush to defend his daughter—a daughter he never visited once in the last decade! On the plane to San Francisco, Connors goes into flashback mode, where we're stuck for the next hour.

Hayward, looking not ten seconds younger than she does at the beginning of the film, is discovered in 1940s flashback to be a promising young artist whose mother is a society matron desperate for her daughter to marry well. When "war hero" Connors fails to be impressed with Hayward's award-winning work, Mama Bette senses that this could be the Perfect Match. But her plan seems to backfire when the two take an instant dislike to each other. It's not until Hayward overhears Connors telling off Davis that she gets interested.

Their courtship and marriage are shown in a cinematic equivalent of shorthand that is both impressively informative and pricelessly silly: Hayward becomes a famous artist who can't seem to sculpt or weld without a colorful scarf on her head, while Connors becomes an infamous lush who scarfs down vodka with his morning OJ. Somewhere during this, they have a child who is, mysteriously, almost never seen before growing up to be every parent's worst nightmare: Joey Heatherton.

When we finally catch up to the present, among the tidbits of helpful information we glean from this film are: (1) No one can roll their eyes in disdain like Bette Davis; (2) juvenile hall must have a beauty parlor on its premises to keep Joey's "bullet hair" in place; and (3) playing "Bones McCoy" on *Star Trek* was not the *only* time DeForest Kelley ever overacted. Here he plays "art critic" and family friend Sam Corwin. How do we know he's a friend of the family? Because he's the only one who ever refers to Hayward's wayward ways before the film's archy, starchy courtroom denouement. Speaking of her work and lifestyle, Kelley labels Hayward, "Sculptress! Pagan! Alley cat!" Connors later tops Kelley by telling Hayward, "You're not a woman—you're a disease!"

At the hearing to determine Heatherton's custody, the truth finally comes out, but not before Hayward gets the chance to screech at Davis, "Will you shut up for once?!?!" (in response to which Davis offers up Her Ultimate Eye Roll). Overcome by the realization that she is as Kelley described her, Hayward at last breaks down to tell the judge that the chisel Heatherton drove into the murder victim (a man both mother and daughter shared as a lover) was actually meant for Mommie Fiercest.

It all ends up at a cemetery, but we'd hate to ruin the surprise of whose funeral it is. Suffice it to say, Heatherton gets in a couple of more "Daddys!" before the bereaved family car departs the graveside.

Dippy Dialogue
Valerie *(Susan Hayward)*: "When you're dying of thirst, you'll drink from a mud hole!"

The Brain That Wouldn't Die

(1959/American International Pictures) **DVD / VHS**

Who's to Blame   CAST: **Herb (Jason) Evers** *(Dr. Bill Cortner)*; **Virginia Leith** *(Jan Compton)*; **Leslie Daniel** *(Kurt)*; **Adele Lamont** *(Doris Powell)*; **Bruce Brighton** *(Dr. Cortner Sr.)*; **Paula Maurice** *(Brunette Stripper)*; **Marlyn Hanold** *(Blonde Stripper)*; **Eddie Carmel** *(The Thing in the Closet)*   CREW: **Written and Directed by Joseph Green; From a story by Green and Rex Carlton**

Rave Reviews
"A great, absurd movie . . . it took 3 years to reach an appalled public."
— **Michael Weldon,** *The Psychotronic Encyclopedia of Film*

"Love is a many-splattered thing [in this] major entry in the Trash Film genre." — *VideoHound's Golden Movie Retriever*

"For bad-movie lovers . . . aided in no small part by The Brain That Couldn't Direct and The Cast That Couldn't Act."
— **Shane Burridge, Online Film Critics Society**

Plot, What Plot? Few of the bad movies given the *Mystery Science Theater 3000* treatment are actually funnier *without* the robots' running commentary. *The Brain That Wouldn't Die* is one of them: an ultra-low-budget cheapy-creepy in which a "mad scientist" decapitates his fiancée in a car accident and pulls just her head from the flaming wreckage. Rushing back to his basement laboratory, the doofy doc puts her head in what looks like a bedpan, attaches it to wires and thingies to keep it alive . . . and then sets out to shop for the most well-endowed replacement body he can find.

Naturally, doc's "body hunt" takes him to sleazy bars, strip joints, and places where scantily clad "models" pose for overly avid photographers. Each of these venues is lingered over in a loving way that suggests writer/director Green may have been quite familiar with them *before* scouting for locations. And, in one of the film's funniest over-the-top touches, all of this sleaze is set to the cheesiest of "jazz" music scores, loaded with insinuating saxophone and piano riffs, often featuring what sounds like a frog in the background repeatedly croaking, "Dig it! Dig it!"

Meanwhile, back at the lab, Jan's Head starts laughing like an over-wound-up doll, developing strange powers and communicating with a mysterious Creature hidden from view inside a closet. Plotting her revenge on the man whose love has made her A Head of Her Time, Jan's Head (JH for short) concocts a scheme to team up with the Creature and stop Doc before he grafts her noggin onto the stacked body of an old high school flame.

Everything ends in flames, as Doc is overpowered just in time by the teamwork of JH and the Creature (who, when revealed, looks like he was given an extra eye and a Silly Putty–shaped egg for a skull by someone unfamiliar with anatomy). As the fire engulfs the lab, JH literally gets the next-to-last laugh, sitting in her bedpan and looking for all the world like a broasting human pot roast. Cackling madly as the flames surround her, JH declares, "I told him he should have let me die!"

Obviously produced on half a shoestring and littered with glaring continuity problems, *The Brain That Wouldn't Die*'s shoddy postproduction saves the very last laugh for us, the audience: It's the only film where the end title card *disagrees* with the main title. In the final 10 seconds of the film, we fade out from JH, guffawing en flambé, to read: "THE HEAD THAT WOULDN'T DIE." This incredible mistake has allowed bad film reference books ever since to list this top-of-the-line turkey under *both* titles.

Dippy Dialogue
Jan's Head *(Virginia Leith)* **to Creature in Closet:** "I am only a head, and you're . . . whatever you are. But together, we're strong!"

Choice Chapter Stop (from non-*MST3K* version)
Chapter 9 ("What Took You So Long?"): Doc comes on to a sleazy blonde stripper, who winds up on the floor in a cleavage-heaving, fists-flying catfight with an even sleazier brunette stripper.

Availability
The Brain That Wouldn't Die is available on both DVD and VHS from Rhino Video, under their MST3K imprint.

Fun Footnote
Seven-foot-eight-inch Eddie Carmel, who plays the Thing in the Closet, had previously starred on TV as the Happy Giant Clown.

Frankenstein's Daughter

(1958/Astor Pictures) **DVD / VHS**

Who's to Blame CAST: **John Ashley** *(Johnny Bruder)*; **Sandra Knight** *(Trudy Morton)*; **Donald Murphy** *(Dr. Oliver Frank/Frankenstein)*; **Felix Locher** *(Carter Morton)*; **Sally Todd** *(Suzie)*; **Special appearance by Page Cavanaugh and His Trio**
CREW: **Directed by Richard Cunha; Screenplay by H. E. Barrie**

Rave Reviews
"Incredibly shoddy teenage-monster movie."
— **Michael Weldon,** *The Psychotronic Encyclopedia of Film*

"A dismal clunker . . . the real monster is the repellent script."
— **S.A.D.,** *Los Angeles Herald-Examiner*

"Wretched Grade Z flick, so compellingly awful it's required viewing for schlock fans."
— **John Stanley,** *Creature Features Movie Guide Strikes Again*

Plot, What Plot? An ultra-low-budget 1958 drive-in quickie, *Frankenstein's Daughter* features a creature so laughably unterrifying that you'll be surprised they ever let you have a good look at her. But the makers of this film are so unaware of their own ineptitude that not only do they frequently show off their "monster" in extended close-ups, they do so for the first time *less than a minute* into the film—supering their main title over what looks like Marjorie Main with Brooke Shields's bushy eyebrows and those wax "vampire teeth" we all loved chewing on as kids at Halloween.

But idiotic as their central character is, she's a Rhodes scholar compared to the mad scientist slowly turning her into something only Boris Karloff could love. The kicker is that the creature being created by "Dr. Frank" was made from the only subject he could find . . . his own teenaged daughter! And he's doing so by injecting her without her knowledge, while she sleeps at night.

Since the transformations get worse as the project progresses, eventually leaving teen Trudy with Ping-Pong balls for eyes and Chiclets for teeth, the film could be seen as some kind of Frankensteinian treatise on teen awkwardness, or that bane of all teenage banes, acne. You think that's a silly notion—wait'll you hear Dr. Frank and his Señor Wences soundalike sidekick Uncle Carter discuss their work. "You fool!" the bad doctor berates Carter. "You've wasted my time. It's a head I need! Everything's ready except the brain!"

Speaking of having no brain, one of this film's subplots involves a citywide "manhunt" after a newspaper headline screams "WOMAN MONSTER MENACES CITY." Heading up the investigation is a detective who could've taught Donald Trump a thing or two about the art of extreme comb-overs, with his own sidekick who looks like a cross-eyed Al Gore. When first told of the marauding "monster," the detective declares, "I might be out of my mind but . . . I believe her!" The other subplot involves Oliver and Carter working on a second "monster" that looks like a melt-faced robotic Santa Claus and walks like Bela Lugosi with lumbago.

Like *Eegah*, everything in *Frankenstein's Daughter* culminates at a poolside barbecue, this one featuring two musical numbers by the Page Cavanaugh Trio. As the Trio sing, "I'm hip, Daddy Bird, let's flip, Daddy Bird, let's hop all day and fly away tonight," both creatures converge on Dr. Frank's patio. The bad doctor is forced to confess, "I'm not just Dr. Oliver Frank—I am Oliver . . . Frankenstein!" But seeing both of his experiments ruined reduces Dr. Frank-enstein to Scooby Speak, getting in one last dig at those darn teenagers: "You satisfied now, you meddling kids?!?"

Barely 85 minutes long, produced on a $60,000 budget using plywood sets and props probably cadged from local trash cans, *Frankenstein's Daughter* is a delightfully dimwitted example of that now dead 1950s film genre: the make-out movie. Find yourself a date with ultra-bushy eyebrows and check it out.

Dippy Dialogue
Dr. Oliver Frank *(Donald Murphy)*, addressing the body on the slab in his lab: "Tonight, you'll be alive again . . . you little vixen!"

The Island of Dr. Moreau

(1996/New Line Cinema) **DVD / VHS**

Who's to Blame CAST: **Marlon Brando** *(Dr. Moreau)*; **Val Kilmer** *(Montgomery)*; **David Thewlis** *(Edward Douglas)*; **Fairuza Balk** *(Aissa)*; **Ron Perlman** *(Sayer of the Law)*; **Neil Young** *(Boar Man)*; **Nelson de la Rosa** *(The Dwarf)*
CREW: **Directed by John Frankenheimer**; **Screenplay by Richard Stanley and Ron Hutchinson; Based on the novel by H. G. Wells**

Rave Reviews
"Legendary for its absurdity. Done up in white powder and wearing prosthetic teeth, Brando looks like Gwen Verdon on a really bad day."
— **Barbara Schulgasser,** *San Francisco Examiner*

"Mr. Brando treats this as an opportunity to play the Queen of England, for reasons that perhaps only he understands."
— **Janet Maslin,** *New York Times*

"*Moreau* won't be seen in its full glory until it shows up on *Mystery Science Theater 3000.*" — **Todd McCarthy,** *Variety*

Plot, What Plot? With his third nomination, Marlon Brando finally "won" a well-deserved Worst Supporting Actor Razzie playing the title role in *The Island of Dr. Moreau*. Given the actor's girth at the time this film was made, we'll leave it up to you to decide *which* title role Brando assayed: Dr. Moreau . . . or the island.

Brando plays, as he did in *Apocalypse Now*, a professed genius whom isolation has driven to madness. Brando brings to this part every eccentricity for which he was infamous, making it difficult to determine whether the comic results of Marlon's efforts here are intentional or not.

Brando doesn't show up until half an hour into the film, making his entrance in a Jeep-cum-Popemobile and genuflecting to his "children," the half-man, half-beast creatures his genetic experiments have created. With his face painted clown white and his head adorned with bee netting topped with a bamboo wimple, for a moment it looks like Brando took his inspiration from one of Oscar winner Sally Field's early roles. When he finally speaks, his voice has an odd, purse-lipped lisp. And you realize . . . he may look like the Flying Nun, but he talks like . . . Elmer Fudd.

Though obviously taken aback by Elmer—er, Marlon's appearance, castaway Edward Douglas (David Thewlis) accepts Brando's invitation to dinner. And in the film's single funniest sequence, Thewlis meets the doctor's family, who look and act like the Waltons in Wookie masks. Thewlis's facial reactions to all this—especially to Brando's literally butt-headed dwarf manservant—are priceless. "This is the most outrageous spectacle I have ever witnessed!" Thewlis declares. "Has it ever occurred to you, you might have totally . . . lost your mind?"

After dinner, for which Brando stretches a pair of white pantyhose over his bald head, he is joined for a piano duet by the dwarf manservant, who plays his own custom-made "baby" grand sitting atop Brando's Baldwin. It is utterly insane images and moments like this, with which *Dr. Moreau* is overflowing, that have endeared this film to bad movie fans everywhere. As ridiculous as Brando's performance in *Island of Dr. Moreau* is, his work here in an odd way justifies his eight Academy Award nominations and two Best Actor Oscars . . . simply because he kept a straight face while appearing in a film like this.

Dippy Dialogue
Edward Douglas *(David Thewlis)*: "I don't see how any of this specious nonsense justifies these monstrous disfigurements."
Dr. Moreau *(Marlon Brando)*: "If, in my tinkering, I have fallen short of the human form by the odd snout, claw, or hoof, it really is of no great import."

Choice Chapter Stop
Chapter 10 ("The Children"): Mr. Douglas meets the Wookie/Waltons.

Fun Footnote
Mike Myers has suggested that his *Austin Powers* character "Mini Me" was inspired by Brando's dwarf sidekick in this film.

Maniac

(1934/Hollywood Producers & Distributors) **DVD / VHS**

Who's to Blame   CAST: **Bill Woods** *(Don Maxwell)*; **Horace Carpenter** *(Dr. Meirschultz)*; **Ted Edwards** *(Buckley/The Ape Man)*; **Phyllis Diller** *(Mrs. Buckley)*; **Thea Ramsey** *(Alice Maxwell)*; **Marvel Andre** *(Marvel)*
CREW: **Directed by Dwain Esper; Written by Hildegarde Stadie; Based on a story by Edgar Allan Poe**

Rave Reviews
"Will be able to render the most hardened room helpless with laughter... encompassing as it does practically everything that is beloved by the seeker after Bad Movies." — **The Bad Movie Report (Web site)**

"Don't pass up the chance to see this incredible old adults-only oddity.... You won't believe it!"
— **Michael Weldon,** *The Psychotronic Encyclopedia of Film*

"The fore-runner of bargain basement sleaze. Any self-respecting schlock watcher must see this."
— **John Stanley,** *Creature Features Movie Guide Strikes Again*

Plot, What Plot? A perfect example of how exploitation films used to use "educational" hooks to get by film censors, 1934's *Maniac* is also one of the most incredibly disjointed, overacted, and deliriously dimwitted "thrillers" ever made.

From the same husband-and-wife writing/directing team as *Sex Madness, How to Undress in Front of Your Husband,* and *Marihuana, Weed with Roots in Hell, Maniac* purports to inform its audience about how to diagnose various "mental illnesses" by illustrating two characters that seem to have every mental disorder known to man. But the interspersed rolling titles discussing psychology are really just excuses to present a lurid, laughable tale of two partners who preserve pulsating human body parts in beakers, raise suicide victims from the dead, and use injections to turn manic-depressives into raving lunatics.

Starring as Maniac #1 is Bill Woods, whose character, Don Maxwell, is apparently a forcibly retired vaudevillian now living with (and beholden to) Maniac #2. Wood's specialty on stage was impersonations, so naturally he's the one chosen to pretend he's the coroner when Dr. Meirschultz (#2) steals a corpse to reanimate with his new elixir. Wood's performance here is so unabashedly over-the-top that one actually cringes at certain points. But silly as his inflections and gestures are, they're topped by Horace Carpenter as Meirschultz. The cliché of being so overwrought as to tear out one's hair is repeatedly demonstrated by Carpenter, who also spends a great deal of screen time cackling as only a "mad scientist" could, and pounding his fists on furniture and props throughout the film's eight-square-foot set of his laboratory. But even Carpenter isn't this film's most overeager overactor—that title goes to Ted Edwards as Mr. Buckley, who, when injected with the wrong serum, writhes and wretches to excruciatingly funny excess as he is transformed into a kind of ape man. He then kidnaps the zombie-like reanimated suicide victim, and the two go on an unforgettable first date.

The two Maniacs have a falling-out when Meirschultz asks Maxwell to kill himself so the heart throbbing away in that beaker can be tested on him. Instead, Maxwell shoots Meirschultz and, being the Great Impersonator, takes his place. As his "mental disorders" worsen, Maxwell decides that Meirschultz's black cat has an "evil eye"—which he plucks out . . . and then eats!

Meanwhile, in what first seems like footage from some unrelated film, a group of scantily clad young female roommates discuss love, money, and the huge inheritance Maxwell has unknowingly come into. When one of the roommates announces she's Maxwell wife (or maybe his sister—it's really *that* disjointed), we follow her to Meirschultz's lab. For no obvious reason, other than that female catfights are a staple of exploitation filmmaking, Maxwell's gal and the ape man's wife are locked in the cellar to fight each other with hypodermic needles. Six reels too late and totally clueless, the police arrive to find Maxwell rambling on madly, the two gals still going at it in the basement, and Meirschultz's body bricked behind a cellar wall. We end on Maxwell, locked up in jail, still ranting and raving.

Less than an hour long, seemingly stitched together from spare parts like Frankenstein's monster and therefore discombobulated to the point of delirium, *Maniac* is a long-lost gem that deserves to reclaim its place in the forefront of Incredibly Incompetent Cinema Classics.

Dippy Dialogue
Mr. Buckley *(Ted Edwards)*, as he transforms into the ape man: "Oh! Stealing through my body! Oooh! Creeping through my veins! Pouring in my blood! Oh, darts of fire in my brain! Stabbing me! Agony!! I can't stand it, this torture! This torment! I won't! I won't . . ." *(Starts making gurgling, babbling "ape man" noises.)*
Mrs. Buckley *(Phyllis Diller)*: "*What* was in that hypo?!?!?"

Choice Chapter Stops and Availability
Maniac is a "public domain" title, meaning it's available from several sources on DVD and VHS, all of which have different chapter stops. Since it's barely an hour long, we recommend you watch it in its entirety.

Fun Footnote
Upon its 1934 release, *Maniac* received the following "warning" from New York censors: "Indecent, immoral, will tend to corrupt morals, will tend to incite to crime."

The Tingler

(1959/Columbia Pictures)   **DVD / VHS**

Who's to Blame   CAST: **Vincent Price** *(Dr. Warren Chapin)*; **Darryl Hickman** *(David Morris)*; **Judith Evelyn** *(Martha Higgins)*; **Philip Coolidge** *(Ollie Higgins)*; **Patricia Cutts** *(Isabel Chapin)*; **Pamela Lincoln** *(Lucy Stevens)*
CREW: **Directed by William Castle; Screenplay by Robb White**

Rave Reviews
"Campish mini-classic . . . enhanced by a tongue-in-cheek flavor."
    — **John Stanley,** *Creature Feature Movie Guide Strikes Again*

"The earliest film depicting an LSD trip. . . . Preposterous."
    — *Leonard Maltin's Movie & Video Guide*

"One of Castle's cheesy best." — *VideoHound's Golden Movie Retriever*

Plot, What Plot? In a day and age as cynical and jaded as our own, it is hard to understand how movie audiences could ever have taken the works of shock 'n' schlock maestro William Castle seriously. But for those of us who deliberately seek out knuckleheaded chuckle fests of the "thrills and chills" variety, Castle's *The Tingler* is his mondo-bizarro masterpiece.

Starring ham-in-high-gear Vincent Price, *Tingler* posits that in moments of abject fear, the human body actually hosts a living, breathing parasite that grips the spine and will let go only if we "scream for our lives." To ensure audience participation in the screaming scenes, super-showman Castle had random seats in theatres showing *Tingler* wired to emit low-frequency buzzes in sync with the film. The process was called "Percepto" and represented the most laughable of Castle's trademark promotional "gimmicks."

"I feel obligated to warn you," Castle himself tells the audience in the prologue, "at any time you are conscious of a tingling sensation, you may obtain immediate relief by screaming. Don't be embarrassed about opening your mouth and letting rip with all you've got . . . a scream at the right time may save your life!" We then see a series of hysterically screaming heads floating through blackness, ending on the face of a man about to go to the electric chair. Performing the criminal's autopsy, Price tells the dead man's brother-in-law about his theory. Willing to be helpful even in a time of grief, "Ollie," the brother-in-law, helps Price name the soon-to-be-discovered creature "the tingler."

Ollie is also inadvertently helpful in that his wife, who runs a silent movie theatre (and must have learned her acting techniques from silent movie masters of overacting) is a deaf-mute with a morbid fear of blood. And being a deaf-mute, no matter *how* terrified she may be, Mrs. Ollie *cannot* scream. We are clearly being set up here, but it's all done with such straight-faced seriousness that we're already anticipating the payoff.

And Castle does not disappoint. After Price himself takes an amazingly acted LSD trip as part of his research, we are led to believe that he accidentally injects Mrs. Ollie with LSD as well. With stiff competition from Price in the overemoting department, Judith Evelyn as the mute gives a performance worthy of a mime on mescaline. So extreme is Evelyn's experience of fear that, even though she's dead, Price is able to extract a living "tingler" from her spine during his autopsy. Blatantly made of rubber and moved by pulling wires, the tingler looks like a cross between a lobster and a cockroach, and is about the size of a dachshund.

Now that it is free from its host, the tingler can "wander about" and eventually gets loose in the silent movie theatre. This sequence, in which the tingler crawls up one patron's leg, then wiggles across the lens of the projector, was the one in which "Percepto" was most clearly used. As the first woman screams, the screen goes black and Price announces, "Ladies and gentlemen, please do not panic . . . but *scream! Scream for your lives!* The tingler is loose in this theater! *Keep screaming!!*" In addition to using the "Percepto" device, this film's exhibitors were encouraged to turn on the house lights at some point in the film and visibly carry out a patron who had "fainted from fright." In reality, the "victim" was a theatre employee. Just imagining the pandemonium in actual movie theatres showing this film forty-five years ago makes this one of the *great* hokey huckster moments in all film history.

In addition to the fun-filled film itself, the DVD of *Tingler* includes original trailers promoting "Percepto" and a wonderfully tongue-in-cheek featurette entitled "Scream for Your Lives." For those of us who fondly recall seeing stuff like this as kids—and being totally suckered by it—*Tingler* is the best of its kind. It'll have you screaming, all right . . . but you'll be laughing at the same time.

Dippy Dialogue
Doctor Chapin's cheating wife *(Patricia Cutts)*: "There's a word for you . . ."
Doctor Chapin *(Vincent Price)*: "There are several for you . . ."

Choice Chapter Stop
Chapter 26 ("Scream!"): The tingler gets loose in the theatre . . . and your seat should start vibrating!

Fun Footnote
Besides "Percepto," Castle also pioneered "Emergo" for 1958's *House on Haunted Hill*. This effect involved running a full-sized, glow-in-the-dark skeleton on a wire over theatre patrons' heads during certain scenes. The only drawback was that younger audience members tended to pelt the skeleton with candy and soda pop—or grab on to its feet and try to pull it down from the wire.

The Adventurers

(1970/Paramount Pictures) **VHS**

Who's to Blame **CAST:** **Bekim Fehmiu** *(Dax Xenos)*; **Candice Bergen** *(Sue Ann Daley)*; **Olivia de Havilland** *(Deborah Hadley)*; **Ernest Borgnine** *(Fat Cat)*; **Charles Aznavour** *(Marcel)*; **Leigh Taylor-Young** *(Amparo)*; **Alan Badel** *(El Rojo)*; **Jaclyn Smith** *(Reporter for* Teen *magazine)*
CREW: **Directed by Lewis Gilbert; Screenplay by Michael Hastings and Gilbert; Based on the novel by Harold Robbins**

Rave Reviews
"Hilariously demented... offers kinks for everyone: Orgies! Drugs! Bloodbaths! Miscarriages! Lesbianism! High Fashion!"
— **Edward Margulies and Stephen Rebello,** *Bad Movies We Love*

"RATED: BOMB. Incredible mess... about fictional South American republic that has a new revolution every two minutes."
— *Leonard Maltin's Movie & Video Guide*

"A classic monument to bad taste... marked by banal, ludicrous dialogue... embarrassing acting... and luridly non-erotic sex." — *Variety*

Plot, What Plot? By 1970, films like *Valley of the Dolls* and *Easy Rider* had broken most of the old Production Code restraints, meaning that the makers of movies from the novels of Harold Robbins could finally show the supposedly sexy tableaux that Robbins had always written about. Among the results is one of the most guffaw-fully funny awful movies ever made from one of hack-meister Harold's books: *The Adventurers*.

Set largely in the mythical kingdom of "Corteguay," a South American nation prone to weekly revolutions, *Adventurers* follows the amorous, glamorous, and decidedly amoral adventures of "Dax Xenos," a child of war first seen at the age of ten, cavorting with a puppy in slo-mo. When soldiers shoot his puppy, then rape and kill his sister *and* his mother in front of him, Dax dedicates himself to a life of vengeance. And when the soldiers who did the deed are put before a firing squad, it's little Dax who pulls the trigger . . . and is then rewarded for being "a man" by getting a kiss—on the mouth—from El Rojo, who will soon be Corteguay's new dictator.

Because he witnessed rape and death at such a young age, Dax forever associates sex with violence, telling his childhood playmate Amparo she is "too young" for them to "do it," adding, "I think I have to kill you afterwards." Entrusted to the care of Ernest Borgnine as Latino revolutionary "Fat Cat" (!), little Dax eventually grows up to be Bekim Fehmiu, an actor *someone* thought would be a big-time movie star. Unfortunately, he looks like a Yugoslavian Ben Gazzara, talks in an unintelligible mumble (even though most of his dialogue has clearly been rerecorded), and has a name that reads like someone had a heart attack at their typewriter.

You may find yourself nearly having a heart attack while laughing at this film's many incredibly inept "dramatic highlights," including a sex scene set in a garden full of naked statues and featuring an in-and-out/faster-and-faster zoom lens simulating an orgasm in a way that's orgasmically idiotic. As Dax reaches his "climax" he sees his screaming sister's face reflected in the swimming pool, and is haunted by the memory. But not so haunted that he can't pursue humping anything and everything female that crosses his path. Enter Olivia de Havilland (!) as a wealthy American woman who hires Dax to be her well-paid gigolo while summering in Rome. The sight of seeing Melanie Wilkes with one of her breasts nearly flopping out from under the bedsheets may haunt *you* forever, but Dax quickly moves on to chasing Candice Bergen, who's described as "the richest girl in the world." At her twenty-first birthday party, Candy and Bekim finally consummate their love in a greenhouse, as the sound goes silent except for the two principals' heavy breathing and the whistling of fireworks bursting overhead (which sound inappropriately like vaudeville slide whistles). All that grunting and groaning creates a baby, but first a pre-nup is in order, and Xenos wants more zeroes on his payment than the family is willing to cough up. Dax then plays the baby card, presenting a letter he says is "from her gine ecologist."

Dax shows up late for his own wedding, but all seems bliss for the happy couple, as they decide to spend her pregnancy on a Mediterranean isle her family happens to own. And when Candy, in a hat that looks like a giant orange Life Saver stuck to her head, asks Dax to push her "higher . . . higher" in a swing, tragedy rears its ugly head: One of the chains on the swing breaks, Candy goes flying like an elephant shot from a cannon, and from the overemoting look on Bergen's face, we know either the baby is lost . . . or Candy is terrified because she's forgotten her next line.

Now that she can no longer provide him an heir, Candy gets an air of doom about her, twisting her fingers into her hospital bedsheets and wracking her shoulders with sobbing as Dax heads on to his next adventure . . . and Intermission. But hang in there, since immediately after Intermission we launch into the funniest, fruggiest, freakiest fashion show ever caught on film, as Dax's old school chum Prince Sergei (pronounced "Sir Gay," get it?) unveils his newest clothing collection in New York. Turns out Candy married Sir Gay on the rebound from Dax (and will later prove to be a gay old soul herself). But first, Dax must return to Corteguay for the unveiling of a statue dedicated to his dead dad, and to visit that playmate he refused to kiss and kill all those years ago. "You and I," he mumbles to Leigh Taylor-Young (yet another whitebread actor unbelievably cast as a Latin character), ". . . was a long time ago." "For me," Leigh replies soulfully, "it was yesterday." "Yesterday," he retorts with deep meaning, "never happen again . . ." Leigh then plays a baby card of her own, introducing Dax to the son he never knew he had. Now he has something to fight for, since as long as her father El Rojo (the guy who kissed Dax at that execution seventeen reels ago) is El Presidente of Corteguay, Leigh/Amparo and their Gerber baby will be held prisoner in a nunnery.

So Dax goes back to his friend Marcel, played by the equally unintelligible Charles Aznavour, who's a whiz at financial matters, but short enough that much of his dialogue is directed at Bekim's navel. The two arrange to ship food to the people of Dax's homeland, negotiating in Marcel's hilariously appointed "secret sex chamber," its walls covered with red velvet, its ceiling cluttered with naked statues whose limbs threaten to put their eyes out, and its furniture shaped like Nomi Malone from *Showgirls* inviting them to lap dance.

Now Dax's *other* old school chum (the one we haven't seen for at least an hour) reappears to tell Dax that Marcel has betrayed him, and is sending guns and ammo along with the relief supplies to Corteguay. So Dax joins up with that week's revolutionary leader El Lobo and waylays the train full of armaments, helping El Lobo to replace El Rojo as leader of their homeland, and effectively setting Amparo and his kid free from their nunnery imprisonment. But Dax's work is still not done, as he's afraid El Lobo may be an even worse leader than El Rojo was, and vows to stay behind, fighting for his people's future. As Amparo and Dax Junior head off in a Jeep with Borgnine (once again appointed El Nannio), Dax surveys the wreckage and waste of war... and a sniper takes aim at him from the roof of the palace...

A nearly three-hour wallow in the ridiculously ribald world of Harold Robbins, *The Adventurers* can boast having not even one believable character, performance, or line of dialogue. But it's all done with such utter sincerity that it's far more entertaining than this same material would be in the hands of anyone but utter incompetents. *Adventurers* struts its empty-headedness like one of those models doing the frug in Sir Gay's fashion show, and it's got more laughs stuffed into its 177 minutes than any of Sir Gay's gowns has sequins. So get your hands on this one, but beware: If you enjoy all those junk-food sex scenes... I think I have to kill you afterwards.

Dippy Dialogue
Reporter for *Teen* magazine *(Jaclyn Smith)*: "Is it true you've made love to every woman in this room?"
Dax Xenos *(Bekim Fehmiu)*, looking soulfully into her eyes: "Not yet..."

Battlefield Earth

(2000/Warner Bros.) **DVD / VHS**

Who's to Blame CAST: **John Travolta** ⊙ *(Terl)*; **Forest Whitaker** ⊙ *(Ker)*; **Barry Pepper** ⊙ *(Johnny "Goodboy" Tyler)*; **Kim Coates** *(Carlo)*; **Richard Tyson** *(Robert the Fox)*; **Kelly Preston** ⊙ *(Chirk)*
CREW: **Directed by Roger Christian** ⊙; **Screenplay** ⊙ by Corey Mandell and J. D. Shapiro; Based on the novel by L. Ron Hubbard

Rave Reviews
"A film that for decades to come will be the punch line of jokes about bad movies!" — **Roger Ebert**, *Chicago Sun-Times*

"One of the worst films ever made. It's that simple. It's *Plan 9 from Outer Space* made with 60 million dollars." — **Mr. Cranky, MrCranky.com**

"I hated this movie, and I had a great time doing it. Hilariously godawful . . . so bad it's actually wildly entertaining!"
— **Rob Blackwelder, SplicedWire.com**

Plot, What Plot? Reportedly John Travolta's "dream project" for more than twenty years, *Battlefield Earth* is based on the novel of the same name by Scientology founder L. Ron Hubbard. When Travolta first started pitching this project to studios, while he was hot off *Saturday Night Fever* and *Grease*, he wanted to play the young protagonist, Johnny "Goodboy" Tyler. By the time he finally found backing, he had to settle for taking the villain role of Terl, a seven-foot-tall "Psychlo" whose race of "superior beings" has taken over Earth in the year 3000. For this role, Travolta wears a codpiece, platform shoes, green grime on his teeth, a mound of Rasta-style hair atop his head, and what look like snot-covered shoestrings dangling from his nose.

Made with the solemn devotion only a religiously inspired film can engender in its makers, this is an extreme example of a vanity production run amok. At several points while watching it, you'll find yourself incredulously wondering if *anyone* was looking at the dailies, or noticed that almost *nothing* about this film works. Its frequent reliance on dizzily akimbo camera angles quickly becomes irritating. Its insistence on transitioning from scene to scene with the same repeated optical wipe device twenty-seven times only serves to call attention to the *one* time the device is *not* used. Its costumes, from the jumpsuits and rags worn by the earthlings to the *Starlight Express*–style outfits adorning the Psychlos, are uniformly hideous, humorous, or both. Its overall look is one of depressing grunge and grime, leaving the audience needing a long, hot shower after sitting though it.

But hang in there! Sprinkled throughout this truly atrocious movie are some of the most laughably lame, inane moments in recent cinema history. Travolta's line readings, almost without exception, suggest he was inspired by both Dishonest John, the villain from the old *Beany and Cecil* cartoon series, and Margaret Hamilton, the Wicked Witch of the West from *The Wizard of Oz*. There's even a moment where, walking through a low-ceilinged set, he whangs his head on a crossbeam, then comments on it. It appears to be an accident the filmmakers left in the final cut, implying that at least *someone* involved in this film did have a sense of humor.

All the characters surrounding Travolta's Terl are equally hammy and embarrassing. Worst Supporting Actor nominee Forest Whitaker as Ker looks like a fugitive from the awful Diana Ross version of *The Wiz*, and speaks many of his lines like he's reading them to first graders. Kelly Preston (Mrs. John Travolta) has a Razzie-"winning" cameo as Chirk, a sort of Psychlo slut coming on to Travolta in a bar by unraveling her eighteen-inch tongue into his lap (!). And Worst Supporting Actor "winner" Barry Pepper, in the role Travolta had originally wanted to play, impressively keeps a straight face, no matter how insipid, illogical, or improbable the situation becomes.

The film's central plot follows Terl's fixation on his own superiority, and how his hubris leads him to train Johnny "Goodboy" to operate the very weapons that will be used at the film's end to challenge the Psychlos' rule over the Earth. Having endlessly told us how intellectually developed Psychlos are, *Battlefield Earth* then contradicts its own basic premise.

In a year in which we presented Razzies in only ten categories, *Battlefield Earth* took *nine* nominations, and wound up with *seven* statuettes. Which helps explain, in part, why the first clip from it at

THE VERY BEST OF THE BERRY WORST

the 21st Annual Razzie Awards was introduced as . . . *Plan 9 from L. Ron Hubbard*.

Dippy Dialogue
Terl *(John Travolta)*, drunkenly bragging in a Psychlo bar: "While you were still learning how to spell your name, I was being trained to conquer galaxies!"

Razzie Credentials
Battlefield Earth got as many Razzie nominations as *Mommie Dearest* (nine) and "won" enough statuettes to tie with our all-time champion *Showgirls* (seven).

Choice Chapter Stop
Chapter 22 ("Blackmailing Planetship"): Mrs. Travolta gives Mr. Travolta a never-to-be-forgotten tongue-lashing . . .

Fun Footnote
At the 21st Annual Razzie Awards, John Travolta's Worst Actor Razzie for this performance was accepted by a nine-inch-tall Talking Terl Action Figure, which said, "You wouldn't last one day at the Academy!"

Body of Evidence 🍓

(1992/MGM) **DVD / VHS**

Who's to Blame   CAST: **Madonna**🍓 *(Rebecca Carlson)*; **Willem Dafoe** 🍓 *(Frank Dulaney)*; **Joe Mantegna** *(Robert Garrett)*; **Anne Archer** 🍓 *(Joanne Braslow)*; **Frank Langella** *(Jeffrey Roston)*; **Jürgen Prochnow** *(Dr. Alan Paley)*; **Julianne Moore** *(Sharon Dulaney)*
CREW: **Directed by Uli Edel** 🍓 **Screenplay** 🍓 **by Brad Mirman**

Rave Reviews
"I've seen comedies with fewer laughs than *Body of Evidence*... excruciatingly incompetent [and] filled with lines that only a screenwriter could love." — **Roger Ebert,** *Chicago Sun-Times*

"It looks as if it wanted to be *Basic Instinct*, though it winds up more like *Ilsa, She-Wolf of the SS* . . . relieved only by unintentional laughter."
— **Vincent Canby,** *New York Times*

"The most enjoyably awful of Madonna's many awful movies."
— **Edward Margulies,** *Movieline* **magazine**

Plot, What Plot? Following fast on the heels of the international hit *Basic Instinct, Body of Evidence* is both a blatant knockoff of it, and an attempt to turn *Sex*, Madonna's best-selling $70 coffee-table book, into a film. The result is one of the funniest, most overheated, over-the-top courtroom sex dramas since Lana Turner retired from the screen.

The movie opens with the camera stealthily moving through a Seattle mansion as rain and thunder rage outside. As we head up toward the master bedroom, we hear a couple indulging in "wild" (and apparently painful) sex. Director Uli Edel, inexplicably unaware that use of a POV camera angle implies that what we are seeing is supposed to be *someone's* point of view, makes the first of his many mistakes when it's revealed that it was only his cameraman, not a character, sneaking up those stairs. Shortly after we reach the bed-

THE VERY BEST OF THE BERRY WORST

room, we see that Madonna has so excited her wealthy, elderly lover that he has died in the throes of passion. We then learn that she had recently been named beneficiary of her now dead lover's $8 million estate. Crackerjack DA Joe Mantegna, unafraid of setting a ludicrous legal precedent, naturally decides to prosecute the Material Girl for murder. Before you can say "She schtupped him to death!" Madonna stands accused of (we kid you not) using her body as a murder weapon. The "Body of Evidence" the title refers to . . . is literally Madonna's. Clever? . . . No!

Cut to the graveside service for the deceased geezer, where Madonna meets the ambulance-chasing defense lawyer played by Willem Dafoe, whose services she's retained. It will soon turn out that he enjoys chasing skirts as well as ambulances, but that's getting ahead of the plot—something almost anyone watching this movie will find themselves repeatedly doing. As the court case proceeds, replete with continual references to handcuffs, nipple clamps, and other "love toys," Dafoe finds himself driven to redefine the lawyer/client relationship with this particular client.

After dropping her off at the windswept houseboat where she lives (and frequently enjoys parading nude before the open windows), Dafoe is suddenly inspired by William Hurt in *Body Heat*, and invites himself in. Groping and grappling their way up the narrow staircase, Madonna and Dafoe finally get to her loft bedroom, which is cluttered with dozens of already lit candles: Is the lawyer being set up, or was Madonna, for once, ahead of the plot herself?

What ensues is one of the most painfully laughable, utterly *un*-erotic seduction scenes ever filmed: Madonna takes Willem's belt off, ties his arms severely behind his back, and goes into an S&M routine. Alternating drips of scalding hot candle wax with splashes of iced champagne, she starts at Willem's chest, "playfully" sucking the champagne and nibbling the candle wax as she slowly works her way south. By the time she gets to his navel, sporting what she thinks is a sloe-eyed come-hither look (but which actually looks like she may arf up what she's already got in her mouth), Madonna's lips are reminiscent of those old floor cleaner commercials warning about "waxy yellow buildup"—and the audience has an uncontrollable case of the giggles. When the hot wax finally hits Willem's willy, theatre audiences (at least all the *male* members!) let out an audible groan. Now that she's scalded the man's scrotum, Madonna's ready to really get down to business.

In the unrated DVD version of the film, Madonna is clearly nude. But before you go getting excited at that prospect, be warned: This was *before* she got so compulsively into physical fitness—and seeing this scene's dailies may have been what convinced her to get into better shape. Simply put, the 1993 nude Madonna looks sadly like the lost love child of Mamie Van Doren . . . and the Pillsbury Doughboy.

Meanwhile, back in the courtroom (filling time till the next kinky sex scene) her dead lover's personal assistant, Anne Archer, archly reveals a dark secret about Madonna's character: "She's a cokehead slut." This bit of testimony apparently so excites Dafoe that he and Madonna now engage in more masochistic sex in the one place no lawyer with a brain would dare risk it: the underground parking lot of the courthouse itself. To afford themselves a modicum of privacy, Madonna smashes an overhead lightbulb, and she proceeds to do the Horizontal Hood Ornament atop his Beemer, with Willem's bare back being ground into the broken glass. Dafoe later defends his client with this priceless bit of firsthand knowledge: "It's not a crime to be a great lay!"

Swayed by this brilliant defense strategy, the jury decides to let Madonna get off in a way she and Dafoe never could. Only after his client is acquitted does it occur to him that, lame as Mantegna's case against Madonna was, she actually *is* guilty. And, as it must to all screen sirens who think they can get away with murder, justice is finally served to Madonna in the film's final moments. As we all know, justice isn't pretty. But when it's served up in a half-baked soufflé like *Body of Evidence*, it *is* pretty funny!

Dippy Dialogue
Rebecca (*Madonna*): "I fucked you, I fucked Andrew, I fucked Frank. That's what I do—I fuck!"

Choice Chapter Stop
Chapter 7 ("White Hot Passion"): The hot candle wax/cold champagne scene (about 40 minutes into the film).

Special Recommendation
Throw a "kinky sex" themed *Body of Evidence* party, complete with dozens of burning candles, iced bottles of champagne, toy handcuffs, nipple clamps, inflatable Madonna dolls, etc. Whenever the movie hits a lull, have everyone pour hot wax and cold champagne on each other.

Exorcist II: The Heretic
(1977/Warner Bros.)   **DVD / VHS**

Who's to Blame   CAST: **Linda Blair** *(Regan MacNeil)*; **Richard Burton** *(Father Lamont)*; **Louise Fletcher** *(Dr. Tuskin)*; **Max von Sydow** *(Father Merrin)*; **Kitty Winn** *(Sharon Spencer)*; **James Earl Jones** *(Kokumo)*; **Paul Henreid** *(The Cardinal)*; **Ned Beatty** *(Edward/Pilot)*
   CREW: **Directed by John Boorman; Screenplay by William Goodhart; Based on characters created by William Peter Blatty**

Rave Reviews
"Everybody's new favorite bad Richard Burton movie. . . . A major financial and critical disaster."
— **Michael Weldon,** *The Psychotronic Encyclopedia of Film*

"There is a very strong possibility that *Exorcist II* is the stupidest major movie ever made." — **John Simon,** *New York* magazine

"An absolute fiasco . . . audiences laughed this hunka-junk off the screen." — **John Stanley,** *Creature Features Movie Guide Strikes Again*

Plot, What Plot? If you're making a sequel to one of the most successful horror movies of all time, you'd better make damned sure it's scary. It also helps if the man you've hired to direct the second installment actually *liked* the film he's making a sequel to. Warner Bros., to their everlasting regret, blew it on both counts when they came up with one of the Truly Great Funny/Bad Films of All Time: *Exorcist II: The Heretic,* or, if you prefer, *Exorcist, Too: The Hilaritic.*
   The original *Exorcist* was the biggest-grossing (and grossest) film of 1973, and was a Best Picture Oscar nominee besides, so making a sequel made perfect sense. But the film that director John Boorman and screenwriter William Goodhart concocted made no sense at all. Jumbled, jump-cut, and overloaded with philosophical mumbo-jumbo, the second *Exorcist* is among the most insanely idiotic sequels ever made.

The movie did draw sellout crowds on opening night, June 17, 1977. But as the film unspooled, the audience—which had come to be scared silly—instead turned on it, finding the movie itself silly, and laughing in all the wrong places. On Hollywood Boulevard, it was reported that moviegoers actually threw things at the screen. By the end of its first weekend, *Exorcist, Too* suffered the humiliation of being outgrossed by the *Jaws* rip-off *The Deep*. Soon it was the laughingstock of the industry, to such an extent that Warners actually flew director John Boorman back from Ireland to recut the entire film, hoping to salvage something from the ashes. But alas, it was too late. The dwindling audiences that still came to *Exorcist, Too* by the time Boorman's recut was ready were coming solely to laugh at it, and they were just as pissed off that this version wasn't funny as opening-night patrons had been that the first cut wasn't scary.

So what exactly was wrong with *Exorcist, Too*? Just about everything. Director Boorman had openly admitted to loathing the first *Exorcist*, and wanted this one to be "uplifting" in its tone. Ellen Burstyn, a Best Actress Oscar nominee for *Exorcist*, essentially said no way in hell when asked to make number two. Jason Miller's character had died at the end of *Exorcist*. And Max von Sydow, who played the priest supervising the original exorcism, would only agree to a cameo appearance. That left chubby-cheeked cherub Linda Blair as the central character. And although she too had been an Oscar nominee for the first *Exorcist*, it was discovered after she was nominated that her most memorable moments all involved body doubles, special effects manipulations, and a "demon voice" dubbed by Mercedes McCambridge.

Exorcist, Too opens with Blair living with Burstyn's "secretary" in a 115th-story high-rise apartment in Manhattan, and undergoing psychotherapy. Unfortunately for her, Blair's mental well-being has been entrusted to Dr. Gene Tuskin, an experimental therapist who's working on a process called Hypno-Sync, which involves wiring two people together and having them mutually "revisit" the patient's past experiences. To make matters worse, Dr. Tuskin is played by Louise Fletcher, who did such a great job with the inmates in *One Flew Over the Cuckoo's Nest*.

Speaking of cuckoo, back in Rome heretical priest Father Lamont wants to investigate von Sydow's exorcism of Regan, apparently hoping to help Blair by proving to be an even worse thespian than she is.

Lamont is played with scenery-chewing, screen-swallowing, hysterical abandon by one of the founding members of Overactors Unanimous, Richard Burton.

Soon Dick, Louise, and Lil' Linda are all hooked together through Hypno-Sync, a device that looks like those two-tin-cans-and-a-string telephones children make, with a throbbing strobe-light-on-a-stick in the center. Together, they take a mental journey back to Regan's old room in Georgetown, where they view a badly restaged version of the exorcism itself. Burton appropriately calls the experience "Horrible, utterly horrible . . . and fascinating!"

Having Hypno-Sunc once, Burton and Blair are now telepathically linked, and when he "flies on the wings of the demon" to find the site of a previous von Sydow exorcism, Blair mentally goes along. This leads to the film's seminal silly moment, when Burton is stoned by primitive priests in Africa while Blair is seen tap-dancing in a high school production of "Lullaby of Broadway." No description can do this scene justice, but it ends with Blair in spasms on the floor, experiencing each blow as obviously rubber rocks bounce off Burton's forehead.

Next, Dick becomes obsessed (one might even say . . . possessed) with the notion of challenging the demon that inhabited Regan, whose name turns out to be Pazuzu (!). Following Regan like a zombie, Burton boards an airplane and they fly back to D.C. through a powerful, conveniently timed thunderstorm. Fletcher realizes Regan has swiped her Hypno-Sync doohickey, and figures out where Linda's heading.

Everyone is reunited in a fun-filled, laugh-laden finale that finds Burton ripping the very heart from the demon and unleashing Blair's inner good, as the entire townhouse topples around them and a "plague of locusts" (actually 10,000 Styrofoam packing squiggles painted brown and shot from vacuum cleaners) swarms around their heads. For some reason, the neighbors all stay inside their homes, more interested in the ending to that night's episode of *Charlie's Angels* than in the devastation going on right next door.

In the original ending, which was greeted with hoots and groans by the opening-night audience, Fletcher greets the now twice-exorcised, doubly good Blair with, "I understand now, Regan. But the world won't . . . not yet!" Then Blair and Burton walk off into a painted backdrop sunrise as the neighbors finally appear. This went over so poorly with audiences that by the 8 p.m. showing the second night, many theatres were emergency-shipped a *new* final reel that simply jump-cut from Blair on the collapsing stairway with a locust on her lip to the end titles, a change so ineptly executed that a ten-year-old child asked the theatre manager in Westwood, "Was this recut!?!?" I know, because *I* was that theatre manager.

Three weeks later, Boorman's complete re-edit was finally ready, and the Westwood theatre where I worked was chosen as the venue where *Exorcist Three* (as wags had dubbed it) would "premiere." When a nattily dressed gentleman came up to me that afternoon and asked for my opinion of the film, I told him that Warners was in such a panic that an "all-new version" would be showing that evening. He then asked if there was anything I thought could be done to salvage the movie, and I snidely replied, "The only thing that could help is if Warners could convince Mel Brooks to put his name on it." The man turned out to be the chairman of the board of Warner Bros.—and the recut played even worse than the tap-dancing, Hypno-Syncing, walk-into-the-sunrise original version.

For the DVD, Warners has thankfully restored the film to its opening-night glory, so you too can now see something so laugh-out-loud lame that you'll be throwing things at your TV set . . . just like those opening-night audiences all those years ago!

Dippy Dialogue
Father Lamont *(Richard Burton)*: "Evil is a spiritual being, alive and living, perverted and perverting, weaving its way insidiously into the very fabric of life!"

Choice Chapter Stop
Chapter 28 ("Torn Out, Torn Apart"): In which Father Dick confronts E-V-I-L and rips the very heart from the Demon Linda Blair, who sits saucily atop her bed wrinkling her nose at Burton in a filmy negligee.

Fun Footnote
Proving that their standards are even lower than those of the Razzies, the Saturn Awards granted *Exorcist, Too* four nominations, including Burton as Best Actor, Blair as Best Actress, and, of course, Best Picture . . .

Glen or Glenda

(1953/Screen Classics)   **DVD / VHS**

Who's to Blame   CAST: **Bela Lugosi** *(Mad Scientist/Narrator)*; **Ed Wood Jr.** *(Glen/Glenda)*; **Lyle Talbot** *(Policeman)*; **Dolores Fuller** *(Barbara)*; **Tommy Haynes** *(Alan/Ann)*; **Timothy Farrell** *(Psychiatrist)*
CREW: **Written and directed by Edward D. Wood Jr.**

Rave Reviews
"The acting is wonderfully ludicrous, made even more so by the solemn, pompous narration . . . an amusing piece of vintage camp!"
— **Howard Kissell,** *Women's Wear Daily*

"Uniformly klutzy—it looks like something Lawrence Welk might make for $1.50!" — **Joseph Gelmis,** *Newsday*

"Even more inept and hilarious than Wood's infamous *Plan 9* . . . could well be the worst movie ever made!"
— *Leonard Maltin's Movie & Video Guide*

Plot, What Plot? Identified by countless bad-movie fans as the worst director of all time (and gloriously saluted in Tim Burton's 1994 biopic), Ed Wood is most often cited for his work on *Plan 9 from Outer Space*, a cheap sci-fi fiasco that is now overexposed and overrated as a trash film classic. Closer to transvestite Wood's heart—and even more odd than *Plan 9*—is this jumbled, brain-boggling tale of two men's efforts to deal with what is now called "gender discomfort." Since Wood himself proudly claimed he stormed the battlefronts of WWII wearing a pink bra and panties under his uniform, he naturally takes one of the woman-wanna-be roles. Under the pseudonym Daniel Davis, Wood plays the title character, a man who finds himself stopping to look longingly in lingerie shop windows, sneaking items from his fiancée's underwear drawer, and literally engaging in a tug-of-war over her fluffy white angora sweater. But even Glen/Glenda isn't willing to go as far as Alan/Ann, who resolves his dilemma by resorting to a sex change operation.

This film was made when Christine Jorgensen had just shocked the world by publicly acknowledging he/she had done just that. But burly men in high heels are *not* this film's most achingly funny element. That distinction goes to Wood cohort Bela Lugosi, playing the film's stentorian mad scientist/narrator. An addled morphine addict when he made this film, Lugosi is supposed to explain the cockeyed stock footage, weird sexual fantasy sequences, and stolid psychological lectures that run throughout the film. Speaking in a voice that sounds like Dracula on downers, Lugosi's every line is memorable.

"Bevare!" he warns, gimlet-eyed. "Diss story *must* be tolt!!" Surrounded by skulls, smoking lab equipment, and other props that look like they were borrowed from Disneyland's Haunted Mansion, Lugosi gives one of the most bizarre performances ever committed to film.

Glen or Glenda's best unintentional running "gag" is its repeated use of a close-up of a newspaper headline, screaming, "WORLD SHOCKED BY SEX CHANGE OPERATION!" This one shot is shown at least twelve times.

Dippy Dialogue
Narrator *(Bela Lugosi)*: "Vat are leetle boys made uff? Bik fat snails? Puppy dok tails? Or maybe . . . brassieres! High heels! Garters!"

Availability and Choice Chapter Stops
Glen or Glenda is a "public domain" title, available on DVD and VHS under numerous imprints, each with different chapter stops. Since it's just over an hour long, we recommend you watch it in its entirety.

Special Recommendations
Show this one to a roomful of friends, and every time one of those close-ups of the newspaper headline appears have everyone scream in shock. Your neighbors'll love it!

The Lonely Lady

(1983/Universal Pictures) **VHS**

Who's to Blame   CAST: **Pia Zadora** *(Jeri Lee Randall)*; **Lloyd Bochner** *(Walter Thornton)*; **Jared Martin** *(George Ballantine)*; **Bibi Besch** *(Veronica Randall)*; **Joseph Cali** *(Vinnie DaCosta)*; **Ray Liotta** *(Joe Heron)*
CREW: **Directed by Peter Sasdy; Screenplay by John Kershaw and Shawn Randall; Adaptation by Ellen Shephard; Based on the novel by Harold Robbins**

Rave Reviews
"Risible concoction, designed to show off the non-talents of a non-star in a film produced by her husband."
           — *Halliwell's Film & Video Guide*

"Typical Robbins sleaze and stupidity. . . . Pia . . . is a classic of non-acting. . . . If you can find this movie, watch it!"
           — Ken Begg, BadMovieNight.com

"A classic Bad Movie howler."
           — **Edward Margulies and Stephen Rebello,** *Bad Movies We Love*

Plot, What Plot? One of my all-time favorite assignments as a trailer-maker was being entrusted to create the entire campaign for Pia Zadora in Harold Robbins' *The Lonely Lady*—knowing the entire time that, come the next spring, it was sure to sweep the 4th Annual Razzies. In rough cut, *Lonely Lady* was one of the funniest bad movies ever made. Sadly, its makers previewed their film in Long Beach a week or two after I saw the rough cut and, realizing what a total turkey they had on their hands, went through the film trying desperately to cut out all the laughs. But without all the laughs, the film was about 17 minutes long. So Universal had to put back in some of the best bad stuff, and, as predicted, *Lonely Lady did* sweep our 4th Annual dis-honors, becoming the first film ever to "win" more than five Razzies.

Adapted from an even trashier than usual Robbins novel, *Lonely Lady* is the story of Jeri Lee Randall, a determined young woman who survives the jungles of Hollywood, all the while struggling to be taken seriously as a screenwriter. And who better to cast as a serious writer than . . . Mrs. Meshulim Riklis, Pia Zadora. Hot off winning a still questioned Golden Globe Award as Best New Star for *Butterfly*—and taking both Worst New Star and Worst Actress Razzies for that same performance—Pia was then riding a wave of publicity largely arranged and bankrolled by her billionaire husband. Apparently when she asked hubby to buy her Harold's book, hubby acquiesced.

The result is a film so shoddily made, so indefensibly inept, and so utterly enjoyable in all the wrong ways that it's a modern classic. Within minutes of the film's opening, we are in flashback mode, traveling inside Pia/Jeri Lee's obviously uncluttered head from this year's "Prestigious Annual Film Awards" back to the day in high school when she won her very first honor, for an essay contest. Wearing an oversized dress, with her hair in pigtails and a rigor mortised grin on her face, Pia looks for all the world like some child molester's idea of the perfect pickup.

Bringing her award to a rich kid's barbecue, Pia is told that it "looks like a penis," and is then violated with a garden hose. Worst Supporting Actress nominee Bibi Besch, as Pia's long-suffering and insufferable mom, decides not to pursue charges of rape, then keeps her opinion to herself when Jeri Lee marries a successful writer roughly three times her age. After a less-than-romantic wedding night, in which a close-up of the couple's feet suggest the groom's pedal extremities are attached to his legs backwards, Pia settles into a glamorous but sexless marriage. Upon publication of her first book, *The Holdout*, Jeri Lee gets her 15 minutes of fame, and the chance to fellate a soap opera actor who wants to option the book. Naturally, this doesn't sit well with Sir Backwards Feet, who trumps his wife's ace by waving a garden hose at her and yelling, "Is *this* more your kick!?!"

Now divorced and "on her own," Pia is thrown over by the soap star and must seek an abortion. But things get progressively worse as she is propositioned by an Italian sex symbol (whose older husband "likes to watch" and, in one of those too-creepy-for-words coincidences, reminds us of Pia's *own* older husband). Next she's hired as a cocktail waitress by sleazy club owner (and Worst Supporting Actor nominee) Joseph Cali, whose idea of a good time is having Pia lie nude atop his pool table while he shoots billiard balls at her crotch (a sequence still referred to by Pia fans as "Eight Ball in the Pia Pocket"). The last straw in the road to Pia's nervous breakdown is when a producer's hefty wife invites Jeri Lee to "join her" topless in a hot tub.

The scene in which Pia literally goes bonkers—featuring her taking a fully clothed shower, smashing every tchotchke in her apartment, and then hallucinating that tiny talking heads are coming at her from the keys of her typewriter—is one of the all-time classic Razzie clips. When this sequence was excised after that Long Beach sneak preview, I threw caution to the wind and told the film's producer how important this scene was to establishing Pia's character and her dilemma. When my client found out what I'd done, he asked why I'd taken such a risk. "Because I *want* that clip for next year's Razzies," I answered, adding, "and besides, if they leave it out, they'll be ruining a perfectly *awful* movie!"

Perfectly awful perfectly describes *Lonely Lady*. From an opening title song that seems to have been written and arranged as a vocal warm-up exercise for the nobody singer who performs it, right through the ending in which Pia accepts a "Best Screenplay" award with an epithet we've endlessly revived in Razzie ceremonies ever since, *Lonely Lady* is an almost nonstop barrage of visual, verbal, and cinematic garbage that makes for one of the all-time great bad-movie-watching experiences.

Dippy Dialogue
Jeri Lee Randall *(Pia Zadora)*, accepting her "Prestigious Annual Film Award" for "Best Screenplay": "I don't suppose I'm the only one who's had to fuck her way to the top!"

Razzie Credential
Lonely Lady was the first film ever to receive more nominations than we had categories: a record-setting eleven nods, when only ten statuettes were given for 1983. It eventually "won" six Berries (also a record at the time) including Worst Song ("The Way You Do It").

Fun Footnote
Lonely Lady was such an awful film to work on that my client and I couldn't resist creating a "joke trailer" for it as a companion to the one we were being paid to produce. It opened with the narration line "They said it couldn't be done . . . too bad they weren't right." If and when MCA Home Video gets around to putting *Lady* on DVD, we'd be glad to provide the joke trailer as one of their Special Features.

Mommie Dearest

(1981/Paramount Pictures)   **DVD / VHS**

Who's to Blame   CAST: **Faye Dunaway** 🍓 *(Joan Crawford)*; **Diana Scarwid** 🍓 *(Adult Christina)*; **Steve Forrest** 🍓 *(Greg Savitt)*; **Mara Hobel** ☉ *(Young Christina)*; **Rutanya Alda** ☉ *(Carol Ann)*

CREW: **Directed by Frank Perry** ☉; **Screenplay** 🍓 **by Robert Getchell, Tracy Hotchner, Frank Perry, and Frank Yablans; Based on the book by Christina Crawford**

Rave Reviews
"The trashiest kind of trash . . . *Bride of Frankenstein* transplanted to the Hollywood suburbs."
— **David Sterritt,** *Christian Science Monitor*

"Flamboyantly gaudy kitsch from beginning to end. . . . For lovers of the outlandish, the inept, the ineffably absurd."
— **David Denby,** *New York* **magazine**

"Dunaway does not chew scenery . . . [she] starts neatly at the corner of the set in every scene and swallows it whole." — *Variety*

Plot, What Plot? The Mother of All Razzie Movies, *Mommie Dearest* is based—incoherently—on Christina Crawford's memoir of life with a monster of a mother. It's also as close to laugh-a-minute incompetence as mainstream Hollywood moviemaking has ever gotten.

The first big laugh comes when Dunaway's Joan Crawford make-up is first revealed. After a five-minute title sequence in which we see her hands, her shoes, and the back of her head but *never* her face, Faye whirls toward the camera for her first full-frontal close-up . . . looking like Tim Curry as Dr. Frank N. Furter in *The Rocky Horror Picture Show*, with eyebrows courtesy of Groucho Marx. And Dunaway's performance is every bit as over-the-top and ridiculous as her makeup. Add in shoulder pads that would do the New York

Jets proud, outrageously styled wigs, and dialogue that could have been written for a 1960s Hammer horror film ("Tina! Bring me the axe!") and you've got a camp classic of the first order.

It's almost impossible to list all of *Mommie*'s hilarious moments, but they include: Joan's axe-wielding/evening-gowned rampage in her rose garden after being fired by MGM; the now legendary "No wire hangers!" sequence, which ends with a priceless expletive from little Christina; and the "Mommie Goes Godzilla" scene, in which Dunaway and Scarwid engage in an off-the-scale catfight and Faye ends up atop Diana, throttling her costar as the younger actress's legs flail every which way, repeatedly revealing her pale pink panties.

The funniest transition in the film occurs when Joan and her two children do a live radio broadcast immediately following the "wire hangers" scene. "Miss Crawford," the announcer breathlessly inquires, "could you tell us what will happen after we leave this evening?" Maybe they'll decorate their Christmas tree...with wire hangers??

Mommie Dearest is one of the all-time Great Bad Movies. Cut down to 90 minutes, it could easily play the midnight movie circuit à la *Rocky Horror*. And think of the convenience: Fans of Faye Dunaway *and* Tim Curry could wear the same makeup to attend *both* films!

Dippy Dialogue
Joan Crawford *(Faye Dunaway)*, addressing a Pepsi executives' meeting: "Don't fuck with me, fellas! This ain't my first time at the rodeo..."

Razzie Credentials
Mommie was the first film ever to "sweep" our awards, winning five tacky trophies from nine nominations. And in 1990, *Mommie* was named Worst Picture of the Decade for the 1980s.

Choice Chapter Stop
Chapter 9 ("No Wire Hangers *Ever!*"): The film's most memorably out-of-control scene, featuring bed straps, wire hangers, Bon Ami, and major eyeball crossing by Dunaway.

Fun Footnote

When *Mommie* bombed big-time its opening weekend, Paramount realized the only way to sell it was as a comedy. So they concocted a print ad for its second weekend headlined "The Biggest Mother of Them All," with a cartoon wire hanger dangling from the film's title. Producer Frank Yablans, who still believed he'd made a serious drama about child abuse, threatened to sue, and the ad was quickly withdrawn.

The Oscar

(1966/Avco-Embassy Pictures) **VHS**

Who's to Blame CAST: **Stephen Boyd** *(Frankie Fane)*; **Elke Sommer** *(Kay Bergdahl)*; **Tony Bennett** *(Hymie Kelly)*; **Jill St. John** *(Laurel Scott)*; **Eleanor Parker** *(Sophie Cantaro)*; **Milton Berle** *(Kappy Kapstetter)*; **Ernest Borgnine** *(Barney Yale)*; **Edie Adams** *(Trina Yale)*; **Peter Lawford** *(Steve Marks)*; **Joseph Cotten** *(Kenneth Regan)*
CREW: **Directed by Russell Rouse; Screenplay by Clarence Green, Harlan Ellison, and Rouse; Based on the novel by Richard Sale**

Rave Reviews
"Should be shown exclusively in theatres that have doctors and nurses stationed in the lobby to attend viewers who laugh themselves sick."
— **Richard Schickel,** *Time*

"Bad movie nirvana beckons in this foot-stompingly funny movie.... Essential, hallucinatory viewing before you ever watch another Academy Awards ceremony."
— **Edward Margulies and Stephen Rebello,** *Bad Movies We Love*

"This bomb has it all: bad story, bad directing, bad dream sequences, bad hair . . . [and] the *absolute* in bad film acting."
— **Michael Sauter,** *The Worst Movies of All Time*

Plot, What Plot? In the pantheon of awful Hollywood movies about how awful Hollywood can be, none shines brighter—or gets viewers laughing harder—than *The Oscar*. Made in 1966 with the full cooperation of the Academy of Motion Picture Arts and Sciences, this is the incredibly shabby tale of how one bad actor made it all the way to being a Best Actor nominee. In a preview of the top-of-the-line/bottom-of-the-barrel cheesiness to come, it opens at an ersatz Oscar ceremony, complete with bleachers full of screaming fans, stars arriving in Buick "limos," and Stephen Boyd as Frankie Fane being interviewed on the red carpet by Hollywood glad-hander Johnny Grant.

Inside, as the house lights dim and Bob Hope launches into his annual monologue about never winning an Oscar, Fane sits in eager anticipation while, across the auditorium, his former best pal Hymie Kelly (!) stares at him in disgust. Played by singer Tony Bennett in what would prove to be both his first *and* his last dramatic role, Hymie begins to narrate the story of how his ex-friend got where he is. Echoing inside his head, we hear Hymie's voice dramatically declare, "You finally made it, Frankie! Oscar night! And here you sit, on top of a glass mountain called success. It's been quite a climb, hasn't it, Frankie? Down at the bottom, scuffling for dimes in those smokers, all the way to the top. Magic Hollywood! Ever think about it? I do, friend Frankie, I do . . ."

From a cheesebag phony Oscar ceremony we're suddenly whisked, through the magic of a B-movie rippling screen effect, to those bygone days when Frankie was promoting hefty, scantily clad stripper Jill St. John, and fighting off crooked club owners trying to screw him out of his dough. In one of the film's more pitiful devices, a string of actual Oscar winners appear in cameo roles, the first of them being Broderick Crawford as a corrupt sheriff scarfing down ice cream as Boyd is roughed up by his deputies. Leaving Nowheresville, Frankie, Hymie, and Laurel head for the Big Apple, where they hope heifer St. John can get a gig as a hoofer, stripping in a club. The club's owner is played by our second slumming Oscar winner, Ed Begley.

But while Laurel works her butt off dancing at night, Hymie and Frankie hang out on her couch or go to "swinging parties in the Village." At one of these, Frankie meets icy blonde (and phonetic English speaker) Elke Sommer as Kay Bergdahl, Frankie's idea of an intellectual. How does he know she's a smart cookie? Because when he asks her where she's from, she brilliantly replies, "Take one from column A and one from column B—you get an egg roll either way!" A fortune cookie couldn't have said it better.

Impressed by her witty repartee, Frankie decides Kay is his kinda woman, and decides to break up with Laurel and support himself for a change. Kay has aspirations of someday being a successful costume designer, and brings Frankie to a rehearsal of the new off-Broadway play she's designing. When Frankie sees an incredibly phony knife fight being rehearsed, he can't help but run up onto the stage to show 'em how it's really done. The violence and passion with which he handles the knife excites Eleanor Parker (merely a former Oscar nominee), as a horny old female agent who looks at Boyd as though he'd make a nice snack. She tells him he's "got something" and decides to mold him into the Next Big Thing.

With the help of Milton Berle as a powerful agent (!), old Eleanor gets Boyd an offer from studio head Joseph Cotten, who refers to his new contract player as "today's meat"—but launches Fane on the road to fame anyway. As Frankie climbs that glass mountain, he brings Hymie out to Hollywood as his sidekick and henchman, but Hymie starts to worry about his pal, who seems to overact everywhere he goes. "Like a junkie shooting pure quicksilver into his veins," Hymie hyperventilates in voice-over, "Frankie got turned on by the wildest narcotic known to man: success!"

But when you're as lousy a heel as Fane, fame can be fleeting. Soon Frankie's nastiness catches up with him, his box office starts slipping, and he hits the skids. Just when he's about to hit Hollywood's rock bottom—he's being asked to do a television series, fer kripesakes—he gets that all-important phone call: He's been nominated for that year's Best Actor Academy Award!

Wall-to-wall with hilariously overheated dialogue and acting so hammy it belongs in a deli display window, *The Oscar* ranks high among the Razzie all-time top ten. Besides the already mentioned charter members of Overactors Unanimous, its cast also includes Oscar winners Ernest Borgnine and Walter Brennan, plus Edie Adams and Peter Lawford. Pickled-pink former screen queen Merle Oberon, hundred-year-old gossip columnist Hedda Hopper, hunchbacked seven-time Oscar-winning costume designer Edith Head, and Ol' Booze Eyes play themselves in cameos at various Hollywood events. But it's the phony Oscar ceremony that provides the film with most of its biggest laughs. As Oberon reads the names of the five Best Actor nominees (wait till you hear the fake film titles appended to names like Lancaster and Sinatra!), Fane's moment of eternal judgment finally comes. Oberon opens the envelope, and the winner is "Frank..." Wanna know which Frank? You'll have to see the film to find out! Like Hymie sez, if you wanna "climb that glass mountain" of Bad Movie Mavenhood, sometimes ya gotta go for the gold—in this case, the Little Gold Naked Man known as *The Oscar*.

Dippy Dialogue
Frankie Fane *(Stephen Boyd)*: "Will you stop beating on my ears! I've had it up to here with all this bring-down!"

Availability
Rarely shown on TV anymore, *The Oscar* is available (with great effort) on VHS. Take our word for it: It's *worth* the effort to see this one!

Showgirls

(1995/MGM/UA) **DVD / VHS**

Who's to Blame CAST: **Elizabeth Berkley** ◉ ◉ *(Nomi Malone)*; **Kyle MacLachlan** ◉ *(Zack Carey)*; **Gina Gershon** ◉ *(Cristal Connors)*; **Robert Davi** ◉ *(Al Torres)*; **Alan Rachins** ◉ *(Tony Moss)*; **Lin Tucci** ◉ *(Henrietta Bazoom)* CREW: **Directed by Paul Verhoeven** ◉ ; **Screenplay by Joe Eszterhas** ◉

Rave Reviews

"An instant camp classic . . . a nearly $40 million movie without anyone who can act!" — **Janet Maslin,** *New York Times*

"A hoot with hooters!" — **Susan Wloszczyna,** *USA Today*

"The first film about Las Vegas that is actually more tasteless *than* Las Vegas!" — **Anthony Holden,** *The New Yorker*

Plot, What Plot? The idea that *anyone* would attempt to make a Serious Drama about lap dancers in Las Vegas is in itself ridiculous. That this idea occurred to the creators of *Basic Instinct* resulted in an all-time Razzie Classic. The central character in *Showgirls* is Nomi Malone ("No Me"—get it?), whom we meet hitchhiking to Las Vegas, where she dreams of Clawing Her Way to the Top in the World of Exotic Dancing. But as any student of bad cinema knows, before she can scale those glitzy heights, she'll have to experience countless humiliations and heartbreaks on the Road to Dreamsville. Before you can say "Whatta slut," Nomi *is* one—dropping her knickers, licking poles, and lap dancing in a dive called the Cheetah Club. Her "big break" comes when she "aces" an audition for an eye-bogglingly tasteless topless revue called "Goddess" at the Stardust Hotel. After her onstage tryout, Nomi also "aces" a second audition in a swimming pool with Kyle MacLachlan in what must rank as one of the funniest sex scenes ever filmed (we don't want to ruin it for you, but think *Flipper Meets Stripper!*). Soon Nomi has her eye on the starring role in

"Goddess," which she'll gladly grab by any means possible. If you've already begun to wonder why there are so damn many shots of the topless dancers traversing the backstage stairs, then you're once again miles ahead of the filmmakers.

By film's end, Nomi's pouty puss is featured on the very same billboard she passed on her way into town, but she's learned a Life Lesson in the process. "Star" Elizabeth Berkley also learned a Life Lesson from making *Showgirls*: Her career has never recovered from this utterly idiotic big-screen debut.

Dippy Dialogue
Al Torres *(Robert Davi)* to Nomi *(Elizabeth Berkley)* backstage: "It must be weird, not having anybody cum onya!"
Henrietta Bazoom *(Lin Tucci)*, appraising Nomi's Stardust costume: "She looks better than a ten-inch dick and you know it!"

Razzie Credentials
Showgirls still holds the All-Time Razzie Record, with thirteen nominations (when only twelve awards were given in 1995) and seven "wins," including Worst Director. Verhoeven set a Razzie precedent by becoming the first Razzie winner *ever* to attend the ceremonies and accept his Tacky Trophy in person.

Choice Chapter Stop
Chapter 23 ("Love for Sale"): In which Nomi visits Zack's backyard pool, and reenacts a sex ed film for dolphins.

Special Recommendation
While we always recommend enabling closed captioning when watching any of the films listed in this book, with *Showgirls* it's even more imperative—seeing Joe Eszterhas's pricelessly puerile dialogue printed out onscreen makes this movie even *more* outrageously funny.

Xanadu

(1980/Universal Pictures)   **DVD / VHS**

Who's to Blame   CAST: **Olivia Newton-John** ☺ *(Kira, the Roller-Skating Muse)*; **Gene Kelly** *(Danny McGuire)*; **Michael Beck** ☺ *(Sonny Malone)*; **Wilfred Hyde-White** *(Voice of Zeus)*; **Coral Browne** *(Voice of Hera)*; **Sandahl Bergman** *(Muse #1)*; **Featuring the music of ELO (Electric Light Orchestra)**
CREW: **Directed by Robert Greenwald**☻; **Screenplay** ☺ **by Richard Christian Danus and Marc Reid Rubel**

Rave Reviews

"Truly a stupendously bad film . . . [in which] Newton-John plays a roller-skating light bulb!" — ***Variety***

"Mushy and limp . . . so insubstantial it evaporates before our eyes!"
— **Roger Ebert,** ***Chicago Sun-Times***

"Flashy but empty-headed. . . . Designed as a showcase for [Newton-John] whose screen charisma is nil!"
— ***Leonard Maltin's Movie & Video Guide***

Plot, What Plot? One of the risks inherent in making a movie designed to cash in on a fad is that if the subject turns out to be a fad-in-the-pan, its popularity can be long dead before the movie ever reaches theatres. One of the briefest fads of the late 1970s, which spawned almost nothing *but* bad movies, was roller disco. And none of the bad movies it spawned were as world-class bad as *Xanadu*, which has the further distinction of being half of the 99-cent double feature that gave me the idea for the Razzies in the first place.

An ill-advised attempt to cash in on Olivia Newton-John's perceived box-office appeal after the mega-hit *Grease*, *Xanadu* is essentially a glitzed-up roller-disco remake of the 1947 Rita Hayworth vehicle *Down to Earth*, the story of a Greek Muse sent to Earth to inspire a mere mortal to follow his dreams. In 1947, the mere mortal was the now forgotten Larry Parks, and the result of the Muse's inspiration was a Broadway musical. In the 1980 remake, the mere mortal is flat-as-cardboard Michael Beck, and the result of the Muse's inspiration is . . . a roller-disco rink called Xanadu.

Filmed with soft lensing techniques so soft that many audience members may be concerned they've suddenly contracted glaucoma, Olivia inspires more laughter than artistry as a daughter of Zeus, the never-before-mentioned Muse "Kira." But then, how could ancient Greeks have guessed that a specific Muse would be needed to oversee the "art" of roller disco?

An inordinate amount of the film is taken up with the trials and travails of Sonny Malone (Michael Beck), a sullen, semi-talented artist who paints billboard-sized reproductions of rock album covers, but dreams of putting his "talent" to work creating the ultimate roller-disco palace. Enter Olivia, who pops out of a wall mural along with her eight sister Muses to the ELO tune "I'm Alive!" (which, in Newton-John's case, may be an overstatement). The other eight sisters all zip off into the stratosphere, leaving neon trails behind them, but Kira/Olivia (K/O) winds up roller-skating in Santa Monica. There she runs into Sonny, who's never before seen a Greek godette on roller skates, and therefore cannot forget K/O.

When Sonny tells a clarinet-playing "beach bum" about his experience, it turns out the bum had a run-in with K/O some forty years ago, when she appeared to him as a big-band singer. In a casting coup that means nothing to the younger audience at whom *Xanadu* was aimed, and proves embarrassing to anyone who *does* recognize him, the clarinetist is played by sixty-eight-year-old Gene Kelly. Of course, Kelly's character is not a bum, but the moneybags backer for Xanadu that movies like this require to propel their plot.

Soon Kelly and Beck are collaborating on bringing their mutual dream to life—both "inspired" by K/O, who keeps popping up at convenient moments and rolling through frame with dopey-looking smiles on her face. When K/O cannot convince Sonny that she's no mere mortal, Sonny pursues his muse right into the wall mural from whence she came. And in one of the film's most eye-irritating sequences, the two of them wind up in an '80s version of Mount Olympus, a neon-glitzed void featuring some of the cheapest-looking bluescreen work ever done. Arguing that they are "in love," K/O and Malone/Beck don't do any better a job of convincing Zeus and Hera than they do of convincing the audience.

And now we've finally arrived at the apotheosis of *Xanadu*'s utter artlessness: the grand opening of the roller disco itself, featuring the single silliest ten-minute musical sequence of all time. It begins with mime-faced jugglers tossing bowling pins at each other as a less-than-lithe Kelly skates toward camera, a frozen smile plastered on his face. Soon a truly odd assortment of skaters ("happy boys" in neon blue outfits, "punks" in zoot suits, and "chicks" in extreme shoulder pads) join Gene in repeatedly yelling the single word "Xanadu!" as they "tap dance" on roller skates, then zip around the club in endless, dizzying circles. Next, the skaters run right over the cameraman and the entire group yells, "Ho!" about a hundred times. Just when you think things can't possibly get any more ridiculous, K/O pops out of a giant neon "X" to sing the title song, showing off how perfectly shaved her armpits are—and risking getting kicked in the head by a group of high-stepping female dancers right behind her, whose kicks repeatedly reveal their underpants.

When the title song ends, we launch into a truly bizarre triplet of "songettes," each featuring Newton-John in progressively hokier, more idiotic costumes. First, she's seen in a razz-berry-and-black outfit, with bows on both ankles, demonstrating that she can tap dance as well as the average eight-year-old. Next, she's seen in formfitting leather-print polyester, her entire body apparently spray-painted with Pam, aptly singing, "Wherever you go, you're a loser!" Then yet another giant neon "X" transitions to a bowlegged, cowboy-clad K/O for a rodeo/square-dance moment. Finally, a third giant neon "X" reveals all eight of K/O's Muse sisters with triangular paperweights stuck to their heads! But wait, they've saved the worst for last: To reprise the title tune K/O comes out in a metallic polyester get-up that makes Olivia look like a Rolls-Royce hood ornament. Just as you're thinking, "What the . . ." all nine sisters are zapped back into their rag-dress costumes from the wall mural, and all but K/O once again zap into space, leaving neon trails behind. From out of nowhere a wind blows up Newton-John's skirt, and suddenly she's blasting off into space, apparently propelled by an Olympic-sized fart . . .

Michael Beck is then seen looking as stunned as all of us feel, and the entire crowd has suddenly disappeared, perhaps fleeing the smell of what's just gone on. Not to worry, though, Zeus and Hera *did* hear their pleas, and Kira is returned to Sonny in the form of a Xanadu cocktail waitress. As they engage in "getting to know each other" dialogue, the music swells and a gargantuan title writes on, reading, "The End, Made in Hollywood, USA."

Dippy Dialogue
Kira *(Olivia Newton-John)*: "It must be frustrating to waste your talents on things that don't really matter to you . . ."

Choice Chapter Stop
Chapter 17 ("Xanadu"): The big, laugh-filled finale.

Fun Footnote
This film was the subject of a famously short review in *Esquire* magazine declaring, "In a word, *Xana*-don't!"

Internet Links for Razzie Movie Guide

For a complete history of the Razzie Awards (or to join up and become a voting member), visit the official Razzie Web site:
www.razzies.com

For a complete history of the Razzies, with links to nominated and "winning" titles' production info on the Internet Movie Database:
www.imdb.com/Sections/Awards/Razzie_Awards/

Getting Your Hands on the Movies Themselves

Most of the titles listed in *The Official Razzie Movie Guide* are available on either DVD and/or VHS through various mail order and Internet services. Below are links for contacting those sources on the Net.

Video Shopping Sites

Amazon.com
The Internet's largest book and DVD emporium, also offering used titles on both DVD and VHS. While you're there, you can buy someone a gift copy of this book:
www.amazon.com

eBay
The world's largest "auction" site, where you can bid on DVDs and VHS tapes, and hope you're the winning bidder. Not immediately gratifying, but a good source for patient buyers:
www.ebay.com

Half.com
An offshoot of eBay that offers instant purchases of DVD and VHS titles, most used, some new:
www.half.ebay.com

Movies Unlimited
One of the larger sites for buying new DVD and VHS titles at or just below full retail:
www.moviesunlimited.com

Video Releasing Companies

Anchor Bay Entertainment
Titles include *Can't Stop the Music, The Car, Duel in the Sun*, and *Supergirl*:
www.anchorbayentertainment.com

Five Minutes to Live Video
An eclectic site devoted to hard-to-find titles like *Impulse*:
www.5minutesonline.com

Image Entertainment
Mostly public domain titles, including *A*P*E* and *Beach Girls and the Monster*.
www.image-entertainment.com

Rhino Video
"The best for buying the worst." Titles include *Orgy of the Dead* Special Edition DVD, and the *Mystery Science Theater 3000 Collection*:
www.rhinovideo.com

Something Weird Video
Specializing in '60s sleaze and "forgotten" stuff like *Wild Wild World of Jayne Mansfield* and *Goliath and the Dragon*:
www.somethingweird.com

Video [DVD] Rental Service

While you can always try your local Blockbuster for titles in this book, you're more likely to find them for rent from the Internet-based mail order service Netflix. As of publication, they carried more than sixty of this book's titles on DVD, and actually have Razzie titles listed under their "Award Winners" subheading:

Netflix
www.netflix.com

Cable Movie Channels

If you'd rather not buy or rent, you can catch some titles on basic cable movie channels. Since they run movies commercially interrupted (and often in expurgated, edited-for-TV versions), we do *not* recommend watching these films on either American Movie Classics or the Sci Fi Channel. Here are links for two basic channels that *do* run some of these films uninterrupted and uncut. Both sites have search engines allowing you to see if a specific title is scheduled to run in the near future:

Fox Movie Channel
All Fox movies, all the time.
www.foxmoviechannel.com

Turner Classic Movies
Mostly MGM, UA, and Warner titles, including *Lylah Clare*.
www.turnerclassicmovies.com

APPENDIX II
THE COMPLETE RAZZIE AWARD HISTORY

"Winners" listed in **BOLDFACE** type

FIRST ANNUAL RAZZIES (1980)

Ceremonies held on Oscar night: Tuesday, March 31, 1981, in Hollywood (Razzie founder John Wilson's living room alcove)

Worst Picture
Can't Stop the Music, *Cruising*, *The Formula*, *Friday the 13th*, *The Jazz Singer*, *The Nude Bomb*, *Raise the Titanic*, *Saturn 3*, *Windows*, *Xanadu*

Worst Actor
Michael Beck, *Xanadu*; Robert Blake, *Coast to Coast*; Michael Caine, *Dressed to Kill* and *The Island*; **Neil Diamond, *The Jazz Singer***; Kirk Douglas, *Saturn 3*; Richard Dreyfuss, *The Competition*; Anthony Hopkins, *A Change of Seasons*; Bruce Jenner, *Can't Stop the Music*; Sam J. Jones, *Flash Gordon*

Worst Actress
Nancy Allen, *Dressed to Kill*; Faye Dunaway, *The First Deadly Sin*; Shelley Duvall, *The Shining*; Farrah Fawcett, *Saturn 3*; Sondra Locke,

Bronco Billy; Olivia Newton-John, *Xanadu*; Valerie Perrine, *Can't Stop the Music*; Deborah Raffin, *Touched by Love*; **Brooke Shields, *The Blue Lagoon***; Talia Shire, *Windows*

Worst Supporting Actor
John Adames, *Gloria*, and Laurence Olivier, *The Jazz Singer* (Tie); Marlon Brando, *The Formula*; Charles Grodin, *Seems Like Old Times*; David Selby, *Raise the Titanic*

Worst Supporting Actress
Elizabeth Ashley, *Windows*; Georg Stanford Brown, *Stir Crazy*; **Amy Irving, *Honeysuckle Rose***; Betsy Palmer, *Friday the 13th*; Marilyn Sokol, *Can't Stop the Music*

Worst Director
John G. Avildsen, *The Formula*; Brian De Palma, *Dressed to Kill*; William Friedkin, *Cruising*; Sidney J. Furie and Richard Fleischer, *The Jazz Singer*; **Robert Greenwald, *Xanadu***; Stanley Kubrick, *The Shining*; Michael Ritchie, *The Island*; John Trent, *Middle Age Crazy*; Nancy Walker, *Can't Stop the Music*; Gordon Willis, *Windows*

Worst Screenplay
Can't Stop the Music, *A Change of Seasons, Cruising, The Formula, It's My Turn, Middle Age Crazy, Raise the Titanic, Touched by Love, Windows, Xanadu*

Worst "Original" Song
"Can't Stop the Music" from *Can't Stop the Music*, **"The Man with Bogart's Face" from *The Man with Bogart's Face***, "Suspended in Time" from *Xanadu*, "Where Do You Catch the Bus for Tomorrow?" from *A Change of Seasons*, "You, Baby, Baby!" from *The Jazz Singer*

SECOND ANNUAL RAZZIES (1981)

Worst Picture
Endless Love, Heaven's Gate, The Legend of the Lone Ranger, ***Mommie Dearest***, *Tarzan, the Ape Man*

Worst Actor
Gary Coleman, *On the Right Track*; Bruce Dern, *Tattoo*; Richard

Harris, *Tarzan, the Ape Man*; Kris Kristofferson, *Heaven's Gate* and *Rollover*; **Klinton Spilsbury, *The Legend of the Lone Ranger***

Worst Actress
Linda Blair, *Hell Night*; **Bo Derek, *Tarzan, the Ape Man*, and Faye Dunaway, *Mommie Dearest* (Tie)**; Brooke Shields, *Endless Love*; Barbra Streisand, *All Night Long*

Worst Supporting Actor
Billy Barty, *Under the Rainbow*; Ernest Borgnine, *Deadly Blessing*; James Coco, *Only When I Laugh* (also Oscar-nominated for this same role); Danny DeVito, *Going Ape!*; **Steve Forrest, *Mommie Dearest***

Worst Supporting Actress
Rutanya Alda, *Mommie Dearest*; Farrah Fawcett, *The Cannonball Run*; Mara Hobel, *Mommie Dearest*; Shirley Knight, *Endless Love*; **Diana Scarwid, *Mommie Dearest***

Worst Director
Michael Cimino, *Heaven's Gate*; John Derek, *Tarzan, the Ape Man*; Blake Edwards, *S.O.B.*; Frank Perry, *Mommie Dearest*; Franco Zeffirelli, *Endless Love*

Worst Screenplay
Endless Love, *Heaven's Gate*, ***Mommie Dearest***, *S.O.B.*, *Tarzan, the Ape Man*

Worst New Star *(New Category)*
Gary Coleman, *On the Right Track*; Martin Hewitt, *Endless Love*; Mara Hobel, *Mommie Dearest*; Miles O'Keefe, *Tarzan, the Ape Man*; **Klinton Spilsbury, *The Legend of the Lone Ranger***

Worst "Original" Song
"Baby Talk" from *Paternity*, "Hearts, Not Diamonds" from *The Fan*, "The Man in the Mask" from *The Legend of the Lone Ranger*, "Only When I Laugh" from *Only When I Laugh*, "You, You're Crazy" from *Honky Tonk Freeway*

Worst Musical Score *(New Category)*
Heaven's Gate, ***The Legend of the Lone Ranger***, *Thief*, *Under the Rainbow*, *Zorro, the Gay Blade*

THIRD ANNUAL RAZZIES (1982)

Worst Picture
Annie, Butterfly, **Inchon***, Megaforce, The Pirate Movie*

Worst Actor
Willie Aames, *Paradise* and *Zapped*; Christopher Atkins, *The Pirate Movie*; **Laurence Olivier, Inchon**; Luciano Pavarotti, *Yes, Giorgio*; Arnold Schwarzenegger, *Conan the Bavarian*

Worst Actress
Morgan Fairchild, *The Seduction*; Mia Farrow, *A Midsummer Night's Sex Comedy*; Kristy McNichol, *The Pirate Movie*; Mary Tyler Moore, *Six Weeks*; **Pia Zadora, Butterfly**

Worst Supporting Actor
Michael Beck, *Megaforce*; Ben Gazzara, *Inchon*; Ted Hamilton, *The Pirate Movie*; **Ed McMahon, Butterfly**; Orson Welles, *Butterfly*

Worst Supporting Actress
Rutanya Alda, *Amityville II: The Possession*; Colleen Camp, *The Seduction*; Dyan Cannon, *Deathtrap*; Lois Nettleton, *Butterfly*; **Aileen Quinn, Annie**

Worst Director
Ken Annakin, *The Pirate Movie*, and Terence Young, *Inchon* (Tie); Matt Cimber, *Butterfly*; John Huston, *Annie*; Hal Needham, *Megaforce*

Worst Screenplay
Annie, Butterfly, **Inchon***, The Pirate Movie, Yes, Giorgio*

Worst New Star
Morgan Fairchild, *The Seduction*; Luciano Pavarotti, *Yes, Giorgio*; Aileen Quinn, *Annie*; Mr. T, *Rocky III*; **Pia Zadora, Butterfly**

Worst "Original" Song
"Comin' Home to You (Is Like Comin' Home to Milk and Cookies)" from *Author! Author!*, "Happy Endings" from *The Pirate Movie*, "It's Wrong for Me to Love You," from *Butterfly*, "No Sweeter Cheater Than You" from *Honky Tonk Man*, **"Pumpin' and Blowin' " from *The Pirate Movie***

Worst Musical Score
Butterfly, Death Wish II, John Carpenter's *The Thing, Monsignor,* **The Pirate Movie**

FOURTH ANNUAL RAZZIES (1983)

Worst Picture
Hercules, Jaws 3-D, ***The Lonely Lady***, *Stroker Ace, Two of a Kind*

Worst Actor
Christopher Atkins, *A Night in Heaven*; Lloyd Bochner, *The Lonely Lady*; Lou Ferrigno, *Hercules*; Barbra Streisand, *Yentl*; John Travolta, *Staying Alive* and *Two of a Kind*

Worst Actress
Loni Anderson, *Stroker Ace*; Linda Blair, *Chained Heat*; Faye Dunaway, *The Wicked Lady*; Olivia Newton-John, *Two of a Kind*; **Pia Zadora, *The Lonely Lady***

Worst Supporting Actor
Joseph Cali, *The Lonely Lady*; Lou Gossett Jr., *Jaws 3-D*; Anthony Holland, *The Lonely Lady*; **Jim Nabors, *Stroker Ace***; Richard Pryor, *Superman III*

Worst Supporting Actress
Bibi Besch, *The Lonely Lady*; **Sybil Danning, *Chained Heat* and *Hercules***; Finola Hughes, *Staying Alive*; Amy Irving, *Yentl* (also Oscar-nominated for this same role); Diana Scarwid, *Strange Invaders*

Worst Director
Joe Alves, *Jaws 3-D*; Brian De Palma, *Scarface*; Brian Herzfeld, *Two of a Kind*; Hal Needham, *Stroker Ace*; **Peter Sasdy, *The Lonely Lady***

Worst Screenplay
Flashdance, Hercules, Jaws 3-D, ***The Lonely Lady***, *Two of a Kind*

Worst New Star
Loni Anderson, *Stroker Ace*; Reb Brown, *Yor, the Hunter from the Future*; Cindy and Sandy (the Shrieking Dolphins), *Jaws 3-D*; **Lou Ferrigno, *Hercules***; Finola Hughes, *Staying Alive*

Worst "Original" Song
"Each Man Kills the Thing He Loves" from *Querelle*, "Lonely Lady" from *The Lonely Lady*, **"The Way You Do It" from *The Lonely Lady***, "Yor's World!" from *Yor, the Hunter from the Future*, "Young and Joyful Bandit" from *Querelle*

Worst Musical Score
The Lonely Lady, *Querelle, Superman III, Yentl, Yor, the Hunter from the Future*

FIFTH ANNUAL RAZZIES (1984)

Worst Picture
Bolero, *Cannonball Run II, Rhinestone, Sheena, Where the Boys Are '84*

Worst Actor
Lorenzo Lamas, *Body Rock*; Jerry Lewis, *Slapstick of Another Kind*; Peter O'Toole, *Supergirl*; Burt Reynolds, *Cannonball Run II* and *City Heat*; **Sylvester Stallone, *Rhinestone***

Worst Actress
Bo Derek, *Bolero*; Faye Dunaway, *Supergirl*; Shirley MacLaine, *Cannonball Run II*; Tanya Roberts, *Sheena*; Brooke Shields, *Sahara*

Worst Supporting Actor
Robby Benson, *Harry and Son*; Sammy Davis Jr., *Cannonball Run II*; George Kennedy, *Bolero*; Ron Leibman, *Rhinestone*; **Brooke Shields (with a moustache), *Sahara***

Worst Supporting Actress
Susan Anton, *Cannonball Run II*; Olivia d'Abo, *Bolero* and *Conan the Destroyer*; Marilu Henner, *Cannonball Run II*; **Lynn-Holly Johnson, *Where the Boys Are '84***; Diane Lane, *The Cotton Club* and *Streets of Fire*

Worst Director
Bob Clark, *Rhinestone*; Brian De Palma, *Body Double*; **John Derek, *Bolero***; John Guillermin, *Sheena*; Hal Needham, *Cannonball Run II*

Worst Screenplay
Bolero, *Cannonball Run II, Rhinestone, Sheena, Where the Boys Are '84*

Worst "Original" Song
"Drinkenstein" from *Rhinestone*, "Love Kills" from *Metropolis*, "Sex Shooter" from *Purple Rain*, "Smooth Talker" from *Body Rock*, "Sweet Lovin' Friends" from *Rhinestone*

Worst Musical Score
Bolero, Giorgio Moroder for *Metropolis* and *Thief of Hearts*, *Rhinestone*, *Sheena*, *Where the Boys Are '84*

Worst New Star
Olivia d'Abo, *Bolero* and *Conan the Destroyer*; Michelle Johnson, *Blame It on Rio*; Apollonia Kotero, *Purple Rain*; Andrea Occhipinti, *Bolero*; Russell Todd, *Where the Boys Are '84*

SIXTH ANNUAL RAZZIES (1985)

Worst Picture
Fever Pitch, ***Rambo: First Blood Part II***, *Revolution*, *Rocky IV*, *Year of the Dragon*

Worst Actor
Divine, *Lust in the Dust*; Richard Gere, *King David*; Al Pacino, *Revolution*; **Sylvester Stallone, *Rambo: First Blood Part II* and *Rocky IV***; John Travolta, *Perfect*

Worst Actress
Arian, *Year of the Dragon*; Jennifer Beals, *The Bride*; **Linda Blair, *Night Patrol, Savage Island*, and *Savage Streets***; Brigitte Nielsen-Stallone, *Red Sonja*; Tanya Roberts, *A View to a Kill*

Worst Supporting Actor
Raymond Burr, *Godzilla '85*; Herbert Lom, *King Solomon's Mines*; **Rob Lowe, *St. Elmo's Fire***, Robert Urich, *Turk 182*; Burt Young, *Rocky IV*

Worst Supporting Actress
Sandahl Bergman, *Red Sonja*; Marilu Henner, *Perfect* and *Rustlers' Rhapsody*; **Brigitte Nielsen-Stallone, *Rocky IV***; Julia Nickson, *Rambo: First Blood Part II*; Talia Shire, *Rocky IV*

Worst Director
Richard Brooks, *Fever Pitch*; Michael Cimino, *Year of the Dragon*;

George P. Cosmatos, *Rambo: First Blood Part II*; Hugh Hudson, *Revolution*; **Sylvester Stallone, Rocky IV**

Worst Screenplay
Fever Pitch, Perfect, **Rambo: First Blood Part II**; *Rocky IV, Year of the Dragon*

Worst Musical Score
Fever Pitch, King Solomon's Mines, Revolution, **Rocky IV**, *Turk 182*

Worst "Original" Song
"All You Can Eat" from *Krush Groove*, "The Last Dragon" from *The Last Dragon*, "Oh, Jimmy!" from *Neil Simon's The Slugger's Wife*, **"Peace in Our Life" from Rambo: First Blood Part II**, "7th Heaven" from *The Last Dragon*

Worst New Star
Arian, *Year of the Dragon*; The New Computerized Godzilla, *Godzilla '85*; **Brigitte Nielsen-Stallone, Red Sonja and Rocky IV**; Julia Nickson, *Rambo: First Blood Part II*; Kurt Thomas, *Gymkata*

SEVENTH ANNUAL RAZZIES (1986)

Worst Picture
Blue City, Cobra, **Howard the Duck and Under the Cherry Moon (Tie)**, *Shanghai Surprise*

Worst Actor
Emilio Estevez, *Maximum Overdrive*; Judd Nelson, *Blue City*; Sean Penn, *Shanghai Surprise*; **Prince, Under the Cherry Moon**; Sylvester Stallone, *Cobra*

Worst Actress
Kim Basinger, *9½ Weeks*, Joan Chen, *Tai Pan*; **Madonna, Shanghai Surprise**; Brigitte Nielsen-Stallone, *Cobra*; Ally Sheedy, *Blue City*

Worst Supporting Actor
Jerome Benton, Under the Cherry Moon; Peter O'Toole, *Club Paradise*; Tim Robbins, *Howard the Duck*; Brian Thompson, *Cobra*; Scott Wilson, *Blue City*

Worst Supporting Actress
Dom DeLuise (as Aunt Kate), *Haunted Honeymoon*; Louise Fletcher, *Invaders from Mars*; Zelda Rubinstein, *Poltergeist II*; Beatrice Straight, *Power*; Kristin Scott Thomas, *Under the Cherry Moon*

Worst Director
Jim Goddard, *Shanghai Surprise*; Willard Huyck, *Howard the Duck*; Stephen King, *Maximum Overdrive*; Michelle Manning, *Blue City*; **Prince, *Under the Cherry Moon***

Worst Screenplay
Cobra, ***Howard the Duck***, *9½ Weeks, Shanghai Surprise, Under the Cherry Moon*

Worst New Star
Joan Chen, *Tai Pan*; Mitch Gaylord, *American Anthem*; **The Six Guys (and Gals) in the Duck Suit, *Howard the Duck***; Kristin Scott Thomas, *Under the Cherry Moon*; Brian Thompson, *Cobra*

Worst "Original" Song
"Howard the Duck" from *Howard the Duck*, "I Do What I Do" from *9½ Weeks*, "Life in a Looking Glass" from *That's Life*, "Shanghai Surprise" from *Shanghai Surprise*, **"Love or Money" from *Under the Cherry Moon***

Worst Special Visual Effects *(New Category)*
Howard the Duck, *Invaders from Mars, King Kong Lives*

EIGHTH ANNUAL RAZZIES (1987)

Worst Picture
Ishtar, Jaws: The Revenge, ***Leonard Part 6****, Tough Guys Don't Dance, Who's That Girl?*

Worst Actor
Bruce the Shark, *Jaws: The Revenge*; **Bill Cosby, *Leonard Part 6***; Judd Nelson, *From the Hip*; Ryan O'Neal, *Tough Guys Don't Dance*; Sylvester Stallone, *Over the Top*

Worst Actress
Lorraine Gary, *Jaws: The Revenge*; Sondra Locke, *Ratboy*; **Madonna,**

Who's That Girl?; Debra Sandlund, *Tough Guys Don't Dance*; Sharon Stone, *Allan Quatermain and the Lost City of Gold*

Worst Supporting Actor
Billy Barty, *Masters of the Universe*; Tom Bosley, *Million Dollar Mystery*; Michael Caine, *Jaws: The Revenge*; Mack Dryden and Jamie Alcroft, *Million Dollar Mystery*; **David Mendenhall, *Over the Top***

Worst Supporting Actress
Gloria Foster, *Leonard Part 6*; **Daryl Hannah, *Wall Street***; Mariel Hemingway, *Superman IV: The Quest for Peace*; Grace Jones, *Siesta*; Isabella Rossellini, *Siesta* and *Tough Guys Don't Dance*

Worst Director
James Foley, *Who's That Girl?*; **Elaine May, *Ishtar*, and Norman Mailer, *Tough Guys Don't Dance* (Tie)**; Joseph Sargent, *Jaws: The Revenge*; Paul Weiland, *Leonard Part 6*

Worst Screenplay
Ishtar, *Jaws: The Revenge*, ***Leonard Part 6***, *Tough Guys Don't Dance*, *Who's That Girl?*

Worst New Star
The Garbage Pail Kids, *The Garbage Pail Kids Movie*; **David Mendenhall, *Over the Top***; David and Peter Paul, *The Barbarians*; Debra Sandlund, *Tough Guys Don't Dance*; Jim Varney, *Ernest Goes to Camp*

Worst "Original" Song
"El Coco Loco (So, *So* Bad)" from *Who's That Girl?*, **"I Want Your Sex" from *Beverly Hills Cop II***, "Let's Go to Heaven in My Car" from *Police Academy 4*, "Million Dollar Mystery" from *Million Dollar Mystery*, "You Can Be a Garbage Pail Kid" from *The Garbage Pail Kids Movie*

Worst Special Visual Effects
The Garbage Pail Kids Movie, ***Jaws: The Revenge***, *Superman IV: The Quest for Peace*

NINTH ANNUAL RAZZIES (1988)

Worst Picture
Caddyshack II, ***Cocktail***, *Hot to Trot*, *Mac and Me*, *Rambo III*

Worst Actor
Tom Cruise, *Cocktail*; Bob "Bobcat" Goldthwait, *Hot to Trot*; Jackie Mason, *Caddyshack II*; Burt Reynolds, *Rent-a-Cop* and *Switching Channels*; **Sylvester Stallone, Rambo III**

Worst Actress
Rebecca De Mornay, *And God Created Woman*; Whoopi Goldberg, *The Telephone*; **Liza Minnelli, Arthur 2: On the Rocks and Rent-a-Cop**; Cassandra Peterson, *Elvira: Mistress of the Dark*; Vanity, *Action Jackson*

Worst Supporting Actor
Dan Aykroyd, Caddyshack II; Billy Barty, *Willow*; Richard Crenna, *Rambo III*; Harvey Keitel, *The Last Temptation of Christ*; Christopher Reeve, *Switching Channels*

Worst Supporting Actress
Eileen Brennan, *The New Adventures of Pippi Longstocking*; Daryl Hannah, *High Spirits*; Mariel Hemingway, *Sunset*; **Kristy McNichol, Two Moon Junction**; Zelda Rubinstein, *Poltergeist III*

Worst Director
Michael Dinner, *Hot to Trot*; Roger Donaldson, *Cocktail*; **Blake Edwards, Sunset, and Stewart Raffill, Mac and Me (Tie!)**; Peter Macdonald, *Rambo III*

Worst Screenplay
Cocktail, *Hot to Trot, Mac and Me, Rambo III, Willow*

Worst New Star
Don (The Talking Horse), *Hot to Trot*; Tami Erin, *The New Adventures of Pippi Longstocking*; **Ronald McDonald (as himself)**, *Mac and Me*; Robby Rosa, *Salsa*; Jean-Claude Van Damme, *Bloodsport*

Worst "Original" Song
"Jack Fresh" from *Caddyshack II*, "Skintight" from *Johnny Be Good*, "Therapist" from *A Nightmare on Elm Street 4*

TENTH ANNUAL RAZZIES (1989)

Worst Picture
Karate Kid III, Lock Up, Road House, Speed Zone, **Star Drek V**

Worst Actor
Tony Danza, *She's Out of Control*; Ralph Macchio, *Karate Kid III*; **William Shatner, *Star Drek V***; Sylvester Stallone, *Lock Up* and *Tango & Cash*; Patrick Swayze, *Next of Kin* and *Road House*

Worst Actress
Jane Fonda, *Old Gringo*; **Heather Locklear, *Return of the Swamp Thing***; Brigitte Nielsen, *Bye-Bye Baby*; Paulina Porizkova, *Her Alibi*; Ally Sheedy, *Heart of Dixie*

Worst Supporting Actor
Christopher Atkins, *Listen to Me*; Ben Gazzara, *Road House*; DeForest Kelley, *Star Drek V*; Noriyuki "Pat" Morita, *Karate Kid III*; Donald Sutherland, *Lock Up*

Worst Supporting Actress
Angelyne, *Earth Girls Are Easy*; Anne Bancroft, *Bert Rigby, You're a Fool*; Madonna, *Bloodhounds of Broadway*; Kurt Russell (in drag) *Tango & Cash*; **Brooke Shields (as herself), *Speed Zone***

Worst Director
John G. Avildsen, *Karate Kid III*; Jim Drake, *Speed Zone*; Rowdy Herrington, *Road House*; Eddie Murphy, *Harlem Nights*; **William Shatner, *Star Drek V***

Worst Screenplay
Harlem Nights, *Karate Kid III*, *Road House*, *Star Drek V*, *Tango & Cash*

Worst "Original" Song
"Bring Your Daughter to the Slaughter" from *Nightmare on Elm Street 5*; "Let's Go!" from *Nightmare on Elm Street 5*; "(I Don't Wanna Be Buried in a) Pet Sematary" from *Pet Sematary*

SPECIAL WORST OF THE DECADE AWARDS
Presented at the Tenth Annual Razzies

Worst Picture of the Decade
Bolero, *Howard the Duck*, *The Lonely Lady*, ***Mommie Dearest***, *Star Drek V*

Worst Actor of the Decade
Christopher Atkins, Ryan O'Neal, Prince, **Sylvester Stallone**, John Travolta

Worst Actress of the Decade
Bo Derek, Faye Dunaway, Madonna, Brooke Shields, Pia Zadora

Worst New Star of the Decade
Christopher Atkins, Madonna, Prince, Diana Scarwid, **Pia Zadora**

ELEVENTH ANNUAL RAZZIES (1990)

Worst Picture
The Adventures of Ford Fairlane and *Ghosts Can't Do It* **(Tie)**, *The Bonfire of the Vanities*, *Graffiti Bridge*, *Rocky V*

Worst Actor
Andrew Dice Clay, *The Adventures of Ford Fairlane*; Prince, *Graffiti Bridge*; Mickey Rourke, *Desperate Hours* and *Wild Orchid*; George C. Scott, *Exorcist III*; Sylvester Stallone, *Rocky V*

Worst Actress
Bo Derek, *Ghosts Can't Do It*; Melanie Griffith, *The Bonfire of the Vanities*; Bette Midler, *Stella*; Molly Ringworm, *Betsy's Wedding*; Talia Shire, *Rocky V*

Worst Supporting Actor
Leo Damian, *Ghosts Can't Do It*; Gilbert Gottfried, *The Adventures of Ford Fairlane, Look Who's Talking Too,* and *Problem Child*; Wayne Newton, *The Adventures of Ford Fairlane*; **Donald Trump (as himself), *Ghosts Can't Do It***; Burt Young, *Rocky V*

Worst Supporting Actress
Roseanne Barr (voice only, *Look Who's Talking Too*; Kim Cattrall, *The Bonfire of the Vanities*; **Sofia Coppola, *Godfather III***; Julie Newmar, *Ghosts Can't Do It*; Ally Sheedy, *Betsy's Wedding*

Worst Director
John G. Avildsen, *Rocky V*; Brian De Palma, *The Bonfire of the Vanities*; **John Derek, *Ghosts Can't Do It***; Renny Harlin, *The Adventures of Ford Fairlane*; Prince, *Graffiti Bridge*

Worst Screenplay
The Adventures of Ford Fairlane, *The Bonfire of the Vanities*, *Ghosts Can't Do It*, *Graffiti Bridge*, *Rocky V*

Worst New Star
Ingrid Chavez, *Graffiti Bridge*; **Sofia Coppola, *The Godfather: Part III***; Leo Damian, *Ghosts Can't Do It*; Carré Otis, *Wild Orchid*; Donald Trump, *Ghosts Can't Do It*

Worst "Original" Song
"He's Comin' Back (The Devil!)" from *Repossessed*, "The Measure of a Man" from *Rocky V*, "One More Cheer for Me!" from *Stella*

TWELFTH ANNUAL RAZZIES (1991)

Worst Picture
Cool as Ice, *Dice Rules*, **Hudson Hawk**, *Nothing but Trouble*, *Return to the Blue Lagoon*

Worst Actor
Andrew Dice Clay, *Dice Rules*; **Kevin Costner, *Robin Hood: Prince of Dweebs***; Sylvester Stallone, *Oscar*; Vanilla Ice, *Cool as Ice*; Bruce Willis, *Hudson Hawk*

Worst Actress
Kim Basinger, *The Marrying Man*; Sally Field, *Not without My Daughter*; Madonna, *Truth or Dare*; Demi Moore, *The Butcher's Wife* and *Nothing but Trouble*; **Sean Young (as the Twin Who Survives), *A Kiss Before Dying***

Worst Supporting Actress
Sandra Bernhard, *Hudson Hawk*; John Candy (in drag), *Nothing but Trouble*; Julia Roberts, *Hook*; Marisa Tomei, *Oscar*; **Sean Young (as the Twin Who's Murdered), *A Kiss Before Dying***

Worst Supporting Actor
Dan Aykroyd, *Nothing but Trouble*; Richard E. Grant, *Hudson Hawk*; Anthony Quinn, *Mobsters*; Christian Slater, *Mobsters* and *Robin Hood: Prince of Dweebs*; John Travolta, *Shout!*

Worst Director
Dan Aykroyd, *Nothing but Trouble*; William A. Graham, *Return to the*

Blue Lagoon; David Kellogg, *Cool as Ice*; John Landis, *Oscar*; **Michael Lehmann, *Hudson Hawk***

Worst Screenplay
Cool as Ice, Dice Rules, ***Hudson Hawk****, Nothing but Trouble, Return to the Blue Lagoon*

Worst New Star
Brian Bosworth, *Stone Cold*; Milla Jovovich, *Return to the Blue Lagoon*; Brian Krause, *Return to the Blue Lagoon*; Kristin Minter, *Cool as Ice*; **Vanilla Ice, *Cool as Ice***

Worst "Original" Song
"Addams Groove" from *The Addams Family*, "Cool as Ice" from *Cool as Ice*, "Why Was I Born (Freddy's Dead)" from *Freddy's Dead: The Final Nightmare*

THIRTEENTH ANNUAL RAZZIES (1992)

Worst Picture
The Bodyguard, Christopher Columbus: The Discovery, Final Analysis, Newsies, ***Shining Through***

Worst Actor
Kevin Costner, *The Bodyguard*; Michael Douglas, *Basic Instinct* and *Shining Through*; Jack Nicholson, *Hoffa* and *Man Trouble*; **Sylvester Stallone, *Stop! Or My Mom Will Shoot***; Tom Selleck, *Folks*

Worst Actress
Kim Basinger, *Cool World* and *Final Analysis*, Lorraine Bracco, *Medicine Man* and *Traces of Red*, **Melanie Griffith, *Shining Through* and *A Stranger Among Us***; Whitney Houston, *The Bodyguard*; Sean Young, *Love Crimes*

Worst Supporting Actor
Alan Alda, *Whispers in the Dark*; Marlon Brando, *Christopher Columbus: The Discovery*; Danny De Vito, *Batman Returns*; Robert Duvall, *Newsies*; **Tom Selleck (as King Ferdinand of Spain), *Christopher Columbus: The Discovery***

Worst Supporting Actress
Ann-Margret, *Newsies*; **Estelle Getty, *Stop! Or My Mom Will Shoot***;

Tracy Pollan, *A Stranger among Us*; Jeanne Tripplehorn, *Basic Instinct*; Sean Young, *Once Upon a Crime*

Worst Director
Danny DeVito, *Hoffa*; John Glen, *Christopher Columbus: The Discovery*; Barry Levinson, *Toys*; Kenny Ortega, *Newsies*; **David Seltzer, Shining Through**

Worst Screenplay
The Bodyguard, Christopher Columbus: The Discovery, Final Analysis, Shining Through, **Stop! Or My Mom Will Shoot**

Worst New Star
George Corraface, *Christopher Columbus: The Discovery*; Kevin Costner's Crew Cut, *The Bodyguard*; Whitney Houston, *The Bodyguard*; **Pauly Shore, Encino Man**; Sharon Stone's "Tribute to Theodore Cleaver," *Basic Instinct*

Worst "Original" Song
"Book of Days" from *Far and Away*, **"High Times, Hard Times" from Newsies**, "Queen of the Night" from *The Bodyguard*

FOURTEENTH ANNUAL RAZZIES (1993)

Worst Picture
Body of Evidence, Cliffhanger, **Indecent Proposal**, *Last Action Hero, Sliver*

Worst Actor
William Baldwin, *Sliver*; Willem Dafoe, *Body of Evidence*; Robert Redford, *Indecent Proposal*; **Burt Reynolds, Cop and a Half**; Arnold Schwarzenegger, *Last Action Hero*

Worst Actress
Melanie Griffith, *Born Yesterday*; Janet Jackson, *Poetic Justice*; **Madonna, Body of Evidence**; Demi Moore, *Indecent Proposal*; Sharon Stone, *Sliver*

Worst Supporting Actor
Tom Berenger, *Sliver*; **Woody Harrelson, Indecent Proposal**; John Lithgow, *Cliffhanger*; Chris O'Donnell, *The Three Musketeers*; Keanu Reeves, *Much Ado about Nothing*

Worst Supporting Actress
Anne Archer, *Body of Evidence*; Sandra Bullock, *Demolition Man*; Colleen Camp, *Sliver*; **Faye Dunaway, *The Temp***; Janine Turner, *Cliffhanger*

Worst Director
Uli Edel, *Body of Evidence*; **Jennifer Chambers Lynch, *Boxing Helena***; Adrian Lyne, *Indecent Proposal*; John McTiernan, *Last Action Hero*; Philip Noyce, *Sliver*

Worst Screenplay
Body of Evidence, Cliffhanger, ***Indecent Proposal****, Last Action Hero, Sliver*

Worst New Star
Roberto Benigni, *Son of the Pink Panther*; Mason Gamble, *Dennis the Menace*; Norman D. Golden III, *Cop and a Half*; **Janet Jackson, *Poetic Justice***; Austin O'Brien, *Last Action Hero*

Worst "Original" Song
"Addams Family (WHOOMP!)" from *Addams Family Values*, "Big Gun" from *Last Action Hero*, "(You Love Me) In All the Right Places" from *Indecent Proposal*

FIFTEENTH ANNUAL RAZZIES (1994)

Worst Picture
Color of Night*, North, On Deadly Ground, The Specialist, Wyatt Earp*

Worst Remake or Sequel *(New Category)*
Beverly Hills Cop III, City Slickers II, The Flintstones, Love Affair, ***Wyatt Earp***

Worst Actor
Kevin Costner, *Wyatt Earp*; Macaulay Culkin, *Getting Even with Dad, The Pagemaster,* and *Richie Rich*; Steven Seagal, *On Deadly Ground*; Sylvester Stallone, *The Specialist*; Bruce Willis, *Color of Night* and *North*

Worst Actress
Kim Basinger, *The Getaway*; Joan Chen, *On Deadly Ground*; Jane March, *Color of Night*; **Sharon Stone, *Intersection* and *The Specialist***; Uma Thurman, *Even Cowgirls Get the Blues*

Worst Screen Couple *(New Category)*
Any Combination of Two People from the Entire Cast, *Color of Night*; Dan Aykroyd & Rosie O'Donnell, *Exit to Eden*; Kevin Costner & Any of His Three Wives, *Wyatt Earp*; **Tom Cruise & Brad Pitt, *Interview with the Vampire*, and Sylvester Stallone & Sharon Stone, *The Specialist* (Tie)**

Worst Supporting Actor
Dan Aykroyd, *Exit to Eden* and *North*; Jane March (as "Richie"), *Color of Night*; William Shatner, *Star Trek: Generations*; **O. J. Simpson, *The Naked Gun 33⅓: The Final Insult***; Rod Steiger, *The Specialist*

Worst Supporting Actress
Kathy Bates, *North*; **Rosie O'Donnell, *Car 54, Where Are You?*, *Exit to Eden*, and *The Flintstones***; Elizabeth Taylor, *The Flintstones*; Lesley Ann Warren, *Color of Night*, Sean Young, *Even Cowgirls Get the Blues*

Worst Director
Lawrence Kasdan, *Wyatt Earp*; John Landis, *Beverly Hills Cop III*; Rob Reiner, *North*; Richard Rush, *Color of Night*; **Steven Seagal, *On Deadly Ground***

Worst Screenplay
Color of Night, ***The Flintstones* (written by 35 people)**, *Milk Money*, *North*, *On Deadly Ground*

Worst New Star
Jim Carrey, *Ace Ventura: Pet Detective*; Chris Elliott, *Cabin Boy*; Chris Isaak, *Little Buddha*; Shaquille O'Neal, *Blue Chips*; **Anna Nicole Smith, *The Naked Gun 33⅓: The Final Insult***

Worst "Original" Song
"The Color of the Night" from *Color of Night*, **"Marry the Mole!" from *Thumbelina***, "Under the Same Sun" from *On Deadly Ground*

SIXTEENTH ANNUAL RAZZIES (1995)

Worst Picture
Congo, *It's Pat*, *The Scarlet Letter*, ***Showgirls***, *Waterworld*

Worst Actor
Kevin Costner, *Waterworld*; Kyle MacLachlan, *Showgirls*; Keanu Reeves, *Johnny Mnemonic* and *A Walk in the Clouds*; **Pauly Shore, *Jury Duty***; Sylvester Stallone, *Assassins* and *Judge Dredd*

Worst Actress
Elizabeth Berkley, *Showgirls*; Cindy Crawford, *Fair Game*; Demi Moore, *The Scarlet Letter*; Julia Sweeney, *It's Pat*; Sean Young, *Dr. Jekyll and Ms. Hyde*

Worst Screen Couple
Any Two People (or Two Body Parts!), *Showgirls*; Billy Baldwin & Cindy Crawford, *Fair Game*; Tim Daly & Sean Young, *Dr. Jekyll and Ms. Hyde*; David Foley & Julia Sweeney, *It's Pat*; Demi Moore & *either* Robert Duvall *or* Gary Oldman, *The Scarlet Letter*

Worst Supporting Actor
Tim Curry, *Congo*; Robert Davi, *Showgirls*; Robert Duvall, *The Scarlet Letter*; **Dennis Hopper, *Waterworld***; Alan Rachins, *Showgirls*

Worst Supporting Actress
Amy the Talking Gorilla, *Congo*; Bo Derek, *Tommy Boy*; Gina Gershon, *Showgirls*; **Madonna, *Four Rooms***; Lin Tucci, *Showgirls*

Worst Remake or Sequel
Ace Ventura: When Nature Calls, *Dr. Jekyll and Ms. Hyde*, ***The Scarlet Letter***, *Showgirls* (remake of both *All About Eve* and *The Lonely Lady*), *Village of the Damned*

Worst Director
Renny Harlin, *Cutthroat Island*; Roland Joffé, *The Scarlet Letter*; Frank Marshall, *Congo*; Kevin Reynolds (with unasked assistance from Kevin Costner), *Waterworld*; **Paul Verhoeven, *Showgirls***

The Joe Eszterhas Dis-Honorarial Worst Screenplay Award
Congo, *It's Pat*, *Jade*, *The Scarlet Letter*, ***Showgirls*** **(written by Joe Eszterhas)**

Worst New Star
Amy the Talking Gorilla, *Congo*; **Elizabeth Berkley, *Showgirls***; David Caruso, *Kiss of Death* and *Jade*; Cindy Crawford, *Fair Game*; Julia Sweeney, *It's Pat* and *Stuart Saves His Family*

Worst "Original" Song
"(Feel the) Spirit of Africa" from *Congo*, "Hold Me, Thrill Me, Kiss Me, Kill Me" from *Batman Forever*, **"Walk into the Wind (a.k.a. Love Theme from the Rape Scene)" from *Showgirls***

SEVENTEENTH ANNUAL RAZZIES (1996)

Worst Picture
Barb Wire, Ed, The Island of Dr. Moreau, ***Striptease****, The Stupids*

Worst Actor
Tom Arnold, ***Big Bully***, ***Carpool***, **and** ***The Stupids***, **and Pauly Shore,** ***Bio-Dome*** **(Tie)**; Keanu Reeves, *Chain Reaction*; Adam Sandler, *Bulletproof* and *Happy Gilmore*; Sylvester Stallone, *Daylight*

Worst Actress
Whoopi Goldberg, *Bogus, Eddie,* and *Theodore Rex*; Melanie Griffith, *Two Much*; Pamela Anderson, *Barb Wire*; **Demi Moore,** ***The Juror*** **and** ***Striptease***; Julia Roberts, *Mary Reilly*

Worst Screen Couple
Beavis & Butt-Head, *Beavis and Butt-Head Do America*; Marlon Brando & That Darn Dwarf, *The Island of Dr. Moreau*; Matt Le Blanc & Ed (The Mechanical Monkey), *Ed*; Pamela Anderson's "Impressive Enhancements," *Barb Wire*; **Demi Moore & Burt Reynolds,** ***Striptease***

Worst Supporting Actor
Marlon Brando, ***The Island of Dr. Moreau***; Val Kilmer, *The Ghost and the Darkness* and *The Island of Dr. Moreau*; Steven Seagal, *Executive Decision*; Burt Reynolds, *Striptease*; Quentin Tarantino, *From Dusk Till Dawn*

Worst Supporting Actress
Faye Dunaway, *The Chamber* and *Dunston Checks In*; Jami Gertz, *Twister*, **Melanie Griffith,** ***Mulholland Falls***; Daryl Hannah, *Two Much*; Teri Hatcher, *Heaven's Prisoners* and *2 Days in the Valley*

The Joe Eszterhas Worst-Written Film Grossing Over $100 Million Award *(New Category)*
The Hunchback of Notre Dame, Independence Day, Mission: Impossible, A Time to Kill, ***Twister***

Worst Director
Andrew Bergman, ***Striptease***; John Frankenheimer, *The Island of Dr. Moreau*; Stephen Frears, *Mary Reilly*; John Landis, *The Stupids*; Brian Levant, *Jingle All the Way*

Worst Screenplay
Barb Wire, Ed, The Island of Dr. Moreau, **Striptease**, *The Stupids*

Worst New Star
Beavis and Butt-Head, *Beavis and Butt-Head Do America*; Ellen DeGeneres, *Mr. Wrong*; *Friends* Cast Members Turned Movie-Star-Wanna-Be's; **Pamela Anderson, *Barb Wire***; The New "Serious" Sharon Stone, *Diabolique* and *Last Dance*

Worst "Original" Song
"Pussy, Pussy, Pussy (Whose Kitty Cat Are You?)" from *Striptease*, "Welcome to Planet Boom! (a.k.a. This Boom's for You)" from *Barb Wire*, "Whenever There Is Love (Love Theme from *Daylight*)" from *Daylight*

EIGHTEENTH ANNUAL RAZZIES (1997)

Worst Picture
Anaconda, Batman & Robin, Fire Down Below, **The Postman**, *Speed 2: Cruise Control*

Worst Actor
Kevin Costner, *The Postman*; Val Kilmer, *The Saint*; Shaquille O'Neal, *Steel*; Steven Seagal, *Fire Down Below*; Jon Voight, *Anaconda*

Worst Actress
Sandra Bullock, *Speed 2: Cruise Control*; Fran Drescher, *The Beautician and the Beast*; Lauren Holly, *A Smile Like Yours* and *Turbulence*; **Demi Moore, *G.I. Jane***; Alicia Silverstone, *Excess Baggage*

Worst Screen Couple
Sandra Bullock & Jason Patric, *Speed 2: Cruise Control*; George Clooney & Chris O'Donnell, *Batman & Robin*; **Dennis Rodman & Jean-Claude Van Damme, *Double Team***; Steven Seagal & His Guitar, *Fire Down Below*; Jon Voight & The Animatronic Anaconda, *Anaconda*

Worst Supporting Actor
Willem Dafoe, *Speed 2: Cruise Control*; Chris O'Donnell, *Batman & Robin*; **Dennis Rodman, *Double Team***; Arnold Schwarzenegger, *Batman & Robin*; Jon Voight, *Most Wanted* and *U-Turn*

Worst Supporting Actress
Faye Dunaway, *Albino Alligator*; Milla Jovovich, *The Fifth Element*; Julia Louis-Dreyfus, *Father's Day*; **Alicia Silverstone, *Batman & Robin***; Uma Thurman, *Batman & Robin*

Worst Reckless Disregard for Human Life and Public Property *(New Category)*
Batman & Robin, ***Con Air***, *Lost World: Jurassic Park*, *Turbulence*, *Volcano*

Worst Remake or Sequel
Batman & Robin, *Home Alone 3*, *The Lost World: Jurassic Park*, *McHale's Navy*, ***Speed 2: Cruise Control***

Worst Director
Kevin Costner, *The Postman*; Jan De Bont, *Speed 2: Cruise Control*; Luis Llosa, *Anaconda*; Joel Schumacher, *Batman & Robin*; Oliver Stone, *U-Turn*

Worst Screenplay
Anaconda, *Batman & Robin*, *The Lost World: Jurassic Park*, ***The Postman***, *Speed 2: Cruise Control*

Worst New Star
The Animatronic Anaconda, *Anaconda*; **Dennis Rodman, *Double Team***; Tori Spelling, *The House of Yes* and *Scream 2*; Howard Stern, *Private Parts*; Chris Tucker, *The Fifth Element* and *Money Talks*

Worst Song
"The End Is the Beginning Is the End" from *Batman & Robin*, **The Entire Song Score from *The Postman***, "Fire Down Below" from *Fire Down Below*, "How Do I Live?" from *Con Air*, "My Dream" from *Speed 2: Cruise Control*

NINETEENTH ANNUAL RAZZIES (1998)

Worst Picture
An Alan Smithee Film: Burn, Hollywood, Burn; *Armageddon*, *The Avengers*, *Godzilla*, *Spice World*

Worst Actor
Ralph Fiennes, *The Avengers*; Ryan O'Neal, *An Alan Smithee Film: Burn,*

Hollywood, Burn; Ryan Phillippe, *54*; Adam Sandler, *The Waterboy*; **Bruce Willis, *Armageddon*, *Mercury Rising*, and *The Siege***

Worst Actress
Yasmine Bleeth, *BASEketball*; Anne Heche, *Psycho*; Jessica Lange, *Hush*; **The Spice Girls, *Spice World***; Uma Thurman, *The Avengers*

Worst Screen Couple
Ben Affleck & Liv Tyler, *Armageddon*; Any Combination of Two Characters, Body Parts, or Fashion Accessories, *Spice World*; Any Combination of Two People Playing Themselves (or Playing *with* Themselves) *An Alan Smithee Film: Burn, Hollywood, Burn*; **Leonardo DiCaprio (as Twins!), *The Man in the Iron Mask***; Ralph Fiennes & Uma Thurman, *The Avengers*

Worst Supporting Actor
Sean Connery, *The Avengers*; **Joe Eszterhas (as himself), *An Alan Smithee Film: Burn, Hollywood, Burn***; Roger Moore, *Spice World*; Joe Pesci, *Lethal Weapon 4*; Sylvester Stallone (as himself), *An Alan Smithee Film: Burn, Hollywood, Burn*

Worst Supporting Actress
Ellen Albertini Dow (as "Disco Dottie"), *54*; Jenny McCarthy, *BASEketball*; **Maria Pitillo, *Godzilla***; Liv Tyler, *Armageddon*; Raquel Welch, *Chairman of the Board*

Worst Director
Michael Bay, *Armageddon*; Jeremiah Chechik, *The Avengers*; Roland Emmerich, *Godzilla*; Alan Smithee (a.k.a. Arthur Hiller), *An Alan Smithee Film: Burn, Hollywood, Burn*; **Gus Van Sant, *Psycho***

Worst Remake or Sequel
***The Avengers*, *Godzilla*, and *Psycho* (3-Way Tie)**, *Lost in Space*, *Meet Joe Black*

The Joe Eszterhas Dis-Honorarial Worst Screenplay Award
***An Alan Smithee Film: Burn, Hollywood, Burn* (written by Joe Eszterhas)**, *Armageddon*, *The Avengers*, *Godzilla*, *Spice World*

Worst New Star
Barney, *Barney's Great Adventure*; Carrot Top, *Chairman of the Board*; **Joe Ezsterhas (as himself), *An Alan Smithee Film: Burn,***

Hollywood, Burn, and Jerry Springer, *Ringmaster* **(Tie)**; The Spice Girls, *Spice World*

Worst "Original" Song
"Barney, the Song" from *Barney's Great Adventure*, "I Don't Want to Miss a Thing" from *Armageddon*, **"I Wanna Be Mike Ovitz!" from *Burn, Hollywood, Burn***, "Storm" from *The Avengers*, "Too Much" from *Spice World*

Special Award: "1998—The Worst Moviegoing Year Ever!" *(New Category, Dis-Honoring the Worst Movie Trends of the Year)*
Gidgets 'n' Geezers (58-Year-Old Leading Men Wooing 28-Year-Old Leading Ladies); If You've Seen the Trailer, Why Bother to See the Movie?!? (Previews That Give Away the Film's *Entire* Plot); 30-Minutes of Story—Conveyed in Less Than 3 Hours! (L-O-N-G-E-R Movies . . . Shorter Plotz); THX: The Audio Is Deafening! (Movie Sound So Loud It Constitutes Assault with a Deadening Weapon); Yo Quiero Tacky Tie-Ins! (Mega-Zillion-Dollar-Cross-Promotional Overkill: *Armageddon, Godzilla,* etc.)

TWENTIETH ANNUAL RAZZIES (1999)

Worst Picture
Big Daddy, The Blair Witch Project, The Haunting, Star Wars: Episode I—The Phantom Menace, **Wild Wild West**

Worst Actor
Kevin Costner, *For Love of the Game* and *Message in a Bottle*; Kevin Kline, *Wild Wild West*; **Adam Sandler, *Big Daddy***; Ah-nold Schwarzenegger, *End of Days*; Robin Williams, *Bicentennial Man* and *Jakob the Liar*

Worst Actress
Heather Donahue, *The Blair Witch Project*; Melanie Griffith, *Crazy in Alabama*; Milla Jovovich, *The Messenger: The Story of Joan of Arc*; Sharon Stone, *Gloria*; Catherine Zeta-Jones, *Entrapment* and *The Haunting*

Worst Screen Couple
Pierce Brosnan and Denise Richards, *The World Is Not Enough*; Sean Connery and Catherine Zeta-Jones, *Entrapment*; **Kevin Kline and**

APPENDIX II

Will Smith, *Wild Wild West*; Jake Lloyd and Natalie Portman, *Star Wars: Episode I—The Phantom Menace*; Lili Taylor and Catherine Zeta-Jones, *The Haunting*

Worst Supporting Actress
Sofia Coppola, *Star Wars: Episode I—The Phantom Menace*; Salma Hayek, *Dogma* and *Wild Wild West*; Kevin Kline (as a prostitute), *Wild Wild West*; Juliette Lewis, *The Other Sister*; **Denise Richards, *The World Is Not Enough***

Worst Supporting Actor
Jar-Jar Binks (voice by Ahmed Best), *Star Wars: Episode I—The Phantom Menace*; Kenneth Branagh, *Wild Wild West*; Gabriel Byrne, *End of Days* and *Stigmata*; Jake Lloyd, *Star Wars: Episode I—The Phantom Menace*; Rob Schneider, *Big Daddy*

Worst Director
Jan De Bont, *The Haunting*; Dennis Dugan, *Big Daddy*; Peter Hyams, *End of Days*; George Lucas, *Star Wars: Episode I—The Phantom Menace*; **"Berry" Sonnenfeld, *Wild Wild West***

Worst Screenplay
Big Daddy, The Haunting, The Mod Squad, Star Wars: Episode I—The Phantom Menace, ***Wild Wild West***

SPECIAL WORST OF THE CENTURY AND DECADE AWARDS
Presented at the Twentieth Annual Razzies

Worst Picture of the Decade
An Alan Smithee Film: Burn, Hollywood, Burn, Hudson Hawk, The Postman, ***Showgirls****, Striptease*

Worst New Star of the Decade
Elizabeth Berkley, Jar-Jar Binks, Sofia Coppola, Dennis Rodman, **Pauly Shore**

Worst Actor of the Century
Kevin Costner, Prince, William Shatner, Pauly Shore, **Sylvester Stallone**

Worst Actress of the Century
Elizabeth Berkley, Bo Derek, **Madonna**, Brooke Shields, Pia Zadora

TWENTY-FIRST ANNUAL RAZZIES (2000)

Worst Picture
Battlefield Earth, Book of Shadows: Blair Witch 2, The Flintstones in Viva Rock Vegas, Little Nicky, The Next Best Thing

Worst Actor
Leonardo DiCaprio, *The Beach*; Adam Sandler, *Little Nicky*; Sylvester Stallone, *Get Carter*; Arnold Schwarzenegger (as the *real* Adam Gibson), *The 6th Day*; **John Travolta, *Battlefield Earth* and *Lucky Numbers***

Worst Actress
Kim Basinger, *Bless the Child* and *I Dreamed of Africa*; Melanie Griffith, *Cecil B. Demented*; **Madonna, *The Next Best Thing***; Bette Midler, *Isn't She Great?*; Demi Moore, *Passion of Mind*

Worst Screen Couple
Any 2 "Actors," *Book of Shadows: Blair Witch 2*; Richard Gere & Winona Ryder, *Autumn in New York*; Madonna & *either* Rupert Everett *or* Benjamin Bratt, *The Next Best Thing*; Arnold (as the *real* Adam Gibson & Arnold (as the *clone* of Adam Gibson), *The 6th Day*; **John Travolta & Anyone Sharing the Screen with Him, *Battlefield Earth***

Worst Supporting Actress
Patricia Arquette, *Little Nicky*; Joan Collins, *Flintstones in Viva Rock Vegas*; Thandie Newton, *Mission: Impossible 2*; **Kelly Preston, *Battlefield Earth***; Rene Russo, *The Adventures of Rocky & Bullwinkle*

Worst Supporting Actor
Stephen Baldwin, *The Flintstones in Viva Rock Vegas*; **Barry Pepper, *Battlefield Earth***; Keanu Reeves, *The Watcher*; Arnold Schwarzenegger (as the *clone* of Adam Gibson), *The 6th Day*; Forest Whitaker, *Battlefield Earth*

Worst Remake or Sequel
Book of Shadows: Blair Witch 2, Dr. Seuss' How the Grinch Stole Christmas, The Flintstones in Viva Rock Vegas, Get Carter, Mission: Impossible 2

Worst Director
Joe Berlinger, *Book of Shadows: Blair Witch 2*; Steven Brill, *Little*

APPENDIX II

Nicky; **Roger Christian, *Battlefield Earth***; Brian De Palma, *Mission to Mars*; John Schlesinger, *The Next Best Thing*

Worst Screenplay
Battlefield Earth, *Book of Shadows: Blair Witch 2*, *Dr. Seuss' How the Grinch Stole Christmas*, *Little Nicky*, *The Next Best Thing*

TWENTY-SECOND ANNUAL RAZZIES (2001)

Worst Picture
Driven, ***Freddy Got Fingered***, *Glitter*, *Pearl Harbor*, *3000 Miles to Graceland*

Worst Actor
Ben Affleck, *Pearl Harbor*; Kevin Costner, *3000 Miles to Graceland*; **Tom Green, *Freddy Got Fingered***; Keanu Reeves, *Hardball* and *Sweet November*; John Travolta, *Domestic Disturbance* and *Swordfish*

Worst Actress
Mariah Carey, *Glitter*; Penelope Cruz, *Blow*, *Captain Corelli's Mandolin*, and *Vanilla Sky*; Angelina Jolie, *Lara Croft: Tomb Raider* and *Original Sin*; Jennifer Lopez, *Angel Eyes* and *The Wedding Planner*; Charlize Theron, *Sweet November*

Worst Screen Couple
Ben Affleck and *either* Kate Beckinsale *or* Josh Hartnett, *Pearl Harbor*; Mariah Carey's Cleavage, *Glitter*; **Tom Green and Any Animal He Abuses, *Freddy Got Fingered***; Burt Reynolds and Sylvester Stallone, *Driven*; Kurt Russell and *either* Kevin Costner *or* Courteney Cox, *3000 Miles to Graceland*

Worst Supporting Actor
Max Beesley, *Glitter*; **Charlton Heston, *Cats & Dogs*, *Planet of the Apes*, and *Town & Country***; Burt Reynolds, *Driven*; Sylvester Stallone, *Driven*; Rip Torn, *Freddy Got Fingered*

Worst Supporting Actress
Drew Barrymore, *Freddy Got Fingered*; Courteney Cox, *3000 Miles to Graceland*; Julie Hagerty, *Freddy Got Fingered*; Goldie Hawn, *Town & Country*; **Estella Warren, *Driven* and *Planet of the Apes***

Worst Remake or Sequel
Crocodile Dundee in Los Angeles, Jurassic Park III, Pearl Harbor, ***Planet of the Apes****, Sweet November*

Worst Director
Michael Bay, *Pearl Harbor*; Peter Chelsom (and Warren Beatty), *Town & Country*; **Tom Green, *Freddy Got Fingered***; Vondie Curtis Hall, *Glitter*; Renny Harlin, *Driven*

Worst Screenplay
Driven, ***Freddy Got Fingered****, Glitter, Pearl Harbor, 3000 Miles to Graceland*

TWENTY-THIRD ANNUAL RAZZIES (2002)

Worst Picture
The Adventures of Pluto Nash, Crossroads, Roberto Benigni's Pinocchio, Star Wars: Episode II—Attack of the Clones, ***Swept Away***

Worst Actor
Roberto Benigni, *Pinocchio*; Adriano Giannini, *Swept Away*; Eddie Murphy, *Adventures of Pluto Nash, I Spy,* and *Showtime*; Steven Seagal, *Half Past Dead*; Adam Sandler, *Adam Sandler's Eight Crazy Nights* and *Mr. Deeds*

Worst Actress
Angelina Jolie, *Life or Something Like It*, Jennifer Lopez, *Enough* and *Maid in Manhattan*; **Madonna, *Swept Away*, and Britney Spears, *Crossroads* (Tie)**; Winona Ryder, *Mr. Deeds*

Worst Supporting Actor
Hayden Christensen, *Star Wars: Episode II*; Tom Green, *Stealing Harvard*; Freddie Prinze Jr., *Scooby-Doo*; Christopher Walken, *The Country Bears*; Robin Williams, *Death to Smoochy*

Worst Supporting Actress
Lara Flynn Boyle, *Men in Black II*; Bo Derek, *The Master of Disguise*; **Madonna, *Die Another Day***; Natalie Portman, *Star Wars: Episode II*; Rebecca Romijn-Stamos, *Rollerball*

Most Flatulant Teen-Targeted Movie *(New Category)*
Adam Sandler's Eight Crazy Nights, Crossroads, ***Jackass: The Movie****, Scooby-Doo, XXX*

Worst Screen Couple
Roberto Benigni & Nicoletta Braschi, *Pinocchio*; Hayden Christensen & Natalie Portman, *Star Wars: Episode II*; **Adriano Giannini & Madonna, *Swept Away***; Eddie Murphy & either Robert De Niro (*Showtime*), Owen Wilson (*I Spy*), *or* Himself Cloned (*The Adventures of Pluto Nash*); Britney Spears & Whatever-His-Name-Was, *Crossroads*

Worst Director
Roberto Benigni, *Pinocchio*; Tamra Davis, *Crossroads*; George Lucas, *Star Wars: Episode II*; **Guy Ritchie, *Swept Away***; Ron Underwood, *The Adventures of Pluto Nash*

Worst Remake or Sequel
I Spy, Mr. Deeds, Pinocchio, Star Wars: Episode II, ***Swept Away***

Worst Screenplay
The Adventures of Pluto Nash, Crossroads, Pinocchio, ***Star Wars: Episode II***, *Swept Away*

Worst "Original" Song
"Die Another Day" from *Die Another Day*, **"I'm Not a Girl, Not Yet a Woman" from *Crossroads***, "Overprotected" from *Crossroads*

TWENTY-FOURTH ANNUAL RAZZIES (2003)

Worst Picture
The Cat in the Hat, Charlie's Angels: Full Throttle, From Justin to Kelly, ***Gigli***, *The Real Cancun*

Worst Actor
Ben Affleck, *Daredevil, Gigli*, and *Paycheck*; Cuba Gooding Jr., *Boat Trip, The Fighting Temptations*, and *Radio*; Justin Guarini, *From Justin to Kelly*; Ashton Kutcher, *Cheaper by the Dozen, Just Married*, and *My Boss's Daughter*; Mike Myers, *The Cat in the Hat*

Worst Actress
Drew Barrymore, *Charlie's Angels: Full Throttle* and *Duplex*; Cameron Diaz, *Charlie's Angels: Full Throttle*; Kelly Clarkson, *From Justin to Kelly*; Angelina Jolie, *Beyond Borders* and *Lara Croft Tomb Raider: The Cradle of Life*; **Jennifer Lopez, *Gigli***

Worst Supporting Actor
Anthony Anderson, *Kangaroo Jack*; Alec Baldwin, *The Cat in the Hat*; Al Pacino, *Gigli*; **Sylvester Stallone (playing 5 roles), *Spy Kids 3-D: Game Over***; Christopher Walken, *Gigli* and *Kangaroo Jack*

Worst Supporting Actress
Lanie Kazan, *Gigli*; **Demi Moore, *Charlie's Angels: Full Throttle***; Kelly Preston, *The Cat in the Hat*; Brittany Murphy, *Just Married*; Tara Reid, *My Boss's Daughter*

Worst Screen Couple
Ben Affleck and Jennifer Lopez, *Gigli*; Eric Christian Olsen & Derek Richardson, *Dumb and Dumberer*; Justin Guarini & Kelly Clarkson, *From Justin to Kelly*, Ashton Kutcher & *either* Brittany Murphy (*Just Married*) or Tara Reid (*My Boss's Daughter*); Mike Myers & *either* Thing One *or* Thing Two, *The Cat in the Hat*

Worst Excuse for an Actual Movie *(New Category)*
2 Fast, 2 Furious, *Charlie's Angels: Full Throttle*, ***The Cat in the Hat***, *From Justin to Kelly, The Real Cancun*

Worst Remake or Sequel
2 Fast 2 Furious, ***Charlie's Angels: Full Throttle***, *Dumb and Dumberer: When Harry Met Lloyd, From Justin to Kelly* (Remake of both *Where the Boys Are '60* and *Where the Boys Are '84*), *The Texas Chainsaw Massacre*

Worst Director
Martin Brest, *Gigli*; Robert Iscove, *From Justin to Kelly*; Mort Nathan, *Boat Trip*; the Wachowski Brothers, Both *Matrix* sequels; Bo Welch, *The Cat in the Hat*

Worst Screenplay
The Cat in the Hat, Charlie's Angels: Full Throttle, Dumb and Dumberer, From Justin to Kelly, ***Gigli***

WORST CAREER ACHIEVEMENT AWARDS

1982: Retired movie star Ronald Reagan
1984: The Master of Disaster Irwin Allen
1986: Razzie Scream Queen Linda Blair
1988: Bruce (the rubber shark) from *Jaws, Jaws 2, Jaws 3-D, and Jaws 4*

Index

Adams, Caitlin: *The Jazz Singer*, 173–74, 331, 332
Adams, Edie: *The Oscar*, 317–20
Adams, Gerald Drayson: *Harum Scarum*, 171–72
Adams, Victoria: *Spice World*, 37, 52–54, 353
Addams Family, The, 345
Addams Family Values, 347
Adventurers, The, 295–98
Adventures of Ford Fairlane, The, 343, 344
Airplane!, 61
Airport 1975, 61–63, 68
Airport '77, 68
Airport '79: The Concorde, 67–69
Ajaye, Franklin: *The Jazz Singer*, 173–74, 331, 332
Alan Smithee Film, An: Burn, Hollywood, Burn, 352, 353–54
Albert, Eddie: *Airport '79: The Concorde*, 67–69
Albertson, Jack: *Poseidon Adventure*, 61, 73–75
Alderton, John: *Zardoz*, 155–56
Aldrich, Robert: *The Legend of Lylah Clare*, 197–200
Alexander, Jane: *The Betsy*, 159–61
Allen, Corey: *Avalanche*, 64–66
Allen, Irwin, 24, 64, 73, 361; *The Swarm*, 76–78
Allen, John, 49
American Idol (TV show), 35
Anaconda, 3–6
Anderson, Bridgette: *Fever Pitch*, 123–24
Anderson, Loni: *The Jayne Mansfield Story*, 91–92
Anderson, Pamela: *Barb Wire*, 243–44, 351
Anderson, Richard: *Kitten with a Whip*, 254–55
Andersson, Bibi: *Airport '79: The Concorde*, 67–69
Andrews, Dana: *Airport 1975*, 61–63
Andrews, John: *Orgy of the Dead*, 264–65
Annakin, Ken: *The Pirate Movie*, 44–45, 334, 335
Annie, 334
Ann-Margret: *Kitten with a Whip*, 254–55

Ansara, Michael: *Harum Scarum*, 171–72
A*P*E, 7–9
Apostolof, Stephen C.: *Orgy of the Dead*, 264–65
Archer, Anne: *Body of Evidence*, 302–4, 346
Archer, Eugene, 259
Armageddon, 353
Armendáriz, Pedro: *The Conqueror*, 165–67
Armstrong, R. G.: *The Car*, 111–13
Arnaz, Lucie: *The Jazz Singer*, 173–74, 331, 332
Arnold, Jack: *High School Confidential*, 125–26
Arrants, Rod: *A*P*E*, 7–9
Arthur 2: On the Rocks, 341
Ashcroft, Ronnie: *The Astounding She-Monster*, 217–18
Ashley, Elizabeth: *The Carpetbaggers*, 191–93
Ashley, John: *Frankenstein's Daughter*, 282–83
Ashton, John: *King Kong Lives*, 21–22
Astounding She-Monster, The, 217–18
Atkins, Christopher: *The Blue Lagoon*, 45, 245–47, 262, 332; *A Night in Heaven*, 262–63, 335; *The Pirate Movie*, 44–45, 334, 335
Atkinson, Michael, 102
Attack of the Killer Tomatoes, 189
Avalanche, 64–66
Avengers, The, 353
Avildsen, John G.: *A Night in Heaven*, 262–63, 335
Aznavour, Charles: *The Adventurers*, 295–98

Bacharach, Burt: *Lost Horizon*, 40–43
Badel, Alan: *The Adventurers*, 295–98
Bailey, Keith, 29, 135
Bailey, Robert: *Yor, the Hunter from the Future*, 153–54
Baker, Carroll: *The Carpetbaggers*, 191–93
Baker, Diane: *Strait-Jacket*, 23, 183–85
Baker, Herbert: *The Jazz Singer*, 173–74, 331, 332; *Sextette*, 269–70
Bakula, Scott: *Color of Night*, 117–19, 347
Barbarella, 219–20

Barb Wire, 243–44, 351
Barrett, Claudia: *Robot Monster*, 232–34
Barrie, H. E.: *Frankenstein's Daughter*, 282–83
Barrington, Pat: *Orgy of the Dead*, 264–65
Barrows, George: *Robot Monster*, 232–34
Barrymore, Lionel: *Duel in the Sun*, 248–50
Barry, Patricia: *Kitten with a Whip*, 254–55
Barsi, Judith: *Jaws: The Revenge*, 18–20
Barty, Billy: *Harum Scarum*, 171–72
Basic Instinct, 321
Bast, William: *The Betsy*, 159–61
Bates, William: *Orgy of the Dead*, 264–65
Batman & Robin, 352
Battlefield Earth, 299–301, 356, 357
Baxter, Anne: *The Ten Commandments*, 79–81
Beach Girls and the Monster, The, 10–12
Beatty, Ned: *Exorcist II: The Heretic*, 156, 305–8
Beau, Sandra: *A Night in Heaven*, 262–63, 335
Beck, Michael: *Xanadu*, xv, 33, 323–26, 332
Beck, Vincent: *Santa Claus Conquers the Martians*, 235–37
Beesley, Max: *Glitter*, 38–39, 357
Begg, Ken, 7, 311
Beller, Kathleen: *The Betsy*, 159–61
Benet, Eric: *Glitter*, 38–39, 357
Bennett, Tony: *The Oscar*, 317–20
Benson, Sheila, 67
Bergen, Candice: *The Adventurers*, 295–98
Bergin, Patrick: *Love Crimes*, 256–58
Berkeley, Xander: *Barb Wire*, 243–44, 351
Berkley, Elizabeth: *Showgirls*, xvi, 321–22, 348, 349, 355
Berkoff, Steven: *Rambo: First Blood Part II*, 177–79, 337, 338
Berle, Milton: *The Oscar*, 317–20
Bernstein, Walter: *The Betsy*, 159–61
Berserk, 23
Besch, Bibi: *The Lonely Lady*, xvi, 311–13, 335, 336
Betsy, The, 159–61
Beverly Hills Cop II, 340
Beyond the Forest, 162–64
Beyond the Valley of the Dolls, 189–90
Big Daddy, 354

Bio-Dome, 350
Bishop, Jennifer: *Impulse*, 127–29
Bishop, Joey: *Valley of the Dolls*, 189, 201, 208–10
Bissell, Whit: *Where Love Has Gone*, 273–75
Black, Karen: *Airport 1975*, 61–63, 175
Blades, Rubén: *Color of Night*, 117–19, 347
Blair, Linda, 361; *Airport 1975*, 61–63; *Exorcist II: The Heretic*, 156, 305–8; *Roller Boogie*, 49–51
Blair Witch Project, The, 354
Blakely, Susan: *Airport '79: The Concorde*, 67–69
Blees, Robert: *High School Confidential*, 125–26
Bloch, Robert: *Strait-Jacket*, 23, 183–85
Blodgett, Michael: *Beyond the Valley of the Dolls*, 189–90
Blue Hawaii, 171
Blue Lagoon, The, 45, 245–47, 262, 332
Bochner, Hart: *Supergirl*, 238–40
Bochner, Lloyd: *The Lonely Lady*, xvi, 311–13, 335, 336
Bodyguard, The, 85–87
Body Heat, 303
Body of Evidence, 302–4, 346
Body Rock, 29–31
Bolero, 336, 337
Bolton, June: *Valentino*, 204–7
Book of Shadows: Blair Witch 2, 356
Boorman, John: *Exorcist II: The Heretic*, 156, 305–8; *Zardoz*, 155–56
Borden, Lizzie: *Love Crimes*, 256–58
Borgnine, Ernest: *The Adventurers*, 295–98; *The Legend of Lylah Clare*, 197–200; *The Oscar*, 317–20; *Poseidon Adventure*, 61, 73–75
Bovasso, Julie: *Staying Alive*, 55–57
Boxing Helena, 347
Boyd, Stephen: *The Oscar*, 317–20
Boyer, Charles: *Lost Horizon*, 40–43
Braden, Kim: *Trog*, 23–25
Brain That Wouldn't Die, The, 279–81
Brando, Marlon: *The Island of Dr. Moreau*, 284–85, 350
Bray, Jim: *Roller Boogie*, 49–51
Breakin', 29
Brian, David: *Beyond the Forest*, 162–64

Bridges, James: *Perfect,* 130–31
Bridges, Jeff, 7
Briggs, Joe Bob, 130, 232, 251, 272
Brighton, Bruce: *The Brain That Wouldn't Die,* 279–81
Brodie, Kevin: *The Giant Spider Invasion,* 13–15
Brodie, Steve: *The Giant Spider Invasion,* 13–15
Brolin, James: *The Car,* 111–13
Bronson, Betty: *The Naked Kiss,* 259–61
Brooks, Richard: *Fever Pitch,* 123–24
Broun, Charles W., Jr.: *The Wild Wild World of Jayne Mansfield,* 211–13
Brown, Bryan: *Cocktail,* 114–16, 340, 341
Browne, Coral: *The Legend of Lylah Clare,* 197–200; *Xanadu,* xv, 33, 323–26, 332
Brown, Peter: *Kitten with a Whip,* 254–55
Brown, Reb: *Yor, the Hunter from the Future,* 153–54
Bruce, Eve: *The Love Machine,* 201–3
Bruce, Nigel: *She,* 180–82
Brynner, Yul: *The Ten Commandments,* 79–81
Buggy, Niall: *Zardoz,* 155–56
Buktenica, Raymond: *The Jayne Mansfield Story,* 91–92
Burke, Paul: *Valley of the Dolls,* 189, 201, 208–10
Burrell, Larry: *The Creeping Terror,* 221–22
Burridge, Shane, 279
Burstyn, Ellen, 306
Burton, Richard: *Exorcist II: The Heretic,* 156, 305–8
Butler, Hugo: *The Legend of Lylah Clare,* 197–200
Butler, Michael: *The Car,* 111–13
Butler, Robert W., 102
Butterfly, 334
Buttons, Red: *Poseidon Adventure,* 61, 73–75

Cable movie channels, 329–30
Caddyshack II, 341
Caine, Michael: *On Deadly Ground,* 70–72, 348; *Jaws: The Revenge,* 18–20; *The Swarm,* 76–78
Calegory, Jade: *Mac and Me,* 229–31, 341
Cali, Joseph: *The Lonely Lady,* xvi, 311–13, 335, 336

Call, John: *Santa Claus Conquers the Martians,* 235–37
Cameron, James: *Rambo: First Blood Part II,* 177–79, 337, 338
Canby, Vincent, 67, 114, 130, 302
Cannon, Dyan: *The Love Machine,* 201–3
Can't Stop the Music, xv, 32–34, 331, 332
Capra, Frank, 40–41
Caresio, John: *The Creeping Terror,* 221–22
Carey, Mariah: *Glitter,* 38–39, 357
Carmel, Eddie: *The Brain That Wouldn't Die,* 279–81
Caron, Leslie: *Valentino,* 204–7
Carpenter, Horace: *Maniac,* 286–88
Carpetbaggers, The, 191–93
Carradine, John: *The Ten Commandments,* 79–81
Carr, Allan: *Can't Stop the Music,* xv, 32–34, 331
Car, The, 111–13
Car 54, Where Are You?, 348
Casablanca, 243–44
Casey, Sue: *The Beach Girls and the Monster,* 10–12
Caspary, Katrina: *Mac and Me,* 229–31, 341
Cassel, Seymour: *Indecent Proposal,* 88–90, 346, 347
Cassidy, Patrick: *Fever Pitch,* 123–24
Castellari, Enzo G.: *Sinbad of the Seven Seas,* 135–36
Castle, William: *Strait-Jacket,* 23, 183–85; *The Tingler,* 289–91
Cat in the Hat, The, 360
Cats & Dogs, 357
Chained Heat, 335
Chamberlain, Richard: *The Swarm,* 76–78
Champlin, Charles, 204, 219
Chapman, Matthew: *Color of Night,* 117–19, 347
Charlie's Angels: Full Throttle, 360
Charo: *Airport '79: The Concorde,* 67–69
Chen, Joan: *On Deadly Ground,* 70–72, 348
Christian, Roger: *Battlefield Earth,* 299–301, 356, 357
Christopher Columbus: The Discovery, 345
Clark, Bob: *Rhinestone,* 46–48, 336, 337
Clark, Robert: *The Astounding She-Monster,* 217–18
Clarkson, Kelly: *From Justin to Kelly,* 35–37

Clery, Corrine: *Yor, the Hunter from the Future*, 153–54
Coates, Kim: *Battlefield Earth*, 299–301, 356, 357
Cobbs, Bill: *The Bodyguard*, 85–87
Cocktail, 114–16, 340, 341
Coffee, Lenore: *Beyond the Forest*, 162–64
Coffman, Jason, 229
Collins, Don: *Rambo: First Blood Part II*, 177–79, 337, 338
Colombani, Marc: *The Pirate Movie*, 44–45, 334, 335
Color of Night, 117–19, 347
Con Air, 352
Conan the Destroyer, 337
Concorde, The: Airport '79, 67–69
Conforti, Donna: *Santa Claus Conquers the Martians*, 235–37
Connery, Sean: *Zardoz*, 155–56
Connors, Mike: *Where Love Has Gone*, 273–75
Conqueror, The, 165–67
Conrad, Robert: *Wild Wild West*, 146, 354–55
Conrad, William: *The Conqueror*, 165–67
Coogan, Jackie: *High School Confidential*, 125–26
Cook, Peter: *Supergirl*, 238–40
Cool as Ice, 345
Coolidge, Philip: *The Tingler*, 289–91
Cooper, Jackie: *The Love Machine*, 201–3
Cop and a Half, 346
Coppola, Francis Ford: *The Godfather: Part III*, 168–70, 343, 344
Coppola, Sofia: *The Godfather: Part III*, 168–70, 343, 344
Corman, Roger: *Avalanche*, 64–66
Cornelius, Joe: *Trog*, 23–25
Corri, Adrienne: *Devil Girl from Mars*, 223–25
Cortese, Valentina: *The Legend of Lylah Clare*, 197–200
Cosby, Bill: *Leonard Part 6*, xvi, *140*, 339, 340
Cosmatos, George P.: *Rambo: First Blood Part II*, 177–79, 337, 338
Costner, Kevin: *The Bodyguard*, 85–87
Cottafavi, Vittorio: *Goliath and the Dragon*, 16–17
Cotten, Joseph: *Beyond the Forest*, 162–64;
Duel in the Sun, 248–50; *The Oscar*, 317–20; *White Comanche*, 105–7
Couples, worst, 85–107
Court, Hazel: *Devil Girl from Mars*, 223–25
Cox, Ronny: *The Car*, 111–13
Crawford, Broderick: *Goliath and the Dragon*, 16–17
Crawford, Joan: *Mommie Dearest* and, 314–16; *Strait-Jacket*, 23, 183–85; *Trog*, 23–25
Creature features, worst, 3–25, 279–91
Crechales, Tony: *Impulse*, 127–29
Creeping Terror, The, 221–22
Crenna, Richard: *Rambo: First Blood Part II*, 177–79, 337, 338
Crenshaw, Marshall, 171
Cristal, Perla: *White Comanche*, 105–7
Crist, Judith, 183
Criswell: *Orgy of the Dead*, 264–65
Crossroads, 358, 359
Cruise, Tom: *Cocktail*, 114–16, 340, 341
Cumming, Alan: *Spice World*, 37, 52–54, 353
Cummings, Bob: *The Carpetbaggers*, 191–93
Cunha, Richard: *Frankenstein's Daughter*, 282–83
Curtis, Jamie Lee: *Perfect*, 130–31
Curtis, Tony: *Sextette*, 269–70
Cutts, Patricia: *The Tingler*, 289–91

Da Brat: *Glitter*, 38–39, 357
Dafoe, Willem: *Body of Evidence*, 302–4, 346
Daigle, Ned, 23, 32
Dalton, Timothy: *Sextette*, 269–70
Damian, Leo: *Ghosts Can't Do It*, 251–53, 343
Daniel, Leslie: *The Brain That Wouldn't Die*, 279–81
Daniels, William: *The Blue Lagoon*, 45, 245–47, 332
Danning, Sybil: *Airport '79: The Concorde*, 67–69
Dante, Michael: *The Naked Kiss*, 259–61
Daredevil, 359
Dare, Michael, 46
Dauphin, Claude: *Barbarella*, 219–20
David, Hal: *Lost Horizon*, 40–43
Davis, Altovise: *Can't Stop the Music*, xv, 32–34, 331

Davis, Bette: *Beyond the Forest,* 162–64; *Where Love Has Gone,* 273–75
Day, Doris: *Julie,* 175–76
De Carlo, Yvonne: *The Ten Commandments,* 79–81
De Havilland, Olivia: *The Adventurers,* 295–98; *The Swarm,* 76–78
De Laurentiis, Dino, 7, 21, 271
Delon, Alain: *Airport '79: The Concorde,* 67–69
DeLuise, Dom: *Sextette,* 269–70
Demarest, William: *Sincerely Yours,* 96–98
DeMille, Cecil B.: *The Greatest Show on Earth,* 194–96; *The Ten Commandments,* 79–81
Denby, David, 314
Dennis, Charles: *The Jayne Mansfield Story,* 91–92
Derek, Bo, 343; *Ghosts Can't Do It,* 251–53, 343
Derek, John: *Ghosts Can't Do It,* 251–53, 343; *The Ten Commandments,* 79–81
Deutsch, Helen: *Valley of the Dolls,* 189, 201, 208–10
Devil Girl from Mars, 223–25
Devils, The, 204
Diamond, Neil: *The Jazz Singer,* 173–74, 331, 332
Die Another Day, 358
Diller, Phyllis: *Maniac,* 286–88
Disaster movies, worst, 61–81
Dmytryk, Edward: *The Carpetbaggers,* 191–93; *Where Love Has Gone,* 273–75
Dobson, James: *Impulse,* 127–29
Donaldson, Roger: *Cocktail,* 114–16, 340, 341
Doran, Ann: *Kitten with a Whip,* 254–55; *Where Love Has Gone,* 273–75
Double Team, 351, 352
Douglas, Gordon: *Sincerely Yours,* 96–98
Douglas, Michael: *Shining Through,* 93–95, 345, 346
Douglas, Scott: *The Astounding She-Monster,* 217–18
Dourif, Brad: *Color of Night,* 117–19, 347
Down, Lesley-Anne: *The Betsy,* 159–61
Down to Earth, 323–24
Driven, 357

Dru, Joanne: *Sincerely Yours,* 96–98
Duel in the Sun, 248–50
Duke, Patty: *The Swarm,* 76–78; *Valley of the Dolls,* 189, 201, 208–10
Dunaway, Faye: *Mommie Dearest,* xvi, 67, 185, 314–16, 332, 333, 342; *Supergirl,* 238–40
Duncan, Kenne: *The Astounding She-Monster,* 217–18
Dunham, Robert: *The Green Slime,* 226–28
Dupont, Elaine: *The Beach Girls and the Monster,* 10–12
Duvall, Robert: *The Betsy,* 159–61; *The Scarlet Letter,* 266–68, 349
Dye, Cameron: *Body Rock,* 29–31

Easton, Robert: *The Giant Spider Invasion,* 13–15
Eastwood, James: *Devil Girl from Mars,* 223–25
Ebersole, Christine: *Mac and Me,* 229–31, 341
Ebert, Roger, 18, 52, 93, 114, 117, 132, 266, 299, 302, 323; *Beyond the Valley of the Dolls,* 189–90
Edel, Uli: *Body of Evidence,* 302–4, 346
Edmiston, Walker: *The Beach Girls and the Monster,* 10–12
Edwards, Nadine, 254
Edward, Ted: *Maniac,* 286–88
Eegah, 120–22
Efroni, Yehudi: *Sinbad of the Seven Seas,* 135–36
Eisley, Anthony: *The Naked Kiss,* 259–61
Elliott, Peter: *King Kong Lives,* 21–22
Elliott, Sam: *Road House,* 132–34
Ellison, Harlan: *The Oscar,* 317–20
Encino Man, 346
Epstein, Marcelo: *Body Rock,* 29–31
Erickson, Leif: *Strait-Jacket,* 23, 183–85
Esper, Dwain: *Maniac,* 286–88
Estrada, Erik: *Airport 1975,* 61–63
Eszterhas, Joe: *Showgirls,* xvi, 321–22, 348, 349, 355
E.T., 229–30
Evelyn, Judith: *The Tingler,* 289–91
Everett, Chad: *Fever Pitch,* 123–24
Evers, Herb: *The Brain That Wouldn't Die,* 279–81

Exit to Eden, 348
Exorcist II: The Heretic, 156, 305–8

Falk, Rosella: *The Legend of Lylah Clare,* 197–200
Farnsworth, Robert: *Rhinestone,* 46–48, 336, 337
Farrant, Trevor: *The Pirate Movie,* 44–45, 334, 335
Farrow, Mia: *Avalanche,* 64–66; *Supergirl,* 238–40
Fehmiu, Bekim: *The Adventurers,* 295–98
Feke, Steve: *Mac and Me,* 229–31, 341
Fell, Norman: *Airport 1975,* 61–63
Ferrer, José: *The Swarm,* 76–78
Ferrigno, Lou: *Sinbad of the Seven Seas,* 135–36
Fever Pitch, 123–24
Finch, Peter: *The Legend of Lylah Clare,* 197–200; *Lost Horizon,* 40–43
Firsching, Robert, 269
Fischer, David Marc, 40
Flashdance, 29
Fleischer, Richard: *The Jazz Singer,* 173–74, 331, 332
Fletcher, Louise: *Exorcist II: The Heretic,* 156, 305–8
Flintstones, The, 348
Fonda, Henry: *The Swarm,* 76–78
Fonda, Jane: *Barbarella,* 219–20
Foreman, Jonathan, 38
Forest, Mark: *Goliath and the Dragon,* 16–17
Forrest Gump, 68
Forrest, Steve: *Mommie Dearest,* 185, 314–16, 332, 333, 342
Forster, Robert: *Avalanche,* 64–66
Forsythe, John: *Kitten with a Whip,* 254–55
Four Rooms, 349
Fox, Ken, 211
Foy, Scott, 70
Francis, Freddie: *Trog,* 23–25
Frankenheimer, John: *The Island of Dr. Moreau,* 284–85, 350
Frankenstein's Daughter, 282–83
Franken, Steve: *Avalanche,* 64–66
Frank, Frederic M.: *The Greatest Show on Earth,* 194–96
Frank, Laurie: *Love Crimes,* 256–58
Freddy Got Fingered, 148, 149, 357, 358

Frederick, Vicky: *Body Rock,* 29–31
Frees, Paul: *The Carpetbaggers,* 191–93
From Justin to Kelly, 35–37
Fukasaku, Kinji: *The Green Slime,* 226–28
Fuller, Dolores: *Glen or Glenda,* 70, 309–10
Fuller, Kim: *From Justin to Kelly,* 35–37; *Spice World,* 37, 52–54, 353
Fuller, Samuel: *The Naked Kiss,* 259–61
Fuller, Simon, 54
Furie, Sidney J.: *The Jazz Singer,* 173–74, 331, 332

Gahagan, Helen: *She,* 180–82
Garcia, Andy: *The Godfather: Part III,* 168–70, 343, 344
Gardner, Joan: *The Beach Girls and the Monster,* 10–12
Garland, Beverly: *Roller Boogie,* 49–51
Garrett, Oliver H. P.: *Duel in the Sun,* 248–50
Gary, Lorraine: *Jaws: The Revenge,* 18–20
Gayle, Nancy: *The Jayne Mansfield Story,* 91–92
Gazzara, Ben: *Road House,* 132–34
Gelmis, Joseph, 309
Germann, Greg: *Sweet November,* 102–4
Gershon, Gina: *Cocktail,* 114–16, 340, 341; *Showgirls,* xvi, 321–22, 348, 349, 355
Getchell, Robert: *Mommie Dearest,* xvi, 67, 185, 314–16, 332, 333, 342
Ghosts Can't Do It, 251–53, 343
Giannini, Giancarlo: *Fever Pitch,* 123–24
Giant Spider Invasion, The, 13–15
Gielgud, John: *Shining Through,* 93–95, 345, 346
Gigli, 359, 360
G.I. Jane, 351
Gilbert, Lewis: *The Adventurers,* 295–98
Girolami, Stefania: *Sinbad of the Seven Seas,* 135–36
Gish, Lillian: *Duel in the Sun,* 248–50
Glen or Glenda, 70, 309–10
Glitter, 38–39, 357
Gloria, 332
Godfather, The: Part II, 169
Godfather, The: Part III, 168–70, 343, 344
Godzilla, 353
Goetz, Peter Michael: *King Kong Lives,* 21–22
Goliath and the Dragon, 16–17
Gone with the Wind, 248

Goodhart, William: *Exorcist II: The Heretic*, 156, 305–8
Gough, Michael: *Trog*, 23–25
Gould, Heywood: *Cocktail*, 114–16, 340, 341
Grahame, Gloria: *The Greatest Show on Earth*, 194–96
Grant, Richard E.: *Spice World*, 37, 52–54, 353
Grease, 32
Greatest Show on Earth, The, 194–96
Green, Clarence: *The Oscar*, 317–20
Greene, Shecky: *The Love Machine*, 201–3
Green, Joseph: *The Brain That Wouldn't Die*, 279–81
Green Slime, The, 226–28
Green, Tom: *Freddy Got Fingered*, 148, 149, 357, 358
Greenwald, Robert: *Xanadu*, xv, 33, 323–26, 332
Greer, Jane: *Where Love Has Gone*, 273–75
Grefe, William: *Impulse*, 127–29
Grey, Virginia: *The Naked Kiss*, 259–61
Griffith, Melanie: *Shining Through*, 93–95, 345, 346
Gross, Linda, 262
Gruber, Frank: *White Comanche*, 105–7
Guarini, Justin: *From Justin to Kelly*, 35–37
Guarisco, Donald, 183
Guest, Lance: *Jaws: The Revenge*, 18–20
Guida, Wandisa: *Goliath and the Dragon*, 16–17
Guillermin, John: *King Kong Lives*, 21–22; *Sheena*, 271–72
Gul, Ayshe: *Yor, the Hunter from the Future*, 153–54
Gullota, Leo: *Sinbad of the Seven Seas*, 135–36
Gurian, David: *Beyond the Valley of the Dolls*, 189–90
Guttenberg, Steve: *Can't Stop the Music*, xv, 32–34, 331

Hackman, Gene: *Poseidon Adventure*, 61, 73–75
Haflidason, Almar, 76
Hale, Alan, Jr.: *The Giant Spider Invasion*, 13–15
Hale, Barbara: *The Giant Spider Invasion*, 13–15

Haley, Jack, Jr.: *The Love Machine*, 201–3
Hall, Arch, Jr.: *Eegah*, 120–22
Hall, Arch, Sr.: *Eegah*, 120–22
Hall, Huntz: *Valentino*, 204–7
Halliwell, Geri: *Spice World*, 37, 52–54, 353
Hall, Jon: *The Beach Girls and the Monster*, 10–12
Hall, Vondie Curtis: *Glitter*, 38–39, 357
Hamilton, George: *The Godfather: Part III*, 168–70, 343, 344; *Sextette*, 269–70
Hamilton, Linda: *King Kong Lives*, 21–22
Hamilton, Ted: *The Pirate Movie*, 44–45, 334, 335
Hanke, Ken, 173
Hanold, Marlyn: *The Brain That Wouldn't Die*, 279–81
Hard Day's Night, A, 52
Hardwicke, Cedric: *The Ten Commandments*, 79–81
Hardy, Ernest, 219
Harewood, Dorian: *Glitter*, 38–39, 357
Hargitay, Mickey: *The Wild Wild World of Jayne Mansfield*, 211–13
Harlem Nights, 342
Harlow, Jean, 191
Harper, Erik, 271
Harrelson, Woody: *Indecent Proposal*, 88–90, 346, 347
Harrington, Richard, 229
Hart, Diane Lee: *The Giant Spider Invasion*, 13–15
Hartford, Margaret, 183
Harum Scarum, 171–72
Harvey, Marilyn: *The Astounding She-Monster*, 217–18
Hastings, Michael: *The Adventurers*, 295–98
Haunted Honeymoon, 339
Hayes, John Michael: *The Carpetbaggers*, 191–93; *Where Love Has Gone*, 273–75
Haynes, Tommy: *Glen or Glenda*, 70, 309–10
Hayward, Susan: *The Conqueror*, 165–67; *Valley of the Dolls*, 189, 201, 208–10; *Where Love Has Gone*, 273–75
Hayworth, Rita, 323–24
Head, Edith, 319
Heatherton, Joey: *Where Love Has Gone*, 273–75

Heaven's Gate, 333
Hecht, Ben, 249
Helgeland, Brian: *The Postman, 145,* 351, 352
Hemmings, David: *Barbarella,* 219–20; *The Love Machine,* 201–3
Henderson, Eric, 79, 191
Henkin, Hilary: *Road House,* 132–34
Henner, Marilu: *Perfect,* 130–31
Hennessey, Kevin, 61, 173
Henry, David Lee: *Road House,* 132–34
Hercules, 135, 335
Herrington, Rowdy: *Road House,* 132–34
Heston, Charlton: *Airport 1975,* 61–63; *The Greatest Show on Earth,* 194–96; *The Ten Commandments,* 79–81
Heyes, Douglas: *Kitten with a Whip,* 254–55
Hickman, Darryl: *The Tingler,* 289–91
Hicks, Andrew, 73
Hicks, Catherine: *Fever Pitch,* 123–24
Hicks, Chris, 70, 93, 229
Hicks, Leonard: *Santa Claus Conquers the Martians,* 235–37
High School Confidential, 125–26
Hinson, Hal, 99, 132
Hogan, David: *Barb Wire,* 243–44, 351
Holden, Anthony, 321
Holden, Lansing C.: *She,* 180–82
Holden, Stephen, 3, 35
Hollywood Production Code, 295
Holt, Joel: *The Wild Wild World of Jayne Mansfield,* 211–13
Holt, Robert I.: *White Comanche,* 105–7
Honeysuckle Rose, 332
Hopgood, Alan: *The Blue Lagoon,* 45, 245–47, 332
Hopper, Hedda, 319
Horowitz, Ed: *On Deadly Ground,* 70–72, 348
Horton, Robert: *The Green Slime,* 226–28
Hotchner, Tracy: *Mommie Dearest,* xvi, 67, 185, 314–16, 332, 333, 342
House on Haunted Hill, 291
Houston, Whitney: *The Bodyguard,* 85–87
Howard, Clint: *Barb Wire,* 243–44, 351
Howard the Duck, 339
Howe, Desson, 18, 88, 168
Hubbard, L. Ron, 299
Hubbard, Reed, 49
Hudson, Ernie: *The Jazz Singer,* 173–74, 331, 332

Hudson Hawk, 344, 345
Hudson, Rock: *Avalanche,* 64–66
Huff, Richard L.: *The Giant Spider Invasion,* 13–15
Hughes, Finola: *Staying Alive,* 55–57
Hughes, Howard, 167, 191–92
Hughes, Ken: *Sextette,* 269–70
Hunter, Ross: *Lost Horizon,* 40–43
Hussey, Olivia: *Lost Horizon,* 40–43
Huston, Walter: *Duel in the Sun,* 248–50
Hutchinson, Ron: *The Island of Dr. Moreau,* 284–85, 350
Hutton, Betty: *The Greatest Show on Earth,* 194–96
Hyde, Jonathan: *Anaconda,* 3–6
Hyde-White, Wilfred: *Xanadu,* xv, 33, 323–26, 332
Hyer, Martha: *The Carpetbaggers,* 191–93

Ice Cube: *Anaconda,* 3–6
Impulse, 127–29
Inchon, 334
Indecent Proposal, 88–90, 346, 347
Ingalls, Don: *Airport 1975,* 61–63
Intersection, 347
Interview with the Vampire, 348
Inwood, Steve: *Staying Alive,* 55–57
Isaacs, Jason: *Sweet November,* 102–4
Iscove, Robert: *From Justin to Kelly,* 35–37
Ishtar, 340
Island of Dr. Moreau, The, 284–85, 350

Jackass: The Movie, 358
Jackson, Mick: *The Bodyguard,* 85–87
Jaeckel, Richard: *The Green Slime,* 226–28
James, Caryn, 99
James, Christopher, 52
Janis, Conrad: *Airport 1975,* 61–63
Jarman, Reginald: *Zardoz,* 155–56
Jarrott, Charles: *Lost Horizon,* 40–43
Jaws: The Revenge, 18–20, 340
Jaws 3-D, 18
Jaws 5, People Zero, 20
Jayne Mansfield Story, The, 91–92
Jazz Singer, The (1980), 173–74, 331, 332
Jeffries, Fran: *Harum Scarum,* 171–72
Jenner, Bruce: *Can't Stop the Music,* xv, 32–34, 331

Jessel, George: *Valley of the Dolls,* 189, 201, 208–10
Jewell, Richard B., 165
Joffé, Roland: *The Scarlet Letter,* 266–68, 349
Johnson, Ben: *The Swarm,* 76–78
Joliffe-Andoh, Lisa: *The Scarlet Letter,* 266–68, 349
Jolson, Al, 173
Jones, Amy Holden: *Indecent Proposal,* 88–90, 346, 347
Jones, James Earl: *Exorcist II: The Heretic,* 156, 305–8
Jones, Jennifer: *Duel in the Sun,* 248–50
Jones, Tommy Lee: *The Betsy,* 159–61
Jorgensen, Christine, 310
Jourdan, Louis: *Julie,* 175–76
Julie, 175–76
Jurassic Park, 153
Juror, The, 350
Jury Duty, 348

Kael, Pauline, 40, 61, 162, 180, 194, 245, 248
Kandel, Aben: *Trog,* 23–25
Kane, Carol: *Valentino,* 204–7
Kasdan, Lawrence: *The Bodyguard,* 85–87
Kay, Gilbert Lee: *White Comanche,* 105–7
Keaton, Diane: *The Godfather: Part III,* 168–70, 343, 344
Kellerman, Sally: *Lost Horizon,* 40–43
Kelley, DeForest: *Where Love Has Gone,* 273–75
Kelly, Gene: *Xanadu,* xv, 33, 323–26, 332
Kelly, Jack: *Julie,* 175–76
Kelly, M. G.: *Roller Boogie,* 49–51
Kelly, Patsy: *The Naked Kiss,* 259–61
Kemp, Gary: *The Bodyguard,* 85–87
Kempley, Rita, 85, 114, 117, 266
Kendal, Felicity: *Valentino,* 204–7
Kennedy, George: *Airport 1975,* 61–63; *Airport '79: The Concorde,* 67–69; *Lost Horizon,* 40–43; *Strait-Jacket,* 23, 183–85
Kerns, Joanna: *A*P*E,* 7–9
Kerr, Bill: *The Pirate Movie,* 44–45, 334, 335
Kershaw, John: *The Lonely Lady,* xvi, 311–13, 335, 336
Kerwin, Bruce: *King Kong Lives,* 21–22
Kestelman, Sara: *Zardoz,* 155–56
Key, Bernard: *Trog,* 23–25
Kiel, Richard: *Eegah,* 120–22

Kier, Udo: *Barb Wire,* 243–44, 351
Kilmer, Val: *The Island of Dr. Moreau,* 284–85, 350
Kilpatrick, Shirley: *The Astounding She-Monster,* 217–18
King Kong (1976), 7–8, 21
King Kong Lives, 21–22
Kingsley, Dorothy: *Valley of the Dolls,* 189, 201, 208–10
Kipp, Jeremiah, 177
Kirkpatrick, Maggie: *The Pirate Movie,* 44–45, 334, 335
Kiss Before Dying, A, 256, 344
Kissell, Howard, 309
Kitten with a Whip, 254–55
Kleiser, Randal: *The Blue Lagoon,* 45, 245–47, 332
Knight, Arthur, 46, 273; *The Wild Wild World of Jayne Mansfield,* 211–13
Knight, Sandra: *Frankenstein's Daughter,* 282–83
Koller, Brian, 194
Kramer, Larry: *Lost Horizon,* 40–43
Kristel, Sylvia: *Airport '79: The Concorde,* 67–69
Kroll, Jack, 245
Kruschen, Jack: *Julie,* 175–76

Ladd, Alan: *The Carpetbaggers,* 191–93
Laffan, Patricia: *Devil Girl from Mars,* 223–25
Lamas, Lorenzo: *Body Rock,* 29–31
Lamont, Adele: *The Brain That Wouldn't Die,* 279–81
Lamour, Dorothy, 10; *The Greatest Show on Earth,* 194–96
Landon, Michael: *High School Confidential,* 125–26
Lange, Jessica, 7
Langella, Frank: *Body of Evidence,* 302–4, 346; *Sweet November,* 102–4
Lanier, Kate: *Glitter,* 38–39, 357
LaSalle, Mick, 3
Latham, Aaron: *Perfect,* 130–31
Lawford, Peter: *The Oscar,* 317–20
Law, John Phillip: *Barbarella,* 219–20; *The Love Machine,* 201–3
LaZar, John: *Beyond the Valley of the Dolls,* 189–90

Leder, Paul: *A*P*E*, 7–9
Legend of Lylah Clare, The, 197–200
Legend of the Lone Ranger, The, 333
Leibman, Ron: *Rhinestone*, 46–48, 336, 337
Leith, Virginia: *The Brain That Wouldn't Die*, 279–81
Leonard Part 6, xvi, *140*, 339, 340
Lessing, Arnold: *The Beach Girls and the Monster*, 10–12
Lester, Mark L.: *Roller Boogie*, 49–51
Lewis, Jerry Lee: *High School Confidential*, 125–26
Liberace: *Sincerely Yours*, 96–98
Liotta, Ray: *The Lonely Lady*, xvi, 311–13, 335, 336
Listen to Me, 342
Llosa, Luis: *Anaconda*, 3–6; *The Specialist*, 99–101, 347, 348
Lloyd, Kathleen: *The Car*, 111–13; *The Jayne Mansfield Story*, 91–92
Locher, Felix: *Frankenstein's Daughter*, 282–83
Logan, Robert: *A Night in Heaven*, 262–63, 335
Lonely Lady, The, xvi, 311–13, 335, 336
Lopez, Jennifer: *Anaconda*, 3–6
Lost Horizon, 40–43
Love Crimes, 256–58
Lovejoy, Frank: *Julie*, 175–76
Love Machine, The, 201–3
Love Story, 102, 103
Lowry, Dick: *The Jayne Mansfield Story*, 91–92
Loy, Myrna: *Airport 1975*, 61–63
Luckinbill, Laurence: *Cocktail*, 114–16, 340, 341
Lucky Numbers, 356
Lugosi, Bela: *Glen or Glenda*, 70, 309–10
Lynch, Kelly: *Cocktail*, 114–16, 340, 341; *Road House*, 132–34
Lyndon, Barré: *The Greatest Show on Earth*, 194–96
Lyne, Adrian: *Indecent Proposal*, 88–90, 346, 347
Lynley, Carol: *Poseidon Adventure*, 61, 73–75

Mac and Me, 229–31, 341
McBroom, Marcia: *Beyond the Valley of the Dolls*, 189–90
McCarthy, Todd, 284
McCutcheon, Bill: *Santa Claus Conquers the Martians*, 235–37
McDermott, Hugh: *Devil Girl from Mars*, 223–25
MacDonald, David: *Devil Girl from Mars*, 223–25
McDonald, Ronald: *Mac and Me*, 229–31, 341
McDowall, Roddy: *Poseidon Adventure*, 61, 73–75
McGinley, John C.: *On Deadly Ground*, 70–72, 348
MacKenzie, Aeneas: *The Ten Commandments*, 79–81
McKern, Leo: *The Blue Lagoon*, 45, 245–47, 332
Mack, Helen: *She*, 180–82
MacLachlan, Kyle: *Showgirls*, xvi, 321–22, 348, 349, 355
McLeod, Duncan: *Beyond the Valley of the Dolls*, 189–90
McNichol, Kristy: *The Pirate Movie*, 44–45, 334, 335
Madonna, 355; *Body of Evidence*, 302–4, 346; *Swept Away*, 358, 359
Mad scientist movies, worst, 279–91
Magnuson, Ann: *Glitter*, 38–39, 357
Majors, Lee: *Strait-Jacket*, 23, 183–85
Major, Wade, 32
Malone, Dorothy: *Sincerely Yours*, 96–98
Maltin, Leonard, 13, 29, 44, 55, 61, 85, 96, 120, 125, 159, 173, 177, 201, 217, 223, 232, 248, 256, 269, 271, 289, 295, 309, 323
Mandell, Corey: *Battlefield Earth*, 299–301, 356, 357
Maniac, 286–88
Man in the Iron Mask, The, 353
Manning, Marilyn: *Eegah*, 120–22
Mansfield, Jayne: *The Wild Wild World of Jayne Mansfield*, 211–13
Mantegna, Joe: *Body of Evidence*, 302–4, 346; *The Godfather: Part III*, 168–70, 343, 344
Man Who Knew Too Much, The, 176
Man with Bogart's Face, The, 332
Marceau, Marcel: *Barbarella*, 219–20
March, Jane: *Color of Night*, 117–19, 347
Marcovicci, Andrea: *Airport '79: The Concorde*, 67–69

Mareth, Glenville: *Santa Claus Conquers the Martians*, 235–37
Margheriti, Antonio: *Yor, the Hunter from the Future*, 153–54
Margulies, Edward, 3, 40, 55, 64, 73, 125, 159, 175, 191, 194, 197, 201, 243, 248, 256, 262, 295, 302, 311, 317
Marine, Craig, 52
Marley, John: *The Car*, 111–13
Marshall, Herbert: *Duel in the Sun*, 248–50
Martin, Duane L., 16
Martines, Alessandra: *Sinbad of the Seven Seas*, 135–36
Martinez, Mike, 153
Martin, Jared: *The Lonely Lady*, xvi, 311–13, 335, 336
Martin, Mardik: *Valentino*, 204–7
Martin, Pamela Sue: *Poseidon Adventure*, 61, 73–75
Maslin, Janet, 70, 93, 117, 123, 243, 284, 321
Maurice, Paula: *The Brain That Wouldn't Die*, 279–81
Mayes, Wendell: *Poseidon Adventure*, 61, 73–75
Meatloaf: *Spice World*, 37, 52–54, 353
Medved, Harry and Michael, 201, 226, 235
Meltzer, Lewis: *High School Confidential*, 125–26
Mercury Rising, 353
Mewborn, Brant, 204
Meyer, Russ: *Beyond the Valley of the Dolls*, 189–90
Millard, Oscar: *The Conqueror*, 165–67
Milner, Martin: *Valley of the Dolls*, 189, 201, 208–10
Mirman, Brad: *Body of Evidence*, 302–4, 346
Mobley, Mary Ann: *Harum Scarum*, 171–72
Moffett, Gregory: *Robot Monster*, 232–34
Mommie Dearest, xvi, 67, 185, 314–16, 332, 333, 342
Monster movies, worst, 3–25
Month, Chris: *Santa Claus Conquers the Martians*, 235–37
Moore, Demi: *Indecent Proposal*, 88–90, 346, 347; *The Scarlet Letter*, 266–68, 349
Moorehead, Agnes: *The Conqueror*, 165–67
Moore, Julianne: *Body of Evidence*, 302–4, 346

Moore, Roger: *Spice World*, 37, 52–54, 353
Morali, Jacques, 33
Moretti, Sandro: *Goliath and the Dragon*, 16–17
Morgenstern, Joe, 208
Morrison, Temuera: *Barb Wire*, 243–44, 351
Moser, Stephen M., 208
Moyle, Allan: *Love Crimes*, 256–58
Mulholland Falls, 350
Murphy, Donald: *Frankenstein's Daughter*, 282–83
Murray, Don: *Ghosts Can't Do It*, 251–53, 343
Musicals, worst, 29–57, 173–74
Musto, Michael, 189
Myers, Cynthia: *Beyond the Valley of the Dolls*, 189–90
Myers, Mike, 285
Mylong, John: *Robot Monster*, 232–34
My Mother the Car, 111
Myra Breckinridge, 269
Mystery Science Theater 3000, 279

Nader, George: *Robot Monster*, 232–34
Nagle, Linda: *The Pirate Movie*, 44–45, 334, 335
Nakano, Desmond: *Body Rock*, 29–31
Naked Gun 33⅓, The: The Final Insult, 348
Naked Kiss, The, 259–61
Napier, Charles: *Beyond the Valley of the Dolls*, 189–90; *Rambo: First Blood Part II*, 177–79, 337, 338
Nashville, 245
Neame, Ronald: *Poseidon Adventure*, 61, 73–75
Neeson, Liam: *Shining Through*, 93–95, 345, 346
Nelson, A. J.: *The Creeping Terror*, 221–22
Nelson, Chris: *Roller Boogie*, 49–51
Nelson, Gene: *Harum Scarum*, 171–72
Nelson, Lori: *Sincerely Yours*, 96–98
Newman, David: *Sheena*, 271–72
Newman, Laraine: *Perfect*, 130–31
Newmar, Julie: *Ghosts Can't Do It*, 251–53, 343
Newsies, 346
Newton-John, Olivia: *Xanadu*, xv, 33, 323–26, 332
Newton, Sally Anne: *Zardoz*, 155–56

Next Big Thing, The, 356
Nicastro, Michelle: Body Rock, 29–31
Nicholas, Kim: Impulse, 127–29
Nichols, Nate, 105
Nickson, Julia: Rambo: First Blood Part II, 177–79, 337, 338
Nicol, Alex: A*P*E, 7–9; Sincerely Yours, 96–98
Nielsen, Leslie: Poseidon Adventure, 61, 73–75
Night in Heaven, A, 262–63, 335
Nightmare on Elm Street 5, 342
Nolan, Jeanette: Avalanche, 64–66
Nordin, Barbara: Orgy of the Dead, 264–65
Nothing but Trouble, 344
Novak, Kim: The Legend of Lylah Clare, 197–200
Novello, Don, 169
Novello, Jay: Harum Scarum, 171–72
Null, Christopher, 168
Nureyev, Rudolf: Valentino, 204–7

O'Connor, Pat: Sweet November, 102–4
Odell, David: Supergirl, 238–40
Ojena, Louis: Orgy of the Dead, 264–65
Oldman, Gary: The Scarlet Letter, 266–68, 349
Olivier, Laurence: The Betsy, 159–61; The Jazz Singer, 173–74, 331, 332
On Deadly Ground, 70–72, 348
O'Neal, Ryan: Fever Pitch, 123–24
O'Neil, Shannon: The Creeping Terror, 221–22
Orbach, Ron: Love Crimes, 256–58
Ordung, Wyott: Robot Monster, 232–34
Orgy of the Dead, 264–65
Oscar, The, 317–20
O'Toole, Peter: Supergirl, 238–40
Outer space movies, worst, 217–40
Over the Top, 340

Pacino, Al: The Godfather: Part III, 168–70, 343, 344
Paget, Debra: The Ten Commandments, 79–81
Paluzzi, Luciana: The Green Slime, 226–28
Panarese, Tom, 44
Parker, David J., 135
Parker, Eleanor: The Oscar, 317–20

Parkins, Barbara: Valley of the Dolls, 189, 201, 208–10
Parry, Frank: Mommie Dearest, xvi, 67, 185, 314–16, 332, 333, 342
Parton, Dolly: Rhinestone, 46–48, 336, 337
Paternity, 333
Patterson, Troy, 32
Paycheck, 359
Payne, Travis: From Justin to Kelly, 35–37
Peck, Gregory: Duel in the Sun, 248–50
Peppard, George: The Carpetbaggers, 191–93
Pepper, Barry: Battlefield Earth, 299–301, 356, 357
Percepto, 289, 291
Perfect, 130–31
Perlman, Ron: The Island of Dr. Moreau, 284–85, 350
Perrine, Valerie: Can't Stop the Music, xv, 32–34, 331
Perry, Frank: Mommie Dearest, xvi, 67, 185, 314–16, 332, 333, 342
Perry, Roger: Roller Boogie, 49–51
Petrie, Daniel: The Betsy, 159–61
Peyton Place, 208
Phillips, Michelle: Valentino, 204–7
Phipps, Kevin, 238
Pichel, Irving: She, 180–82
Pickens, Slim: The Swarm, 76–78
Pigozzi, Luciano: Yor, the Hunter from the Future, 153–54
Pinocchio, 358
Pirate Movie, The, 44–45, 334, 335
Planet of the Apes, 357, 358
Plan 9 from Outer Space, 265, 309
Platt, Oliver: Indecent Proposal, 88–90, 346, 347
Plowright, Joan: The Scarlet Letter, 266–68, 349
Poetic Justice, 347
Pola, Allen and Claude: Avalanche, 64–66
Poseidon Adventure, 61, 73–75
Postman, The, 145, 351, 352
Powell, Dick: The Conqueror, 165–67
Pratt, Doug, 223
Presley, Elvis: Harum Scarum, 171–72
Preston, Kelly: Battlefield Earth, 299–301, 356, 357
Price, Vincent: The Tingler, 289–91

Primus, Barry: *Avalanche,* 64–66
Prochnow, Jürgen: *Body of Evidence,* 302–4, 346
Product placement, 229, 230
Prosky, Robert: *The Scarlet Letter,* 266–68, 349
Psycho, 353
Puchalski, Steven, 269
Purdy, Jack, 251
Puzo, Mario: *The Godfather: Part III,* 168–70, 343, 344

Quinn, Anthony: *Ghosts Can't Do It,* 251–53, 343

Raffill, Stewart: *Mac and Me,* 229–31, 341
Railsback, Steve: *Barb Wire,* 243–44, 351
Rain Man, 115
Rambo: First Blood Part II, 177–79, 337, 338
Rambo III, 341
Rampling, Charlotte: *Zardoz,* 155–56
Ramsey, Thea: *Maniac,* 286–88
Randall, Shawn: *The Lonely Lady,* xvi, 311–13, 335, 336
Ray, Billy: *Color of Night,* 117–19, 347
Raye, Martha: *Airport '79: The Concorde,* 67–69
Razzie Awards: brief history of, xv–xvi; Worst Career Achievement Awards, 361; 1st (1980), xv–xvi, *137,* 331–32; 2nd (1981), xvi, 332–33; 3rd (1982), 334–35; 4th (1983), xvi, 335–36; 5th (1984), *138,* 336–37; 6th (1985), *139,* 337–38; 7th (1986), 338–39; 8th (1987), 339–40; 9th (1988), 340–41; 10th (1989), *141,* 341–43; 11th (1990), *142,* 343–44; 12th (1991), 344–45; 13th (1992), 345–46; 14th (1993), *143,* 346–47; 15th (1994), 347–48; 16th (1995), *144,* 348–49; 17th (1996), 350–51; 18th (1997), 351–52; 19th (1998), 352–54; 20th (1999), 354–55; 21st (2000), *147,* 356–57; 22nd (2001), *148,* 357–58; 23rd (2002), *150, 151,* 358–59; 24th (2003), *152,* 359–60
Read, Dolly: *Beyond the Valley of the Dolls,* 189–90
Read, James: *Love Crimes,* 256–58
Reagan, Ronald, 361

Rebane, Bill: *The Giant Spider Invasion,* 13–15
Rebello, Stephen, 40, 55, 64, 73, 159, 175, 191, 194, 197, 201, 248, 256, 262, 295, 311, 317
Reddy, Helen: *Airport 1975,* 61–63
Redford, Robert: *Indecent Proposal,* 88–90, 346, 347
Red Sonja, 338
Reeves, Keanu: *Sweet November,* 102–4
Repossessed, 344
Return of the Swamp Thing, 342
Reynolds, Debbie: *The Bodyguard,* 85–87
Reynolds, Peter: *Devil Girl from Mars,* 223–25
Rhinestone, 46–48, 336, 337
Rhodes, Cynthia: *Staying Alive,* 55–57
Richardson, Joely: *Shining Through,* 93–95, 345, 346
Rich, David Lowell: *Airport '79: The Concorde,* 67–69
Ringmaster, 354
Ritchie, Guy: *Swept Away,* 358, 359
Road House, 132–34
Roberts, Eric: *The Specialist,* 99–101, 347, 348
Roberts, Tanya: *Sheena,* 271–72
Roberts, Tony: *The Beach Girls and the Monster,* 10–12
Robinson, Edward G.: *The Ten Commandments,* 79–81
Robinson, Phil Alden: *Rhinestone,* 46–48, 336, 337
Robot Monster, 232–34
Robson, Mark: *Valley of the Dolls,* 189, 201, 208–10
Rock, Oz: *Body Rock,* 29–31
Rocky IV, 179, 337, 338
Roller Boogie, 49–51
Romance movies, worst, 85–107
Roman, Ruth: *Beyond the Forest,* 162–64; *Impulse,* 127–29
Rose, Ruth: *She,* 180–82
Ross, Charles: *The Wild Wild World of Jayne Mansfield,* 211–13
Ross, Katharine: *The Betsy,* 159–61; *The Swarm,* 76–78
Roth, Eric: *Airport '79: The Concorde,* 67–69
Rouse, Russell: *The Oscar,* 317–20

Rouveral, Jean: *The Legend of Lylah Clare*, 197–200
Royle, Selena: *Robot Monster*, 232–34
Rubinstein, John: *The Car*, 111–13
Ruffo, Eleanora: *Goliath and the Dragon*, 16–17
Rush, Barbara: *Can't Stop the Music*, xv, 32–34, 331
Rush, Deborah: *A Night in Heaven*, 262–63, 335
Rush, Richard: *Color of Night*, 117–19, 347
Russell, Ken: *Valentino*, 204–7
Rutigliano, Nick, 211
Ryan, Robert: *The Love Machine*, 201–3
Ryder, Winona, 168

Sahara, 336
St. Elmo's Fire, 337
St. John, Jill: *The Oscar*, 317–20
St. John, Theodore: *The Greatest Show on Earth*, 194–96
Salamon, Julie, 123
Salmaggi, Robert, 259
Sand, Paul: *Can't Stop the Music*, xv, 32–34, 331
Santa Claus Conquers the Martians, 235–37
Sargent, Joseph: *Jaws: The Revenge*, 18–20
Sasdy, Peter: *The Lonely Lady*, xvi, 311–13, 335, 336
Saturday Night Live, 55, 56
Sauter, Michael, 96, 130, 238, 317
Scarlet Letter, The (1995), 266–68, 349
Scarwid, Diana: *Mommie Dearest*, xvi, 67, 185, 314–16, 332, 333, 342
Scheib, Richard, 7, 21, 23, 217
Schickel, Richard, 197, 317
Schneider, Barry: *Roller Boogie*, 49–51
Schulgasser, Barbara, 284
Schwarzenegger, Arnold: *The Jayne Mansfield Story*, 91–92
Scott, Donovan: *Sheena*, 271–72
Scotti, Tony: *Valley of the Dolls*, 189, 201, 208–10
Scott, Martha: *Airport 1975*, 61–63
Scott, Randolph: *She*, 180–82
Screen couples, worst, 85–107
Seagal, Steven: *On Deadly Ground*, 70–72, 348

Seltzer, David: *Shining Through*, 93–95, 345, 346
Selznick, David O.: *Duel in the Sun*, 248–50
Semple, Lorenzo, Jr.: *Sheena*, 271–72
Seros, Alexandra: *The Specialist*, 99–101, 347, 348
Sextette, 269–70
Shameless roles, 159–85
Shanghai Surprise, 338
Shapiro, J. D.: *Battlefield Earth*, 299–301, 356, 357
Sharkey, Ray: *Body Rock*, 29–31
Shatner, William: *Impulse*, 127–29; *White Comanche*, 105–7
She, 180–82
Sheena, 271–72
Shields, Brooke: *The Blue Lagoon*, 45, 245–47, 332
Shining Through, 93–95, 345, 346
Shire, Talia: *The Godfather: Part III*, 168–70, 343, 344
Shore, Pauly, 355
Showgirls, xvi, 321–22, 348, 349, 355
Shryack, Dennis: *The Car*, 111–13
Shue, Elisabeth: *Cocktail*, 114–16, 340, 341
Siff, Greg: *From Justin to Kelly*, 35–37
Silliphant, Robert, 12; *Poseidon Adventure*, 61, 73–75
Silliphant, Stirling: *The Swarm*, 76–78
Silver, Fawn: *Orgy of the Dead*, 264–65
Silverstein, Elliot: *The Car*, 111–13
Simon, John, 189, 305
Sinbad of the Seven Seas, 135–36
Sincerely Yours, 96–98
Sindelar, David, 120, 264
Slate, Laura: *The Car*, 111–13
Slater, Helen: *Supergirl*, 238–40
Smight, Jack: *Airport 1975*, 61–63
Smith, Jaclyn: *The Adventurers*, 295–98
Smith, La Ron A.: *Body Rock*, 29–31
Smith, Neil, 38, 168
Snodgress, Carrie: *A Night in Heaven*, 262–63, 335
Sokol, Marilyn: *Can't Stop the Music*, xv, 32–34, 331
Sommer, Elke: *The Oscar*, 317–20
Southern, Terry: *Barbarella*, 219–20
Space movies, worst, 217–40
Specialist, The, 99–101, 347, 348

INDEX 376

Speed Zone, 342
Speed 2: Cruise Control, 352
Spice Girls: *Spice World,* 37, 52–54, 353
Spice World, 37, 52–54, 353
Spiers, Bob: *Spice World,* 37, 52–54, 353
Spradlin, G. D.: *The Jayne Mansfield Story,* 91–92
Spy Kids 3-D: Game Over, 360
Stadie, Hildegarde: *Maniac,* 286–88
Stallone, Frank: *Staying Alive,* 55–57
Stallone, Sylvester, 343, 355; *Rambo: First Blood Part II,* 177–79, 337, 338; *Rhinestone,* 46–48, 336, 337; *The Specialist,* 99–101, 347, 348; *Staying Alive,* 55–57
Stanley, John, 21, 23, 221, 282, 286, 289, 305
Stanley, Lauren: *Mac and Me,* 229–31, 341
Stanley, Richard: *The Island of Dr. Moreau,* 284–85, 350
Starnes, Dene: *Orgy of the Dead,* 264–65
Starr, Ringo: *Sextette,* 269–70
Star Trek V, 341, 342
Star Wars: Episode I—The Phantom Menace, 355
Star Wars: Episode II, 358, 359
Staying Alive, 55–57
Steiger, Rod: *The Specialist,* 99–101, 347, 348
Steiner, John: *Sinbad of the Seven Seas,* 135–36; *Yor, the Hunter from the Future,* 153–54
Steiner, Max, 163
Stephens, A. C., 265
Sterling, Jan: *High School Confidential,* 125–26
Sterritt, David, 211, 314
Stevens, Stella: *Poseidon Adventure,* 61, 73–75
Stewart, Douglas Day: *The Blue Lagoon,* 45, 245–47, 332; *The Scarlet Letter,* 266–68, 349
Stewart, James: *The Greatest Show on Earth,* 194–96
Stiles, Victor: *Santa Claus Conquers the Martians,* 235–37
Stiller, Jerry: *Airport 1975,* 61–63
Stoddard, Samuel, 135
Stoltz, Eric: *Anaconda,* 3–6
Stone, Andrew L.: *Julie,* 175–76

Stone, Sharon: *The Specialist,* 99–101, 347, 348
Stop! Or My Mom Will Shoot, 345, 346
Story of Mankind, The, 76
Strait-Jacket, 23, 183–85
Stranger Among Us, A, 94, 345
Striptease, 267, 350, 351
Stroker Ace, 335
Stupids, The, 350
Sullivan, Barry: *Julie,* 175–76
Summers, Jimmy, 262
Sunset, 341
Supergirl, 238–40
Susann, Jacqueline, 201, 208
Swanson, Gloria: *Airport 1975,* 61–63
Swarm, The, 76–78
Swayze, Patrick: *Road House,* 132–34
Sweet November (2001), 102–4
Swept Away, 358, 359
Swift, Jessica: *Zardoz,* 155–56
Szwarc, Jeannot: *Supergirl,* 238–40

Talbot, Lyle: *Glen or Glenda,* 70, 309–10
Tamblyn, Russ: *High School Confidential,* 125–26
Tarzan, the Ape Man, 333
Tate, Sharon: *Valley of the Dolls,* 189, 201, 208–10
Taylor, Elizabeth, 164
Taylor, Samuel: *The Love Machine,* 201–3
Taylor-Young, Leigh: *The Adventurers,* 295–98
Temp, The, 347
Ten Commandments, The, 79–81
Terrio, Deney: *A Night in Heaven,* 262–63, 335
Tewkesbury, Joan: *A Night in Heaven,* 262–63, 335
Texada, Tia: *Glitter,* 38–39, 357
Theron, Charlize: *Sweet November,* 102–4
Thewlis, David: *The Island of Dr. Moreau,* 284–85, 350
Thomas, Kevin, 10
Thomas, Trevor: *Sheena,* 271–72
Thompson, Howard, 235
Thompson, Tim: *Rhinestone,* 46–48, 336, 337
Thornton, Billy Bob: *On Deadly Ground,* 70–72, 348; *Indecent Proposal,* 88–90, 346, 347

Thourlby, William: *The Creeping Terror*, 221–22
Thumbelina, 348
Tighe, Kevin: *Road House*, 132–34
Tingler, The, 289–91
Todd, Sally: *Frankenstein's Daughter*, 282–83
Tognazzi, Ugo: *Barbarella*, 219–20
Tomelty, Joseph: *Devil Girl from Mars*, 223–25
Took, Barry, 76
Toomey, Regie: *Beyond the Forest*, 162–64
Towering Inferno, The, 64, 76
Towers, Constance: *The Naked Kiss*, 259–61
Travers, Peter, 88, 102, 132
Travolta, John: *Battlefield Earth*, 299–301, 356, 357; *Perfect*, 130–31; *Staying Alive*, 55–57
Trog, 23–25
Trump, Donald: *Ghosts Can't Do It*, 251–53, 343
Tucker, Phil: *Robot Monster*, 232–34
Turan, Kenneth, 243
Turner, Lana, 273–74
Tuttle, Lurene: *Sincerely Yours*, 96–98
Twister, 350
Two Moon Junction, 341
Tyner, Adam, 7
Tyson, Cicely: *Airport '79: The Concorde*, 67–69
Tyson, Richard: *Battlefield Earth*, 299–301, 356, 357

Ullmann, Liv: *Lost Horizon*, 40–43
Undari, Claudio: *Goliath and the Dragon*, 16–17
Under the Cherry Moon, 338, 339

Vaccaro, Brenda: *Supergirl*, 238–40
Vadim, Roger: *Barbarella*, 219–20
Valentino, 204–7
Valley of the Dolls, 189, 201, 208–10
Van, Bobby: *Lost Horizon*, 40–43
Van Cleef, Lee: *The Conqueror*, 165–67
Van Doren, Mamie: *High School Confidential*, 125–26
Van Gelder, Lawrence, 38
Van Patten, James: *Roller Boogie*, 49–51

Van Peebles, Mario: *Jaws: The Revenge*, 18–20
Verhoeven, Paul: *Showgirls*, xvi, *144*, 321–22, 348, 349, 355
Video releasing companies, 328–29
Vidor, King: *Beyond the Forest*, 162–64; *Duel in the Sun*, 248–50
Village People: *Can't Stop the Music*, xv, 32–34, 331
Villareal, Phil, 35
Voelker, Kurt: *Sweet November*, 102–4
Voight, Jon: *Anaconda*, 3–6
Von Sydow, Max: *Exorcist II: The Heretic*, 156, 305–8

Wagner, Robert: *Airport '79: The Concorde*, 67–69
Walker, Albert, 127
Walker, Arnetia: *Love Crimes*, 256–58
Walker, Jimmy J.J.: *Airport '79: The Concorde*, 67–69
Walker, Nancy: *Can't Stop the Music*, xv, 32–34, 331
Wallace, Irving: *Sincerely Yours*, 96–98
Wallach, Eli: *The Godfather: Part III*, 168–70, 343, 344
Wall Street, 340
Walters, Thorley: *Trog*, 23–25
Ward, Jonathan: *Mac and Me*, 229–31, 341
Ward, Simon: *Supergirl*, 238–40
Warren, Lesley Ann: *Color of Night*, 117–19, 347; *A Night in Heaven*, 262–63, 335
Wass, Ted: *Sheena*, 271–72
Waterworld, 349
Watson, Minor: *Beyond the Forest*, 162–64
Wayne, John, 191; *The Conqueror*, 165–67
Web sites, 327–30
Webster, Nicholas: *Santa Claus Conquers the Martians*, 235–37
Wehling, Bob: *Eegah*, 120–22
Weldon, Michael, 10, 13, 76, 91, 105, 111, 120, 127, 221, 226, 235, 279, 282, 286, 305
Wendt, George: *Spice World*, 37, 52–54, 353
Wenner, Jann: *Perfect*, 130–31
West, Mae: *Sextette*, 269–70
West, Red: *Road House*, 132–34
Wexler, Jodi: *The Love Machine*, 201–3
Wexler, Norman: *Staying Alive*, 55–57

What Ever Happened to Baby Jane?, 183
When the Boys Meet the Girls, 97, 98
Where Love Has Gone, 273–75
Where the Boys Are, 35
Where the Boys Are '84, 336
Whitaker, Forest: *Battlefield Earth*, 299–301, 356, 357
White Comanche, 105–7
White, Robb: *The Tingler*, 289–91
Who's Afraid of Virginia Woolf?, 164
Who's That Girl?, 339–40
Widmark, Richard: *The Swarm*, 76–78
Widom, Bud: *The Green Slime*, 226–28
Wilde, Cornel: *The Greatest Show on Earth*, 194–96
Wild Wild West, 146, 354–55
Wild Wild World of Jayne Mansfield, The, 211–13
Williams, Bill: *The Giant Spider Invasion*, 13–15
Williams, Edy: *Beyond the Valley of the Dolls*, 189–90; *The Naked Kiss*, 259–61
Willis, Bruce: *Color of Night*, 117–19, 347
Wilson, Owen: *Anaconda*, 3–6
Winters, Shelley: *Poseidon Adventure*, 61, 73–75
Wloszczyna, Susan, 266, 321
Wolf, William, 254
Women in Love, 204
Woodard, Bronte: *Can't Stop the Music*, xv, 32–34, 331
Wood, Ed, 70, 217, 221; *Glen or Glenda*, 70, 309–10; *Orgy of the Dead*, 264–65; *Plan 9 from Outer Space*, 265, 309

Woods, Bill: *Maniac*, 286–88
Woods, James: *The Specialist*, 99–101, 347, 348
Woodward, Joan, 273
World Is Not Enough, The, 355
Wright, Brian J., 153
Wuhl, Robert: *The Bodyguard*, 85–87
Wyatt Earp, 347
Wybenga, Roland: *Sinbad of the Seven Seas*, 135–36

Xanadu, xv, 33, 323–26, 332

Yablans, Frank, 316
Yani, Rosanna: *White Comanche*, 105–7
Yapp, Nate, 264
Yiasomi, George: *King Kong Lives*, 21–22
York, Michael: *Lost Horizon*, 40–43
Yor, the Hunter from the Future, 153–54
Young, Karen: *Jaws: The Revenge*, 18–20
Young, Neil: *The Island of Dr. Moreau*, 284–85, 350
Young, Sean: *Love Crimes*, 256–58

Zabriskie, Grace: *Body Rock*, 29–31
Zadora, Pia, 170, 343; *The Lonely Lady*, xvi, 311–13, 335, 336; *Santa Claus Conquers the Martians*, 235–37
Zardoz, 155–56
Zimbalist, Efrem, Jr.: *Airport 1975*, 61–63
Zobda, France: *Sheena*, 271–72
Zugsmith, Albert, 125
Zunser, Jesse, 175

About the Author

In his fifty years on planet Hollywood, John Wilson has seen more than 4,000 movies, many of them as the founder of the Golden Raspberry Award Foundation and the creator of the Razzie Awards, which were recently saluted by E! TV as "the foremost authority on all things that suck on the big screen."

A graduate of UCLA's prestigious movie/television studies program, Wilson has spent more than twenty-five years as a producer, copywriter, and creative consultant for many entertainment industry clients. In 1990 he won the Hollywood Reporter Key Art Award for Comedy Trailers. He has created hundreds of major movie campaigns, including those of the first three *Star Wars* films; three of the four *Superman* movies; such classic Disney reissues as *Pinocchio, Lady and the Tramp*; the animated versions of both *The Jungle Book* and *101 Dalmatians*; and, in a bit of Razzie serendipity, the trailer and TV spots for Pia Zadora's bad film classic *The Lonely Lady*. He has also worked for PBS and the Playboy Channel, and helped create CBS-TV's fall preview print ads, a three-minute retrospective look at MGM/UA's renowned video library, and the electronic press kit for the 67th Annual Academy Awards.

Wilson lives with his wife, Barbara (whom he met while working at a movie theatre), their son, Parker, their cat, Nora, six VCRs, a 537-volume film reference library, and more than 2,000 videotapes and DVDs in an ever-more-crowded ranch-style home in a quiet suburb of Tinseltown.